THE L ND

Fat of the Land

GARBAGE IN NEW YORK
THE LAST TWO HUNDRED YEARS

BENJAMIN MILLER

FOUR WALLS EIGHT WINDOWS
NEW YORK/LONDON

© 2000 by Benjamin Miller

Published in the United States by
Four Walls Eight Windows
39 West 14th Street, room 503
New York, NY 10011
http://www.4W8W.com

Joseph Mitchell's literary executor, Sheila McGrath, and Pantheon Books, a division of Random House Books, have generously given permission to reprint a passage from *Up in the Old Hotel*. Copyright 1992 by Joseph Mitchell. Parts of several chapters of the present work appeared in somewhat different form in the journal *Social Research* 65, no. 1 (spring 1998). © 1997 by the New School for Social Research

Library of Congress Cataloguing-in-Publication Data:
Miller, Benjamin, 1953–
Fat of the land : garbage in New York : the last two hundred years.
        p. cm.
ISBN: 1-56858-172-6
1. Refuse and refuse disposal—New York (State)—New York—History. 2. Refuse and refuse disposal—Health aspects—New York (State)—New York. 3. Refuse and refuse disposal—Social aspects—New York (State)—New York. I. Title.

TD788.4.N72 N454 2000   363.72'85'097471—dc21   00-056191

Design and type composition by Ink, Inc., New York.
Printed in Canada

10   9   8   7   6   5   4   3   2   1

Contents

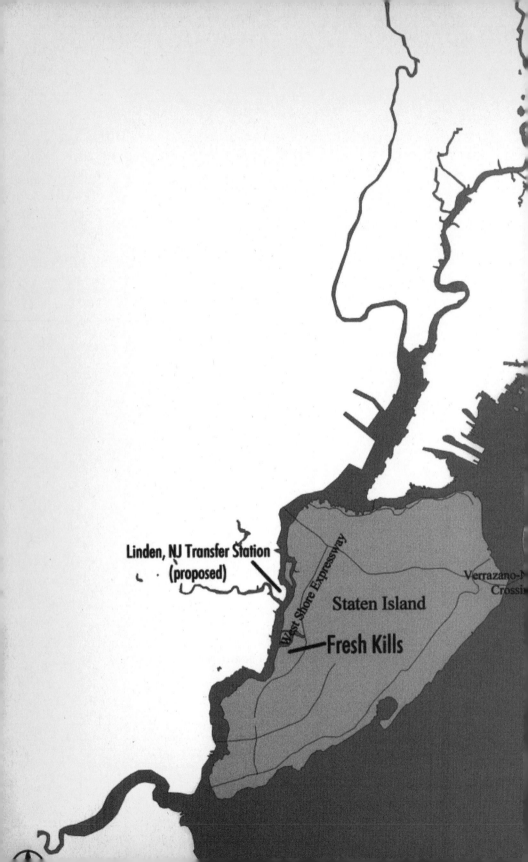

Bronx

Harlem River Railyards   Sound View

Rikers Island

Central Park   LaGuardia Airport

hattan   Randalls Island/   Corona Meadows
             Triborough Bridge

Brooklyn Navy Yard   Queens

Brooklyn

                    Jamaica Bay

Ocean Parkway

Barren Island

Belt Parkway

Base Map Sources: NYC Dept. of
City Planning, Bytes of the Big Apple
ESRI, Inc.

2   0   2   4 Miles

Acknowledgments

I would like to thank the staffs of the following libraries and archives: Brooklyn Public Library, Columbia University Library, the former Engineering Societies Library, Long Island/Brooklyn Historical Society, Municipal Archives, Municipal Reference Center, New York Academy of Medicine, New-York Historical Society, New York Public Library, Queens Historical Society, and the Staten Island Institute of Arts and Sciences. Special thanks are due Robert Bernstein, MTA Bridges and Tunnels Records manager, for granting me access to Robert Moses's Triborough Authority papers.

For assistance well beyond the call of duty I would like to thank: Ruth Deutsch, of the Queens County Clerk's office, who willingly went on a fishing trip for me to find in the vaults the papers from the *William L. Baxter vs. John Brady et al.* suit of 1850, which no doubt otherwise would have been lost to all time; Kenneth Cobb, director of the Municipal Archives, who deserves (and has) my most profound gratitude for his help and courtesies over the years; Harry Szarpanski, who, among other kindnesses, has offered unfailingly amiable assistance with computer problems; and my agent, Malaga Baldi, for whose steadfast support I am very grateful.

One of the things this book suggests is that the history of waste management planning in New York has been very checkered indeed. There have been few heroes. Yet, among our contemporaries, I would like to acknowledge the well-meaning efforts of the following individuals—even though the results achieved may not have been all that they might have wished. James T. B. Tripp, general counsel of the Environmental Defense Fund (and former chairman of the Citywide Recycling Advisory Board) and Eric Goldstein, senior attorney, Natural Resources Defense Council, stand out for their unstinting efforts on behalf of more rational waste management planning. And though I did not agree with all of their decisions, former deputy mayor Norman Steisel and former sanitation commissioner Steven M. Polan have my respect for their dedicated energy and intelligence. I enjoyed working with both of them—most of the time.

On a personal level, I would like to express my gratitude to Bob and Jeanne Cumming for many things, including the use of the island cottage in which some of this was written. Jim Meyer, my colleague and partner for ten years, shared all of the work described in Part IV. He used his selfless and uncommon skills to make significant contributions to the City of New York, and to me. My parents have waited patiently for this book to appear, and have my thanks for (among many other things—including my incomparable siblings) their tact in rarely mentioning it. My children, Jonah and Rebecca, have grown up with garbage and appear not to resent it overly. And they have provided many profoundly satisfying excuses for me to step away from it for a while. Jan, my long-beguiling wife, may not know how much her understanding support of this project has meant to me, nor how much she herself does. If not, I would like to try to make these things clear.

Chronology

1853   George Waring tours Maine and Vermont, lecturing on the merits of fertilizer.

1854   A by-product of the Crimean War is Florence Nightingale's demonstration that sanitary techniques can save lives.

1854-70 Under the patronage of Louis-Napoléon, Eugène Haussmann clears swathes of medieval neighborhoods to make Paris a place for boulevardiers; beneath the boulevards he builds sewers, and at their ends, parks. One of these, the Parc des Buttes-Chaumont, is the former garbage dump, Montfaucon.

1850   Frederick Law Olmsted, seeking an escape from his farmer's life on Staten Island, takes a walking tour of England, Scotland, France, Belgium, Holland, and Germany and is much impressed by his introduction to European parks.

1853   Engineer Egbert Ludovickus Viele surveys the watercourses under the land chosen for the new Central Park. Because of the fever-inducing miasmatic conditions he finds there, he pronounces the site "perhaps the most unpropitious that could have been selected for such a purpose on the whole continent."

1858   Olmsted and his partner Calvert Vaux receive the commission for designing Central Park and Olmsted replaces Viele as chief engineer. Olmsted inherits Viele's deputy, George Waring.

1864   Griscom heads the Citizens' Association's survey on "the Sanitary Condition of New York City." Viele's map of underground watercourses and waste-filled land is its centerfold.

1865   Louis Pasteur proves that contact with specific organisms can cause disease.

1868   In the course of designing Brooklyn's Prospect Park, Olmsted and Vaux exceed their mandate and start planning for the larger region in which their park is embedded. In so doing, they invent the "park-way." Ocean and Eastern Parkways, which connect Prospect Park to Coney Island and eastern Long Island, respectively, are the first such roads built. Olmsted, in collaboration with Andrew Haswell Green and others, goes on to plan parkways and other roads in northern Manhattan, the Bronx, and Staten Island.

Between 1930 and 1960, Robert Moses will build some of them, including the West Shore Expressway in Staten Island.

Andrew Green proposes a "Greater City" to encompass all the municipalities and unincorporated territory around the Port of New York.

1874 The first incinerator is built in Leeds, England, in response to a cholera epidemic.

1882 Thomas Edison flips a switch in Drexel, Morgan and Company's Wall Street offices and incandescent lights go on in buildings downtown. By the turn of the century, electricity is also being used to power the transit lines that are snaking across the city, bringing residential development in their wake and creating powerful economic incentives for landfilling refuse on wetlands and shorefronts to create saleable property. Edison's invention is also the motive power behind the combined utility/transit franchises that exert a stranglehold on the city.

1885 The first permanent incinerator in the United States is built on Governor's Island in New York Harbor.

1888 A cross-harbor rail freight tunnel to connect New York to the continent is proposed. On the strength of promises that the Greater City would accomplish this objective, Staten Islanders vote in 1894 to accept Andrew Green's plan to consolidate the five boroughs of New York City.

1895 Under a Reform administration, George Waring is appointed commissioner of the Department of Street-Cleaning. Waring experiments with mandating source-separated recycling and incineration, but his most lasting waste disposal legacies are new contracts to continue the practice of waste "reduction" (to produce glycerin, grease, and fertilizer) on Barren Island.

1898 Andrew Green's Greater City is born. Tammany Hall surges back into City Hall. George Waring, out of office, is sent to Cuba to clean up after William Randolph Hearst's Spanish-American War. He contracts yellow fever there and dies.

1902   William J. Wilgus conceives the plan for Grand Central Station.

1903   The Brooklyn Rapid Transit consortium creates a company called Brooklyn Ash with partners William Greve, William Reynolds, and Frank Bailey. Brooklyn Ash hauls refuse on streetcar rails and dumps it off the end of the line.

1905   William Randolph Hearst forms the Municipal Ownership Party to take power from the transit/utility "trust" and runs for mayor on the Municipal Ownership line. One of the planks in the party's platform is a pledge to develop municipally owned refuse-to-electricity plants. Ballot-dumping in the East River by Tammany toughs gives the mayoral election to George Brinton McClellan, Jr.

   The first municipal refuse-to-energy plant goes into operation, lighting the Williamsburg Bridge. Street-Cleaning Commissioner John McGaw Woodbury proposes a network of additional refuse-to-electricity plants.

1906   Mayor McClellan proposes building an international seaport in Jamaica Bay.

   William Wilgus designs a system of tunnels between New Jersey and New York to bring containerized freight in and out of the city, and to haul refuse out of the city. One element of the spider-web-like radial-and-circumferential rail network he proposes is a tunnel across the Verrazano Narrows.

1911   Wilgus drafts bills for the New York and New Jersey legislatures to create a Port Authority of New York and New Jersey. The New York version is enacted in 1911, New Jersey in 1917.

1912   Frederick Law Olmsted, Jr. helps prepare a plan for Brooklyn that includes a road looped around the borough's waterfront, and an industrial/commercial Jamaica Bay port with a "marginal" railroad rimming the shore.

1913   Edward Bernays, a father of the public relations industry, invents the "influence-leader technique" while staging a play about venereal disease. Belle Moskowitz participates in the public-relations campaign to promote *Damaged Goods*.

1914   After the New York State legislature, led by Al Smith and Robert F. Wagner, kills a bill that would have allowed the city to produce and sell electricity generated from refuse, Mayor John Purroy Mitchel contracts with his friend William Reynolds to build a plant ("Metropolitan By-Products") at the mouth of the Fresh Kills that will transmute garbage to glycerin, grease, and fertilizer. Although the plant's nauseating odors foment near rebellion on Staten Island, its output is critical to the allied war effort in Europe.

1917   Hearst's puppet, John ("Red Mike") Hylan, promises Staten Islanders that, if elected mayor, he will close the garbage plant.

1918   Mayor Hylan closes the Metropolitan By-Products plant on Staten Island. After almost seventy years of operation, the last Barren Island garbage plant is also closed. Violating the 1888 Marine and Harbor Protection Act, the city resumes dumping refuse at sea.

    In France, Wilgus uses the railways Haussmann built as a "belt" around Paris to move the men and materiel that win the war. Ex-mayor Mitchel dies in a training accident (while flying his plane upsidedown without a seatbelt). Congressman Fiorello LaGuardia becomes a major in the air corps and develops a lifelong passion for aviation and airports.

    Belle Moskowitz hires a young civil-service reformer, Robert Moses, as executive director of Governor Al Smith's Reconstruction Commission.

1921   Al Smith, a commissioner of the newly formed Port Authority of New York and New Jersey, puts Belle Moskowitz in charge of an "influence-leader" campaign in support of the authority's plan for a cross-harbor rail-tunnel between New York and the Penn Central's New Jersey yards. Wilgus campaigns instead for the Staten Island route, which offers many advantages. Wilgus loses the propaganda war.

1922   Charles Dyer Norton, Frederic Delano, and others found the Committee on the Regional Plan (which in 1929 will become the Regional Plan Association) to develop a comprehensive plan for the greater metropolitan region.

1931   William Francis Carey begins expanding North Beach Airport (which in 1939 will be re-named LaGuardia Field) with refuse mined from Rikers Island and hauled across Flushing Bay on a pontoon bridge.

1933   The New York City Board of Estimate agrees to buy Brooklyn Ash, its network of twenty-two incinerators, and the Corona Meadows ashfill through which New York State Parks Commissioner and Triborough Bridge Authority Chairman Robert Moses plans to build an access road ("parkway") to the Triborough Bridge. The board also approves the mayor's plan to dump the city's refuse in Jamaica Bay to build the islands needed for Mayor Mitchel's great industrial seaport.

1934   After taking its case to the Supreme Court, the State of New Jersey finally compels New York City to stop dumping refuse in the ocean. As a result, the city sends more of its waste to Rikers Island (which will soon tower 140 feet above Flushing Bay), and to eighty-eight other landfills scattered across the city where Robert Moses needs fill to make parks.

1936   Bill Carey is appointed sanitation commissioner—presumably at the behest of Robert Moses.

1938   Moses prods Carey to move his department's dumping operations away from Rikers Island before the nearby World's Fair begins, but opposes Carey's plans to dump refuse in Jamaica Bay instead. Moses secretly proposes starting a new landfill at Fresh Kills in Staten Island as an alternative, then denies it.

1943   Under the slogan "Save Some Scrap to Kill a Jap," Mayor LaGuardia leads the drive to recycle materials in support of the war effort. But because of the high costs of collecting these materials, the city is relieved to receive federal permission to end the scrap drive before General MacArthur lands in Japan.

1946   Robert Moses makes a deal with the Staten Island borough president to build the West Shore Expressway in exchange for approval to build the Fresh Kills landfill.

1948   Moses begins landfilling at Fresh Kills with the secret goal of
        building an access road for the Verrazano-Narrows Bridge. He
        promises the Staten Island borough president that the landfill will
        not accept raw garbage after 1951, by which time all of the city's
        refuse will be burned in a network of eleven upgraded and five
        new incinerators. By the time the last of the new incinerators
        actually opened (in 1962), two-thirds of the city's refuse is still
        being landfilled.

1962   Rachel Carson's *The Silent Spring* launches the modern environ-
        mental movement.

1964   Moses' Verrazano-Narrows Bridge opens.

1966   DDT spraying by the Suffolk County Mosquito Commission leads
        to the founding of the Environmental Defense Fund in 1967.

1967   Sanitation Commissioner Samuel Kearing announces that New
        York City will build a six-thousand-ton-per-day waste-to-energy
        plant at the Brooklyn Navy Yard. Because the city is still negotiat-
        ing with the Navy to acquire the yard, the announcement embar-
        rasses the Lindsay administration. Kearing is fired.

1970   Ralph Nader invents the concept of "Public Interest Research
        Groups." Money is siphoned automatically from college students'
        tuition payments to fund the ongoing work of statewide staffs of
        professional organizers. The New York Public Interest Group—
        NYPIRG—is formed in 1973.

1971   Jerome Kretchmer, administrator of the New York City Environ-
        mental Protection Administration, announces that the city will not
        build the Brooklyn Navy Yard incinerator. Instead, refuse will be
        mounded at the Fresh Kills landfill. The term coined for this waste
        disposal technique is "landscape-sculpture."

1977   In a fireside chat about the energy crisis brought on by the Organ-
        ization for Petroleum Exporting Countries' oil embargo, President
        Jimmy Carter declares the "moral equivalent of war" and estab-
        lishes a multibillion-dollar grant program to encourage the devel-
        opment of "alternative energy" sources such as refuse-to-energy
        facilities.

Norman Steisel is appointed sanitation commissioner.

A pharmaceutical plant in Seveso, Italy explodes: dioxin is in the air.

1979   Norman Steisel closes the Pelham Bay landfill in the Bronx: its
        slopes are too steep for garbage trucks to climb. With the support
        of federal grants, the Sanitation Department proposes building a
        three-thousand-ton-per-day refuse-to-energy incinerator in the
        Brooklyn Navy Yard.

1981   UOP, Inc., is selected to build the Navy Yard incinerator. In 1983,
        UOP is acquired by Wheelabrator-Frye. The company's name is
        changed to Signal Environmental Systems and then to Wheel-
        abrator Environmental Systems. Before the end of the decade,
        Wheelabrator is acquired by Waste Management, Inc.

1982   Former presidential candidate Barry Commoner moves his Center
        for the Biology of Natural Systems to New York and announces
        plans to develop urban energy cooperatives fueled by refuse-
        derived methane.

        Dioxin is detected at an incinerator in Hempstead, Long Island.

1985   The Board of Estimate approves the proposed contract with
        Wheelabrator Environmental Systems to build the Brooklyn Navy
        Yard incinerator. Norman Steisel resigns as sanitation commis-
        sioner to join the financial firm of Lazard Frères, which numbers
        Wheelabrator among its clients.

1987   Lowell Harrelson launches the *Mobro*. After a two-month, six-
        thousand-mile voyage, it returns to New York and its contents are
        burned in an incinerator built by Robert Moses.

1989   Mayor Ed Koch asks the US Department of the Interior for per-
        mission to keep open the Fountain Avenue landfill in Brooklyn,
        which had been deeded to the federal government by the Lindsay
        administration as part of Gateway National Park. His petition is
        refused. The city's inventory of waste-management facilities
        dwindles to three one-thousand-ton-per-day incinerators built in
        the 1950s by Construction Coordinator Moses and two landfills
        (the 144-acre Edgemere landfill, in Queens, started by Sanitation

Commissioner Carey in 1938, and the 3,000-acre Fresh Kills land-fill in Staten Island, started by Moses in 1948).

A law is passed that commits New York City to recycle 25 percent of its refuse by 1992 and requires New Yorkers to divide their refuse into separate categories.

Mayoral candidate David N. Dinkins, one of whose advisors is Barry Commoner, pledges to institute a five-year moratorium on constructing the Brooklyn Navy Yard incinerator if he is elected mayor. This stand is castigated by his opponent, Rudolph W. Giuliani, as an example of political cowardice. Dinkins defeats Giuliani by fewer than fifty thousand votes.

1990   Dinkins appoints Norman Steisel, who has become one of the foremost incineration lobbyists in the country, first deputy mayor.

1991   In response to a declaration by Sanitation Commissioner Steven M. Polan in an interview with the *New York Times* that the city is committed to incineration as its predominant waste management strategy, Barry Commoner, the New York Public Interest Research Group, the Environmental Defense Fund, and the Natural Resources Defense Council (among other environmental groups) decide to join forces to insist that no refuse-to-energy facility, including the Brooklyn Navy Yard incinerator, be built in New York City until the city has demonstrated that it has achieved the maximum feasible level of recycling.

1992   After thirty-four of the City Council's fifty-one members vow that they will never approve the administration's waste management plan (which includes building the three-thousand-ton-per-day Brooklyn Navy Yard incinerator), the council nonetheless approves it by a substantial margin. Among the promises made to obtain votes in favor of the plan, the Dinkins administration commits to closing two of the city's three existing one-thousand-ton-per-day incinerators, and to build no refuse-to-energy incinerator other than the Navy Yard plant without the council's express approval.

While the plan is being debated, the first in a series of trains carrying refuse intended for disposal in midwestern landfills leaves New York; like the *Mobro*, it circles around the country for weeks before coming back to New York, where its containers are buried at the Fresh Kills landfill. The train, and its sisters, spur a renewed congressional debate about enacting laws to prohibit states from exporting refuse to other states.

Fresh Kills, the last remaining landfill in New York City, has a remaining capacity of some hundred million cubic yards, which, depending on the rate of filling, will last twenty to fifty years.

1993   Rudy Giuliani defeats Dinkins.

1996   Guy V. Molinari, George E. Pataki, and Rudy Giuliani agree to close the Fresh Kills landfill by December 31, 2001. Only the month before, the Giuliani administration had submitted a permit application to the New York State Department of Environmental Conservation asking for a twenty-year permit for landfilling at Fresh Kills on the grounds that there was no feasible alternative, and in its supporting environmental analysis specifically concluded that it would be infeasible to export any significant portion of the city's waste. There is no plan for where New York City's waste will be disposed after 2001, who will manage it, or how it will be paid for. The law that embodies this agreement also forbids building the Brooklyn Navy Yard incinerator.

2000   As of May 2000, there is not an approved plan for managing the city's thirteen thousand tons per day of solid waste after the closure of the Fresh Kills landfill.

Fat of the Land

GARBAGE IN NEW YORK
THE LAST TWO HUNDRED YEARS

Garbarge

The first news story appeared on the morning of April 6, 1987, when the *Charlotte Observer* reported that a barge filled with New York garbage had been turned away from a privately owned port near Morehead City, North Carolina. Two days later, *New York Newsday* revealed that the barge was "somewhere out in the Atlantic" and believed to be headed for Louisiana. Two weeks later, its daily progress was being covered by most news media in the country. Before the month was out, the garbage had become famous from London to Beijing.

Lowell Harrelson, a fifty-three-year-old heating and air-conditioning contractor still owned the biggest house in Bay Minette, Alabama, but his business had seen better times. He had defaulted on two government-backed business loans, the second of which was for 8.2 million dollars. Other debts were mounting, and it was becoming difficult to keep up his forty-acre estate with its swimming pool, tennis court, three-hole golf course, and man-made lake stocked with catfish and bass. "He was not a shyster," one of his supporters said, "things just keep happening to him." He was a gambler whose weakness, another friend said, "is [that] he does not know how to judge and handle people." He was a better salesman than a money manager, said others. Everyone seemed to agree that he was ruled by enthusiasm.

Inventions were one of his enthusiasms. In the summer of 1976 he watched a farmer use methane from a manure pile to generate electricity to run his milking machines. Methane—natural gas—is produced when any organic waste (such as refuse in a landfill) decomposes. If there were a way of concentrating the waste so that each cubic foot gave off a rich supply of methane, it occurred to Harrelson, an entrepreneur would be able to kill two birds with one stone—dispose of garbage and recover profit from methane at the same time.

Another of Harrelson's enthusiasms was high school football. Part of Harrelson's local popularity came from his work with the Quarterback Club, an organization that raised money for the high school team and helped students get football scholarships. One of the beneficiaries of this civic enthusiasm was Rick Byrd, who later got into the refuse-hauling business. When the New York Legislature passed a law in 1983 that banned new landfills on Long Island and ordered existing landfills to close by the end of 1990 (a measure designed to protect the aquifers that supply Long Island's drinking water), it attracted the attention of refuse-haulers all over the country. The going price for shipping refuse was about fifty cents a ton-mile. Long Island produced eight thousand tons of refuse a day, and the nearest available off-island landfills were over a hundred miles away. Islip was one of the first towns where the new law would have an effect. Its landfill was almost full, and the State Department of Environmental Conservation had refused to give the town permission to extend it by twelve and a half acres to provide space until the waste-to-energy incinerator the town was building was in operation. As a stopgap measure, Islip closed its landfill to waste generated by private businesses and advertised for bids to take this waste somewhere else. Rick Byrd wanted to bid on this contract, but the town required all proposers to post a twelve-million-dollar bond. Byrd did not have the resources to get a bond of that size. Then he thought of his old friend Lowell Harrelson. Harrelson listened to Byrd's plan to bale each ton of Islip's commercial refuse into a three-foot cube for easy shipping, heard a way to solve the methane-generation problem he had contemplated, and got the bond.

Since Long Island is the suburban backyard for New York's major mafia families, it is not surprising that its refuse-hauling industry (as was common elsewhere in the country) has had long and extensive mafia connections. In 1984, a number of carters and local officials were indicted for collusive practices and coercive threats. In November 1986 (while these individuals were still under indictment), Harrelson and Byrd flew to New York and checked into the Bay Shore Capri Motel in Islip. At the last minute, the town officials announced that they were postponing the bidding. Harrelson and Byrd flew home to Alabama and then back to Islip again, but the town postponed the bidding a second time. Harrelson then discovered that, bypassing an open bidding process altogether (contrary to state law), the town had signed a contract to pay eighty-six dollars for each ton of commercial refuse to a newly formed local firm. The firm, Waste Alternatives, Inc., was owned by Thomas Hroncich, who until a few months before had been Islip's environmental control commissioner, and who was said to have ties to the Lucchese and Gambino crime families. Among those negotiating with the town on behalf of Waste Alternatives was James Corrigan, the head of the Private Sanitation Industry Association on Long Island, who was one of those who was under indictment. Complicating matters further, Hroncich and his associates did not have a landfill.

A few days before Christmas, Harrelson gave Hroncich a call. "Tommy," Hroncich heard the stranger drawl, "I've got a great idea for you. There's an awful lot of barges sitting down here in Louisiana...." They arranged to meet in early January. On the appointed evening, Hroncich waited in the bar of the Islip Ramada Inn. It was a cold night. Harrelson's cab from the airport ran out of gas on the Long Island Expressway. Finally, he walked into the bar. Since he was wearing what Hroncich would later describe as a "forty-five-gallon" hat, Hroncich spotted him right away. Harrelson lit up a low-tar cigarette, ordered a Canadian whisky, and started talking about barges and balefills, suitable subsoils and methane conversion, on-site power plants and four-dollar-a-cubic-yard profits. Harrelson, Hroncich said later, "seemed to know what he was talking about." Without raising any issues that might disturb Harrelson's confidence—such as where the landfill was that Harrelson planned to use, or whether he had contractual access to it, or whether the landfill was legal, or how the methane would be recovered—Hroncich signed an agreement whereby Harrelson would take all of Hroncich's refuse for three years for thirty dollars a ton. Harrelson offered to let Rick Byrd in on the deal, but at thirty dollars a ton Byrd was not interested.

Hroncich's economics were relatively straightforward. Apart from his payments to Harrelson, he had some minor trucking and transfer expenses; on every ton of refuse, he was going to double his investment. Harrelson's end of the bargain also seemed simple. Hroncich and his associates in the private carting business would deliver the refuse to a pier in Long Island City, Queens, where it would be baled and stacked on a barge. A Louisiana barge could hold over three thousand tons of baled refuse. Harrelson could lease the barge, a tug and a four-man crew from a firm called Harvey Gulf &

Marine for about five thousand dollars a day. All he needed was a landfill.

In early March, he found one outside New Orleans that would take his refuse for five dollars a ton. A few days later, he found a closer one in Jones County, North Carolina, a rural community thirty-five miles from the coast. He offered the county four dollars and ninety cents a cubic yard to dump one hundred thousand yards of refuse in its landfill. Larry Meadows, the county administrator, was encouraging, but not (he later told reporters) definitive. "Yeah," (he said he said) "that sounds good, but you got to meet in a regular meeting of the Jones County Board of Commissioners." Without any further encouragement, Harrelson instructed Harvey Gulf & Marine to "go up and get us a load."

In addition to waste from Islip, Harrelson and his partners also opened their doors to anyone else who was willing to pay thirty dollars a ton to get rid of commercial refuse. Within ten days of opening his business, Harrelson and company had acquired 1,238 tons of waste from their Islip contract, and 1,968 tons of commercial waste from New York City and Nassau County. These 3,206 tons left Long Island City by barge on the morning of March 22. The barge was called the *Mobro 4000*, its tug was called the *Break of Dawn*, its captain was named Duffy St. Pierre. Within a month, they would all be famous.

Four days after setting out, the tug and barge arrived in the port of Morehead City, North Carolina, while the Jones County commissioners were in Raleigh, the state capital, getting advice from the state's environmental experts. While the experts and the county commissioners deliberated, the citizens of Morehead had time to wonder what a 240-foot barge of New York refuse was doing in their harbor. Their reaction was negative. "Oh my land," as Sonny Lane of Lane's Marina put it, "when the wind blows in the right direction, you can smell it." Harrelson knew which way the wind was blowing. Before he was formally ordered out of the state on April 3, he told the county health commissioner that he "was just stopping in North Carolina to show the cargo to some tobacco farmers who were interested in setting up landfills." Telling reporters that Louisiana had been his real destination all along, he instructed his crew to head down the coast.

The environmental officials who had ordered the barge out of North

Carolina's waters jumped to the phones to warn their colleagues in other states that the barge was headed south. Alabama reacted with dispatch, getting a court order against the barge well before it was within striking distance. As the *Mobro* and its crew tried to enter the mouth of the Mississippi (en route to the private landfill Harrelson had earlier found just beyond New Orleans), they were met by state police and officials of the Louisiana Department of Environmental Quality who had flown down from Baton Rouge to tell them that the barge could not be unloaded in Louisiana—even though Governor Edwin W. Edwards was not yet sure of the state's authority to keep the barge out. "If we don't have the legal authority," he explained to a group of reporters, "then we can't line the National Guard on the banks of the river and shoot at them."

In *City of Philadelphia v. New Jersey*, the Supreme Court had determined that refusing to accept waste from other states imposed an unreasonable restraint on interstate commerce. Since Harrelson threatened to sue Louisiana on these grounds, the Louisiana Department of Environmental Quality had to find a legal excuse for its position. The state's obligations to protect public health and the environment seemed a plausible argument. Assistant Secretary Dale Givens repeatedly told the press that "smelly puddles" were leaking from the barge, that the barge was covered with thousands of flies and mosquitoes, that it appeared to contain medical wastes. When the barge was finally unloaded and its contents inspected bit by bit, none of these allegations turned out to be true, but that did not affect their enthusiastic acceptance by the news media, or Louisiana's ability to obtain a court order within hours.

The Department of Environmental Quality gave Harrelson a week to get out of the state's three-mile territorial waters. Captain St. Pierre moored the *Mobro* to a sweet gum tree in the lower Mississippi for a few days, and then the barge disappeared. After a brief but frantic search, Louisiana officials found it moored to an oil platform in the Gulf of Mexico. By April 22, the barge had disappeared again, and so had Harrelson. When he turned up again two days later, he revealed that he was in the process of negotiations with a Caribbean country, but he would not say which country or where the barge was. The Mexican navy added a dash of drama to Harrelson's sprinkling of mystery: when it spotted the barge coming toward Tampico, it sent four ships, two planes, and a helicopter to intercept it. That evening, on the *Tonight Show,* Johnny Carson added a touch of comedy. Using a marker and a map of the world, he drew a course for the barge from Florida to Gibraltar, through the Suez Canel, into the Red Sea, and told St. Pierre to "do a U-ey at Yemen" and continue up the Gulf of Persia to Iran. (Iran's Ayatollah Khomeini was much in the news because his government had mined the Gulf of Persia and had secretly purchased US military hardware with funds covertly transmitted by Marine Colonel Oliver North to support Nicaraguan rebels.)

On April 27, there were reports that the Central American country of Belize might be willing to take the refuse, but Belize officially refused it the next day after discovering that the methane project Harrelson had been talking about involved the famous barge from New York. By the beginning of May, the barge was back off the coast of Florida, circling aimlessly, it seemed, although there were rumors that it was heading back to New York. A Florida businessman offered to use the refuse to build a private island off the Bahamas, but the Bahamas Ministry of Health refused to grant a permit. The *Miami Herald* interviewed Captain St. Pierre's mother, while at least one other paper found space to print some of St. Pierre's favorite Cajun recipes.

On May 12, the rumors that had appeared since the beginning of the month were confirmed. The barge was coming home. Frank Jones, Islip town supervisor, told reporters that the town planned a "gala" welcome for the garbage, and that he and his constituents would "tie yellow ribbons around the gates of the Islip dump."

The state's governor, Mario Cuomo, who was being mentioned as a likely candidate in the upcoming presidential election, made no such satisfied announcement. Nonetheless, he too had reason to be pleased. It appeared that Cuomo had been embarrassed by the situation his environmental commissioner, Hank Williams, had indirectly caused, and had asked Williams to make an arrangement with Islip to take the refuse back. Such an arrangement, of course, would mean reversing William's prior decision to limit the capacity of the Islip landfill. Meanwhile Jones, who had been appointed Islip town supervisor to fill the unexpired term of his predecessor eight days after the *Mobro* left the Long Island City dock, faced his first election in November; Jones seemed to think that he could strengthen his electoral chances by solving the crisis which, he had said, made Islip "the laughingstock of the Eastern Seaboard." But after the consent order to expand the capacity of the Islip landfill was signed (an order that did not mention Islip's agreement to accept the contents of the barge), both sides downplayed the seeming coincidence of Commissioner Williams's change of heart. Supervisor Jones said that while the barge highlighted the issue, "It almost became secondary to the solution." Commissioner Williams said he knew "that the chronological relationship of these events certainly puts things in a cast where people say, 'All you're trying to do is get out from under this barge and selling your soul.' But we don't think so because the issues are more substantial than that."

Not everyone was so sanguine about the solution. Islip planned to charge Harrelson forty dollars a cubic yard for accepting the waste (its standard fee, which was about ten dollars a yard more than Harrelson had been paid to take the refuse away in the first place). That amounted to about 124,000 dollars, in addition to unloading and trucking costs of another 110,000 dollars or so. Thomas Hroncich, who was in a good position to appreciate the discrepancy between those costs and Harrelson's financial resources after accruing a fifty-one-day tug-and-barge bill, asked "Who's going to pay the fees?" Harrelson, reached at home in Bay Minette, was asked whether he planned to return the waste to Islip. He did not mince words. "No sir, I'm not."

Harvey Gulf & Marine, the owner of the barge and tug, had received a 150,000-dollar retainer from Harrelson before the voyage started. Its expenses, however, had been more than three times that, and Harrelson's ability to pay the remainder appeared dubious. Robert Guidry, the president of Harvey Gulf, put his foot down, and announced two days later that the barge would indeed return to New York. Harrelson concurred. "It was foolish of me to object unless I had a better plan," he said, "and right now I don't." But a Ralph Nader-inspired group, the New York Public Interest Research Group (NYPIRG), filed a lawsuit to prevent disposing the barge's contents in Islip on the grounds that the consent order violated a law that forbade the expansion of a landfill without a permit and prior public hearings. The barge's troubles were just beginning.

Captain Duffy St. Pierre, who had not seen his wife or children for eight weeks, who had traveled six thousand miles with a bargeload of refuse, and had been formally rejected by six states and three countries, finally sighted the New York City skyline on Saturday, May 17. "Let them try to stop me," he told reporters. "I think they'll have to have gunboats." At nine o'clock that evening, just three miles south of the Statue of Liberty, under the vast span of the Verrazano-Narrows bridge, he was stopped by three armed vessels of the New York City Police Department. "This is garbage without a home and I don't want it to squat anywhere in New York City," First Deputy Mayor Stanley Brezenoff told reporters. The sanitation commissioner, Brendan Sexton, insisted that the refuse could be transferred through New York City only if it were unloaded directly into covered trucks and the trucks left as soon as they were loaded. The mayor, Edward I. Koch, seconded Sexton's strictures in characteristic fashion. "We are treating the garbage like Germany treated Lenin," Koch repeatedly told reporters. "He had to be in a sealed train as he went through Germany and Poland, until he got to Finland. This garbage has to get onto sealed trucks until it gets to Islip." In light of these conditions, the owner of the Long Island City transfer station—who had loaded the refuse in the first place—refused permission to use his pier. The mayor matched his refusal by forbidding the use of a city-owned pier.

His fellow local elected officials followed suit. Hours before the police cruisers intercepted the barge, Claire Shulman, the new borough president of Queens (whose predecessor had stabbed himself through the heart in a depression associated with an investigation into his role in a political corruption scandal that eventually sent five other politicians to jail), obtained an injunction to prevent the refuse from passing, however fleetingly, however sealed, through her borough. "In the tropical sun for eight weeks?" she explained. "Fifth-generation insects?" Supervisor Jones, whose robust persona was epitomized by his use of the nickname "Sayville Fats," was outraged that Shulman would try to sabotage his statesmanly solution to the laughingstock crisis. "I heard her say Islip's garbage will never travel the streets of Queens. And she presides over the corruption capital of the universe. If she wants to get porky about it, we'll identify how much of it is hers and we'll leave it on the dock for her."

By then, however, the tension between the Queens borough president and the Islip town supervisor, though still newsworthy, had become somewhat academic, since NYPIRG and the citizens of Islip had succeeded in obtaining their injunction against unloading the *Mobro* in Islip. As Commissioner Williams's and Supervisor Jones's solution collapsed, doors slammed shut on other potential options even before they had been opened. The junior councilperson from Staten Island, twenty-eight-year-old Susan Molinari, filed for and received a temporary restraining order to prevent the barge from being unloaded in Staten Island and its contents buried at the Fresh Kills landfill, the three-thousand-acre onetime marsh that former City Parks Commissioner Robert Moses had started to build before she was born (over the protests of her grandfather, Assemblyman Robert Molinari), and which the actions of successive city administrations had conspired to make the primary depository for all of New York City's twenty-four-thousand-tons-a-day of refuse. Commissioner Williams asked a private company to dispose of the refuse in its new waste-to-energy facility sixty miles up the Hudson River in Peekskill; John Sullivan, president of the company (which had also won the contract for a waste-to-energy plant that the City of New York wanted to build in the Brooklyn Navy Yard), agreed to the request, but the local county executive vetoed the deal.

When it seemed that New York officials were incapable of making any headway on the problem, two Ohioans tried to step into the breach. The mayor of Columbus offered the services of his incinerator, but he wanted to charge three hundred dollars a ton for the privilege (which was ten times more than Harrelson had been paid, and seven-and-a-half times what Islip wanted). Representative Thomas Luken, chairman of the House Subcommittee on Transportation, Tourism, and Hazardous Materials sent Mayor Koch and Supervisor Jones a letter informing them that "there has been too much posturing, petulancy and petty parochialism shown by the local officials in the New York area. The parties involved have had more than sufficient time to date to put an end to this international embarrassment. If no agreement to dispose of the 3,200 tons of rotting garbage has been reached by June 24, I expect you to be in my office that morning...." Mayor Koch declined the invitation, citing its "unfortunate and inexplicable" tone.

Under these circumstances, when the joke had gone on so long that even the most jocular of publicity seeking politicians had grown irritable in the extended glare of the national spotlight, and it was clear that no help could be hoped for from outsiders, Conservation Commissioner Williams's embarrass-

ment grew more desperate, as did his dependence on New York City to come
up with a plan. The plan that the city's sanitation department came up with,
however, created new problems for him. Sanitation Commissioner Brendan
Sexton's proposal was to burn the refuse in one of the city's three remaining
1950s-era incinerators (which were also a legacy of the Robert Moses era),
and then to bury the ash in a landfill on the Rockaway Peninsula in Queens.
Accepting this plan, as Sexton well knew, would put Commissioner Williams
in an awkward position. Not only did the fifty-year-old landfill have few safeguards to protect the adjacent waters of Jamaica Bay or the underlying Long
Island aquifer from pollutants leaching from its refuse, but sanitation officials
had recently discovered that thousands of hazardous waste drums had been
buried there. Borough President Shulman's constituents had fought for years
to get the landfill closed; the discovery of the drums had raised their protests to
a new level. Sanctioning the use of this landfill would require Williams to
make another embarrassing reversal of a prior decision. Sexton's plan, under
the circumstances, was attempted blackmail.

On the evening of June 17, after eighty-eight days with the barge, Captain
St. Pierre, his crew, and his wife Esther (who had flown to New York a
month earlier, after understanding a television newscaster to suggest that
Duffy was about to haul the barge to Europe), cast off from the *Mobro* and
headed *Break of Dawn* home to Louisiana. They were incongruously replaced
(but not in the affections of the news media) by a pleasure boat that Harvey
Gulf bought to carry on the watch. With Duffy St. Pierre and his now famous
crew out of the picture, supplanted by a rotating crew of solo sailors on eight-
hour shifts, much of the human interest was drained from the news story,
which readers were tiring of anyway. For all concerned, the fun was gone.

Commissioner Williams refused Commissioner Sexton's extortionate
proposal to dispose of *Mobro* incinerator residue at the city's Rockaway
landfill. He found Frank Jones's offer to dispose of the ash in Islip's little
landfill less embarrassing. But in closed negotiations with the conservation
department staff—and with the new commissioner, Thomas Jorling, who
took over from Williams while the controversy still raged—New York City
Sanitation Department officials continued to press for a quid pro quo: the
city would burn the refuse if the state would give formal permission to keep
the Rockaway landfill open. To the conservation department, which had

recently claimed that Williams's reversal of his earlier decision on the Islip landfill had nothing to do with the *Mobro*, the causal linkage in the city's new proposal appeared much less direct. Once again, the conservation commissioner could claim that a simultaneous *Mobro* plan and permission for a landfill to remain open were just a coincidence.

Predictably, the plan that finally offered to relieve Lowell Harrelson's prolonged public anguish and the embarrassment of public officials from Islip to Albany was not equally received in all quarters. The Brooklyn borough president, Howard Golden, whose relations with the mayor had long since soured, immediately filed for an injunction. He had been advised by his environmental experts, he said, that "that once you touch the garbage, it sets into the air the motion for bacteria and a lot of other health hazards." Barry Commoner, a former presidential candidate and *Time* magazine cover subject who was currently the director of the Queens College Center for the Biology of Natural Systems, was the foremost of these advisers.

For four years, Commoner had vocally opposed the sanitation department's plan to reduce the city's dependence on its rapidly filling landfills by building a series of incinerators. While the *Mobro* was languishing in the lower harbor, Commoner had appeared in the conservation department's regional headquarters in Long Island City to oppose the granting of a construction permit for an incinerator that the sanitation department wanted to build in the Brooklyn Navy Yard. Unlike those who had prevented the *Mobro* from unloading at each of its previous ports of call because they were afraid of accepting New York garbage in their localities, Commoner made no objection to disposing of the waste in New York City. Commoner's primary interest in the borough president's suit seemed to be the platform it offered for his crusade against the generic evils of incineration.

The second *Mobro* trial began in Kings County Supreme Court on July 27. Commoner was the first witness. He went straight to the anti-incineration argument he had been honing for the past four years. Dioxin, a compound whose public significance derives from its association with Agent Orange, the defoliant used in Vietnam, is created in incinerators. Incinerators are "dioxin factories" because large corporations make profitable chlorinated organic compounds that, when burned, combine to form a substance not found in nature, and for which no practical use exists. Dioxin is one of the most potent causes of cancer, Commoner's argument continued, and is especially pernicious because it is not a direct "initiator" of cancer (that is, a substance that acting alone upon a cell will cause cancer) but a "promoter," a substance that exacerbates the effects of other compounds that do cause cancer directly. Because dioxin is a man-made product, it does not break down in the environment, but is instead accumulated in, among other things, human fat. New York City, as part of the industrialized Northeast, could be said to have the highest concentration of dioxin in body fat in the country as well as the highest concentration of other cancer-causing pollutants. For this reason, minimizing the sources of dioxin in New York is especially important. Refuse should therefore be recycled rather than burned.

This particular refuse, however, Commoner testified, was likely to include infectious medical waste, and should be handled as little and as quickly as possible. The *Mobro*'s cargo, he concluded, should not be recycled or incinerated, but buried at the Fresh Kills landfill on Staten Island.

There were few scientists who would have agreed with Commoner's line of reasoning, or with the premises upon which it was based. (Commoner himself attributed this to the fact that most of the other scientists who had paid any attention to these issues "work for incinerator companies," while only a handful, like himself, approached them from a completely independent perspective.) For example, his assertion that dioxin is "especially pernicious" because it is a cancer "promoter" rather than "initiator" is contrary to the standard epidemiological view that the degree of relative health risk from promoter substances is less than that from initiators. Recycling is a feasible waste-management alternative only for that fraction of municipal solid wastes that can be reused in the manufacture of new products. And if the *Mobro* did indeed contain infectious medical wastes, unloading its bales at the Fresh Kills landfill—where they would be dropped by cranes onto the ground, picked up by front-end loaders, dropped into open-topped wagons, hauled a mile or so over rough roads by slow-moving caterpillars, then dumped to tumble down a bank of refuse, crushed by the heavy bladed wheels of a compactor, and finally, covered by dirt—would not be the most effective way to minimize the potential for exposure to disease-bearing pathogens.

When all the testimony had been taken, the judge ordered that the barge's contents be burned in the Southwest Brooklyn incinerator, which had been built twenty-five years earlier by City Construction Coordinator Robert Moses. His order included several specific requirements. One, each bale was to be inspected for hazardous materials before it was burned. Two, the sanitation department had to provide an opportunity for any private recycling company that wished to to take whatever portion of the refuse it wanted. Three, the city was to take whatever measures were possible to recover its costs from the private firms and individuals who had been parties to the *Mobro* venture.

The inspectors who examined every bale found nothing in the waste that was hazardous or infectious, nothing not commonly found in household and commercial trash, no appreciable odor, no insects, no seeping liquids; the only item deemed newsworthy was a yo-yo found by Sanitation Commissioner Sexton, which, dangling from his middle finger made the front pages of two of the city's dailies. The sanitation department placed three newspaper ads advising any interested party of the opportunity to take *Mobro* refuse to be recycled. No one accepted the invitation, but a Virginia novelty company asked for sixty pounds of the *Mobro*'s contents to be sealed in little plexiglass cubes and sold as souvenirs, offering to split its profits with the city. The city said it would try to recover its costs of processing the *Mobro*'s waste (about seventy-five thousand dollars), but no payments were ever made.

What was left—the ash—ended up at the same Islip landfill where the refuse would have gone in the first place if, by insisting that it be closed before any long-term replacement was available, the upstate regulators had not opened the door to the kind of ingeniously ad hoc entrepreneurial activity that had long characterized the porous relationship between public and private enterprise in the downstate region.

The "barge heard round the world" was generally perceived as a warning of an impending nationwide garbage crisis that could threaten our environment, economy, and public health. It was not. It was just a bit of garbage that got away—out of the usually closed orbit of municipal-operations-as-usual into a spotlight that cast intense embarrassment on the hapless actors who once again had failed to fulfill the essential public task entrusted to them. The fruitless voyage reflected a fundamental incapacity to plan adequately for the basic functions that define our cities' physical space, determining their efficiency and their appeal. It also put on prominent display a range of anxious attempts to control the chaos we seem to feel our refuse represents, the sense of fear in which our perception of our refuse is embedded, and the varying objectives that our collective discomfiture with our offscourings can advance.

In *Fat of the Land*, refuse is used as a lens for examining how some of our most fundamental institutions have functioned over the past couple of hundred years. Caught in the push-pull between the classes, between conflicting entrepreneurial ambitions, between competing visions of the future, this disgust-inducing stuff has played crucial, if largely unseen roles in determining some of the most basic features of our physical environment, has helped shape our transportation systems, our land use patterns, our land itself, while the conflicts it has induced have helped to mold the political and economic environments in which we also live. And the discrepancies between what we *thought* we were doing with our waste—protecting our health, saving our planet, building something, making a buck—and what we have actually achieved, offer humbling insights into the nature of the planning processes through which we have tried to control our destiny.

Is it disconcerting, or in a strange way reassuring, to discover that, in the end—of course the story, one hopes, will never be over—despite the fluctuations in institutional relations, despite the shifting technological circumstances in which we find ourselves, when it comes to how we actually interact with this ineluctable stuff, little has really changed?

PART I

Engineering Reform

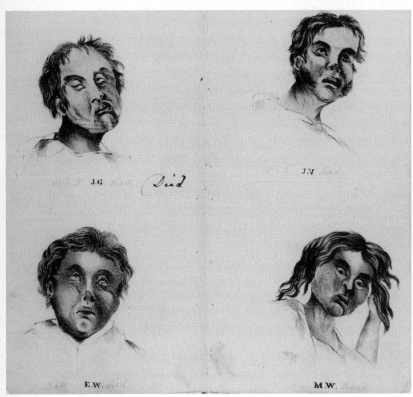

J.G. aged 31, admitted 6 o'clock...July 17.... in a state of collapse...died. E.W. aged 43, born in Ireland, laborer,...Died at half past one... being ill only 7 hours and a half. J.V. aged 32, born in England, blacksmith. Purging came on yesterday, and spasms and vomiting this morning; countenance sunken; surface cold; pulse scarcely perceptible; tongue cold and covered with yellow fur; spasms in the legs....Died at half past 8 o'clock... after an illness of 10 hours. M.W. Born in New-York, lives in Goeric Street; intemperate... Cured.

CHAPTER I

The Greatest Happiness

James Reyburn, a fifty-five-year-old Wall Street lawyer and cotton broker who was widely admired for his good works and infectious good humor, had a premonition that he would die of cholera. As the epidemic spread through New York City in the late spring and early summer of 1849, he suffered from the mental unease that his contemporaries considered one of the predisposing causes of the disease. He felt a heightened awareness of his bodily functions and was alert for the signs of gastrointestinal upset that were the cholera's first symptoms. Friday, July 13, was the hottest day in ten years; at 2 PM the temperature was ninety-five degrees. To all appearances in the peak of health, Reyburn went about his business as usual. But he felt weak from a slight case of diarrhea. He went with a friend to Delmonico's to have a glass of port wine and fruit juice. After drinking it, he was relieved to find that he felt much better. He went home. Several hours later he was struck with severe cramps. Doctors were called immediately; they applied every remedy medical science could prescribe. On Saturday, after he had passed through the stage of violent vomiting and diarrhea that wring from the victim a thin white, "rice water," discharge, his pulse had weakened to imperceptibility, and his skin had turned the cold, wrinkled blue that marks the final collapse, his physicians covered his body with hot salt in a desperate attempt to stimulate his peripheral circulation and restore some sign of vitality. He died that night.

His death, along with the deaths of fifty-four other cholera victims, was reported in Monday's papers. The weekend's toll, which in addition to Reyburn included several other eminent members of "the respectable classes, including even ladies," rent the walls of calculated insouciance that New York's powerful had erected as a bulwark against the disease. Until then, the ranks of cholera victims had been safely filled by unfortunate members of the lower classes whose degraded physical and moral circumstances, it seemed, were bound to provide fodder for plague. The nervous whistling sort of composure the city had maintained in the face of mortality reports from its more wretched quarters had become (as James Gordon Bennett put it in the editorial that described Reyburn's death) Almost A Panic.★

If there remained understatement in the *Herald's* characterization, there were good reasons: the flight from the city by those who could afford to seek shelter elsewhere was already costing its merchants millions. If one of the preventive measures being discussed were enacted—quarantining incoming ships with their fresh supplies of trade goods and immigrant laborers—the effects on the city's mercantile economy would be even more devastating. But financial fears were not enough to damp the terror cholera caused.

It was awful for the *way* it killed: striking its victims with sudden force (a survivor of the 1832 epidemic reported that he felt nothing at all until he was suddenly pitched forward in the street "as if knocked down with an axe"), to produce a sudden death ("she was struck while putting on her makeup to go out, and was dead two hours later" a reporter wrote of an unlucky prostitute), of excruciating horror ("One often thought of the Laocoön," a New York physician recalled, "but looked in vain for the serpent").

Equally unsettling was the mystery of *how* it was transmitted. Many diseases clearly passed from person to person. Measles and chickenpox could be avoided by staying away from those who were infected. Syphilis could be avoided by abstaining from promiscuous intercourse. (And could be exacerbated, found the empirically minded public-health pioneer Alexandre-Jean-Baptiste Parent-Duchatelet, on the basis of in-depth personal research, by wading up to one's thighs in the Paris sewers.) Smallpox could be given to Indians with gifts of infected blankets, as Lord Jeffrey Amherst demon-

---

★ Bennett continued: "The public feeling began to be excited in a very extraordinary degree yesterday, on the publication of the usual reports upon the cholera. This excitement grew out of the aggregate number of deaths, as well as the character of some of the casualties which are now beginning to affect the higher classes of society.... The increase in the number of deaths may be attributed chiefly, if not altogether, to the sudden and extraordinary variations in the weather which we have experienced in this city in the past week.... Other causes may be assigned, in connection with the above, as exercising a great deal of influence. These are, carelessness, inattention, over exertion of body, and, above all, fear acting upon the mind. It is, therefore, very important that every person who is now in the enjoyment of health, should keep cool and pluck up courage, and not abandon himself to alarms...."

strated; alternatively, it could be avoided—a trick picked up in Egypt a century before by an English ambassador's wife—by scratching oneself with a needle dipped in the pus of someone else's pox. (Jenner's discovery, fifty years later, that cowpox picked up on a milkmaid's fingers gave a milder and more foolproof immunity—"vacca": cow: vaccine—simply refined the technique.) But the mechanism of cholera, like that of yellow fever before it, was so mysterious that it split the medical profession into violently opposed camps called "contagionist"—those who believed that the disease was passed from person to person and could be controlled through quarantines—and "anticontagionists"—who believed that the disease was due to some "miasmatic" element in the environment. (In the City of Brotherly Love, the conflict was institutionalized in two mutually exclusive organizations, with those in the former camp founding the College of Physicians and those in the latter the Academy of Medicine.) For those who were not physicians, the hopelessness of seeking a cure from someone who was one helped to place the medical profession in a disrepute that in retrospect is difficult to imagine.

But the most unsettling aspect of the disease was that it seemed to grow out of the very problems that were overwhelming civilization in so many other ways. Cholera first left its native India to make a global circuit in 1832, riding the swift frigates that mercantilism, empire, and immigration drove, finding fine hosts in the concentrated squalor that the mushrooming urban centers had produced. In the Old World, the Industrial Revolution had torn peasants from the land, pushing them into cities where they survived, if at all, at the very margins of society. Paris's population nearly doubled between the turn of the nineteenth century and its midpoint, while London's was about two million (one and a half times) greater than it had been at the century mark. In the New World, waves of immigration were producing even steeper growth, as those uprooted who did not move into their own cities instead sought their fortunes on American shores. Between 1820 and 1850, Baltimore's population tripled and Boston's quadrupled; Philadelphia's census grew fivefold between 1800 and 1850, while New York's population grew ten times bigger, from sixty thousand at the turn of the century to over half a million at its midpoint—and passed a million by 1860. While the cities had never been clean, their sanitary defects had at least remained modest in scale. But now the uncollected heaps of domestic refuse and street dirt, the stagnant undrained puddles, the drinking water fouled by sewage and industrial discharges, were no longer just unaesthetic and disgusting, but terrifying sources of mortal vulnerability.

As disquieting as the physical squalor—the thick stench that could kill ("all smell is disease," according to the widely read Edwin Chadwick)— were the new people themselves. The refugees from the impoverished south and the degraded Irish were unlike any previous Londoners, the peasants from Languedoc and Auvergne were as foreign to their fellow Parisians as if they had come instead from North Africa—almost as foreign as the German and Irish peasants were to Old New Yorkers. It was not just the strange accents, the lack of literacy, the crushing poverty, but the intemperance, prostitution, and criminality that seemed to flourish in their midst. The dangerous physical uncleanness was matched if not outstripped by a frightening immorality: whether a contagionist or a miasmist, every educated person believed that the cholera was most likely to strike a constitution that had been weakened through depravity. The mortality data that were beginning to be collected—"statistics" were a new method of quantifying demographic and economic information pertaining to the power of the state— supported the assumption that epidemic diseases primarily struck the iniquitous poor. And yet this tinder risked the lives of presumed innocents like Reyburn, and even ladies.

John Hoskins Griscom, a forty-year-old physician and crusading public-health pioneer, had recently served a two-year stint as city inspector, a post created in the wake of the 1803 yellow fever epidemic. Almost as terrifying as cholera, yellow fever was another of those warm-weather diseases that sprang up in the spring and died down in the fall, that jumped from one spot to another without apparent effects in intervening districts, that seemed to prefer victims of lowly station and unwholesome habits. And as in the case of cholera, educated opinion was torn between the conflicting contagionist and miasmatic camps.

Like most, Griscom was heartily on the miasma side. In compiling a history of the city's yellow fever epidemics, Griscom pointed out that the fever had struck hardest near places that had been used for dumping "all manner

of filth, street dirt, dead animals, &c," killing those who had "inhal[ed] the poison evolved from such a seething mass of corruption." More generally, Griscom found that diseases of all sorts were more common in cities than in less densely peopled places, "proving conclusively that the congregation of animal and vegetable matters, with their constant effluvia...is detrimental to the health of the inhabitants." His solution—which he offered to the mayor in his official capacity as city inspector—was the creation of a "Health Police" capable of enforcing measures to achieve "Sanitary Reform" and thus *preventing* the disease that he and his colleagues were incapable of curing. The mayor, a reform-seeking Democrat, referred the recommendation to the Common Council, whose greedy Whigs promptly concluded that the inspector's services were no longer needed.

Griscom's martyrdom was widely noted. In London, Poor-Law Commissioner Edwin Chadwick, perhaps the most well-known bureaucrat of the day, read a paper to the Statistical Society in which he approvingly noted Griscom's attempt to save lives and money by getting the city to adopt a street-cleaning machine invented by Joseph Whitworth, and lamented that he himself had instead been "swept away from his office." The admiration was mutual. It was no coincidence that the published version of Inspector Griscom's report was entitled "The Sanitary Condition of the Laboring Population of New York, With Suggestions for Its Improvement": Chadwick's "Report on the Sanitary Condition of the Laboring Population of Great Britain," published the previous year, had been the most widely read government publication in English history. In case his allegiance was not sufficiently clear, Griscom made it explicit:

> No one can rise from the perusal of the works of Edwin Chadwick of London or of Parent-Duchatelet of Paris . . . without feeling a portion of the ardor which inspires them, and wishing he had been thrown into the same pursuit, that some of the leaves of the same laurel might encircle his own brow. It is the cause of Humanity, of the poor, the destitute, the degraded, of the virtuous made vicious by the force of circumstances, which they are now investigating, and exposing to the knowledge of others.
>
> . . . But Chadwick and Duchatelet, especially the former, are diving still deeper into the subject of moral and physical reform. They are probing to the bottom the foul ulcers upon the body of society, and endeavoring to discover the causes of so much wretchedness and vice, which fill the prisons and work-houses.

Chadwick and Griscom had bigger fish to fry than just public health. The whole political economy needed rationalizing, a reordering that by saving lives would save money. According to Griscom,

> Fathers are taken from their children, husbands from their wives, 'ere they have lived out half their days,'—the widows and orphans are thrown upon public or private charity for support, and the money which is expended to save them from starvation, to educate them in the public schools, or perchance, to maintain them in the work-house or the prison, if judiciously spent in improving the sanitary arrangements of the city, and instilling into the population a knowledge of the means by

Jeremy Bentham
Listening to Griscom, many educated New Yorkers would have recognized the strains of Jeremy Bentham, father of the political philosophy of utilitarianism.

Edwin Chadwick
It was Bentham, who preached social control through rational institutional structures, who had put Chadwick on his course.

which their health might be protected and their lives prolonged and made happy, would have been not only saved, but returned to the treasury in the increased health of the population, a much better state of public morals, and, by consequence, a more easily governed and respectable community.

Listening to Griscom, many educated New Yorkers would have recognized the strains of Jeremy Bentham, father of the political philosophy of utilitarianism, coiner of the maxim that the goal of all legislation was "the greatest happiness of the greatest number." It was Bentham, who preached social control through rational institutional structures, who had put Chadwick on his course. He chose Chadwick—when he was still a struggling young barrister who preferred penny-a-line journalism to the law—to be his live-in secretary, and dictated to him the closing sections of his *Constitutional Code*. To Chadwick (along with his colleague and competitor, Unitarian-minister-turned-physician Southwood Smith) fell the task of easing the diminutive old man through his final days. (Fortunately for Chadwick, only Southwood Smith was qualified to perform the last offices Bentham requested—which was that he be eulogized in an operating theater, so that his friends could have the final benefit of seeing his cadaver simultaneously dissected. Smith reportedly performed both tasks with fluent aplomb. Afterward, again following Bentham's instructions, his skeleton was dressed in his own clothes, his head remolded from wax, and his favorite walking stick stuck in his hand.) It was Chadwick whom the self-infatuated bachelor offered a lifetime legacy to be caretaker of his intellectual estate. But despite his devotion and his need for a steady income, Chadwick was too ambitious to spend the rest of his days as just an acolyte to the old man's memory. Instead, while maintaining lifelong fidelity to his mentor's views, he found more direct means than Bentham had discovered to put utilitarian principles to actual use.

The insidiously complex intermingling of public and private interest inherent in their common precepts is perhaps best depicted by the grand scheme of Bentham's maturity, which became the obsession of his old age. The "Panopticon" was an architectural idea he conceived while visiting his brother, a diplomat posted to Russia, after inspecting his brother's workshop on Prince Potemkin's estate. Its object was the exact opposite of the painted-backdrop-village Bentham was shown, which the prince had built to fool Catherine the Great. Instead of screening her subjects from the ruler's sight (leaving them free to the squalor of their own devices), the purpose of the Panopticon—a poorhouse shaped like a wagon wheel, in whose mirrored hub the hidden keeper could stare simultaneously and unblinking to the cells around the rim—was to know everything its occupants did, instilling in the process (through the awareness that every act was known before it could be completed) a moral control so perfect that it would guarantee the greatest contentment to the greatest number. A spider surrounded by its happy flies.

Surreal as was this vision of the power of the centralized state, Bentham was committed to its execution. In the opening lines of his first public announcement of the idea (a publication subsidized, because of its pressing need for more poorhouses, by the government of Ireland), he promised

Morals reformed, health preserved, industry invigorated, instruction diffused, public burthens lightened, Economy seated, as it were upon a rock, the gordian knot of the Poor-Laws not cut but untied—all by a simple idea in Architecture!

In a second treatise on the subject (published in 1798), he elaborated on the earlier concept by proposing the establishment of a private, profit-making National Charity Company with "undivided authority" over the "whole body of the burdensome poor" wherever they might occur throughout England (carefully leaving open the possibility of expansion, as needed, to any of the Empire's remaining colonies). Through its agency, two-hundred-fifty Panopticons would be erected to house five-hundred-thousand poor, and their children, for life. In these perfectly efficient workhouses, no effort would be stinted to ensure that the inmates would produce as much profit as working sixteen and a half hours a day could yield.

Not least striking of the Panopticon company's particulars was Bentham's intent to run these poorhouses himself. By avoiding stockings, shirts, hats, and bedding, by feeding the inmates mainly on potatoes they themselves would grow, he expected to make a 100-percent profit on the women, 200 percent on the men, and much more on the able-bodied "apprentice" children under the age of twenty-one, who (to ensure that there would always be more of them) would be encouraged to marry as soon as they were physically capable of reproduction. The highest glory of the scheme, however, was its combination with an invention of his brother's (designed in the same Russian workshop that birthed the Panopticon itself), an automated milling machine, which, unfortunately, could not conveniently be made to run on steam: the brothers Bentham would run a vast industrial enterprise on the strength of human-powered treadmills. He drafted a bill for this privilege that was speedily approved by both houses of Parliament, but after Bentham had obtained the deeds for the land necessary for building the Panopticons, George III's treasury refused to ratify his contract. Bentham fought unsuccessfully for twenty years to have the decision reversed; finally, in his eighties, he revenged himself by writing a book on the subject of the madness of George III; in Bentham's version (*History of the War between Jeremy Bentham and George III*), the failure to execute the Panopticon contract was the result of the king's anger over Bentham's efforts to achieve peace with Russia.

Death and Taxes

Although the chimerical Panopticon left few traces, one of these was on Edwin Chadwick. His entrée to public life came with an assistant's post to Lord Grey's 1832 Poor Law Commission. England's industrialization in the eighteenth century had created social disruptions on a scale unparalleled since the fall of the Roman Empire (an historical pageant with which Gibbon had recently regaled his countrymen). The problems that the displaced peasants and artisans brought with them threatened to overwhelm any physical or institutional bulwarks the old society had erected for its support. Not least of these were the Poor Laws Elizabeth had enacted in 1601 to counter the displacements her father's Reformation had caused by closing down the convents and monasteries on which English charity, like other civilized nations', had always depended. Elizabeth's Poor Law provided relief to the old or infirm as well as to the able-bodied unemployed through taxes ("poor-rolls") levied by every local administrative unit (the parishes). Parishes distributed this relief to the able-bodied in their homes ("outdoor relief") in the form of subsidized wages, food, or cash grants, and to the disabled in poorhouses, where they were made to occupy themselves as best they could to produce goods that would help to offset the cost of their care.

Among the problems the Poor Law administrators faced were steep escalations of the poor-roll rates, gross inequities in the distribution of the pauper population due to a proscription against migration between parishes, and a payment system that not only encouraged having more children but, since it was often more remunerative than working, kept families on the rolls for generations. Chadwick, undoubtedly the most energetic of the assistants, found here a full field in which to exercise his utilitarian inclinations. His vigor soon brought a promotion that made him one of the commissioners, and he became more responsible than anyone else for the shape the New Poor Law took. Following Bentham, he insisted that the law establish a single administrative system encompassing all of England, set relief rates low enough to exclude automatically anyone who could find employment, eliminate outdoor relief so that the only way to receive aid was by living in a poorhouse, and make the standards for poorhouse life so grim that they would scarcely maintain life. (Unlike the Panopticon, however, the new poorhouse rules were *not* designed to produce a captive breeding population: even in the case of married couples, no contact was allowed between the sexes.) To those with any empathy—for instance, Charles Dickens, whose family had found life in the Marshallgate Poorhouse dreary enough under the old regime—Chadwick was a monster.

Five years after the passage of the new restrictions, Chadwick—who had become one of the least popular men in England—was removed from an active role in the Poor Law administration by a newly appointed and hostile chief commissioner. Just then a providential outbreak of influenza and typhoid—and the fear that cholera might return—provided a new outlet for his ambition. After local Poor Law commissioners had cleaned up the dangerously stagnant pools and the refuse piled in London's East End, and the central auditors had refused to reimburse them for their expenses, the commission was forced to consider the implications of "the sanitary problem." Chadwick took charge. As usual, his tack was utilitarian and economically reductionist. "In general," he wrote, "all epidemics and infectious diseases are attended with charges, immediate and ultimate, on the Poor Law Rates. Labourers are suddenly thrown by infectious disease into a state of destitution, for which immediate relief must be given. In the case of death, the widow and the children are thrown as paupers upon the parish. The amount of burthens thus produced is frequently so great as to render it good economy on the part of the administrators of the Poor Laws to incur the charges for preventing the evils where they are ascribable to physical causes, which there are no other means of removing."

From there a course was set in which his contempt for physicians and their squabbling inability to identify either causes or cures was equalled by an enthusiasm for engineering preventive solutions. Like his plan for "preventive police" to eliminate crime before it could be committed, Chadwick developed a new credo directed toward the "removal of nuisances" before their smell could kill, the killing could cost money, and society's net quotient of happiness thereby be reduced. The international Sanitary Reform Movement was born.

Chadwick was scarcely alone in his belief in "epidemic atmospheres." Most of the English medical establishment agreed. Foremost among the proponents were the prominent researchers he had recruited for the Poor Law Commission. They led the way in documenting their case, not just for public officials and their peers, but more importantly, for the upper- and middle-class publics whose support would be needed to effect any comprehensive legislative reforms. Their richly descriptive case studies grabbed the attention of thousands of gentle readers, showed them things beyond their imagination, told startling stories about the kinds of living conditions that Charles Dickens in his own way and out of his own experience was trying to portray (despite his personal distaste for the man, Dickens admitted that the sanitation report was a solid piece of work), and captured the passionate admiration of Americans like John Griscom. Though Chadwick received most of the credit for the renowned report, it was based on the work of the physicians who had conducted the surveys, including Bentham's dissector, Southwood Smith. For his part, Smith was quite certain he knew the mechanisms by which an epidemic atmosphere killed.

> Wherever animal and vegetable substances are undergoing the process of decomposition, poisonous matters are evolved which, mixing with the air, corrupt it, and render it injurious to health and fatal to life. But wherever human beings live together in communities, these large masses of animal and vegetable substances, the refuse of food and of other matters essential to human existence, must necessarily be always decomposing. If provision is not made for the immediate removal of these poisons, they are carried by the air inspired to the air-cells of the lungs, the thin delicate membranes of which they pierce, and thus pass directly into the current of the circulation. It has been shown that by the natural and ordinary flow of this current, three distinct and fresh portions of these poisons must necessarily be transmitted to every nook and corner of the system in every eight minutes of time. The consequences are sometimes death within the space of a few hours, or even minutes; at other times a progressive and rapid, or a progressive but slow deterioration and corruption of the whole mass of the blood; a consequent disorganization of the solid structures of the body, and the excitement of those violent commotions of the system which constitute fevers, choleras, dysenteries and other mortal epidemics. . . .

Through a dangerous alchemy, things were not what they seemed. The delicate membranes that separated and distinguished one thing from another were easily pierced, allowing constant transformations of matter that could turn grapes to wine, hay to manure, decaying animal matter into poisonous gases which, absorbed through the lungs into the blood could become yellow fever, dysentery, or something else, or turn a relatively mild disease (such as "cholera morbus"—a form of bilious diarrhea that was rarely fatal) into a more serious affliction (such as the real cholera). The fluidity of matter, the permutability of disease, the delicate dependence of a human system's internal balance on the airs, waters, and places of the environment in which it lived (in the still accepted Hippocratic view)—and the congruence between mental, moral, and physical states—provided an invaluable construct for the sanitary reformers who wanted to reshape society through engineered interventions in the urban environment.

One of the most famous of these reformers was Florence Nightingale, the wellborn young nurse who had astounded the medical world during the Crimean War by demonstrating that lives could be saved through a starched-and-pressed approach to field hospital hygiene. Chadwick's relations with her were not uncomplicated: the haughty socialite was good enough to oblige his request for an invitation to discuss his sanitary ideas with the German Prince Royal over dinner, but a similar request to meet the Empress Léonie, Napoléon III's consort, at Windsor Castle was ignored. But on the plane of sanitary theory, the bureaucrat and the nurse were of one stubborn mind. Well after Pasteur and his successors had established that diseases are the products of specific, identifiable causes, Nightingale continued to insist that her rules for controlling a hospital environment were the only safeguard against a mortally dangerous chaos. "I was brought up," she wrote,

> by scientific men and ignorant women distinctly to believe that
> smallpox was a thing of which there was once a specimen in the world,
> which went on propagating itself in a perpetual chain of descent, just as
> much as that there was a first dog (or first pair of dogs) and that smallpox
> would not begin itself any more than a new dog would without there
> having been a parent dog. Since then I have seen with my eyes and
> smelled with my nose smallpox growing up in first specimens, either in
> close rooms or in overcrowded wards, where it could not by any
> possibility have been 'caught' but must have begun. Nay, more, I have
> seen diseases begin, grow up and pass into one another. Now dogs do

not pass into cats. I have seen, for instance, with a little overcrowding, continued fever grow up, and with a little more, typhoid fever, and with a little more, typhus, and all in the same ward or hut. For diseases, as all experiences show, are adjectives, not noun substantives. . . .

The specific disease doctrine is the grand refuge of weak, uncultured, unstable minds, such as now rule in the medical profession. There are no specific diseases: there are specific disease conditions.

And thus while John Snow, the Queen's own anaesthesiologist, was about to discover through a masterful analysis of morbidity statistics that cholera is transmitted through drinking water, Chadwick had his staff dashing about London flushing all the filth they could find into the Thames, the city's only water supply. His belief that flushing away nuisances was the solution to sanitary problems also led him to have a new kind of sewer made. Rather than an open ditch or a box-shaped tunnel in which water either stood still, or, when its surface moved, left ever thicker layers of silted sediment behind, the new system was made of glazed ceramic and had an egg-shaped narrow-gauged channel in which the entrained material was propelled with surprising force. Maintaining this force, however, required a steady supply of water. Chadwick therefore began to see water supply as another critical sanitary priority. But in combining the design of water supply and sewerage to produce a unified system, his driving concern remained not the purity of the drinking water that entered the city, but the pressure of the polluted flow that left it.

A noble German chemist had recently astonished the world with his theory that plants, like other living things, needed food. Baron Gustav von Liebig pointed out that the matter in plants had to come from somewhere; since it did not come out of the air, plants had to get food substances from the soil. Like the simple architectural idea that offered Bentham the apparent power to untie the Poor Laws' gordian knot, Liebig's insight gave Chadwick an idea for squeezing a return from the hydraulic fluid his costly egg-shaped sewers carried: he proposed building pipelines from London to the agricultural districts that fed it. The economic viability of the overall sanitary system proposed in his famous 1843 report, in fact, depended on successfully realizing this vision. But when Chadwick went to Munich to get the baron's blessing, he came away disappointed: Liebig insisted that in a country as wet as England a "liquid manure" would only be washed away.

There was some validity in the scientific assessment. The concentration of agriculturally available phosphates, potassium, and nitrogen in such a slurry would have been far too low to have an offsetting effect on the overall system's economics. Still Liebig's disparagement was a very personal blow to Chadwick, who had either put his money where his mouth was, or was using his position to gain his own fortune: liquid manure was the secret to the hoped-for success of the "Towns Improvement Company" that he and his partners had formed to sell water-and-sewer systems. (One of these partners was the same Joseph Whitworth who had tried to sell street sweepers to Inspector Griscom in New York.) But neither could it be said that Liebig's lack of enthusiasm was completely disinterested: he also owned part of a fertilizer company, and the success of *his* depended on the market primacy of a dry product.

The world's leaders in turning excrement to profit through the use of dry commercial processes were the French. Paris and its already famous (though woefully inefficient) sewers were the source of the world's greatest supply of the raw material used to make a product known with some delicacy as *poudrette*. This *powder* was easy enough to make—the sewage was dried and lime and other compounds added to improve its effectiveness and reduce its odor—but problems with storing and transporting it launched the career of the other reformer whose laurels Inspector Griscom envied. Like Chadwick, Alexandre-Jean-Baptiste Parent-Duchatelet was temperamentally unfit for the profession for which he had been trained. Appointed to a position on the faculty of the École de Médecine de Paris after his graduation from it, he found himself too shy to lecture. Even sitting on an examination panel before which hapless students appeared one by one was too much: he shook with fear and stuttered nervously when he had to ask a question. But he got the gift of a new métier the day (in 1821) he was asked to investigate the deaths of half the sailors on a poudrette ship en route to Guadaloupe. He concluded that the men closed below decks were asphyxiated by the gases the fermenting material gave off. Within a few years his further researches would make him the world's foremost practitioner of the science of smell.

Unlike Chadwick, who largely relied on the first-hand reports of others, Parent did all his fieldwork himself. His first major assignment as a member of the Health Council of the City of Paris was to deal with a sewer emer-

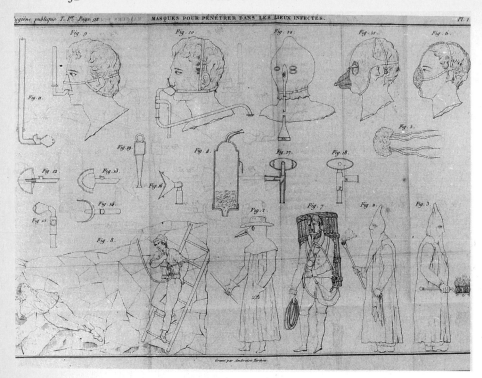

Precautions against dangerous odors

gency: the Amelot stretch, which had not been scraped for decades because of its reputation as the most dangerous in the city, was emitting gases so noxious that its cleaning could no longer be postponed. Experience made it seem inevitable that some of the city's brave sewer workers, who waded up to their thighs in the muck dragging scrapers behind them, would be sacrificed to this dragon's breath. Parent was asked to supervise the enterprise in the hope of reducing the mortal toll. He made a close study of the system, spending his days in the tunnels with the workers, supervising their nutrition, their rest periods, ensuring that they took breaks to breathe fresh air, that they stayed warm and dry under a tent when they went above ground in inclement weather. To his profound joy, not one man died.

Parent found below ground the company of a small band united in a thrillingly repulsive and dangerous task, working in a world that no civilian could enter or imagine, dependent for survival upon the watchful support of their fellows, and possessed of a sensitivity and intellectual curiosity, of a love of literature and of family rarely found above ground. In the sewers the shy man had found real happiness. He would slip away from dinner parties to descend again. "I would almost say," his friend Leuret would write after his early death, "that he loved them."

Among contemporary historians there are those who believe that the excruciating skin disease that kept Jean-Paul Marât huddled in the bath where Charlotte Corday stabbed him was something he picked up in the Paris sewers while hiding from Lafayette's counterrevolution squads. Along with much other popular wisdom, Parent would have disputed this. The sewer workers themselves, he said, believed the ooze through which they trod was a beneficial, moisturizing unguent. Upon examination, this seemed true—they had fewer rashes and cutaneous eruptions than were commonly found, and any cuts they had healed quickly. Admittedly the slime appeared to aggravate the effects of syphilis, but since his friends were generally careful to avoid contracting the disease, this was not a significant problem. The sewers, in short—contrary to the folktales about the danger of the evil smells themselves—could be safely negotiated if basic precautions were taken.

Henceforth Parent would maintain his empirical approach to all the public health and sanitary tasks to which he set himself. Always his own guinea pig, he put Chadwick's "All smell is death" directly to the test time and again. In twenty-seven consecutive experiments, for example, he tried to establish what would happen if he ate meat that had been hung in a closed chamber with the rankest odors he could find. "The disgust that necessarily accompanies such experiments, as one can readily imagine, did not allow me to repeat them *as often as I would have wished*," [emphasis added] but there was obviously no effect on health: smells that went into the meat could go out of it again (the pieces he ate tasted mainly of the chlorine he used as a precautionary fumigant before cooking them), and the odors' passage through the meat had obviously not affected its rate of putrefaction or healthfulness. These tests were good preparation for sharing meals with the workers of Montfaucon, the hill outside Paris where the city's dead horses and other offal were taken. He called the meat cut from the horses there "very good and very savory." (He didn't try the cat carcasses, though he admitted that, neatly dressed on a plate, they did not look unpalatable.)

His most fearsome experiment, judging by the anxiety he candidly reported, was sleeping in a room filled with wet hemp. To be made into rope, hemp plants had first to be soaked for days or weeks until their fibers could be retted (rotted) from the stalk, producing all the while an intensely disagreeable odor. If odors themselves were dangerous, the material that gave off the odor was presumably the source of the harm. To test this, Parent drank some of the retting liquor. When he found no adverse effect, he expanded his experimental pool by slipping some of the broth into hospital patients' medications. No one was the worse. Parent then tested the effect of the other exposure route. He filled his laboratory with wet hemp, shut himself up in it, and tried to sleep. He had a most unquiet night: he woke often, clutching his chest and fighting for air, until gradually he realized that he had simply been "under the empire of the imagination," stifled by the unsettling stories he had heard about hemp water's hazards. To confirm his finding, he brought his five-year-old son into the room the following night. His son's three-year-old brother came along the next. On the fourth night, he added his last child, a fifteen-month-old baby, whose mother "insisted on coming along to nurse him." The whole family survived.

His interest in the relationship between the most basic functions and public health provided his other major field of research, prostitution. In the course of exploring this subject, he tested the only element of Bentham's Panopticon that the English prison system ever adopted, the human-powered "wheel à l'Anglaise" whose application had been extended to penitentiaries for Parisian prostitutes. His medical colleagues found it a particularly barbarous punishment. But after spending an afternoon in it, Parent pronounced it better than any mineral water. He also sat through the religious services that incarcerated prostitutes were made to attend: even when the scripture was read in the vulgar tongue, and supplemented by clerical explanations, the experience, he found, was useless. In perhaps his most famous formulation, Parent wrote that prostitution is "as inevitable, in an agglomeration of people, as sewers, cesspools, and refuse dumps." The goal of the public health authorities should be the same for both prostitutes and refuse dumps: "to hide them, to relegate them to the most obscure corners, in a word, to render their presence as imperceptible as possible."

Original lithograph from Parent's *Recherches et considérations sur l'enlèvement et l'emploi des chevaux morts*, 1827. (Note the baby in the carcass.)

When cholera came in 1832, Parent was asked to monitor what was presumed to be the city's most dangerous quarter, the sewage and dead horse dump on Montfaucon. The inhabitants believed themselves healthy, Parent reported, but naturally his inquiries did not stop there. He took detailed family histories, conducted physical examinations, and closely observed the circumstances in which they lived. Families had maintained themselves on Montfaucon for healthy generation after generation, their members living to ripe old age, blessed with plenty of descendants. As an example, Parent pointed to a woman whose family worked in the thick of the cutting up and dismembering and who was always pregnant. To keep her youngest child nearby for nursing, she kept it stuffed inside a carcass. Certainly there was unpleasantness: for example, the fields where layers of horseflesh were left to putrefy until the whole surface of the ground writhed with maggots to be harvested for poultry feed and fish bait (a passing drunk who lay down and fell to sleep there lost both sight and hearing), or the rats that swarmed over the cutting grounds. But there was nothing inherently dangerous in this work, nothing that, with sensible precautions, could not be managed even in the heart of Paris. That year twenty thousand Parisians died of cholera. Not one was from Montfaucon.

Nuisance Removal

Chadwick's famous dictum clearly was wrong. But somehow the lesson was missed. Parent died young—aged forty-six, of overwork, his friends said—in 1835. Louis Pasteur would one day begin to crack the mystery of cholera by discovering that microorganisms were what made things rot (a discovery that Liebig would mock with caricatures of little animals shaped like distilleries: "As to the opinion which explains the putrefaction of animal substances by the presence of microscopic animalcula," he said, "it may be compared to that of a child who would explain the rapidity of the Rhine current by attributing it to the violent movement of the many mill wheels at Mainz"). In 1849, however, when cholera came to Paris again, Pasteur was still hanging his head with his colleagues' in the attics over hospital wards, sampling the air to find the smell that killed. Chadwick's response in London was to have passed a "Nuisance Removal Act" meant to get all refuse out of town. And back in New York, in the Whig-filled chambers of the municipal administration, the man in Griscom's old city inspector post that cholera July was a short, slight, fortyish druggist named Alfred W. White who was a Whig himself. Without benefit of either medical training or license, he had taken to calling himself *Dr.* He was equally ambitious in carrying out his regulatory responsibilities.

In June, White had cracked down on the hogs that ran through the streets, or were penned in basements and backyards, living on garbage and offal and excrement, and on which thousands of the poor in turn subsisted. With a liberal application of police clubs, he succeeded in driving several thousand hogs from the populous lower portions of the city to the wide-open spaces of what was then uptown. But the slaughterhouses and bone-boiling industries were a more intractable problem. Unlike the poor man's hog, these businesses provided services without which the city clearly could not manage. Moreover, their owners were substantial citizens who had significant investments in these "nuisances." They were already located as far north as the city proper extended; moving them even farther would be costly, and, from their point of view, unfair, since they had erected their buildings when their neighborhoods were virtually unpopulated—the burgeoning slum population had pushed into the stockyard districts, not vice versa. Still, White did what he could. He investigated the complaints he received, and found,

> hid away in densely populated neighborhoods, . . . shanties and out-
> buildings, in which are boiled up together, in large cauldrons, the refuse
> of the streets and markets, the bones and scraps of animal substances,
> found about these places, and every particle of dead and putrifying
> animal matter, that the scavengers of the city collect in hand-carts and
> bags, by raking the gutters and purlieus of offal and filth. The carrion of
> horses, and oxen, cows, hogs, rancid fat, bought or begged at the
> markets, are all thrown into the cauldrons and boiled, for various
> purposes of traffic. From these places the most intolerable stench arises,
> which, mingling with the atmosphere, is brought into the dwellings of
> the neighborhood, their sick rooms and nurseries, in a greater or less
> state of dilution. So dense and persistent is the stench created by these
> places, that I have been led, when ferreting out their secluded abodes,
> for a long·distance, with no other guide.

White had the authority to close businesses that, in his judgment, were hazards to public health; he closed as many as his ferreting found.

But on the panic-filled Monday following Reyburn's death, he felt impelled to seek a broader and more permanent solution. He asked for an ordinance to forbid bone boiling anywhere within the city. While the Common Council appointed a committee to study the issue, White went ahead and ordered all bone boiling and bone-burning businesses closed for the duration of the epidemic. The immediate public reaction was one of relief, but it quickly changed. White himself freely confessed that his ad hoc solution was unsatisfactory. The result, he admitted when the season had passed, was just "another evil": with nowhere else to go, the rotting carcasses of horses and cattle were simply tossed into the rivers surrounding the city, where they remained for weeks, stinking and bloated, floating in and out with the tides. As the warm weather of 1850 approached, bringing with it the renewed possibility of plague, White stepped up his campaign to rid the city of dangerous impurities.

One of these was a manure pile on the corner of Thirty-third Street and Tenth Avenue, in the heart of the animal district. It was owned by William C. Lent, a stagecoach superintendent who sold fertilizer as a sideline. When he got White's order to rid himself of his inventory, Lent strode into White's City Hall office to complain. If a pile of horse manure was unacceptable in the middle of the stable and slaughterhouse district, Lent said, nowhere in the city would do. White agreed. In that case, Lent replied, a place should be designated outside the city that would be large enough to handle all the city's animal droppings, and all of the bones, carcasses, and offal as well. Inspector White paused for a moment, Lent later testified. Then he said, "there is the greatest chance for a fortune I ever saw."

Because White's official position constrained his ability to operate as a private businessman in the field he regulated, he asked Lent to find this place. Lent looked, but not fast enough to suit his prospective partner. White broadened the net by having Lent arrange a meeting with another manure dealer, a Queens farmer named William L. Baxter. When the three met for the first time, White tried to impress Baxter by bragging that "he had the city government under his thumb," mentioned a new law the state legislature had adopted in the wake of the epidemic to give him extraordinary powers to close businesses that, in his judgment, might endanger public health, or that caused complaints, and pointed out that he had received a number of such complaints recently and had reason to expect more in the near future. Then he made his pitch: if they would form an association with him, they could each make a hundred thousand dollars before the remaining two years of his term were up. He would use his official influence on behalf of the firm, would invest in it, and share in its profits. For their part, they would run the business and keep his role secret.

Over the next few weeks, White suggested several other prospective partners, and his colleagues, after interviewing them, agreed to take three more members into the firm. John Brady was a contractor; James D. Morgan ran a stationery store, but had liquid assets and useful connections. The third, like White himself, became another silent partner. Heman W. Childs, the commissioner of the Department of Streets and Lamps, had responsibilities (for cleaning the streets and administering the public markets) that clearly recommended his usefulness to his fellow partners; for his part,

Childs could scarcely be called a reluctant bridegroom—he seemed to understand the matter at once and told Baxter, who had been delegated to feel him out about the scheme, that it was just the sort of thing that he "would like to go into secretly," adding, "that is the way to make a fortune," and "that is the way we do things up here."

Meanwhile the associates continued their search for an acceptable location. Using an assumed name, Inspector White visited Wards Island in the East River with his colleagues one April Sunday. The associates ruled it out as too close to civilization, but they decided that South Brother Island, three miles farther upstream, did suit their purposes. They bought it for 3,200 dollars on the first of May and quickly set up a series of large open kettles, dug a trench to the river into which the waste liquid from the kettles could be drained, built houses for their laborers, assembled a small fleet that included barges, sloops, and a steamship, and landed several thousand hogs. Assistant Alderman Oscar W. Sturtevant, the head of the Special Committee on Nuisances that had been created the previous summer to consider White's proposal to ban bone boiling within the city limits, kindly produced the desired ordinance. The partners were ready to begin business.

Sugar refiners and fertilizer manufacturers wanted blood.

Bones were a valuable commodity. The best were used for handles and buttons. The next best were ground and charred to be used by sugar refiners to filter the dark liquid they pressed from the cane; bone black was also used to make pigments and china. Even the least desirable bones fetched an attractive price from the emerging industry for commercial fertilizers, whose promising future seemed to offer an eternal new life for the urban eastern seaboard's exhausted market garden soils. Ninety percent of the marrow could be converted to tallow that was valuable to chandlers and soap makers and to the rapidly expanding chemical industry. The remaining parts of the carcass could also be sold. Sugar refiners and fertilizer manufacturers wanted blood. Flesh, boiled, was another material sought by the tallow industries. Hooves were used for gelatin, and in the dye known as Prussian blue. Hides and hair had their uses. Whatever remained was hog food.

Baxter, Brady, Lent & Company bought the bones, offal and carcasses that were now banished from the city. At the city inspector's East Twenty-third Street pier they paid about a dollar-twenty for each dead horse and a dollar-fifty for each cow carcass; they bought kitchen waste under contract from the major hotels; and they bought bones for a few cents apiece wherever they found them. Their steamship towed their scows up the river to their island where the garbage was thrown on the shore for the hogs, the hides skinned from the carcasses, and the bones boiled. The business brought a liberal profit of about a hundred dollars a day. But for two problems, its future would have been rosy.

The first problem was interpersonal. William Baxter knew boats and had learned the channels and currents of New York's rivers and harbor by sailing sloops filled with manure. His partners therefore welcomed his offer to oversee their marine operations and to supervise the steamship *Boston*. But despite his obvious enthusiasm for the work (or perhaps, because of it) his relations with the other five soon soured. The *Boston*'s daily round trip to the island took only a few hours, but it had to sail with the tide in order to negotiate the treacherous currents through the "Hell Gate" at the mouth of Long Island Sound. The partners discovered that they could make extra money in the *Boston*'s otherwise dead hours by chartering her for excursions to Coney Island and other resort destinations. When their dispute began, Baxter claimed that his presence was required on board the *Boston* at all times; his partners claimed that the boat's pilot was fully capable of managing her, and that because Baxter was never ashore, they had to do all of the real work. Baxter claimed that his attention to pleasure trips simply reflected his desire to maximize the boat's profitability and to fulfill the obligations the firm had assumed under its arrangement with an excursion company; his partners claimed that the trips were his idea, not theirs, and that his devotion to resort excursions made his availability for the firm's primary purpose—moving its highly perishable cargo in timely fashion through the tide gates—too unreliable. His partners claimed that Baxter was not turning over to the firm his hundreds of dollars of excursion receipts and was instead squandering the money on lavish food, wines, and liquors for his friends; Baxter claimed that he used the receipts from ticket sales to pay the boat's expenses, and that he ran a strictly cash bar. Baxter's partners claimed that he maintained onboard a band of loose women, "including even common prostitutes," with whom his friends caroused and otherwise disported themselves to such an extent that the *Boston* was known about the harbor as the North River Brothel; Baxter maintained that his wife—along with Brady, Lent and Morgan and their wives—generally accompanied him on his excursions, that he never "caroused," that he had never heard any such opprobrious term applied to the *Boston*, and that it was Brady and Lent who had hired the prostitutes.

The predictable upshot was that by mid-August the other five wanted Baxter out of the partnership, while Baxter himself was reluctant to give up his congenial work, particularly without adequate compensation.

The second problem was with the neighbors. South Brother Island was just half a mile from the south shore of the Bronx, where a handful of wealthy New Yorkers—including such luminaries as tobacconists Jacob Lorillard and William H. Leggett—had established their country estates, and almost as close to the more modest villages of northern Queens. The partners claimed that they took care to throw their garbage below the high-water line (so what the hogs did not eat would be washed away with the tide rather than remaining to become an objectionable nuisance), but the neighbors were fussy about flotsam. The partners claimed that they did not accept "offal," only kitchen garbage from hotels (food "of the same description as that ordinarily bestowed upon" hogs), hides that were "clean and well preserved, and free from any offensive substance or vermin" and bones that were "uniformly fresh and free from taint," which "were incapable of becoming offensive, however long they might lie," but citizens in these adjacent jurisdictions claimed that odors from the island were depriving them of health, happiness, and the enjoyment of their property. The partners claimed that they had stopped accepting carcasses after the first week in August, but a landing party from the Bronx said that they found a scowful of putrefying horse carcasses, and maggot-infested hides and entrails on the evening of the fifteenth, and that the stench forced them to flee within minutes. The partners claimed that one of them (Lent) had moved to the island so that he could personally supervise operations there at all times, but the Queens-shore Board of Health nonetheless issued a resolution condemning the operation as a hazard to health.

The Queens County Supreme Court awarded injunctions to both Baxter and the neighbors. The partners were forced to close their South Brother Island business. But the injunctions, along with a parallel development in the East River, inspired an even more rewarding idea.

Blood and entrails—since city ordinance now forbade their processing or storage within the city limits—were usually dumped into the East River at the city inspector's pier. Despite the action of tide and currents, a viscous accumulation had so filled the channel that it impeded navigation, not to mention the olfactory effect in the immediate vicinity of East Twenty-third Street. The Common Council unimaginatively tried to placate angry constituents by moving the dumping pier a few blocks away, only to have other constituents raise objections to the new location. Frustrated in its attempt at governance, the council handed the problem to City Inspector White, who (in the words of George Washington Plunkitt, a sanitary official and state legislator of the next generation) saw his opportunities and took them. With the assistance of Board-of-Assistant-Aldermen President Oscar Sturtevant, White created a contract for removing all "soap-boiler's nuisances" from the city. Its most creative features were that the contract holder had the right to claim all offal in the city, and that instead of paying for this privilege, the city would pay him for exercising it. Of the handful of bids the city inspector received in response to his advertisement, three were from dummies for Brady, Lent & Co; White made sure that one of these won. To ensure that his firm's new monopoly rights were adequately safeguarded, Inspector White hired nineteen new "health wardens" to catch offal poachers, who were subject to a fine, a term in jail, or both.

From that point, the contract began to develop a powerful inertia. Commissioner Childs, ailing, resigned from the Department of Streets and Lamps; his diminished role in the firm ended with his death a few months later. Inspector White, with his official powers, and his friend James Morgan, with his financial resources, were thus left in control of the contract. And Oscar Sturtevant was due a reward for his many kindnesses. Accordingly, White and Morgan engineered the re-assignment of the contract, cutting Sturtevant in as a new secret partner and eliminated Lent and Brady (even though they had loyally perjured themselves on White's behalf by claiming that he had never been a partner in the firm; the claim was rejected in three successive layers of judicial review, and Lent and Brady eventually revoked their testimony). The new front man, William B. Reynolds, was a friend of Morgan's whose only business experience was in selling hardware.

With the East River islands now off bounds, the new operation needed a new location. White and Morgan found it twenty-eight miles from City Hall, down New York Harbor, through the Narrows and along the southern shore of Brooklyn in the mouth of Jamaica Bay. There, on an island of white sand covered with sedge and cedar, William Reynolds got a ten-year lease for a hundred dollars a year and established an operation that consisted of an unloading dock and a wooden factory building, scores of laborers, and several thousand hogs. When his contract came up for renewal in 1852, Oscar Sturtevant (now elevated from assistant alderman to alderman) again slipped it through the Common Council with unseemly dispatch, its length mysteriously increased from one to five years, and its annual cost by tenfold; the feat was the more remarkable for the fact that other qualified proposers had offered to do the work at little or no cost to the city. Indeed, three of them later testified before the comptroller, they would have been willing to pay fifty thousand dollars a year for the exclusive right to the twenty thousand tons of offal the city produced.

Such testimony probably would not have been gathered—he might never have encountered difficulties with the comptroller, no matter how excessive his bills, or how fraudulent the award of his contract—if William

Reynolds had simply performed the work assigned to him. But ironically, the absurdly inflated fees he received from the city for removing animal parts made the relatively mundane profits he could get from processing the materials for other uses seem almost trivial. Gaspar Goldstein, a German immigrant who spoke no English, sat at Reynolds's Hudson River pier and pulled a rope to release the drop-away bottom on a barge he kept permanently moored there. Between that expedient and a number of even simpler ones—Goldstein often helped the butcher's helpers empty their offal carts off the pier in such a way that they avoided the half-submerged barge altogether—the result was that all but the most valuable commodities (bones, chiefly) ended up in the river, creating the same problem for the city that its exorbitantly expensive contract was ostensibly meant to prevent.

Although the comptroller eventually succeeded in abrogating Reynolds's contract, Reynolds and company continued to operate their factory. The city's new offal contractor opened *his* plant on Barren Island as well. Within a decade, the island had the largest concentration of offal industries in the world, and the white sand, sedge, and cedar were transformed into loading docks and smoke stacks and factory buildings and workers' shacks. The island that the Indians had called Equindito (Broken Lands—a reference to the sandy fingers surrounded by marsh), and that the Dutch had called Beeren (Bears Island—separated by a narrow channel from the island they called Konynen: bears and rabbits), the English settlers, through a natural linguistic evolution, called Barren. In spite of the scores of souls who lived there, the island was cut off almost entirely from the outside world. With the exception of a weekly mail boat, the only vessels that approached it were scows filled with offal. But to any visitor who might have reached the island, the landscape would have appeared barren indeed.

CHAPTER 2

Grease

Minute globules of complex organic acids wrapped in tissue—fat cells—are found in varying quantities in all plants and animals. The fat can be liberated with heat and pressure, by dissolving the cells with solvents such as benzene or kerosene, or by breaking them down with acids. Candle makers were the first to use the simple heat-and-pressure approach. In colonial New York, door-to-door fat-and-bone collectors boiled their gleanings in open kettles. In these high temperature environments, the tissue of the cell walls broke down, the expanding fat molecules burst free, and the liquid fat, less dense than water, rose to the surface to be skimmed off. Making candles required little more than cooling this tallow in a mold, although inventive artisans developed a variety of more elaborate devices to mass-produce a smoother, more evenly shaped product. To make soap (a product that even European monarchs rarely used before the French Revolution), the acids in tallow are combined with an alkali (soda ash) and water. (The French Revolution liberated, among other things, the patent for making soda ash from Nicolas Leblanc, a court physician who had developed the first method for making it in commercial quantities. Since Leblanc's method used sea salt, which was in greater supply than the forests that had to be burned to make potash—the original form of soda ash—his discovery made the commercial production of soap feasible.) After the alkaline soda ash has combined with some of the acids in the tallow to form solid or semisolid soap curds, the remaining acids are left in the form of a clear, sweet-tasting liquid that the French chemist and soap maker Michel Eugène Chevreul in 1814 named glycerin ("sweet oil"). The discovery a few years later of clean-burning stearin candles (made from fat that had been pressed through cloth filters to isolate the crystalline acids) produced another source of glycerin. The steadily expanding supply of this unwanted residue begged for commercial applications. In 1847, an Italian chemistry professor named Ascanio Sobrero found that glycerin could be combined with nitric

The French Revolution liberated the patent for making soda ash from Nicolas Leblanc; his discovery made the commercial production of soap feasible.

acid to produce an unstable compound he named nitroglycerine, for which he saw no utility. In 1863, a Swedish munitions maker, Alfred Nobel, figured out what nitroglycerine could do, and thereby made possible New York's subways and skyscrapers, the Panama Canal, and World War I.

As the role of candles shrank to dinner tables and birthday cakes, glycerin became a basic building block in the burgeoning chemical industry, which was transforming industrial society with its countless new products. Manufacturers soon discovered glycerin's usefulness as a moisturizing agent for textiles, leather, chocolate, modeling clay, tobacco, paper, and adhesives; as a vehicle for inks, cosmetics and medical preparations; as a lubricant for clocks, guns, and delicate machinery; as an antifreeze in meters and compasses; as a preservative for meat, eggs, fruit, and scientific specimens; as a means of extracting essences from hops and perfume ingredients; and as an (illegal) additive in wines and liqueurs. But nitroglycerine never lost its role as its most important commercial application. In 1878, about twenty-two million pounds of glycerin (valued at five cents a pound) were produced worldwide; within a decade, production quadrupled. Four decades later—at the height of World War I—when it was worth seventy cents a pound,

American producers sent fifteen million dollars' worth to Europe to be blown up as quickly as possible.

Meanwhile, a parallel technological evolution was underway. Bird droppings—specifically, the excrement of anchovy-fed cormorants, pelicans, and gannets on islands untouched by rain—were propelling President Millard Fillmore's administration to the brink of military adventures off the coast of Peru. Provisioning the ballooning Eastern Seaboard cities had exhausted the soils of their horticultural hinterlands. Long Island's light, sandy loam, a major source of New York City's subsistence, was particularly vulnerable; the luxuriant foliage that so struck visitors was an illusion created by the industrious application of manure. But if a farmer could feed all his crops to his animals and then plow their droppings back into his land, he would still be fighting a losing battle. When he succumbed to the inevitable attraction of an expanding metropolis and abandoned his subsistence farming to produce products for an urban market—when his Long Island hay was used to fuel metropolitan transportation—the depletion effects on his soil were even more dramatic. Even though farmers usually filled their empty hay-carts with manure from city stables for the trip back to the island, they were losing ground. But the crucial difference fertilization made (a farmer in Riverhead could get over a hundred bushels of potatoes from an acre if he fertilized it, but only sixty if he did not) impelled market farmers to greater and greater lengths to feed their land. Long Island farmers in the middle of the century typically spent forty to fifty days a year catching fish to throw on their soil, not to mention the time they spent gathering horseshoe crabs, seaweed, swamp muck, and other fertilizing agents.

This demand turned fertilizers into a commercial commodity; farmers were fully caught up as producers in a market system, selling their output to the city, and buying back from the city fertilizers from commercial brokers such as William Baxter and William Lent. In 1840, Queens County farmers sold about half their hay (their principal cash crop), to gross 280,000 dollars, and bought back 230,000 dollars' worth of manure from New York City. At first brokers like William Lent conveyed this material by barge, but as railroads stretched out onto the island, they became the primary conduit for this trade.

The excrement of anchovy-fed cormorants, pelicans, and gannets

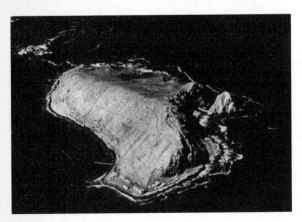

on islands untouched by rain were propelling President Millard Fillmore's administration to the brink of military adventures off the coast of Peru.

The expanding commerce in fertilizers was buttressed not only by the empirically observable effects of applying soil nutrients (which Native Americans had been the first to demonstrate to the early settlers), but by the theories that the new journals dedicated to "scientific agriculture" were bringing to a wide audience of farmers, gentlemen farmers, and interested laymen. American readers of journals such as *The Country Gentleman* and *The Working Farmer* had become as familiar with von Liebig's work as their European contemporaries were. James J. Mapes, publisher of the latter (who, along with steel magnate Peter Cooper, was one of the sponsors of Griscom's 1844 Sanitary

At first brokers like William Lent conveyed manure by barge, but as railroads stretched out onto the island, they became the primary conduit for this trade.

Report and ran a New Jersey poudrette factory on the side) was one of the foremost proponents of the new gospel. Among his young disciples was George E. Waring (a Pound Ridge, New York, native, whose grandfather and great-uncle had owned the eponymous "Brother" islands at the mouth of Long Island Sound before Inspector White and his partners bought one of them), who spent part of his twenties travelling around Maine and Vermont lecturing on the new theories. (Contrary to his mentor's commercial interests, Waring would later promulgate a Chadwickian scheme to pump liquid sewage from New York City directly onto Long Island fields.)

As Parent well knew, there is enough ammonia in manure to produce a powerful aroma. Ammonia, of course, contains the nitrogen Liebig found was essential. But there were problems with using the stuff scooped from New York streets. In the first place, there was so much dirt and rubbish in it that the percentage of this active ingredient was uneconomically low. And even high-grade manure that came from stables with well-fed horses was mostly water—which raised the same problem Chadwick faced with his hydraulic fluid: the cost of getting such a bulky mass from the stable to the farm and out onto the fields was greater than its fertilizing value. Even so, there was not enough to meet the demand. An even greater problem was that manure alone, since it supplied little potassium and phosphate, was not enough to maintain the fertility of soil. Ashes were a known source of potassium (the word comes from potash, the potassium carbonate residue left in iron pots in which wood ashes have been boiled), but the output of the region's potash works and of the city's fireplaces was not enough to meet the demand. An English gentleman farmer, Colonel St. Leger, discovered the fertilizing value of bones in 1775; English proselytizers for bone fertilizer later declaimed the usefulness of their product as a source of phosphates by pointing to the dense vegetation on the battlefields of Waterloo. However, it was not until French bone buyers discovered in American sugar refineries a cheap source of bone meal (spent bone black that could absorb no further impurities) that American farmers decided to try it. But this supply, too, was limited, which is why the commercial discovery of Peruvian guano in the 1840s was so important. Besides making the Towns Improvement Company's odds as remote as the Panopticon's, it also had diplomatic consequences.

Native American agriculturalists were using guano by the second century BC. Europeans discovered it in the early 1600s, but it had no commercial value until the English began to import it from the Chincha Islands off the coast of Peru in the 1840s. A few years later, a whaling captain found another guano island off the coast of Africa; this new supply created a glut in the English market that suddenly made guano available in the United States. Like the discovery of gold in California, Americans' discovery of the powers of this "white gold" drove eager young men off to seek their fortunes. The Union annexed California as the thirty-first state soon after the discovery of its mother lode; the guano hunt through foreign seas, which created security risks to American lives and investments, also aroused expansionist sentiments. In one episode, a New York merchant named Alfred G. Benson went off to claim the Lobos islands forty miles off the coast of Peru and ran into trouble with the Peruvian navy; in the process he inveigled Secretary of State Daniel Webster to send a US naval vessel to his defense. President Fillmore, weighing the jurisdictional evidence and finding that ownership claims were likely to be decided in Peru's favor (and considering, perhaps, the possibility that—as William Cullen Bryant charged—Webster had a personal interest in Benson's speculative venture), cancelled the naval order to defend the islands. To reduce the odds that this might happen again, Benson

Guano had no commercial value until the English began to import it from the Chincha Islands off the coast of Peru in the 1840s.

successfully lobbied for a federal law to authorize protection for any US citizen who discovered a guano deposit. Within four years, over fifty islands
had been claimed under the Guano Island Act, most of which were held by
companies tied to Benson.

Another guano fortunate was William Russell (W. R.) Grace. A teenage
refugee from the 1846 Irish potato famine, Grace had the good fortune to
emigrate directly to Peru. There he set himself up in the business of supply-
ing and provisioning ships' crews. Recognizing the importance of the
standing-room-only queues of ships waiting their turns at the guano chutes
on the Chincha islands, young Grace got himself a scow, filled it with his
wares, had it towed out to the guano grounds, and threw down his anchor.
His business thrived. He soon acquired his own fleet of guano ships and set
up a parallel business exporting another raw material used in making commercial fertilizers, nitrates from the Chilean desert. At the age of thirty-
three he married a Yankee ship captain's daughter and moved to New York,
where his ships and his wealth earned him the sobriquet "Pirate of Peru,"

Another guano fortunate was William Russell (W. R.) Grace. On a platform of bringing "rational business principles" to municipal administration, Grace was elected for two (nonconsecutive) terms as mayor of New York City. Today the company he founded is ranked 180 on the Fortune 500 list of the top American corporations. In the 1980s, W. R.'s descendant and successor as CEO of W. R. Grace, J. Peter Grace, headed a commission that advised the federal government on how to implement more efficient business practices in its operations. The company still makes fertilizer.

and where his years of seasoning before the mast stood him in good stead. When the steamer *Seawanhaka* blew up in the Hell Gate of the East River in 1880, dozens of people out on a pleasure cruise panicked and burned to death or drowned. But Grace coolly stuffed his wife's diamonds into his pocket before jumping overboard with her and their child to be saved. He was elected mayor four months later.

The physical discomforts, logistical difficulties, and political obstacles of the guano trade, and most importantly, the exhaustion of the guano supplies that had taken hundreds of years to accumulate, led to a search for substitutes to supply the newly evolved global market. Rather than viewing them as end products to be recycled directly into the soil, American entrepreneurs, like Parent's compatriots, began to see city wastes as a raw material for manufacturing more sophisticated fertilizers. Old-time manure brokers like William Baxter and John Brady, who had been the only link between horse and farmer, were replaced by sophisticated industrialists. Urban alchemists succeeded to some extent in replicating this white gold (or so their salesmen said) with products they sold under labels such as bone guano (ground bone that had been treated with sulfuric acid to make the phosphates more soluble), blood guano, and *guano à cheval* (made by boiling flesh in acid).

Barren Island soon surpassed even Montfaucon to become the world capital of the artificial guano trade. Leffert Cornell, William Reynolds's successor to the contract for New York City's offal, had a monopoly on Brooklyn's as well. With the largest plant on the island, Cornell made a product that he shipped to London to be made into nitro-phosphate fertilizers. William Reynolds, meanwhile, continued to operate his factory on the island, too, making fertilizers for vineyards on the Rhine. Reynolds also made oils that he and his partners Frederick Devoe and Charles Pratt used to make paint. (Pratt's skills with acids and oils later led to the partnership with John D. Rockefeller that created Standard Oil.) Other factories on the island made oils and fertilizers from the fish on which Long Island farmers had so long depended. In the 1860s, some new players muscled their way onto Barren's shores. Junk dealer Patrick White (no relation to *Dr.* White, who by this time had moved to Brooklyn to practice medicine) and his sons Andrew and Thomas joined forces with Brooklyn grocer Francis Swift. Swift got the contract for Brooklyn's offal away from Cornell; by the beginning of the 1870s, the Whites also had the exclusive contract for the offal from New York City.

The technology of the Barren Islands factories was simple. It was derived from the fat rendering of early candle and soap making, to which had been added the refinements of the pressing and filtration techniques used in making stearin candles and extracting fish oil, and the further refinement of adding sulfuric acid to the boiling mixture to release the final quotient of fat and to enhance the solubility of phosphates. The usual arrangement was a series of vertical steel cylinders about fifteen feet high and five feet in diameter, the top of which could swing open to receive charges of offal, water, and solvents, the bottom of which tapered to a point from which waste liquid could be drained (after the contents of the vat had been boiled in water or solvents or pressure-cooked with steam) while the grease rose to the top to be skimmed off. The semi-dry solids left in the vats were removed and placed in flat layers, covered with burlap, and then squeezed by a hydraulic press to remove the remainder of the grease and water. But simple as the basic technique was (and so remained), as competitive entrepreneurs grappled with their fleshly material and their steamy vats and presses down the remaining slope of the century, new patents, each containing the germ of some minor improvement, snowballed out of the patent office, all reflecting attempts to squeeze the slight advantage of some tighter efficiency.

Microbes

All his life General Egbert Ludovickus Viele (he carried the unusual name with pride, clear evidence of his link to a venerable Old New York heritage) had a reputation as a difficult man. Intemperate in speech (he was infamous for swearing even around women), impolitic (he had no qualms about reporters quoting his characterizations of colleagues as "liars," "drunks" or "thieves"), and bitter from decades of failure (other men stole the credit for building what he had been the first to envision—including such masterworks as New York's Central Park, Brooklyn's Prospect Park, and the New York subway system), he was a classic example of a man out of step with his times—born too late for his fellows to tolerate willingly his feudal arrogance, too soon for them to appreciate his insights into the technological future that lay ahead.

In death, as in life, Viele characteristically fused ancient forms and modern functions with his own firmly held ideas. A believer in the afterlife, his last rites must almost have rivaled Jeremy Bentham's in unconventionality. But there would be no public dissection for him. Instead he made sure that there would be an electric alarm buzzer within easy reach of the West Point bier on which he would be laid to rest beside his long-suffering wife in their Etruscan-style sphinx-flanked tomb.

A different, but equally unconventional end awaited the mortal remains of Viele's lifelong rival, Colonel George E. Waring, who died of yellow fever contracted in Cuba: his body was hermetically sealed in a metal casket and incinerated on a man-made quarantine island in New York Harbor. Since Waring had never thought to protect himself from mosquitoes, and the rare precautions bestowed upon his remains protected no one else, he managed with his death to demonstrate both the futility of the miasma theory he had spent his career so stubbornly defending and the limitations of his opponents' contagionist views. It is unlikely that Viele, who outlived the

Chutes and digesters at Barren Island, circa 1905.

Garbage being pressed after boiling at Barren Island, circa 1897.

younger man, shared his fellow citizens' mourning for the nation's foremost sanitary reformer, since he was on record as saying, "The sooner the city is rid of Colonel Waring the better for the city."

But if Viele's dislike for Waring was visceral, he no doubt felt pure hatred for Waring's mentor, Frederick Law Olmsted. Waring, after all, had only been Olmsted's assistant. *Olmsted* was the one who had taken from Viele the commissions—and the fame and fortune that might have followed—for designing both New York's Central and Brooklyn's Prospect Parks. Of the three, only Olmsted (after a last decade of senility and madness had finally passed) would be interred in conventional fashion, in the ground, under a traditional stone marker. But despite his conventional funerary arrangements, Olmsted was a thoroughgoing Benthamite.

Like Chadwick, Olmsted spent much of his career in the effort to prove Bentham's central contention that the same things that made for happiness could *prevent* the problems to which society, in their absence, was so susceptible. From Bentham's *The Means of Preventing Crimes*, he took the thought that "Any innocent amusement that the human heart can invent is useful under a double point of view: first, for the pleasure itself which results from it; second, from its tendency to weaken the dangerous inclinations which man derives from his nature." This truth was demonstrable. His own Central Park proved it: "No one who has closely observed the conduct of the people who visit the park, can doubt that it exercises a distinctly harmonizing and refining influence upon the most unfortunate and most lawless classes of the city,—an influence favorable to courtesy, self-control, and temperance."

Olmsted also admired Chadwick's sanitary work. He was impressed with *The Health of Towns*'s statistical demonstration that clean water and adequate sewerage reduced urban mortality. But he also shared Chadwick's miasmist view that population density itself inevitably produced (as Olmsted put it) a "certain gas" so corrupt and irritating that "even metallic plates and statues corrode and wear away," and which therefore must still make city dwellers' lives shorter and more painful than those of their rural contemporaries. Chadwick's proposed solution to this problem distinctly recalled the Panopticon: to complement the water supply and sewage removal functions of his Towns Improvement Company, he had formed a Pure Air Company. The idea was to erect giant tubes reaching hundreds of feet into the heavens and to charge city dwellers for the supplies of fresh air pumped down through them. *Olmsted's* solution to this difficult sanitary problem, though he styled himself a wholly "unpractical man" (a judgment with which Egbert Viele, who was for a while his Central Park supervisor, wholeheartedly agreed) was distinctly more practical: building public parks could make human lives longer and happier not only by preventing crime, but by discouraging disease as well—by offering, as the editorialists campaigning for Central Park put it, "ventilation for the working man's lungs."

Building parks and broader streets to bring air and light and trees to crowded city spaces was not a completely new idea. The Great Fire of 1666 had cleared the way for the first semblance of open space planning in London. Louis-Napoléon, with the Baron Haussmann, had done for Paris what his uncle had not had time to do ("If heaven had given me twenty-one years of leisure men would have looked in vain for the old Paris," the aging former emperor told Las Cases on St. Helena). With sweeping strokes they cut routes where a new world of boulevardiers and buildings would grow, replacing with straight lines and uniform facades crooked idiosyncratic streets. Parks to provide healthful exercise and relaxation were among the recommendations of Chadwick's famous sanitary report, spurring London's town council to rebuild great sanctuaries like Hyde and St. James Park. Parent-Duchatelet had seen how much the workers relished their Sunday strolls beyond the city gates, even when the breezes blew the stench of Montfaucon into their lungs and they had to thread their way past piles of offal. Haussmann—to provide great green destinations at the ends of his streets—had built more than four thousand acres of parks, lavishing as much care upon the Bois de Boulogne as upon the sewers beneath his boulevards.

Wandering through Britain in 1850 (and before returning home, France, Belgium, Holland, and Germany), collecting impressions that would be used in his *Walks and Talks of an American Farmer in England*, the thirty-two-year-old Olmsted found himself irresistibly drawn to these new creations, spending as much time wrapped in their contemplation as he did the agricultural innovations that ostensibly he had gone to visit. The restful, gracefully planned spaces no doubt soothed the young neurasthenic's nerves: his brief career already had been checkered with the frustration of repeated failures, as a student (he had had to leave Yale because of poor eyesight and "nervous prostration") and as a mercantile clerk, apprentice engineer, and magazine publisher. The Staten Island farm he was now escaping (as he had done earlier to travel through the slave-holding South)—a last-ditch investment by his father to help him earn a gainful living—was driving him mad with boredom. When sitting by a seaside hotel in Connecticut one afternoon, finishing the manuscript on his travels abroad, he chanced to meet an old school pal of his brother's who was a member of the Central Park's Board of Commissioners, and heard that the board was looking for a superintendent to oversee the park's construction. Olmsted suddenly imagined a new career opportunity. With immediate resolve, he seized it.

But the situation he found in the muddy wasteland at the center of Manhattan was untidy, to say the least. After securing recommendations from as many politically connected contacts as his literary credentials could command (Washington Irving's signature, since Irving was on the Board of Commissioners, was the last boost his application needed) the Common Council confirmed his appointment to the superintendent's post. Approaching the park offices the next morning to pay his respects to his new superior, dressed with all the dignity his new position demanded, he found the chief engineer, Lieutenant Viele, seated behind a desk before which a crowd of work-booted job seekers clustered, each clutching the recommendation of some Common Council member. Viele took the note his clerk handed him, glanced wordlessly at the dapper morning-coated figure standing a bit apart from the other job seekers and continued reading the stack of recommendations on his desk. Olmsted waited the rest of the day without getting the opportunity to speak to Viele, then taking the seat beside Viele on the streetcar running back to the city, introduced himself. Viele gruffly replied that he "would rather have a practical man." When a few days later Olmsted again produced himself in Viele's office, Viele again ignored him, then finally ordered one of his assistants, whom he introduced as "a practical man" to show Olmsted his duties. For the next several hours (Olmsted would write) this "conductor exhibited his practical ability by leading me through the midst of a number of vile sloughs in the black and unctuous slime of which I sometimes sank nearly half-leg deep."

Frederick Law Olmsted   General Egbert Ludovickus Viele

Viele was indeed the hard-crusted epitome of a self-styled "practical man." Yet he was given to staking his efforts and his pedestrian competence on visionary schemes that, though they often enough paid off for someone, never did for him. Given his interest in the geological foundation of the city as well as in the flows of its physical economy, it is no surprise that he was among the first to promote an underground railroad to take New Yorkers quickly up- and downtown. The efficacy of the invention would be amply demonstrated in London, Paris, and Manhattan—several decades after his Arcade Under-Ground Railway Company went bust. The obsession of his final decades (his Panopticon, his Towns Improvement Company) was his East Bay Land Improvement Corporation, founded in the belief that

> [t]he Harlem River will be to the New York of the future much more than the Seine is to the Paris of the present, every foot of its water line will be in great demand and of great value. From the balconies and porticos of the clustered villas that adorn the surrounding heights a splendid scene of active life and industry will be presented in the vast ampitheatre below that will be at once an epitome of the nation's wealth, and an exposition of the city's prosperity.

In this vision the South Bronx would become the nexus of what we would now call an "intermodal freight transfer" operation unequalled in the history of the world, where grain and ore and lumber hauled through the Erie Canal would meet the railway network stretching north, south, and west, and the trans-Atlantic and coastal steamships that had made New York the world's greatest transfer point. It was another promising idea—particularly after Viele succeeded in convincing the federal government to blow up the mixture of Manhattan schist and Inwood marble that blocked the channel through the Hell Gate—but the city and federal government instead decided to focus their port-development work on the great harbor that Jamaica Bay (home to Barren Island) offered, and when these plans failed to materialize, the Erie Canal and the Port of New York would slowly lose their importance, while the railroads too would be strangled by the inability of the city to build the river crossings upon which their future depended.

Before either of these ventures, however, Viele wanted to build parks, and before Frederick Law Olmsted came along, he was doing quite well at it. After West Point, and duty in the Mexican War, he had left the army to practice engineering, first with an appointment as engineer to the State of New Jersey, then in his own consulting firm. But one of the biggest jobs that lay ahead was the Central Park that New Yorkers had been talking about since William Cullen Bryant had suggested in the mid-1840s that the sanitary problems of the city demanded the staking out of a preserve of light and air and foliage. The 1849 epidemic that took the lives of even ladies helped to concentrate attention on the urgency of the city's sanitary needs. By 1852, the scuffling Common Council had decided between two warring sets of real estate operators, rejecting the well-favored Jones's Wood, a shady bank of the East River, for a desolate stretch of rock and marsh uptown that was covered by dogs and pigs and people, most of whom were squatters living in shacks and—despite Inspector White's injunctions—plying their trades of scavenging, bone boiling, and hog feeding.

On the straightforward theory that the way to get the job was to just go do it, Viele set out at his own expense to draw up a plan for the park, cudgel and deodorizers in hand to protect himself from the "Gauls" who lived there ("people who...were...principally of foreign birth, with but very little knowledge of the English language, and with very little respect for the law.

Like the ancient Gauls, they wanted land to live on, and they took it. . . .").
As usual, he could not disguise his view that those in charge were idiots: the
site the Common Council had selected was "perhaps the most unpropitious
that could have been selected for such a purpose on the whole continent."
But the worst of it, he found—worse than the fact that scarce a blade of grass
remained and that there were heaps of dung and refuse everywhere—was the
fact that the ground itself was so soddened by underwater streams that it
would inevitably give rise to the forms of fever that (in his judgment) caused
more than half of all the epidemic mortality in the world.

Unlike the Romantic-inspired "greensward" plan that Olmsted would
eventually draw up for the visible surface of Central Park (an artist's attempt
to produce an environment conducive to physical, mental, and social well-
being), the blunt focus of Viele's design was on the park's basement. His
foremost concern, as a "sanitary engineer," was simply on keeping the
park's users alive.

When Viele became the first park engineer and began to build its drainage
system, George Waring was his assistant. From the outset, relations between
the two were tense. The crusty, no-nonsense engineer was first of all annoyed
by his subordinate's flamboyant ostentation—his habit, for instance, of trot-
ting his splendid pair of white horses around the park roads every morning.
He was further put out by Waring's insistence that his name appear beside
Viele's on the cover of the final drainage plan to which he had contributed.
Relations were scarcely improved when Viele accused Waring of selling
drainage pipe purchased for the park (which he further claimed had been purchased to meet specifications with which only Waring's favorite bidder could
comply) and then pocketing the proceeds. The final break in their relations
came when the Park Board selected Olmsted's "Greensward" plan over
Viele's drainage-focused drawings and those of their fellow competitors, hired
Olmsted and his partner Calvert Vaux to superintend the building of the park,
and sent Viele packing. While Waring continued happily on in Olmsted's
employ, Viele had to skulk off to Brooklyn, where he managed to land the
consolation prize of the contract to build that city's Prospect Park.

But Viele's work on *that* project too was interrupted when the Civil War
came along. While he went off to become a brigadier general of volunteers,
Waring became a major of the Garibaldi Hussars, before being promoted to

Major George E. Waring
(before his promotion to colonel):
*"It is a pleasant thing to be a colonel of
cavalry in active field service. . . . To be
the head of the brotherhood, with the
unremitting clank of a guard's empty
scabbard trailing before one's tent-door
day and night."*

a colonel of Missouri cavalry. Even in war, Waring landed on his feet, and
when it was over, he could scarcely contain his wistfulness. "It is a pleasant
thing," he wrote in an essay published in *The Atlantic Monthly,*

> to be a colonel of cavalry in active field service. . . . We may not have
> confessed it even to ourselves; but on looking back to the years of the
> war, we much recognize many things that patted our vanity greatly on
> the back,—things so different from all the dull routine of equality and
> fraternity of home, that those four years seem to belong to a dream-land.
> … To be the head of the brotherhood, with the unremitted clank of a
> guard's empty scabbard trailing before one's tent-door day and night;
> with the standard of the regiment proclaiming the house of chief
> authority; with the respectful salute of all passers, and the natural
> obedience of all members of the command; with the shade of deference
> that even comrades show to superior rank; and with that just sufficient
> check upon coarseness during the jovial bouts of the headquarters' mess,
> making them not less genial, but void of all offense,—living in this
> atmosphere, one almost feels the breath of feudal days coming modified
> through the long tempestuous ages to touch his cheek, whispering to

him that the savage instinct of the sires has not been, and never will be, quite civilized out of the sons."

There is good reason to believe that Olmsted, too, was in some measure relieved to be able to take a break from *his* boss, Andrew Haswell Green, the brittley autocratic bookkeeper who was president of the Central Park Board of Commissioners. In any event he clearly welcomed the opportunity to remove to Washington to become secretary of the US Sanitary Commission, a new entity established by American sanitary reformers modeled after the British Sanitary Commission that grew out of Florence Nightingale's experience in the Crimean War.

Though the Sanitary Commission had its work cut out for it—conditions in the camps were such that it was hard to tell what proportion of the war's casualties were caused by disease and what by enemy fire—its services could have been put to good use on the homefront as well, where it was equally clear that "the savage instinct of the sires" had *not* been "civilized out of the sons." In fact, things were so far from orderly that in July 1863, thousands of Irish laborers rampaged through the streets chasing and lynching African-Americans and putting the torch to the property of as many abolitionist sympathizers as they could find. Meanwhile, because of the city administration's complete abdication of responsibility for the conditions of the city's streets, they were as filthy as ever, and the death rate that everyone assumed was directly tied to their cleanliness was higher than it had ever been: one in every thirty-five New Yorkers would die that year, a rate greater than that of any other major city in the western world. Before the month was out, a frightened band led by industrialist Peter Cooper had formed a new self-defense organization whose democratic-sounding name was somewhat misleading, since "the Citizens' Association" included only one hundred of the city's richest inhabitants.

Like the Chadwick report upon which it was modeled, Griscom's Citizens' Association survey "upon the Sanitary Condition of the City" was an urgent attempt to draw the gentler classes' attention to conditions in their midst that, should they continue to be left unmanaged, threatened to knock the "social economy" dangerously out of control. In addition to avoiding "the insensible and certain *loss of millions*" to the "interests of commerce" through the prevention of pestilential outbreaks of disease, new sanitary regulations aimed at prevention could cut the Gordian knot (as Bentham might have put it) in the "fatal connection between physical uncleanness and moral pollution." "The mobs that held fearful sway in our city during the memorable outbreak of violence in the month of July 1863 [the Association's Committee on Sanitary Inquiry wrote]

> were gathered in the overcrowded and neglected quarters of the city.... [where, quoting a contemporary newspaper report] '[t]he high brick blocks...seemed to be literally *hives of sickness and vice*. It was wonderful to see, and difficult to believe, that so much misery, disease, and wretchedness can be huddled together and hidden by high walls, unvisited and unthought of, so near our own abodes. Lewd but pale and sickly young women, scarcely decent in their ragged attire, were impudent and scattered everywhere in the crowd. But what numbers of these poorer classes are deformed! what numbers are made hideous by self-neglect and infirmity! Alas! human faces look so hideous with hope and self-respect all gone! And female forms and features are made so frightful by sin, squalor, and debasement! To walk the streets as we walked them, in those hours of conflagration and riot, was like witnessing the day of judgment, with every wicked thing revealed, every sin and sorrow blazingly glared upon, every hidden abomination laid before hell's expectant fire.'"

At the request of this committee (which, among others, included John Jacob Astor, Jr., August Belmont, Hamilton Fish, and Robert B. Roosevelt), Griscom organized a team of twenty-four physician-surveyors, many of whom were already familiar with local conditions through their work in the city-run dispensaries that offered the only medical care the poor could afford. These volunteer "sanitary inspectors" fanned across the city meticulously recording the physical conditions that affected every resident in every building on every block. Like Parent-Duchatelet (the committee appreciatively noted), the inspectors did not hesitate "to sacrifice personal ease and comfort, and deny themselves many social enjoyments," and "exposed themselves to repulsive and nauseous scenes." So meticulous were their observations that, like Parent, some of them even *tasted* the food their less fortunate fellows ate.

Dr. Ezra R. Pulling, the dispensary physician in the Lower East Side district that gave birth to Boss Tweed, was one of these:

The 'fresh-ground coffee' used here has never been fanned by the
breezes of 'Araby the blest.' It is innocent of the slightest association
with swamps of Java or Brazilian plains. It may be interesting to some
portions of the public to know something of its history previous to its
assuming its status and title as a beverage. It runs somewhat in this wise:
That professional chiffonier, the New York ragpicker, derives the
emoluments of his calling from several distinct sources. The products
extracted from the dubious mines in which he delves, viz., the gutter,
the garbage-box, the ash-barrel, &c., are various, having only this in
common, that they are all extremely filthy. Thus the textile contents of
his bag and basket go to the paper mill and shoddy factory. Bones find
their destiny in saponaceous and fertilizing compounds; metallic articles
are transferred to the junk shop; and even bits of coal find their
appropriate uses. But there still remains a residuum which his
professional genius has contrived to make a source of profit. This
consists of fragments of bread and other farinacious food, decaying
potatoes, cabbages, &c., interspersed with lifeless cats, rats, and puppies,
thus introduced to a *post mortem* fellowship. I shall not stop to trace the
occasional metamorphosis of the latter into the familiar sausage, but
proceed to state that much of the above miscellaneous collection is
supplied to certain sailors' boarding-houses, and enters into the
composition of bread puddings, and of a sort of '[s]long-shore lobscouse'
which Jack loves 'not wisely but too well.'

There is, however, a *debris* of material too thoroughly saturated with
street-mire to be considered savory, even in the above compound; but
this is by no means destined to be wasted. It is sold to the manufacturers
of cheap coffee. It is dessicated, partially carbonized, mingled with a
small proportion of chickory, &c., ground, and is ready to fulfill its
destiny.

Some of my professional brethren who have a down-town practice,
when belated in the vicinity of Chatham St. may possibly have sought
refreshment in the popular form of 'coffee and cakes' at some of the
numerous night saloons in that neighborhood, and thus have had an

opportunity to test the merits of the above-described beverage. If so, the uproar into which the digestive organs were subsequently thrown, doubtless left a lasting impression on the memory.

Everywhere the inspectors found that "garbage" was "one of the principal sources of impure air," the air that, as Dr. Guido Furman put it, gave "*spontaneous* birth to...maladies." (Like Nightingale, Furman insisted that "specified diseases *did not* spring from an original unit! They arise from a chemical combination of materials in certain proportions or equivalents.... [These] materials are violations of hygienic laws, and *may* very often coexist without developing any disease; inasmuch as absence of the exact equivalents of the elementary exciting causes, to cooperate in union with proper combining forces or affinities, are accidentally wanting.") Unfortunately, however, "a little more than one-fifth" of Furman's district (the Chelsea neighborhood that Clement Moore, author of *The Night Before Christmas*, had done his best to develop into a model residential quarter)

is reclaimed ground from the Hudson River; the materials used for this purpose being bricks, mortar, slate, gravel, ashes, coal-dust, street-sweepings, oyster, clam, lobster, and egg shells, pig's hair, shavings, straw, glass, carpets, brooms, refuse materials from tanneries, crockery, bones, dead animals—as cats, rats, and dogs; shoes, boots, feathers, oyster cans, old tin roofs, tin clippings, etc., etc.; and includes the whole of that section lying between Twentieth and Twenty-sixth Streets and the Tenth Avenue and the Hudson River.

Most of the other inspectors reported similar geological findings in their districts.

Egbert Viele not only claimed credit for being the first to point out (via his Central Park drainage plan) that conditions below the ground were dangerous, but suggested that since the new Metropolitan Board of Health that was the outgrowth of the Citizens Association's sanitary survey of the city (which featured Viele's map of Manhattan's watercourses as its centerfold) had been copied by localities across the country, *he* had "materially affect[ed] the health and happiness of all the people." ("Thus the promoters of the Central Park builded better than they knew.")

As usual, Viele's claims were a bit overblown, but at least it was true that the Citizens' Association finally did succeed in ridding the city of the depredations of its incumbent city inspector—Francis I. A. Boole. Defending himself against the association's charges in a hearing before the governor, Boole argued that awarding contracts to the low bidder violated his most strongly held principles, which committed him to give as much money to the poor as possible. And if he gave to his political friends rather than to his enemies, after deliberations conducted in secret, well—wasn't this simply the way of democracy, as President Jackson and our secret jury system had demonstrated? (Mad with disappointment, according to his moralizing obituary in the *Times*, he died three years later of "softening of the brain" in a Utica asylum.) The new Metropolitan Board of Health that replaced Boole in 1866 was not granted jurisdiction over the cleaning of the streets, refuse collection, or waste disposal. Those functions were assigned to the police department, which was supposed to be an institution free from political influence. But since George Washington Plunkitt was a deputy police inspector, and Boss Tweed was still at the height of his power, the change in the look and smell of the city, if any, was imperceptible.

In 1870, after his arrest and conviction, Tweed escaped the Ludlow Street jail and fled to Spain before being recaptured and returned to New York to spend his final days in captivity, his "ring" broken with him. The advantages of a "cleaner" government, however, were scarcely apparent at the curb— and what little the police did manage to remove from the streets they put down again in a place that was almost as awkward for a city that depended on its maritime economy: the harbor. In 1880, elected mayor in the wake of his *Seawanhaka* showing, shipping magnate W. R. Grace took a leaf from his predecessor (Peter Cooper's son Edward), and expanded an investigation of the police commissioners that focused on their preposterously negligent management of "the waste-disposal question." His chief prosecutor was his secretary, William Mills Ivins. Ivins's counterpart, the police commissioners' lead defender, was Elihu Root (who earlier had tried to defend Boss Tweed). Under Ivins's skillful examination, Root had few options. He drafted a bill to relieve his defendants of their street-cleaning responsibilities, and Ivins took the lead in lobbying for it. With its passage—after intense partisan debate about who would control the new body and its patronage ("What I want to protect is the health of my family," an angry J. P. Morgan said, "I don't care anything about the mayor's politics," while Assemblyman Theodore Roosevelt contemptuously dismissed the concerns of his fellow Republicans that the Democrats would control its spoils)—the Department of Street-Cleaning was born.

George Waring, for good reason, became the most famous commissioner the new department ever had. He got the job after another wave of reformers—a "Committee of Seventy" modeled after the one that threw Tweed out—brought down another corrupt and incompetent administration in the 1894 elections. The police, as usual, were a big part of the problem, attracting public outrage by (among other things) protecting prostitutes in return for payoffs, while arresting innocent women in order to collect ransoms for their release. (The public's interest in these goings-on was fanned by a Presbyterian minister named Charles Parkhurst who trolled the Tenderloin at night dressed in disguise, listening outside doors and bursting in at opportune moments, collecting in this fashion material for sermons that greatly enlarged his congregation.) As was also usual, problems with how refuse was collected and disposed of also motivated the reformers. Though Waring had a considerable reputation before he took office, his predecessor's was more colorful. William S. Andrews, a Texas native, was the son of a well-known spiritualist and had been an actor, lecturer, and journalist before becoming a professional politician. When his street-cleaning days ended, he was ousted from the New York Commandery of the Loyal Legion for "conduct unbecoming a gentleman"—such as, for example, accepting a one-thousand-dollar "loan" from George Washington Plunkitt, who had a contract with the department.

What made such behavior not just a question of bad manners (like Viele's habit of swearing around women) was that the department Andrews presided over—whose budget had more than doubled in recent years—was leaving the streets unspeakably filthy (as journalist Jacob Riis's photographs attest), keeping fears of epidemics uppermost in the public mind. To make matters worse, most of what his patronage-bloated troops did sweep up—on calm days—was pushed off open-deck scows into the harbor, causing all the problems to navigation and nuisances to shorefront property owners

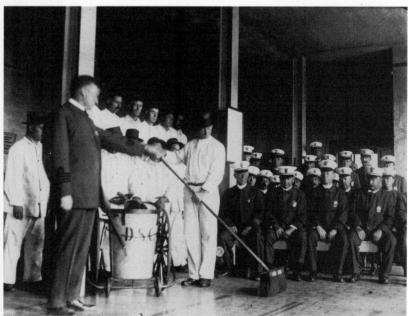

Street-sweeper discipline before and after George Waring. (The bucket on wheels was designed by Mrs. Emily Waring.)

that the federal Marine Protection Act of 1888 (which forbade the ocean dumping of any refuse) and Root and Ivins's 1881 bill (establishing the Street-Cleaning Department), had been meant to avoid. On stormy days (which included most of the winter months), when "the Italians," (in Andrews's phrase) were "too scared to go out" (a sign of good judgment, since despite their compatriots' efforts to "trim" the heterogeneous cartloads of refuse that rained down on their heads into some semblance of seaworthiness, the boats were notoriously unsteady), Andrews had devised a new expedient: piling up the stuff on a little island nestled between Queens and the Bronx in the entrance to Long Island Sound. Rikers Island was about three thousand feet from where General Viele's East Bay Company was in the process of developing what Viele fondly hoped would become the greatest seaport in the world.

General Viele was not alone in deploring the Rikers Island situation. But his outrage was more than a little hypocritical, since the East Bay Land Improvement Company was building its "land" out of the same stuff that would eventually make the island tower 140 feet over the East River, its area four times greater than it was when the filling began (even though, earlier in his career, Viele had told the Citizens' Association that making refuse-filled land of the type that caused half the deaths in the world "was the height of folly.") But the mayor's correspondence from the other neighbors reeked with sincerity. It smells like the "burning of dead horses," said one. "Our house is filled with the foul stench that is present when an old house drain is cleared of its cheesy slime," said another. Annie E. Bigelow, a teacher in the Bronx, wrote to her local health officer,

> The air in school today is simply unsufferable. We keep the windows closed and endure the heat and breaths of the children in preference to the polluted atmosphere outside. . . . We will hardly be able to stand the remaining two weeks of school unless we can have fresh air in our classrooms. Forty-eight children averaging twelve years of age in a close room in such warm weather is in itself enough to breed disease.
> . . . If I have been too blunt or emphatic, pray excuse it; the children are sick and nervous and so am I.

And it was no better for the children once the summer vacation began.

Before Waring: Morton Street, "Corner of Bedford, Looking Toward Bleecker Street, March 17, 1893," by Jacob Riis; after Waring: "The same street, May 29, 1895."

George Waring wrote: "About twenty Italians unload the cargo of a deck-scow in about two and one half hours. In 1896 over 760,000 cubic yards of refuse were disposed of in this manner, on 1,531 scows, at an average cost of 17.9 cents per cubic yard."

[I]t smells as horrible as if you'd live in a dirty, old yard closet that the dirt hadn't been cleaned for a thousand years or more.

Last summer, I was sick with a lot of contagious diseases from that smell, and could not enjoy my vacation, and I think that is the reason why I was not so smart in school this term.

[A] girl of thirteen years, like me, and as delicate, surely cannot stand it.

In response to all this election year outrage, Mayor Gilroy took the usual course: he set up a committee to study the problem. The 1894 Gilroy Commission promptly began to ferret out the latest and most scientific principles of waste management. They sent a questionnaire to municipal officials in

"all the cities in the US where modern [waste disposal] methods are known to be employed, concerning the merits, defects, and cost of systems in use." They placed newspaper ads inviting any and all comers to propose waste disposal schemes for their consideration. And they visited waste disposal facilities in Alleghany City, Atlanta, Boston, Canarsie, Chicago, Cincinnati, Coney Island, Montreal, Philadelphia, St. Louis, Wilmington, and Yonkers. One of their number even made a tour of incineration facilities in Chadwick's England, where the first modern incinerator had been built twenty years before in response to a bout of cholera. (Chadwick was still alive; though long turned out of power, his moral influence and renown were greater than ever, since a new generation saw the old man's sanitary accomplishments as a beneficent herald of modern views, while the chilling origins of it all in the Poor Law reforms and his often venal ambition and offputting lack of humor had been all-but-forgotten.)

The Gilroy commissioners received seventy responses to their newspaper notice. The technical feasibility of the proposals varied (eight involved conventional incineration, several others proposed burning at sea, four simply called for "self-dumping" oceangoing barges, seven suggested reduction technologies to produce grease and fertilizer.) So did the eloquence of their salesmen. The Sanitary Cyclone Garbage Cremator Company's M. J. Fenton was the most florid:

> At the dumpage all filth and nastiness is immediately consigned within the confines of the cremator where the work of destruction is performed completely. The Terrestrial parts, in primary particles only, are delivered in different classes, as separated within at the base of the furnace. All gases and vapors heavy and light, are collected at the top part of the Furnace Tower and saved within pipes, cylinders and tubes, separately, so that the air passes out highly elevated, clear and free from smoke or fumes, renewed by regenerating work of a furnace operating by powers of affinity, gravity, vacuum, magnetic attractions and electrical actions, for an approved annihilation of offensiveness and a healthy restoration of useful materials.

The committee's final recommendations called for an end to the obstructing, wasteful, and unsightly practice of ocean dumping (not an act of particular courage or insightfulness since ocean dumping was popularly viewed with something akin to our modern views on child abuse), expressed a preference for the technology known as "reduction" (i.e., what happened on Barren Island, by which profitable grease and fertilizer were frugally squeezed from garbage) over incineration, and suggested that in order to best accomplish this reduction, the refuse be separated by householders into separate receptacles for kitchen waste and dry trash. But since they were not presented to the mayor until after the election in which he was defeated, their immediate effect was negligible.

Nonetheless, since the Committee of Seventy seconded the Gilroy commissioners' recommendations in its own analysis of the waste management problem, there was a clear path in 1895 for the new mayor and his new commissioner, George Waring, to follow. But from Mayor Strong's perspective, Waring was not following it fast enough. Instead he seemed to focus on showy displays, like outfitting his men in new uniforms of white canvas duck and parading them down Fifth Avenue, himself resplendent on a white stallion in the lead. Strong was never a patient man: he gave Waring his first public dressing-down for not getting the city's foul snow obstructed streets cleaned quickly enough only six weeks after Waring had received command of his undisciplined troops. But Strong had larger grounds for anger in September when Waring still had not signed a contract for the waste reduction facility that he had promised in February would be up and running in March.

The promise had been made after a heated public hearing on a bill introduced by Dr. Alonzo Bell (a Bronx Assemblyman who had been one of Griscom's sanitary-reforming colleagues earlier in the century) to forbid refuse-dumping either on Rikers Island or anywhere else in the city. General Viele sat impassively in the hearing chamber while one after another of his angry fellow citizens excoriated the Department of Street-Cleaning's waste disposal operations.

Colonel A.H. Rogers, a former deputy commissioner of the Street-Cleaning Department, began the testimony by declaring that landfilling on Rikers Island could not be offensive since the nastiest parts of the refuse were removed before the garbage scows left the dumping piers, and that these materials in any event were not a threat to health.

Now the bones, the rags, etcetera, which are certainly the most offensive and most detrimental to health, are collected and stored under the various dumps [dumping piers], and for that privilege the City receives 1,760 dollars a week, besides the services of from 180 to 200 Italians, men, women and children, gratuitously.

Now the people who trim these scows at the various dumps are on the tops of those scows from morning till night. The ashes, garbage and refuse is almost literally deposited upon the backs and the heads of these people who stand there as fast as each cart load is dumped and spread these valuable materials for which the City is paid this vast amount. These people also live, eat, sleep and have their sole habitation under the dumps of the Street Cleaning Department.... It has never yet been charged that those people who are employed in this business have become sick, that they have spread contagion, or that they have bred an

epidemic; but, on the contrary, they seemed to thrive in their habitations and upon the places in which they live. (Laughter.)

(The *New York Times* was condescending in its coverage of Rogers's testimony: "He attempted to argue that garbage was delightful and productive of health. . . . Col. Rogers went on to say that the Italians who trimmed the scows at the dumps were healthy. 'Why they thrive on it,' he declared enthusiastically. This statement called forth groans.")

Rogers's account was disputed by the next speaker:

Now as to the men who collect the garbage, or spread it on the dumps, being healthy and rugged and all that sort of thing. It may be that those men cannot be affected by the garbage, in the same sense that one scow load of garbage could not be affected by another. (Great laughter.) . . . Those men are completely saturated, their whole system is permeated with garbage, and there is not a man in this party here who values his own sense of decency or cleanliness, or his sense of what is just and right in the community, or who values the feelings of his family who would want his wife or his daughter, or allow himself to sit in the same street car with them. They are offensive in appearance, offensive in smell, offensive in everything that goes to make manhood, and if you want to build up such characters as that in the community it is a very sad condition of things.

Now I have visited those dumps, and I challenge the gentleman to go on that one dump with me at the foot of Seventeenth Street East and stay for one hour among those men. He cannot do it. He does not look like a man who could; he isn't built that way. I have seen the cart coming from Bellevue hospital carrying the plaster casts from ulcerated sores, the wrappings from cancer operations, with rank and filth of all kinds that you can possibly imagine and beyond the imagination of any man except one coming from a hospital. In the same cart there was kitchen garbage, legs of chickens, heads of fish, ends of sausage, all in one cart dumped over there, and those men scrambled for it and picked out the stuff and put it to one side and ate it and took it home.

Do you, Mister Mayor, want to sit beside or have a member of your family sit beside that animal, with his pockets full of that stuff, taking whatever may come from the hospital and carrying it broadcast through this City?

Nor were the trimmers taking out *all* of the things that made the air stink. Judge Ernest Hall spoke next.

I desire to speak upon this practical question.... Rikers Island is situated from one-half to three-quarters of a mile off the shore.... There are in that [shore] district 120,000 people. Last summer we held meeting after meeting. There were present clergymen, doctors, lawyers, people who lived in palaces and people who lived in tenements. They begged us as we loved our section, they begged us as we loved the health of our children, that we would take some action that might preserve the lives of themselves and their children.... I live, Mister Mayor, two miles from Rikers Island on the highest point of land in the Twenty-third Ward, in the most healthful and magnificent location that there is, and I say to you as a fact, as I stated last year, my wife and family were driven from their homes absolutely; but there were thousands and tens of thousands of people that could not be driven from their homes because they had not the means of leaving them to go elsewhere. The physicians at the meeting which we held, at which hundreds of people attended, without a single dissenting voice, reported that the sickness, the malarial diseases, the dyptheretic diseases and all diseases arising from that condition of things, existed to such an alarming extent that in some families they were kept busy having the doctors attend their children and the undertakers take them to the graveyard.

J. H. Hildreth continued.

Living on 138th Street, . . . I had the full benefit, exceedingly full, of the nuisance and the smell which arose to the nostrils of the community from that nuisance. It is a fact, as Judge Hall has borne witness here, that we had to get up in the night time, aroused from our sleep by the stench that filled our nostrils beyond endurance. . . . The silver on the door knobs, and other metallic substances in and about the houses in that section were turned and spotted with some black substance that would not respond to the polishing of servants or anybody else.

Now if such things, such microbes, are floating in the air to be breathed into the lungs of humanity, must there not be some permanent injurious result? If metal can be so affected, what must the effect be upon a healthy lung?

Commissioner Andrews had already been forced to consider the possibility that the material the department handled could cause infection. The solution he effected—in part to prevent his indictment by the Queens County Board of Health, which attributed a diptheria outbreak to his Rikers Island dump—was a patented system sold by an inventor named Albert E. Woolf. The product it made was called "Woolf's Electrozone"; it was first introduced to treat the city's Croton water supply during a typhoid outbreak in 1893. Woolf got thirty thousand dollars for installing a plant on Rikers Island. Charles T. Bell, who with Judge Hall and General Viele was an active member of the North Side (i.e., South Bronx) Board of Trade, described it in action.

Now I have heard some of the gentlemen on this question of
disinfecting; whether it could be disinfected before it was put on the
Island; whether it could be disinfected after it was put on the Island. I
have given this question a little examination. I went over on that Island
last year one night with my brother. We went in such a state that it
would be difficult for anyone to find out who we were or why we were
there—[we] went there as fishermen. I examined the disinfecting plant.
I looked over that disinfecting plant and I got some information from
the engineers there as to how it worked and I believe from looking at
the thing very carefully that disinfecting plant is of no use at all. The
process used there simply consists in passing electricity through salt
water, decomposing the salt and generating in one vat chlorine gas
which passes off, and on the other side caustic soda. Now this soda in
very weak form is what is pumped on this garbage. I also saw some of
the men squirting this stuff on it. I found three fellows towards dusk on
the Island who probably did not expect us to come along. I found them
with hose in their hands and stepped up and talked to one of them. He
was then squirting a stream about as large as my little finger, by actual
measurement five paces long, on this mass of garbage, just a little splash,
and on the mud around it. I looked over this huge mass, acres in extent,
and was astonished that they would attempt to disinfect so huge a mass
in that manner. I talked with the men there. Their general opinion
seemed to be that it was a pretty good thing for somebody, but wasn't
any good for them.

The "microbe" and disinfection notion obviously reflected the work
that Pasteur, Koch, and Lister had done over the past three decades. It represented an advance over the original miasma theories upon which Viele
and Waring had built their reputations. But the advance was modest. Olmsted had blamed "certain gases" arising from urban density for the erosion
of stone and metal. Sulfur dioxide from coal fires would do that. The rot-
ten-egg smell that was discoloring J. F. Hildreth's doorknobs beyond the
polishing of any servant was hydrogen sulfide, made by anaerobic bacteria
chewing garbage under water (part of the same process that, a century later,
Lowell Harrelson hoped would produce enough methane from landfilled
refuse to make him rich). Hydrogen sulfide adds aroma to the methane in

"sewer gas"—the stuff that Parent-Duchatelet had worked so hard to protect his friends from, and which George Waring had spent the better part of his career fighting with his own sewer designs. (Waring's diatribes against sewer gas, a contemporary said, made people fear "it perhaps more than they did the Evil One.") After the Koch and Lister discoveries, Waring mildly modified his original miasmic formulation to reflect the possibility that the active evil ingredient in the gas was microbes. But his concession to microscopic life did not go far. For some reason, though garbage stank for much the same reason that sewer gas did, Waring did not believe there were any harmful bugs in this emanation. And as for the presence of dangerous bacteria on the garbage itself, he pronounced that fear the "great bugbear of the uninformed." They were harmless, he said, because such little creatures could not "escape" from the moist "substance to which they are attached."

Perhaps that is why he had no second thoughts about the prospect of confining women and children along with the men who worked on an island whose stench—as the Brooklyn Health Department reported—carried with "a range, flatness of trajectory and penetration equal to that of our modern coast defense rifles." Perhaps he knew (though he seems never to have cited him) that Parent-Duchatelet had found no deaths from the smell of Montfaucon. But this result—the Barren Island reduction plant he had promised (at the close of the Bell Bill hearing) would be up and running within a month—took longer than expected to produce.

A month later, nothing had happened, except that Waring's sharp tongue had gotten him in political hot water for (among other things) referring to his fellow Civil War veterans in the Grand Army of the Republic (the fraternal organization that was resisting on behalf of its members Waring's efforts to establish discipline among his patronage-addled pensioner troops) as "a bunch of drunken bums." The bad press gave Viele an opening to jump in, claiming that Waring's honesty could not be trusted, and resurrecting the charge that Waring had profited from the drainage pipe for Central Park. Waring's response: "I have studiously avoided taking notice of anything General Viele has said for thirty-eight years."

But Viele's charges had a ring of truth; the mayor's apparent discomfiture (one witness reported that never "in the history of the city had a subordinate received such criticism from the Mayor of New-York") suggested that he too suspected the worst of Waring's intentions. Whatever these intentions were, the *appearance* was that he was doing everything he could to further the interests of his brother-in-law, Herbert Tate, who had a contract for recovering the saleable metals, rags, and paper from the city's waste. Separating such "unreduceable" materials from the rottable portion of the waste stream was a prerequisite to the use of the reduction technology that the city sought, but Waring's contract specifications were structured in such a way that only Tate had rights to this material. When the city controller disallowed a form of bid that did not allow bidders to propose a way of managing the entire waste stream, Waring had to begin the cumbersome competitive procurement process all over again.

By the time he had finished issuing and re-issuing bid forms, three different contractors each claimed victory.

Mayor Strong had been elected in large part through the efforts of two of the city's leading Republican lawyers, Elihu Root (who as secretary of war four years later would lend the Army dredges needed to dig General Viele's channel between the Hudson River and Long Island Sound) and Joseph Choate (who four years later would become McKinley's ambassador to England). They represented two of the competing bidders. The third was in the hands of a former congressman named John J. Adams.

Waring had tried to reject the lowest bid, from the American Reduction Company (which had plants in Pittsburgh, Reading, and York, Pennsylvania), on the grounds that the firm used sulphuric acid in its process. (His substantive reasons for this decision, if any, were opaque, since acid was commonly used not only to extract the grease and make the nutrients in the residuum more available as fertilizer, but to minimize the production of noxious waste water.) Waring then tried to award the contract to the second lowest bidder, the New-York Sanitary Utilization Company. Elihu Root, counsel for the third bidder (the Merz company, which had plants in Buffalo, Detroit, Milwaukee, and St. Louis), filed a mandamus motion against the proposed award. But Root's suit (which must have offered plausible grounds for success since Waring had tried to accept Merz's previous low bid in a round of proposals that had been thrown out on a technicality and initially had made an unauthorized selection of Merz's present bid) was denied.

Waring's contract specifications gave only Tate rights to this material.

The ultimate decision belonged to the Board of Estimate, a body that included the mayor, the comptroller, and the president of the Board of Aldermen. In the final round of argument before the board, Choate (who had recently won the case that postponed the imposition of the federal income tax for nearly two decades) represented New-York Sanitary Utilization, Adams represented American Reduction. Adams pressed Choate for details on his client's technical process, since the American Reduction Company's claim for primacy was the odor-free effluent that its patented use of sulphuric acid produced. Choate refused to be drawn into this line of argument. Eventually Adams held up a vial of what he claimed was the liquid discharge from one of his client's plants. The fluid was clear and had no

Joseph Choate:
"Why the babies of Philadelphia cry for this!"

perceptible odor. Then the chemist from the Sanitary Utilization Company held up a vial of waste water from his company's Philadelphia plant. The fluid was dark and emitted a nauseating caramel odor. "Why the babies of Philadelphia cry for this!" Choate declaimed with a broad mock-solemn flourish, but none of the board would allow the vial closer.

At this point Commissioner Waring spoke up and threatened to resign if any more discussion of waste water was allowed. Mollifying Waring, the mayor introduced a motion in favor of the New-York Sanitary Utilization Company. It carried.

The firm that got New York City's contract was called the New-York Sanitary Utilization Company, but it was based in Philadelphia, where its only operating plant was. Partly on the strength of its New York contract, it would soon have affiliates known as the Boston Sanitary Product Company, the Baltimore Sanitary and Contracting Company, and the Reading Sanitary Reduction Company, and others that held monopoly contracts for the garbage of Washington, Wilmington, Newark, and Atlantic City. The primary political operative behind the national company was the Republican boss of Pennsylvania, "Dave" Martin, whose ingenuity Lincoln Steffens memorialized for posterity in the *Shame of the Cities*. Its primary financial backers were a group of Philadelphia bankers. Its most important New York partners were Thomas and Andrew White, who, with their father Patrick, had operated factories to process the city's offal on Barren Island for over thirty years. The Whites's network of well-placed local investors included Walter V. and Frederick L. Cranford, who in the past few years had become the leading public works contractors in Brooklyn; DeLancey Nicoll, a politician who had recently served as the city's corporation counsel; Alderman Anthony N. Brady, a major railroad financier; and Alderman Patrick McCarren, the deputy chief of the Brooklyn Democratic party. The Whites also had their own political talents: Thomas had a judgeship in Brooklyn and his fellow fertilizer manufacturer, former mayor W. R. Grace, had given Andy a judgeship in Manhattan. (Andy later gave up his seat on the bench to accept a commissionership in the patronage rich Docks Department even though the term was shorter and the pay less, a decision that a state commission appointed to investigate municipal corruption would find most interesting.)

When the Whites got the contract for their new enterprise, Barren Island already had some five hundred souls and several times more hogs. When the new factory opened three months later, another three hundred lumpen proletarians were added to their domain, a society as mixed (African-American, Irish, Italian, Polish; men, women, and children) as any on the mainland. Within a decade, the factories of Barren Island were receiving three thousand tons of garbage a day, plus all the dead animals and offal from Manhattan, Brooklyn, and the Bronx, and the menhaden that, though in diminished amounts, local fishermen were still hauling in, and producing fifty thousand tons of oils and tens of thousands of tons of grease and fertilizers and other products worth over ten million dollars a year. None of the physical details of the manufactories or of the materials they processed were unique, but in their aggregate, they may well have made on Barren Island the largest, most odorous accumulation of offal, garbage, and alienated labor in the history of the world.

The New-York Sanitary Utilization Company's original five-year contract for all of New York's eight hundred tons of garbage a day was worth

Unloading scows at Barren Island, circa 1905

Cutting floor, Barren Island, 1920

Barreling Barren Island oil

89,990 dollars a year, plus another 1,440 dollars a day for the grease and 5,600 dollars for the fertilizer ingredients it would produce. Two years later, the New-York Company got the exclusive contract for Brooklyn's garbage for an additional 120,000 dollars a year. Three years later, (Mayor Strong's autocratic administration having been replaced by a resurgent Tammany Hall, Commissioner Waring having been replaced by a saloon-owning protege of Tammany Boss ["King Richard"] Croker) the Sanitary Utilization Company's contract was renewed for another five years, at a price that had been inflated by over 130 percent. (The increase was due not to higher costs or lower profits, but to the fact that "Percy" Nagle, Waring's successor, prevented competition by waiting until two days before the expiration of the first contract to advertise for new bids. After the new contract was awarded, Nagle treated the braves of his Tammany Kanawha Club to a whisky sodden celebratory picnic.)

In 1897, there were five factories and four saloons on Barren Island, one store, one road, no doctor, nurse, or pharmacist, no church, no electricity, no post office, no social hall, no reading room, and a one-room school (the first floor of a Polish tenement house) into which some fifty of the school-age children on the island crowded for their daily lessons. The school was frequently closed on account of typhoid and diptheria epidemics, from the latter of which the inhabitants of the island tried to protect themselves by wearing chunks of salt pork wrapped in flannel around their necks. After an 1899 storm destroyed the school (driving the wornout schoolmaster to such a depression that he was found days later wandering in a "demented condition" on Fulton Street in Brooklyn), a new one-room schoolhouse was built to occupy the hours when the children of the island were not earning their keep by clambering over the piles of newly arrived garbage, picking out cans and bottles and buttons and anything else that might have any value. Eighteen years after their first schoolmaster was hospitalized for a depression, a new schoolmistress, Jane Shaw, arrived. For the next nineteen years, the energetic Miss Shaw was the island children's guardian angel. She bought a piano with her own money to give them dancing lessons, taught them cooking in her own kitchen, and got their parents interested in sprucing up their houses with curtains and paint, while meanwhile she monitored the city's construction of new roads and water mains. In April 1921, she took her charges on a trip to Viele and Olmsted's Prospect Park in Brooklyn so that they could see what grass and trees looked like; it was the first time most of them had ever been off the island. In 1936, when Robert Moses evicted everyone from the island so that he could build his Marine Park, Parkway, and Bridge, she fought to buy enough time for her charges to finish the school year; despite the odds of going against the famously ruthless parks commissioner, she succeeded.

The children of Thomas and Andrew White needed no such missionary attention. Thomas's daughter Grace married Howard Croker, the son of Tammany Hall's King Richard. Croker's daughter Ethel, after an unhappy elopement with her riding instructor, married Thomas White, Jr., Grace's brother. In 1907 Boss Croker moved to Glencairn Castle in Ireland, leaving his Fifth Avenue townhouse and his ten-million-dollar Florida estate in order to avoid an unpleasant investigation that had to do with the sort of public works projects in which associates such as the Whites and Cranfords were engaged; when his wife died a few years later, the seventy-three-year-old Croker decorously waited several weeks before marrying a twenty-three-year-old entertainer named Bula Benton Edmonson. When Boss Croker died, leaving his money, his castle, and his thoroughbreds to his young wife, the White and Croker children sued the estate. Although, from their point of view, the Croker suit was never satisfactorily resolved, it did not much matter because there had never been any question about their access to the White fortune. Thomas White died in 1904, leaving an estate worth more than a million dollars. Thomas Jr. inherited three companies (Andel Soap, the Manhattan Export Company, and the Products Manufacturing Company) and spent most of his time playing polo, riding to the hounds, and steeplechasing near his fourteen houses on Long Island. Andrew White died in 1900 after falling between a train and the platform on a twenty-fifth wedding anniversary trip to Montreal, leaving his four children, in addition to his share of Barren Island, enough real estate in more fashionable neighborhoods to make them very comfortable.

The New-York Sanitary Utilization Company's contracts continued to be renewed without interruption until 1917, twenty-one years after its chemist opened the noxious vial that foreshadowed the billions of gallons of polluted effluent the company would discharge into Jamaica Bay, sixty-five years after Inspector White and William Reynolds first set up shop on the island. The reason for the eventual termination of the Barren Island contracts had nothing to do with their costs to the city's treasury, to the public health, or to the environment. Nor were there any changes in waste disposal technology, or a decline in the markets for grease or fertilizers (the European war, in fact, had pushed demand and prices higher than ever before). But other developments had altered the landscape, and shifted the political winds.

In 1884, a German bacteriologist—Robert Koch—on the trail of the infectious agent that causes cholera, chased it down in an Egyptian epidemic. Now it was certain that what had killed Reyburn was not a secret lapse in morals, and that, though it may have been related to sanitary nuisances such as refuse, drainage, and sewer gas, Parent was right, Chadwick and White wrong: it was not the smell itself that killed.

George Waring's wife, Emily, (who in her own way had helped to clean New York City's streets by designing the wheeled bucket in which the men dumped their sweepings) had bad luck with yellow fever. When she was a child, the rest of her family died during an outbreak in New Orleans. When President McKinley asked her husband to go to Cuba after the Spanish American War to fight the yellow fever that had caused the vast majority of US casualties, she lost him, too. His death, which left vacant a slot on the Citizens Union slate in New York City's 1898 municipal elections, preceded by a few months Walter Reed's definitive proof that the *Aedes aegypti* mosquito, rather than anything inherent in the material itself or in the gases its putrefaction in damp circumstances gave off, was another reason why refuse had to be disposed of carefully. Egbert Viele died in bed three years later, not knowing if his death was permanent, but knowing at least one factor to which it was not due.

PART II

Expanding Opportunities

CHAPTER 3

Friends

William H. Reynolds (no relation to Barren Island's William B. Reynolds), by temperament and instinct was ideally suited to the opportunities and ethos of the turning century. Known by the public as "Senator Reynolds" in deference to two years spent in the state legislature while still in his twenties, his legions of friends called him "Billy." Big, brash, bull-necked and bullet-headed, he had a huge appetite for amusement, loved horses and gambling, boxing and musical comedy, was exciting to women and irresistible to men. He was a talented amateur boxer and had some of the world's greatest fighters as friends and sparring partners. An avid racing enthusiast, he founded the Jamaica Jockey Club and built the Jamaica Raceway. He built the Montauk Theatre in Brooklyn and ran the Garrick and Casino theaters in Manhattan. He owned copper mines in Arizona and Colorado, timberlands in Washington, and oil fields in Texas. Many of his male friends were politicians; happily for them, many of his female friends were actresses. For their mutual amusement he organized dinners and entertainments, cross-country trips by private railcar, European tours with hired jesters. He built the largest amusement park in the world on an empty spit of sand, and a new city on another. He sold a plot of land to Walter Chrysler complete with architectural drawings of the art deco building that would one day bear the automobile maker's name. More than anything else, his contemporaries were awed by his way of looking at an empty landscape and imagining new possibilities.

If Reynolds's imagination for acquisition was innate, as his early exploits would suggest, the gift did not come through his father's line. Born in 1868, the son of a Brooklyn building contractor, by the age of fourteen he was charging his father's creditors a commission for inducing his parent to pay his bills more promptly. These commissions produced enough capital for the young Reynolds to begin building his own houses at the age of eighteen. By the age of twenty-one he had already lost his first fortune in an

William H. Reynolds
Brash, bull-necked and bullet-headed, he
was exciting to women, irresistible to men.

adventurous year on Wall Street, but within another three years he had
made a quarter of a million dollars in Brooklyn real estate and his father was
working for him. By the time he was forty, he had made twenty times more
by building acres of houses on what had been farmland in Flatbush and Bedford and other new neighborhoods.

His partner in this enterprise was Frank Bailey, a dour banker who, until
he met Reynolds, had scarcely had a moment's fun in his life. Bailey had
been a poor, rail-thin boy from upstate who came to the city when a friend
of his mother's found him a job clerking in a mortgage office. By dint of all
work and no play, forgoing even his meals to hoard his savings, the dull boy
had become a very dull but reasonably successful man. Looking for a loan,
Reynolds one day blew into Bailey's office like the Ghost of Christmas and
began to transform the incipient Scrooge. ("Wherever Reynolds is," Bailey
said later, "there is trouble. Not trouble in its annoying, vexatious sense, but
rather in its tumultuous, turbulent, animated sense—the kind of trouble
which the Scriptures teach us is given to mankind for his happiness.")

The banker and the builder became inseparable. At night they played:
Reynolds introduced Bailey to the world of Manhattan nightlife—Broadway shows and prizefights, casinos and restaurants, politicians, pugilists,

Frank Bailey
*A dour banker who, until he met Reynolds
had scarcely had a moment's fun in his life.*

gamblers, and actresses. In the mornings they took their exercise: riding in Prospect Park, Reynolds, endlessly, inexhaustibly inventive, would spin new plans while Bailey listened. One by one, during the business part of the day, they put them to work—and together helped to create new ways of thinking about real estate.

Big things were happening in Brooklyn, New York's chaste little sister, the City of Churches. Every nook of old New York, all the way up to Da Line (Fourteenth Street in underworld parlance, a four-lane boundary between respectability uptown and poverty downtown) was swelling from the flow of an unflagging immigrant stream. The population of Manhattan had surged, since the tidegates opened at midcentury, from just over half-a-million to nearly two million at its close—almost doubling every decade. But by then Brooklyn was growing even faster. The steamboat connecting the two Fulton Streets named after the ferry's maker had shuttled commuters from bedroom Brooklyn to the workaday world for seventy years without dramatically affecting the differential population pressure on the two shores of the East River. But with the opening of the Brooklyn Bridge (in 1883), and then the Williamsburg and Manhattan bridges (in 1903 and 1909), the overflow from downtown Manhattan found an outlet. With the spread of rail lines, first across the bridges and on out to the farther fields and towns on the Brooklyn side, and then with tunneled subways tying the suburbs even more tightly to the centers, the climb in Brooklyn real estate's value was dizzying.

Reynolds and Bailey, with their respective skills and connections, were conveniently situated to take advantage of these forces of centrifugal expansion. A tract of farmland in Bedford (a town Brooklyn was beginning to engorge) had been chosen as the site of a new park for the burgeoning metropolis, but the plans had not come to fruition. With the city's intent unclear, title to the property was muddled: its owners were in the unfortunate position of holding property that it might not be within their power to sell. This was the type of difficulty that was very likely to come to Frank Bailey's attention, since he and his banking partners, besides financing mortgages, had developed a lucrative subsidiary specialty: investigating titles and selling guarantees that they were sound. Reynolds's contribution to the scheme was a set of political connections that could simultaneously keep the current owners in fear while ensuring that there would be no governmental challenge to their claim if the property were transferred to his partner and himself. Reynolds and Bailey built several hundred houses on these "Eastside Parklands." They repeated this process on a larger scale by buying a tract called Borough Park from financier Jay Cooke, where they put up over a thousand houses. The houses were not really very well built, Bailey later admitted, but after a short advertising campaign, "people began coming out in droves to the new development by trolley car every Sunday, to be beguiled by the explosive personality of Billy Reynolds until they meekly signed on the dotted line."

From there, the pair parlayed their techniques into new developments in Bensonhurst and Laurelton through a vehicle they called the Realty Associates, which became one of the largest producers of low priced houses in the world. With the turning of the new century, they were ready to move outward to the next frontier, Brooklyn's south shore, where they and some of their political associates saw some of the city's greatest development opportunities.

One of these was something that Reynolds, Bailey, and a handful of partners built with three and a half million borrowed dollars on Coney Island. Their project was a grander version of something that their neighbor,

George Tilyou, had invented a few blocks away. The Reynolds enterprise, an amusement park called Dreamland, took to the hilt his showman's sense of style and atmosphere, creating a kind of walk-through theatrical space dense with overripe and unexamined classical conceits (Sigmund Freud, who visited it one September night in 1909, was presumably better prepared than most to fathom its attractions). Dreamland opened its gates on May 15, 1904 to the thousands who came, as they did every day from then on, to gawk at the lushly bosomed caryatid holding up the grand entry arch and the three-hundred-seventy-five-foot tower covered with an extravagant display of a hundred thousand electric lights, to experience the sensation of riding the Shoot the Chutes, to feel the pull of the crowd.

Although the crowds were real enough, their setting was as artificial as a movie set, made of the same materials—"stuff and lath" (straw-laced plaster of paris and thin wood strips)—and as flammable as the era's nitrate film. During the night of May 26, 1911, it burned to the ground. In terms of both

spectacle and financial return, the fire was its greatest moment. In 1915, Reynolds and his partners sold the less valuable half of the ash-covered land to the city for 80 percent more than they had paid for the entire parcel just over a decade before, even though the year of the fire they had sworn to the tax commission that there had been no increase in land values since their purchase, and despite the fact that the city's own appraisers had assessed the land at less than half the purchase price.

The partners also made a backdoor to Dreamland on the other side of Coney Island creek. Called Harway Basin, Reynolds imagined it a "Venice-on-the-Bay"—a sort of residential yacht club composed of luxurious villas nestled among canals. Like Dreamland, Harway was completely artificial. The land was made of ashes and rubbish hauled on the rails of the Brooklyn Rapid Transit Company (a syndicate in which Reynolds, Bailey, and friends were partners) and dumped off the end of the line.

Greater City

Of the millions of men in New York City in 1903, perhaps the very *last* one people could have imagined would be gunned down on the street by a jealous lover was eighty-four-year-old Andrew Haswell Green, best known to his contemporaries as "the father of Greater New York," the man to whom, more than anyone else (not even excepting Frederick Olmsted) the planned shape of the city's expansion since midcentury was due. And yet Cornelius M. Williams, an African-American handyman, enraged that his erstwhile lover, Hannah Elias, had become the mistress of a white-bearded octogenarian, fired five bullets at him as he approached his house at 91 Park Avenue, one of which tore into his temple, killing him instantly.

But as in the case of James Reyburn on a previous Friday the 13th, death made a mistake. In his confusion, Williams had stalked the wrong white-bearded octogenarian. If anything, Green (it appears) was interested in men, although his libido seems to have been very much suppressed. If sublimation there was, it would help to explain the fastidious attention to nickels and dimes that had sorely tried the patience of men as different as Frederick Olmsted and Boss Tweed, as well as his more visionary obsessions.

In Olmsted's case, the tensions had begun back in 1858 with an order for eighteen-cents-worth of pencils for which he sought reimbursement from Green in his capacity as president of the Central Park Board of Commissioners. The tensions between Green and Olmsted (who tended toward a prickly independence in his relations with any superior) continued as Green persisted in his old maidish oversight of every detail of the park's management. The two also quarreled over how the park should relate to the world outside its cut-stone walls: Olmsted's proposal for revamping the city street system, Green said, was "inexpedient."

But even here their disagreements were more of style and degree than of real substance—compared to almost all of their contemporaries, the two were of astonishingly like mind about all that mattered to them most: their shared vision of the city's future. So alike were their objectives, in fact, that one cannot imagine either successfully achieving any portion of what each actually accomplished—or of having any claim to posthumous fame—without the other.

Despite disagreements about the details, Olmsted and Green agreed that the

Andrew Haswell Green
Death made a mistake. Williams had stalked the
wrong white-bearded octogenarian.

1811 grid plan—the square network laid out by the street plan commissioners
appointed in 1807, the first and only large-scale, long-term planning until then
visited on the surface of New York by the city government—should be
altered. Although the plan (presciently, for its time) mapped streets all the way
north to Forty-second Street, it did little to suggest the direction of routes farther uptown. Both Olmsted and Green lamented (Olmsted, as usual, more
extremely) the deadening effect of the rectilinear geometry that had been
imposed on the undulating planes of New York, drawing unfavorable parallels
between New York's grid plan and the beaux arts design that Napoléon III and
Haussmann had recently bestowed upon Paris. (Ironically, Napoléon's diago-
nal patterns were as divorced from any humanistic concerns as New York's
grid was, drawn as they were with an equal disregard for his city's existing fabric, and for reasons as much military as aesthetic: one of Napoléon's primary
objects was to make it no longer possible for revolutionaries to throw barri-
cades across narrow streets.) But the tractable bedrock below Forty-second
Street that had allowed buildings and streets to march in straight parallel ranks
relatively unimpeded became unruly above the park, all but forcing the park
commissioners (who at Green's request had been authorized to develop plans
for the whole uptown territory) to consider other solutions.

Rather than contemplating only the convenience of real estate developers, Olmsted and Green conceived plans that addressed a range of objectives. Healthfulness was one. The 1835 fire that wiped out a generous swathe of downtown Manhattan demonstrated how far flames could leap. The fundamental premise behind the new park was that sunlight, air, and trees were the disinfectants needed to cleanse the workingman's lungs. Wider streets were the solution to both these concerns. Plotting them with respect to natural topography (rather than impeding the flow of the underground streams that Viele found so threatening) would resolve another. And not leveling the stubborn schist that pushed so far above the plains would make the streets more attractive as well as less costly. Designing roadways into and out of the park (thinking always of the comfort and convenience of carriage riders), Olmsted and Green were forced to consider where their routes eventually would lead. A rider could follow Seventh Avenue all the way north from Houston Street to enter the park at its splendid Fifty-ninth Street gate, follow the carriage road up through the park, come out on 110th Street, and continue north all the way to the Harlem River where the Croton water came over the High Bridge from Westchester County. Here, the horseman would be forced to dismount, to cross the bridge, if he chose to, on foot, or to board a ferry that plied the swift currents.

The huge granite High Bridge carrying water down from the Croton Reservoir was the first solid link between the city and its growing outskirts. As with the water systems that cities like Boston and Philadelphia were also developing, it provided an initial impetus for organizing a larger form of metropolitan government. The roads that Green and Olmsted were designing were another. (The actual building of the roads—with all the accompanying plunder this might entail—was carried out by Boss Tweed after he had removed this authority from Green and Olmsted.) Criminals (as Tweed's imminent flight from justice would soon demonstrate yet again) were no respecters of the inked lines that separated one jurisdiction from another— which was why (along with upstate Republicans' horror over the Tammany depredations of Mayor Fernando Wood) the first metropolitan institution devised to integrate the counties of downstate New York was a police commission. (The Metropolitan Police Commission's first action was facing down the mayor's parochial force in a tense standoff on City Hall's steps.)

Nine years later—in 1866—the mingled causalities of miasma and quarantine, contagion and environment had led to the formation of the Metropolitan Board of Health that encompassed the same expansive territory.

Criminals and air pollution and water supply and sewage and tide-tossed refuse, Green observed, all refused to respect the welter of jurisdictional boundaries that carved up the region:

> We cannot parcel out the air among us nor partition the fleeting tides. In defiance of enactment by council and mayor of one city, malaria will evolve from the limits of another, float thence upon the free winds, and precipitate into the general atmosphere, for inhalation by distant patients, exotic microbes, bacteria, and all varieties of poisonous germ life. The procession of tides marches through the limits of all the municipalities, impartially collecting and distributing everywhere offal and sewerage loaded with contagion. Each community has done full duty to itself in injecting its smoke, stenches, and sewerage into another province or mayoralty, so that some of our people live in the interchange of reciprocal nuisances or medley of conglomerate nauseas.

It was time, Green argued—as had Chadwick in London and Haussmann in Paris—to bring the region's outmoded institutional arrangements under unified control.

Though improving the healthfulness of the environment was crucial, the most important benefits Green promised concerned the way the city was connected to others. Green's primary focus was transportation. New York's primacy depended upon its port. The way refuse was disposed of was just one of many reasons for putting an end to the current system of competing "shrievalties" that affected shipping in New York Harbor.

> The water front of no municipality here belongs to it to be extended, filled in, or aligned as its authorities may determine. This front has relation to the water front of all the other municipalities. Artificial change in one section creates, by natural operation, change often prejudicial in another.... The rogueries of garbage and mudscow boatmen in making the channels dumping places for all sorts of waste are past finding out. From Sandy Hook to Yonkers all the shore and all the water space is open to lawless enterprise. Every little district has its

marauders, who by encroachment, appropriation, and misuse deplete the general system, to transfuse its vitalities into some niggard scheme or individual profit.

Parasite companies, usurping the name of giant corporations, stake broad lines far out in this common domain and bid the waters come no further, and they obey.

Without unified control over its rivers and harbor—especially since the railroads were creating new nexes that could make or break a city's fortunes—the city would inevitably fall behind in its race with others for commercial supremacy. Boss Tweed made former General George Brinton McClellan the first chief engineer of the new Department of Docks, a body that had been created in 1870 to build a wall around lower Manhattan, to prevent at least its own garbage from further impairing its deep water access. (Another former general, Egbert Viele, submitted a plan for how this bulkhead should be constructed; it was not accepted.) But though its wall finally stopped the expansion of Manhattan itself, the docks department did nothing to prevent even New York from continuing to foul its own waterways with refuse, and it did nothing to advance the overall management of the port to protect New York's commercial supremacy.

Had the docks department chosen to fulfill its larger responsibilities, the first thing it might have done—now that trains were beginning to overtake ships as the most important means of moving passengers and freight—would have been to take steps to develop some form of railroad infrastructure. Chicago—the fast rising city on the plains, whose port seemed connected with rail lines to every city on the continent—was the object of New Yorkers' wonder. Visiting it on a midwestern tour in 1857, Andrew Green wrote to his sisters back in Worcester that it was the only place he had seen since leaving New York where he would be willing to live: "Great is the activity, the stir, the upturning, of this place...." But the idea that it might soon supplant New York as the nation's most populous city (and in that case, what would prevent the lifeblood of New York's economy—its banks and brokerage houses—from moving there?) was too fearsome to contemplate. From 1870 on, it had become obvious that the Port of New York was losing market share to those that had better rail connections to the mainland. The harbor and river system—when the Erie Canal at its northern end was the only way across the Alleghenies into the interior—were what had made New York great. Now, with the rise of the railroads, these same waters were a moat that had begun to seal the city off.

Though the fortunes that had come from managing most of the country's railroads were in New York City, none of their termini were. The famous Erie and New York Central lines came only as close as Piermont (twelve miles up the Hudson, where Erie freight and passengers debouched onto the pier by the mountain to board ferries to the city), and Selkirk, where the Central's first bridge crossed the river. The only railroad that directly entered any part of the city was the Baltimore & Ohio's route from New Jersey into Staten Island, but there it stopped. What was needed to connect the harbor to the rest of the continent was a tunnel to Brooklyn where the Narrows pinched the Lower Bay. This obvious solution was first proposed in 1888; Green's Greater New York plan—which, after a twenty-year hiatus, in 1889 finally began to attract widespread support—by making both ends of the tunnel part of one city, would provide the means for accomplishing this critical connection.

But if the planning rationality of wrapping the city all around New York Harbor—New York's "imperial destiny" according to Mayor Abram Hewitt in 1888—was clear, the politics of the enterprise were murkier. The promise of a Narrows tunnel that would bring Staten Islanders into the city's rapid transit orbit was a significant factor in securing their support. The rapid transit operators in the other boroughs also saw clear self-interest in a Greater City. William Reynolds, for instance, who was planning a "marginal" railway along the Brooklyn shore, foresaw greater demand for his transit enterprises. A Greater New York, in fact, would suit all of Reynolds's plans. And so he joined the Brooklyn Consolidation League and led its efforts to make equal assessment and taxation on real estate a part of the consolidation referendum, so that assessments for building sewers and roads to his new developments would be reduced by spreading the tax over a larger base. But for the same reason, Manhattan real estate developers wanted to keep things the way they were, so that the valuable real estate downtown would subsidize only *their* uptown holdings.

To keep the Manhattanites on board, Green (who, as chairman of the Greater New York Commission, controlled the referendum-drafting process) sided with them against Reynolds (with whom privately he agreed). Without this incentive, getting Brooklyn's accord for the consolidation was little short of a miracle: the referendum carried by just 277 votes out of 129,000 cast (a winning margin of just two-tenths of a percent.) And after that, the politics got even tougher, since the legislature had to approve not just a bigger pie, but the way it would be sliced. Green, however (now serving on the charter revision commission with Calvert Vaux, Olmsted's former partner, since Olmsted himself had long since left New York in disgust) maintained idealistic hopes that the addition of new native-born voters in the outer boroughs (Brooklyn, for example, was dominated by New England-born men like himself) would dilute the influence of unscrupulous ward heelers over easily led immigrants enough to keep machine-style politics out.

Municipal Ownership

Adding more "American" votes to the melting pot was not enough to roust Tammany Hall in 1898. Instead, it made the possibilities of plunder all the more attractive, and the difficulties of coordinating a reform coalition even greater. So instead of keeping a reform administration in power (some had proposed George Waring as the replacement for his too cantakerous boss, but the prevailing opinion was that his elitist military-discipline approach to personnel management would do nothing to win the working man's vote), Tammany bounced back in to run the Greater City first. The depredations of its first Greater City term, however (it was Tammany Street-Cleaning Commissioner Percy Nagle, for example, whose renewal of the Barren Island contract was the occasion for inebriated celebration by his entire Kanawha Club) created a wave of public disgust that made it possible to insert another reform administration, that of Columbia president (and former Brooklyn mayor) Seth Low. Low's street-cleaning commissioner was another military sanitarian, Major John McGaw Woodbury, whose specialty was bacteriology. The public reputation Woodbury earned through his efficiency in keeping the streets clean kept him in office beyond the next election, though Seth Low and the Tammany boss who had reaped the spoils of the past decade and a half (Richard Croker, now safely in Ireland), were not so fortunate.

The reappointment of an effective sanitarian as street-cleaning commissioner by an incoming Tammany administration reflected the promise made by Boss Croker's successor, Charles Murphy, to refine his party's manners.

Charles Murphy
*A poorly educated product of the Lower East
Side, the portly new boss nonetheless affected
a dark-suited patrician image.*

A poorly educated product of the Lower East Side, the portly new boss
nonetheless affected a dark-suited patrician image. His best friend was the
Harvard-educated socialite J. Sargeant Cram. Like Reynolds and Bailey,
they were a seemingly mismatched pair who nonetheless saw eye to eye
(Cram through a monocle, Murphy through pince-nez), sharing a motivating vision that combined outward elegance with dissembling rapacity. Tammany contemporaries mocked their mutual regard and Murphy's transparent pretensions with a couplet: "Charlie Murphy wore his trousers with
cuffs, ate his peas with a knife, tried Sargeant Cram's monocle, and said,
'how noice.'" Murphy's mayor was another exemplar of the "New Tammany," the thirty-eight-year-old Princeton-educated son of Civil War general George Brinton McClellan, Sr. Lincoln Steffens, surveying the scene,
declared that he preferred his Tammany unvarnished and predicted that no
good would come from this patina of respectability.

Steffens's prediction was soon borne out. Murphy put Cram in charge of
the Board of Docks, whose budget increased by 300 percent in four years
without any noticeable increase in either its responsibilities or its effectiveness; the only evident change was that commissionerships became so cov-
eted that Judge Andy White (co-owner of the Barren Island factories) left

Murphy's mayor, the thirty-eight-year-old son of Civil War general George Brinton McClellan, Sr., was another exemplar of the "New Tammany." Lincoln Steffens declared that he preferred his Tammany unvarnished.

the bench to join the board. His fellow docks commissioner, Alderman James Gaffney (whose business partner was Murphy's brother John), blackmailed the builders of the Pennsylvania Station by withholding a necessary aldermanic vote until his company got the excavation contract at five times its competitor's price. Murphy's handpicked utilities commissioner, by secretly signing a contract that Mayor McClellan had rejected, committed the citizens of New York City to pay more for their gas than did the inhabitants of any other city in the world, while by accepting lion-sized chunks of transit stock, Murphy and his partners helped to make the trams they rode on the most crowded and expensive and the least safe.

Though the criminality of Crams and Gaffney was richly remunerative (even Gaffney's wife became a millionaire through "her" business ventures), the take from their entrepreneurial approach to municipal governance was only a modest percentage of the profits from the interconnected utility/transit interests' arrangements.

The knots between utility and transit franchises started with the lines
Thomas Edison laid. When Edison began to set up the first system for delivering electricity from a centralized power plant to a network of individual
customers, although he had not yet invented the dynamo, the fuse, the
meter, the lamp, or the socket upon which it would depend (much less
decided how much voltage, resistance, or energy loss he should design for),
he was fairly certain that he could make the idea work. Many others, however, were not so sure. Most scientists working in the field believed that the
only possibility permitted by the laws of physics was the existing arc-light
system, in which a constant current was delivered to a series of lamps, such
as street lights in a row. To "subdivide" a current into separate, independ-
ently operating lamps (the conventional wisdom held) would be like trying
to build a perpetual-motion machine, since each customer's bulb would just
drain off light from his neighbors'. Edison's new system depended on the
revolutionary notion of using Ohm's understanding of resistance to *vary* the
flow (current) as needed, while keeping the *force* (voltage) from a variable-
capacity generator constant.

He chose for this demonstration a square mile on New York's Lower
East Side, largely because of its proximity to the Wall Street financiers upon
whom the next phase of his electrical revolution would depend. Edison
worked day and night for the better part of a year, snatching naps when he
could on an overcoat thrown over a pile of tubing stacked in his Pearl Street
power plant, to make sure that the lights would go on, as they did, when he
flipped the switch in Drexel, Morgan and Company's office at the beginning of September in 1882. On the strength of this demonstration, the
Board of Aldermen gave him a franchise to supply electricity for an unlim-
ited period anywhere within the city (overriding the mayor, who tried to
veto their bill on the grounds that a payment of a penny per lineal foot of
street cut open to lay wiring was inadequate compensation). Two more
franchises were granted twenty-one days later, overriding mayoral vetoes on
the same grounds. (One of these was to Edison's foremost competitor,
Charles Brush, whose alternating-current idea offered distribution efficiencies over Edison's original direct-current system.) Ten other firms also got
Manhattan franchises during the next decade and a half, but the absurdity of
having competing companies capitalizing separate systems in overlapping

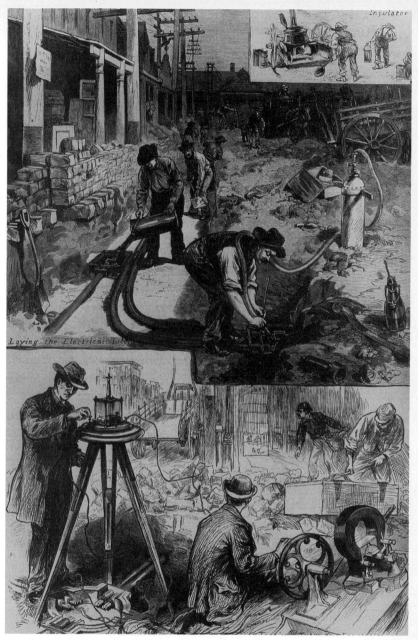

Insulator

Laying the Electrical Tubes

The Board of Aldermen overrode a veto cast by the mayor on the grounds that a total payment of a penny per lineal foot of street cut open was inadequate compensation.

geographic areas quickly became so apparent that by the time the New York Edison Company (the re-organized successor of the original Edison firm) was incorporated in 1901, it serviced Brush's customers and had swallowed up all but two of the other firms, while its sister, the Edison Electric Illuminating Company of Brooklyn, controlled all service in that borough, and between both and their predecessor gas companies any semblance of distinction in ownership had all but disappeared.

The growth of electric utilities changed the way street-railways were run. The elevated tracks were one of the problems. In the most built-up areas of the city, the streets were often so clogged with carts and carriages, vendors and pedestrians, that trams—most of which were still horse-drawn when the Edison company was formed—were frequently reduced to cubicles that bore more resemblance to stationary steambaths or refrigerators than to any form of rapid transit. In the 1880s, a tram trip from City Hall to Forty-second Street, a distance of fifty-six blocks, was likely to take an hour. A natural solution was to get the tracks out of the middle of the road and up in the air over it. By 1888, ninety-four miles of such elevated lines for steam-powered engines had been built in Manhattan. But then the els, too, began to reach their capacity. The number of trains they carried was fixed by the distance that safety dictated be between them, and the size of the locomotives that pulled them dictated their length and speed. This size, in turn, was severely constrained by the cost of strengthening the els' steel structures. Constructing additional lines was equally implausible, given the public resentment the existing lines' noise and visual nuisance caused: trying to sleep, eat, or learn to read when one's bedroom, kitchen, or classroom window was within a hundred or so feet of the clattering roar of a passing train—as tens of thousands of New Yorkers did daily—was a stressful exercise in patience or futility. Electric power solved this problem because electric motors under each car eliminated the need for locomotives and made possible faster, more fuel-efficient trains as long as the length of the station platforms would allow.

Electric motors were easier to adapt to trains that flew over streets and stopped only at stations than they were to trains that started and stopped, speeded and slowed at every cross street, wearing down the copper brushes and steel commutator shafts faster than they could be replaced. It was also easier to develop a means of maintaining an electrical contact that could keep cars mov-

Trying to eat, sleep, or read within a hundred feet or so of a passing train was a stressful exercise in patience or futility.

Roughly the same set of financiers (chief among them Anthony N. Brady, William C. Whitney, and the aptly named Thomas Fortune Ryan) gained control of both the rail and electric systems.

ing without killing living things. But once the carbon-brush motor and the under-running cable-contact device were invented, and the basic concept of using electricity to power trains had been accepted (against the judgment of some of the best minds in the business—a surge, a short, a flash, a leap, and Jay Gould refused ever again even to contemplate electric trains), the efficiencies offered by electricity ensured its adoption for street-level trams too.

To power lines like those that were snaking out to new neighborhoods in Brooklyn, new generating plants were required. These increased the capital requirements of the franchise-fixed routes, making ever more inevitable their control by monopolies and the evolution of closer links between "transit" and "utility" corporations. When, as soon happened, roughly the same set of financiers (chief among them Anthony N. Brady, William C. Whitney, and the aptly named Thomas Fortune Ryan) gained control of both the rail and electric systems, the ordinary citizens of the city (as opposed to the members of an interlocking network of stock-sharing politicians and real estate speculators) were caught in a double stranglehold.

"Enemy of the utility trusts" therefore was a role guaranteed to make

popular anyone who played it as well as William Randolph Hearst did. Hearst, whose *New York Journal* would fan a war to sell the news, began by attacking the gas trust in a series of campaigns that were almost as successful as was his crusade for a *Cuba libre*. A taxpayer suit he filed in 1896 kept the mayor from signing an inequitable franchise agreement; his plan to construct a municipal gas plant in 1899 threatened the gas companies into rolling back their prices; and his suit to overturn the contract secretly signed by McClellan-and-Murphy's utilities commissioner produced a 20 percent rate reduction. Six months after the start of this last gas battle, Hearst returned to New York from the defeat of his presidential aspirations at the 1904 Democratic national convention to found, with reform Judge Samuel Seabury, a new party they called Municipal Ownership, whose platform called for replacing private utilities with public ones. After an initial show of reluctance, Hearst agreed to head the party's ticket in its challenge of Mayor McClellan's re-election. But for Charlie Murphy's toughs—ballot dumping in the East River apparently reversed the electoral tide—he may well have won.

Most representatives of the city's educated classes shared at least some reservations about the foremost proponent of the kind of journalism that was named after a cartoon ("The Yellow Kid"). But in addition to Seabury, Hearst

Most representatives of the city's educated classes shared at least some reservations about the foremost proponent of the kind of journalism that was named after a cartoon ("The Kid in the Yellow Shirt").

had some very respectable allies in his war on Tammany Hall. His near success against McClellan had depended on a bolt upright, thin lipped Puritan sort— Mayor Grace's corruption-stalking secretary, William Mills Ivins—who served Hearst's purposes on the Republican line, siphoning off voters who had neither the stomach to vote for Hearst nor the complacency to vote for Tammany. (Ivins's lackluster appearance on the Republican slate was due to a deal between Hearst and the state Republican boss, Governor Benjamin Odell, who promised not to stand in Hearst's way in return for the Municipal Ownership party's support for other Republican candidates.) Despite losing the mayoralty prize (with Ivins as his counsel, Hearst after two years succeeded in getting the state legislature to authorize a recount, only to have the law declared unconstitutional before it could be conducted; he therefore had to content himself with the use of quotation marks around the word "mayor" whenever McClellan's name appeared in his papers), the combined Republican-Municipal-Ownership forces won a two-to-one majority in the Board of Aldermen. They soon found a way to exploit their advantage.

What began in January 1906 as a modest inquiry into why the Street-Cleaning Department had taken so long to respond to a snowstorm, with the help of numerous newspaper articles, including one in the *World* alleging that ten million dollars had been "stolen and wasted" under Woodbury's command, had, by March become a scandal of politically promising proportions. The opportunity for further embarrassing the mayor (and for getting some leverage on the department's enormous patronage potential) made the new aldermen drool. For William Mills Ivins, the opportunity was particularly welcome. He eagerly accepted the aldermen's invitation to serve as special prosecutor because he believed that the department's private waste disposal contracts were likely to demonstrate (in reverse) the virtues of Municipal Ownership.

Ivins hired as his bloodhound Henry Klein, the *World* reporter who had broken the scandal story. Their talents and temperaments made the two a dangerously well-matched pair. Ivins's penchant for dogged cross-examination would one day culminate in a forty-hour grilling of Teddy Roosevelt in a libel suit that some thought contributed to the ex-president's death shortly thereafter, while Klein, it was apparent to those who knew him, "loved an investigation better than a professional Irishman loves his mother." Together they found Reynolds and Bailey at the bottom of a boondoggle known as the Harway Basin.

One way of getting rid of the city's waste—a sensible way, to reform-oriented minds—was to burn it, as the major European cities had been doing for over a decade, producing as by-products steam and electricity for public purposes such as lighting streets and running trams. The double-edged logic of this system, it seemed, showed Municipal Ownership in its purest, most beautiful form. Why, Ivins wondered, was it not happening in New York?

What he and Klein discovered was that a handful of people had good reasons to keep waste disposal a private affair. Klein found that the renewal of the Barren Island contract not only had made former commissioner Percy Nagle rich, but that Woodbury had himself conspired to ratify the contract against the advice of the city's attorney and, as Nagle had done, had held up advertising for the succeeding contract so that the White-Cranford crew again won it by default. But more important, both in the scope of its vision

"loved an investigation better than a professional Irishman loves his mother."

and the scale of its impact, was a new contract that Woodbury made. Like the Barren Island business, it had seemed to begin innocently enough. Woodbury was approached by a young man named Milton Kennedy, who had an idea for hauling refuse on tram lines at night when they would not otherwise be in use. At the end of these lines the refuse would be tipped onto privately owned property. The idea was welcome on two accounts: the Department of Street-Cleaning had all but run out of city-owned dumping grounds (particularly those that could be reached by scows), and the trams would clearly be more efficient than the department's horse-drawn carts.

But, as Klein's investigations soon showed, every aspect of the deal was somewhat more complicated than it had at first appeared. In the first place (a street-cleaning official admitted under cross-examination from Ivins), the bid specifications had been drawn in such a way that only Kennedy could compete; to achieve this end, Kennedy had paid thirty thousand dollars to his one likely competitor to secure control over all potential "land dumps"

William Mills Ivins
*Why, Ivins wondered, was municipally owned
incineration not happening in New York?*

near the trolley lines. In the second place, within a few months it was no
longer Kennedy's contract, but had fallen under the control of Anthony
Brady, who, having joined the enterprise with the promise to provide capital, had instead used his resources to force Kennedy to accept a fifty-thousand-dollar buyout. (Since Brady controlled the Brooklyn Rapid Transit
Company, which owned all the equipment and facilities needed to do the
work, he could blackmail Kennedy with the threat of forfeiting his sixty-
thousand-dollar bond on the contract; when Kennedy complained to
Woodbury about the unexpected treatment from his erstwhile partner, he
was told, "I am glad you got out all right, Kennedy. This damned octopus
can't fool Commissioner Woodbury.") And in the third place, while
Kennedy had sought Brady's financing in order to build the covered cars
and stone-and-steel loading stations that the contract required for minimizing neighborhood nuisance, when Brady took over he ran open cars and
put up wood-and-corrugated-iron sheds that did little to suppress dust,
noise, or odor.

One of the more sensational findings of the investigation was that state
senator Patrick Henry McCarren, the Brooklyn Democratic boss, had
demanded twenty-five thousand dollars for helping to deliver the deal.
McCarren, on the witness stand, denied that he had accepted the money, but

not that he had been asked for his help in arranging the transaction, or that he had come to hold an important stake in the companies that now controlled the contract. Other prominent parties to the arrangement, Ivins established, were Billy Reynolds and his friend Frank Bailey, and a gaggle of other politicians that included two governors, a judge, and another state senator.

Although hauling refuse by train should have been cheaper than the Street-Cleaning Department's old methods, the cost of waste disposal in Brooklyn after four years under the contract was ten times higher than it had been before. This increment, of course—along with the refuse itself—went straight to the consortium that soon became known as Brooklyn Ash. The fees from the city would no doubt have been enough to keep the enterprise afloat, but the money that could be made from the refuse itself—as Ivins pointed out—was the key to understanding the deal. Joseph Marrone (or Morrone, Maroni, or "Mary Brown"—a sister-in-law, whose name, for reasons best known to himself, he generally used on contracts) paid his crews of Italian laborers as little as ten cents an hour (plus lunch, supper, and any food they found in the course of their work that they wanted to keep) to work twelve-to-fourteen-hour days pulling paper, rags, glass, and metals from the waste, but he paid Brooklyn Ash an estimated three-quarters of a million dollars a year for this privilege. Brooklyn Ash itself burned the remaining refuse in its three incinerator-boilers and sold for several thousand dollars a year the excess steam that it could not use to power equipment in its own repair shops; and they charged fellow real estate developers Oliver Harriman, William Engeman, and former governor Timothy Woodruff some thousands of dollars each to fill in wetlands. But they profited most from the real estate that they made for themselves. A Reynolds-and-Bailey-led group known as the Harway Associates (in which Brady and McCarren were also partners) had purchased a hundred acres of marshland for less than six hundred dollars an acre in 1902. Now, four years and two million cubic yards later, that tract was five feet higher and ten times more valuable.

Meanwhile, because of the electric utilities' stranglehold over their customers, there were no takers at any price for the electricity that a new, state-of-the art, municipally owned and operated incinerator that Woodbury had built was producing. Since utility-beholden state legislators had enacted a law to preclude the city from using this electricity itself, Woodbury's flag-

Joseph Marrone paid his crews of Italian laborers as little as ten cents an hour to work twelve-to-fourteen-hour days pulling paper, rags, glass, and metals from the waste.

ship plant, instead of advancing his plans for waste-fired boilers to produce light and power for municipal purposes all over the city, Ivins claimed, was costing the city over a hundred dollars a day.

Klein's probing also found that James Gaffney and John Murphy were leasing municipal docks from the Cram/Gaffney/White Docks Commission and then leasing them back to the Street-Cleaning Department at a rate that represented a 350 percent clear profit; that state senator George Washington Plunkitt had passed legislation that gave him three long-term contracts for providing stables to the department ("I seen my opportunities and I took 'em"); and that the franchises for salvaging recyclable materials from the city's scows were being awarded to racketeers like Marrone for a fraction of their value.

The "incompetency, inefficiency, [and] favoritism" they had uncovered,

Ivins and Klein wrote in their report to the aldermen—not to mention the "violation of the provisions of the city charter"—argued for Woodbury's removal, and for ending the Brooklyn Ash contract in favor of a municipal operation. The aldermanic majority agreed.

The vote put McClellan in an awkward position. He had no love for the independent and impolitic Woodbury (like Waring, Woodbury was wont to disingratiate himself with unguarded comments, such as his reference to the Board of Aldermen as "an illiterate body of rum-soaked bums")—a reporter overheard McClellan telling a friend on the Staten Island ferry that Woodbury "is a whelp I will whip"—but firing him would mean that he accepted the truth of the Hearst-Ivins campaign theme that at least some part of his administration was corrupt. And though he had his own reasons for getting rid of Brooklyn Ash so that the city could dispose of its own waste, adopting Ivins's conclusions about the role of private interests in the department's operations would create another set of political difficulties.

His own reasons for getting rid of Brooklyn Ash had to do with the evolution of maritime technology. In 1905, the Cunard Line built the *Coronia*, which extended six hundred seventy-five feet and weighed twenty-one thousand tons. With the other major steamship companies, Cunard representatives told McClellan that, without longer docks, they could no longer stay in New York. The War Department, on the grounds that it would imperil navigation, denied McClellan's application for permission to extend the city's piers farther into the Hudson. He got around the immediate difficulty by digging into the shoreline farther north than his father's bulkhead had extended, and—gratifying a sentimental desire to finish the work his father had begun—completed the granite wall around the island. But looking ahead to continuing demands for expanded docking capacity, which he felt critical to the city's future growth, McClellan could not help noticing that, with just a little dredging, the shores of Jamaica Bay, which were just twenty minutes away from blue water, would provide space for more ships than all of Manhattan's perimeter could hold—without requiring War Department approval. The steamship companies told him (he said) that they would gladly move to Jamaica Bay if he could accomplish his plan.

"The first necessary move in the work," McClellan recounted years later, was the acquisition of options on this shore property, all of which was in private hands. I realized that these options must be secured without letting the owners know for what purpose they were intended if prices were to be kept within reason. Accordingly, I discussed the matter in confidence with the comptroller and the president of the Board of Aldermen, and we agreed to try to secure them informally without any action of the Board of Estimate, and we placed the work of buying the options in the hands of Douglas Robinson, a well-known real estate man, who was brother-in-law of Theodore Roosevelt. Unfortunately too many people knew our secret, someone had talked and Robinson found options on every piece of real estate adjoining Jamaica Bay had been secured by a little syndicate of Democratic politicians, friends of Charlie Murphy.

McClellan's self-serving account was wrong in two particulars: *he* had not been the one to develop the plan (so there was not much of a secret to leak), and the options were held not by *Murphy's* friends, but by his own.

Andrew Green was among the many who had helped develop plans for Jamaica Bay. His assumption that Jamaica Bay would be the key to New York Harbor was the reason the Greater City's boundaries had been drawn to encompass it. One day shortly after the consolidation, a young civil engineer found himself sitting on a train next to the white-bearded octogenarian and they began talking about the future of the Greater City. On hearing Green's enthusiastic prediction that Jamaica Bay—connected with the East River and Long Island Sound by a great ship canal across Queens to Flushing Bay—would become "the greatest shipping center in the world," the engineer could scarcely wait to make his first site survey and within days had begun sketching port-construction plans. Seth Low, the former Brooklyn mayor who had preceded McClellan as mayor of the Greater City, appointed a commission to draw up a more formal plan for how the city's new territory should be developed. This effort stretched beyond his term of office and was completed in the second year of McClellan's administration. Making Jamaica Bay into an industrial port well-served by a tunneled rail connection to Staten Island and the rest of the continent was one of its central features. The Low planners (The New York City Commission) called for building big islands in the center of the bay (using as fill, naturally, the sort of low-cost material—ash and refuse—that had already been used to such effect to expand Rikers Island). And McClellan's comptroller, Edward M. Grout, had already been on record as saying that the most important form of municipal ownership was ownership of the shoreline of Jamaica Bay.

As for the "little syndicate" that held options on the land, its ringleaders included Reynolds, Bailey, and politically connected friends like Patrick Henry McCarren.

As so many New Yorkers before him had done, McClellan decided to get the land he wanted the old-fashioned way.

> The syndicate thought that it had a stranglehold on the city, a stranglehold that I determined to break. I found that under an old law the city owned in fee simple the land abutting on Jamaica Bay between high and low water, which was a very wide strip. I therefore abandoned the old plans that had been drawn and moved the bulkhead line to low water mark, which left in the possession of the city sufficient land not only for a wide marginal street but also for deep warehouses in the rear. The syndicate was left literally high and dry with options on land far inland from the marginal street.

And so McClellan was in the same boat as Reynolds and Bailey and company: holding acres of water-covered land waiting for waste.

The political problem that would be caused by dismissing Woodbury was another of McClellan's father's legacies. Thanklessly dismissed from his command of the Army of the Republic ("If McClellan is not using the army," Abraham Lincoln had said, "I should like to borrow it for a while"), "Little Mac" had then failed in his quest (as the 1864 Democratic nominee) to unseat his former boss. It was a failure that his devoted son intended to avenge with the satisfaction of his own presidential ambitions. But getting from the New York's City Hall to the White House would require, in addition to the luck that had carried him so far at such an early age, all the hereditary mastery of tactics he could muster. After bungling his first term by letting Murphy pull the strings, McClellan felt that the only way to restore his reputation in his second was to declare his independence from the Murphy machine. After that, the plan was to run for governor in 1910, and for the

COPPERHEADS WORSHIPING THEIR IDOL.

McClellan's late father, thanklessly dismissed from the Army of the Republic, had then failed in his quest for the presidency as the 1864 Democratic nominee.

CAN THEY OVERTHROW HIM?

MAYORALTY PEDESTAL.

When after the break with McClellan Murphy had with alacrity made up with Hearst, McCarren was truly the only game in town.

presidency in 1912. But to take on Charlie Murphy—and still survive in politics—meant forming an alliance with another power capable of counterbalancing Tammany's strength. Recent events had demonstrated that there were only three men in New York who had any real political clout. Murphy was one. Hearst was another. Patrick McCarren, the Brooklyn boss, was the third.

McCarren's support in McClellan's first-term election (defying Boss McLaughlin's stricture against any alliance with his Tammany rivals across the East River) unleashed a coup that dethroned McLaughlin and put McCarren in his place. McCarren's commitment to McClellan's re-election was what had kept Charlie Murphy (who would have preferred a new, more loyal mayoral nominee) in McClellan's camp. So when Murphy made up with Hearst after McClellan's break with Murphy (Murphy gave Hearst the 1906 nomination for governor), McCarren—whom Ivins and Klein had

Senator Patrick Henry McCarren
His liabilities, to everyone's surprise, threatened to
outweigh the possibility of even humble bequests
to his aged female relations.

determined was a partner with Reynolds and Bailey in Dreamland, Harway, and Brooklyn Ash—was truly the only game in town.

But when McCarren came to McClellan that fall to complain that Major Woodbury's Brooklyn superintendent (who also happened to control more than a thousand jobs) was supporting Hearst's gubernatorial campaign, McClellan was relieved of his indecision. Woodbury (after too many cocktails at lunch) hotly told the mayor that he refused to dictate the political affiliations of his subordinates, left the room, and then, aware that he had made a fool of himself, started to walk back to City Hall to make amends. Before he got there, however, he bumped into a friend who convinced him to threaten his resignation instead. To his surprise and distress, it was readily accepted, leaving McCarren in control of street cleaning in Brooklyn.

No one was more devastated than Mayor McClellan when the seemingly fit sixty-two-year-old McCarren collapsed with appendicitis in the middle of a conversation and died a few days later. Anthony Brady managed to salvage something of his friend's estate (whose liabilities, to everyone's surprise, were well in excess of a million dollars) to allow some humble bequests to McCarren's aged female relations, but there was nothing anyone could do to save George Brinton McClellan's public career. It was over, as his father's had been, well before he had achieved the ends he sought. Like his father, he retired to

Napoléon at Fontainebleau on March 31,   Mussolini al tavalo di lavoro, 1944
1814, after receiving news of the entry of
the Allies into Paris

Princeton, where he taught Princeton boys and wrote about Napoléon and Mussolini, two strongmen he much admired. Because Napoléon had been dead for a hundred years, McClellan's esteem for the emperor—to whom his diminutive father frequently had been compared—was perforce unrequited; in gratitude, however, Il Duce made him a Grand Officer of the Order of the Crown of Italy on his seventy-second birthday.

After he was dismissed from city government, Major Woodbury spent the last four years of his life working for the General Electric Company, where his work with electrical power could continue. Only Billy Reynolds and his friend Frank Bailey, and William Randolph Hearst and his once-and-future henchman Henry Klein, continued their respective labors in the best of health.

CHAPTER 4

Enemies

John Purroy Mitchel was the epitome of the ambitious young reformer. Like McClellan, he had a family background in politics and civil warfare (his uncle, Henry Purroy, along with Andy White, was disciplined by Richard Croker for perceived disloyalty, which led them both to team up with W. R. Grace's County Democracy before returning to the Tammany fold; his grandfather, John Mitchel, was an organizer of the 1848 Irish rebellion; two uncles died defending the Union against foes such as his father, a Confederate captain). His tastes and aptitudes matched his family's bellicose reputation: like Reynolds, he loved boxing, a sport in which he had been welterweight champion while at Columbia, and he was an avid collector of handguns who never went anywhere without one. When he was twenty-eight, Mayor McClellan (then in his anti-Tammany second term) asked him to investigate the borough president of the Bronx; Mitchel's relentless prosecution ended with the removal from office of three of the five borough presidents, and charges that would have removed a fourth had not his term already been completed. His renown from this work made him president of the Board of Aldermen when he was thirty. By the time he was thirty-four, in 1913, he was mayor.

At first Hearst was one of the young mayor's supporters. He found in Mitchel's pronouncements on the municipal ownership question symptoms of mutual sympathy and good copy in his attacks on municipal corruption. But the honeymoon was short-lived. Some said Hearst's enmity began when Mitchel refused to appoint his wife to a mayoral commission: however the feud started, both soon had more reasons for continuing it.

One reason was Mitchel's relationship with Billy Reynolds, who had become one of the mayor's closest companions. As two prominent players in the workings of municipal government (Mitchel, for instance, sat on the Board of Estimate when Reynolds first offered to sell his burned-out Dreamland to the city), they had known each other for years. With Mitchel's elevation to

John Purroy Mitchel
He was an avid collector of handguns, who never went anywhere without one.

Mrs. William Randolph Hearst
Some said Hearst's enmity began when Mitchel refused to appoint his wife to a mayoral commission.

mayor, their ties seemed to grow closer. The public's awareness of their relationship was heightened by headlines when—getting out of his car after a Sunday's drive in the country—the mayor accidentally shot Reynolds in the groin.
Obviously bearing the mayor no ill will, Reynolds later offered him a cost-free
partnership in an Arizona copper company (which Mitchel sensibly refused).
When Reynolds and Bailey (along with William Greve, their "scamp of an
office boy" who had become president of the Realty Associates) were indicted
for defrauding the government after a Hearst-and-Klein-fanned investigation—the district attorney decided that the sale of Dreamland and some
Jamaica Bay shoreline for parks was indeed criminal—Mitchel's publicly
acknowledged friendship continued unchanged. He flaunted it, in fact, by
attending a 140-dollar-a-plate testimonial dinner in Reynolds's honor at the
Sherry-Netherlands hotel. Nor did it help that the mayor appeared unrepen-
tant in face of an affronted public. "Those who do not like my friends," he told
reporters, "can go to hell."

John Purroy Mitchel:
"Those who do not like my friends can go to hell."

Another impediment to the Mitchel-Hearst relationship was the way waste management was practiced. Hearst had been pleased with the Mitchel administration's early attempts to develop a municipally owned network of incineration facilities. But under the young-Tammany leadership of Al Smith and Robert F. Wagner, the state legislature killed the bill that would have allowed the city to sell the electricity that these facilities could produce and squelched the funding needed to build them. The effective foreclosure of the incinerator option left the city with only two waste disposal choices—both of which, as Mitchel's competent street-cleaning commissioner well understood, were unacceptable from any rational public policy perspective, but each of which was (as the members of the state legislature understood equally well) pretty good for business-as-usual.

One of these inevitable choices, of course, was to extend Brooklyn Ash's lucrative contract, which by now was costing the city twice as much as it was paying for waste disposal in any other borough. The other choice was continued use of Barren Island-style reduction. But here there was not such unanimity among the members of the status quo. Precisely because of the effectiveness of the first decade of Brooklyn Ash's operations in making land that could be sold for people to live on, there was increased sensitivity in some quarters—most notably in Billy Reynolds's—to the debilitating odors that the White-and-Cranford factories were producing in South Brooklyn. For a man of Reynolds's connections and resourcefulness, the solution to this problem posed no great challenges of either imagination or implementation. He and Bailey simply had the Board of Estimate write its specifications for the next five-year garbage contract in a way that precluded the use of any location "within the confines of Jamaica Bay," which, of course, was Barren Island's home, as William Greve in a gleefully unguarded moment confessed to reporters who sought to trace the pulling of the proverbial strings ("There is no veiled reason for giving up the Barren Island plant. We own great properties in the Jamaica Bay section," he said).

But Reynolds, never satisfied to profit from just half an opportunity, did not rest with a victory for his South Brooklyn real estate interests. He also took the trouble, with Bailey, Greve, James Gaffney, and the president of Brooklyn Ash, to obtain the next reduction contract for himself.

The name the partners selected for their new venture—the Metropolitan By-Products Company—revealed some of the same promotional flair that had gone into naming Dreamland. Their choice of a site, in some respects, was similarly inspired. It was a lonely plot of salt meadow on Staten Island, the city's least populated borough, a place not yet tightly tied by bridges and tunnels to the expanding metropolis, where real estate speculation was not yet a game to interest high-stakes gamblers like themselves. The only people there, in fact, were citizens who considered it home. But that, of course, could make its own kind of problem.

Although precisely the sort of circumstance that Bailey and company, with their professional title-guaranteeing expertise, should have foreseen, the property in which the Metropolitan By-Products Company were interested had a complicated history. Through long-accepted tradition, a man named J. Sterling Drake believed it his to sell, but a local real estate broker named Edward P. Doyle knew of a charter made by Queen Anne to a friend of hers (for a bushel of wheat to be paid every year at Windsor) for much of the land under water around the island—including the site Drake now believed his. Doyle bought this title, and by erecting a shed and stationing a watchman, laid claim to it. At 11 o'clock the night before the real estate transaction was to be concluded, Doyle's watchman was kidnapped and replaced by a gang of thugs; at 3 o'clock that morning, Doyle counterattacked and hauled the gang off at gunpoint to the local police station under citizen's arrest. Since Drake was unable to swear that he was in possession of the property, the sale did not go through. Similar events occurred checkerboard fashion up and down the Arthur Kill (the river that separates the west shore of Staten Island from New Jersey) as the Metropolitan By-Products Company tried to land on spaces covered by Doyle's title, until finally it dug in on a dry spot called Lake Island that stuck up from the Fresh Kills Creek, an inlet off the Arthur Kill, and, with thirty private detectives and ninety city police—an occupying force transferred from Brooklyn and billeted on the island for the duration—prepared to make a final stand. These troops did not allow Doyle to land with a load of lumber and a building permit for building a "bungalow." After sinking his two-hundred-foot barge in front of them, he found himself charged with obstructing navigation.

When he surrendered the next day, Doyle found that many of the island's more prominent residents had come to make his bail and sweep him away a hero. His last hurrah—which managed to convey at once a realistic recognition of defeat and a wry refusal to submit—was to turn the property adjacent to Lake Island into a perfectly legal rifle range for target shooting. He arrayed the targets, naturally, along the Metropolitan By-Products boundary.

With that sort of preliminary, Mayor Mitchel spared no precautions in seeing that the contract between the Metropolitan By-Products Company and the city would not be blocked. To prevent an inevitable outpouring of hundreds of Staten Islanders in the Board of Estimate chambers, Mitchel scheduled the contract hearing for a day not normally devoted to Board of Estimate business. The Staten Island borough president was notified of the meeting—he was in his office on Staten Island—just an hour and a half in advance. He arrived in time to cast his losing vote (it had only one partner, made by Manhattan's borough president, who found the lack of advance notice unsporting). And then the Staten Islanders, responding to the Paul Revere-like improvised alarm they were able to employ, began to arrive in the chamber. In the middle of one of their members' testimony, the Islanders' lawyer dashed in with a freshly obtained order signed by the Chief Justice of the Appellate Division that restrained execution of the contract. Having anticipated just such an outcome, Mitchel had kept his street-cleaning commissioner standing by his office telephone, and so the contract had been signed the instant—before the Islanders' arrival—the authorizing resolution had passed. Not wishing to incite a riot, Mitchel made a pretense of reading the restraining order, then calmly announced that since the Board was enjoined from any *further* action, the hearing was adjourned.

All this left a bad taste in Staten Island mouths, a taste made more bitter because the most notable party to the contract was the mayor's well-known friend. But to add further insult to injury, the Islanders' worst fears about the possible effects of the plant's operation soon were realized. Like the implementation of the Brooklyn Ash contract, every shortcut that could be taken to reduce costs had been. The plant that was contractually required to process up to two thousand tons of garbage a day had been built large enough to handle just eight hundred—when all the equipment was working well, which often it was not (since the exhaust pipes were too small, the vapor condensers were of the wrong type, and the doors to the "reducers" were often broken). This meant that refuse that was supposed to be unloaded promptly from covered barges (which in fact were never covered) was simply left to rot for up to six months in the sun. Commuters on the Staten Island ferry lost their breakfasts. People trying to sleep on porches and in rooms with open windows, even in the far-off bedroom communities on the north shore, could not. Golfers at the fashionable hilltop country club four miles downwind lost their pleasure in the game. Edwin Markham, whom his employer William Randolph Hearst had made the most famous poet in America, felt that "a corner in Arcady" had been "transformed into the Valley of Gehenna."

Hearst himself, of course, followed the whole affair closely, as did his

John Hylan
With his wooden, deadpan delivery, he was Hearst's perfect puppet.

handpicked candidate for Mitchel's job, a little known Brooklyn justice named John ("Red Mike") Hylan who, with his wooden, deadpan delivery, was Hearst's perfect puppet. The protest rallies to which thousands of aggrieved Islanders came were ready-made campaign forums for Hylan. He reminded voters that three of the principals in the deal were "now under indictment in the Rockaway [and Dreamland] land steal" and promised his listeners that "the health of the people of Staten Island will be given prior consideration to the profits of Reynolds, Greve, and Bailey. The next Health Commissioner of this city," he added, "will deal with the garbage situation with an iron hand."

Mitchel's counterattack charged that the protests were fanned by the Cranfords of Barren Island (a likely, and ironic, possibility, but the nuisances were such that the public reaction probably would have been much the same anyway). Mitchel's rejoinder to Hylan's use of "Reynolds-Greve-Bailey" as a campaign slogan was "Hylan-Hearst-and-Hollenzollern"—a reference at once to Hylan's Svengali-like relationship with Hearst, and to Hearst's well-known anti-interventionist, pro-German sympathies. (Throughout the 1917 campaign, Mitchel pushed his patriotism past the point of political prudence, appearing, for example, on posters in full military uniform, which, since he was not a soldier, was contrary to federal law, and which, in any event, many of his German, immigrant, and socialist-leaning constituents found distasteful.)

On election day, two out of three Staten Islanders voted for Hylan. The rest of the city followed suit, not out of sympathy with the reduction-plant problem, of course, but largely because Hearst and Hylan had succeeded in focusing the public's irritation on Mitchel's public and private intimacy with men like Reynolds and his overarching "public-be-damned" attitude. Mitchel put on a real uniform within days of his successor's inauguration and died three months later—thirteen days short of his thirty-ninth birthday—in a fall from the training plane he was flying upsidedown without a seatbelt. Hylan, good to his word, had the Staten Island plant closed by order of his new health commissioner (over the protests of the War Department and Food Commissioner Herbert Hoover that the allies desperately needed the grease and glycerin in Belgium). Until Thomas Cranford could arrange for the family's Barren Island plants to re-open a month later, New York's garbage was once again dumped in the sea.

Things were not as bad for the Brooklyn interests as they might have been, however, because, thanks to their persistent efforts (those of the *Eagle*, the Realty Associates, and their common lobbying organization, the newly formed Brooklyn Chamber of Commerce), Hylan was unable to make any headway on his proposed incineration program, which was designed, as Mitchel's original plan had been, to replace the need for reduction plants. (It did not help Hylan's odds that all six of the incinerators were punitively proposed for Brooklyn neighborhoods.) And soon, the Barren Island operation, too, was closed, this time forever. But the Brooklyn Ash Removal Company's increasingly lucrative monopoly contracts continued, despite Hylan's personal antipathy toward its parent company (which had fired him twenty years earlier for crashing a train.)

Brooklyn Ash's continued good fortune under the Hylan administration could not have been hurt by the fact that a key figure in his administration, his first personal secretary and second police commissioner, Grover Whalen, was an heir of one of the partners in the firm. Or that John A. ("Fishhooks") McCarthy, one of the mayor's strongest Tammany supporters, was the company's treasurer. It was thus during the otherwise forgettable Hylan years that Brooklyn Ash's most lasting monument (of sorts) was created. On a hundred-fifty swampy acres in northern Queens called Corona Meadows, the company was dumping what eventually amounted to millions of cubic yards of smoldering waste, from which poured thick clouds of foul-smelling smoke. By the summer of 1923—though it would continue for another decade—the transformation was in full operation. F. Scott Fitzgerald, commuting between Great Neck and Manhattan to rehearse a new play, began work on a novel he planned to call *Among the Ash-Heaps and Millionaires*, but which Max Perkins, his editor, eventually convinced him to call *The Great Gatsby*. He found the meadows an apt background for introducing Tom Buchanan's sad mistress: "a valley of ashes—a fantastic farm where ashes grow like wheat into ridges and hills and grotesque gardens; where ashes take the forms of houses and chimneys and rising smoke and, finally, with a transcendant effort, of men who move dimly and already crumbling through the powdery air."

By then, Billy Reynolds had long since lost interest in the possibilities of that kind of landscape. He had gone on to found Long Beach, a new town in Long Island, and to be twice again indicted while serving as its first mayor. He soon thereafter lost interest in Long Beach, too, so that when he died, in 1931, he was living just a stone's throw from the gleaming art deco tower, just opened, whose footprint and blueprint he had sold to Walter Chrysler. Long Beach's residents were hurt that their founder chose not to have his funeral in their town. They considered erecting a monument to him anyway, but then decided against it.

PART III

Public Work

CHAPTER 5

Roads and Rails

Like everything else he touched, Robert Moses carefully stage-managed the paper trail through which he controlled his empire. The long foolscap pages covered with a quick pencil, the script elegantly spare, the phrases precise and to-the-point, were swept up by a fleet of efficient secretaries to be turned into clean white originals and a pile of filmy carbons or—if the distribution instructions were more extensive (the typist often found a scrawled note, "copies to City Hall press room and Chief Editorial Writers and Metropolitan Editors at all dailies, including Brooklyn and Queens")—crisply cut into stencils to be mimeographed in brown ink onto hundreds of dun-colored pages. After the original and the copies were off to their intended targets, the papers that remained were filed away in neatly labeled folders, one for each of his offices (his parks department headquarters at the Arsenal in Central Park, his New York State office at 270 Broadway, his Long Island park commission office in Bethpage State Park, and his flagship headquarters nestled out of sight under the Triborough Bridge). When, after thirty-odd years, it was all over, and Robert Moses had to relinquish his powers, equally efficient hands went back through the files, stripping them clean of anything that might cause the boss embarrassment, sanitizing them of any subject that might disturb his place in history. The official city files, the ones required by law to be placed in the Municipal Archives, hold but dry bones. The only place to find an angry memo from his putative boss (Mayor LaGuardia), say, is to find the carbon in the mayor's own files—where, on the backs of memos Moses sent him, the Little Flower (after learning his lesson the hard way) made his own pencil scrawls to check the addition on Moses's requests.

Moses's *real* files, the only workaday records whose bones were not scraped clean by the scalpels of his Securität, are buried in a cavernous shed beneath the Triborough Bridge, in a vast chilly space next to giant snow-

plows with wheels eight feet high, surrounded by drab filing cabinets in
rows as long as football fields—the battered originals from his flagship office,
carted from the paneled sanctum next door, their contents apparently as
intact as on the day they were put there. Inside—nary a pink sheet in sight,
the folders plump with their original stuffing—can be found an unbowdler-
ized archive of the Triborough Bridge and Tunnel Authority, from its
inception in 1936 as the simple "Tunnel Authority" ("leave the son of a
bitch off" LaGuardia had told his Corporation Counsel when Moses tried to
get a seat on it) through the putsch in which Moses purged it of its original
appointees to absorb it into his own Triborough empire. (The story is chillingly told in the daily meeting log kept by the original authority directors in
cabinet #186. After a sudden summons to the mayor's office, the authority's
counsel and chief engineer were surprised to find that Moses was inside
with the mayor. In the discussion that followed, "Mr. Moses made a number of remarks about what an unsatisfactory project the Queens tunnel was,
and that the Battery Tunnel would likewise be a failure, but for the Circumferential Highway. The Mayor [to the authority men's surprise] seemed to
agree with these remarks...." Within a few days, all the original authority
personnel had been removed, and Moses was in complete control.)

But even amidst such rich files, one is struck more by what is missing (or
cannot be found) than by what is there. Nowhere is there a trace of a comprehensive game plan—the complex critical path chart that Moses must
have carried around at least in his head—the strategy that plotted in
advance, as in a chess game, the layers of moves he would make (for that he
did indeed devise long-term stratagems to accomplish specific ends in a specific order, outwitting his opponents through indirection, patiently waiting
for the desired conditions to develop, or changing his tactics in response to
unforeseen circumstances, is clear from the evidence that remains). And
though secrecy from its intended victims was this critical path's raison
d'être, no indication can be found that he shared these thoughts with *anyone*. Did he somehow manage to orchestrate a vast bureaucratic machine
with thousands of human parts without anyone else knowing exactly what
he or she was really doing—or why?

Another type of absence is any indication of the source of his plans.
Where did they come from? How were they developed, these engineering

drawings and right-of-way alignments that fill the files? The lack of any planning context is not so surprising from a man who expressed nothing but contempt for planners and plans—"dusty volumes lying on a shelf" when what was needed, and too rarely found, were "men of action." (Like himself, he always seemed too modest to add, though in context the clarification would have been redundant.) Still, for a man who among all his other boasts never claimed any originality for his ideas (though somehow he managed to leave the impression with many of his listeners that many of them *were* new), it is striking to find nowhere among his personal papers (much less in any published writing or public remarks) any allusion to those whom he had to have realized were the source of the blueprints for the works he built one by one over the course of a forty-year career.

It is understandable perhaps that the Regional Plan Association, with which he so frequently feuded, might not get credit for putting on paper the lines for virtually all of the roads and crossings he built, but why not acknowledge the sources behind *those* plans, especially since their germ (and much of their substance) came from Frederick Law Olmsted, the nation's first transportation planner, as well as its first great parks architect—a popularly revered forebear with whom one would have imagined a consummate egotist like Moses might have felt a rush of sympathetic identification? But Olmsted, who had dedicated his life to building parks—the parks for which Moses as New York City's Parks Commissioner would become the steward—and the roads to bring people to them, who had shared Moses's predilection for personal (as opposed to mass) transport modes, whose commitment to the social utility of recreation in a carefully cultivated, artificially natural environment had so eerily paralleled his own, appears never to have been so much as mentioned anywhere in the Moses files. The omission is amazing.

Instead, the scant references to predecessors tend to center on the heroic past. The draining of the Pontine marshes—the Emperor Trajan's grand miasma-eradication project (which Mussolini finally completed in 1932)—is the comparison he often used to characterize the scale and impact of his own work making dry land from New York City's refuse. Indeed, apart from the Roman Emperor, there is only one historical personage whom Moses ever implicitly suggested was a worthy predecessor: Baron Haussmann, Prefect of the Seine.

Haussmann's Rue de Rivoli, opposite the Tuilleries Gardens

His choice is brilliant. In the objects of their vast ambitions; the ways they used their sweeping powers; their dependence on the one man who brought them to their appointed offices (with their too obvious disdain for the citizens whose physical destiny they so dramatically controlled, neither would have had a chance at elected office); the flamboyance of their entertaining; their attractiveness to women; their parallel intellectual enemies (without doubt the Brothers Goncourt would have hated Moses as much as Jane Jacobs would have hated Haussmann); their capacity for work; their managerial styles; their penchant for clandestine manoeuvers against their opponents' positions; the strengths and limitations of their political skills; their family positions (the Haussmanns a well-connected, well-to-do Protestant family in Catholic France, the Moses a well-connected, well-to-do Jewish family in Protestant America)—down to the very roots of their personalities and their deepest obsessions—the two are brothers.

In the summer of 1941 Moses assigned a staffer to prepare a dossier on his totemic relation. (His motive for doing so is not clear—was he planning an article, a speech, or was he just indulging his interest?) The result can be found in cabinet #1123 in the Triborough warehouse. Of especial interest,

Moses' Shore Parkway at the Narrows, with bicycle path and promenade

perhaps, are the parallel pictures, eight-by-ten glossies suitable for publication, depicting some of Haussmann's greatest works, alongside photographs of some of Moses's own creations. The staffer consulted André Morizet's seminal analysis of Haussmann's oeuvre and reported, "Among Haussmann's greatest works are the boulevards, . . . the Inner Belt Highway, the parks (including the Bois de Boulogne), the water system; and the enlargement of the city limits to include many suburbs."

What appeared to impress the staffer most were Haussmann's financial methods. Haussmann created a state bank, he told Moses, called the *Caisse des Travaux de Paris*—"which functioned very much as our own RFC [Reconstruction Finance Corporation]," through which he issued bonds to pay for his public works. Although the staffer was impolitic enough to use

Paris's Montfaucon (Haussmann's Parc des Buttes-Chaumont)

the phrase "World's Fair theory" to explain Haussmann's belief in "'productive expenses'" ("'extraordinary expenditure...if it is intelligently applied... enriches rather than impoverishes a community and leads to a general increase of revenue'")—Moses's 1939 World's Fair, the armament of excuse on which he had hung more than fifty-nine million dollars of infrastructural expenditures had just lost tens of millions of dollars—he did not point out that (like Moses's) the methods used by Haussmann to channel private capital into his public works circumvented any legislative controls and permitted the enrichment of his allies through means both legal and illegal, and eventually led to his downfall. (In Morizet's phrase, Haussmann "fell by his finances.")

For some reason, Moses's researcher paid no attention to the transportation innovations Haussmann evolved, the spiderweb-like network of interconnected radial and circumferential railways—the "Petite" and "Grande" Belts—that formed the basic organizing principle for the integrated rail/road circulation flows of Napoléon III's Paris.

New York's Corona Meadows (Moses's Flushing Meadow Park: Connecting Loop at the south end)

Nor did the staffer notice the transformation Haussmann had wrought on Parent-Duchatelet's teeming Montfaucon, which the order-loving Baron had tidied up into the Parc des Buttes-Chaumont, so that children could gambol on slopes where their predecessors, while their parents flayed hides from hack horses, had curled, asleep, in carcasses. Had he been more prescient, *that* might have been the most fitting achievement to have highlighted for his empire-building boss, whose most lasting contribution to New York's landscape—at any rate, whose *largest*—would be a three-thousand-acre two-hundred-foot-high plateau on the site of the old Metropolitan By-Products plant that one day would far surpass Montfaucon and Barren Island as the world's greatest repository of refuse.

Pale Blue Lines

If Haussmann was Moses's spiritual brother, there could have been no greater antithesis than William John Wilgus, the anti-Moses, whose plans for New York, had they been built instead of Moses's, would have made of the city both of them adopted a vastly different place.

As a boy in upstate New York in the late 1870s, William John Wilgus had often risked his neck grabbing onto freight trains as they slowed to climb the hill that ran behind his father's little farm, clinging to the sides as they picked up speed on the downgrade, waiting until the last possible moment to fling himself off. When he got older, he followed the trains farther, setting off to make his fortune with sixty dollars in his pocket and a letter of introduction to a relative who worked for the Minnesota & Northwestern. Starting as a rodman, he laid out lines in the iron and coal country, moved on to Iowa and Missouri with the Duluth & Winnipeg and the Chicago Union Transfer, and then returned east with the New York Central and Hudson River Railroad—by this time, still in his early thirties, as vice president in charge of building and maintaining all its tracks.

His father, too, worked for the Central. For fifty years he was its agent for Buffalo's freight. He had often taken his young son to the yards and to the adjacent harbor where the steamers that carried coal and ore and grain docked. The flow of material over the water and onto trains, of trains over the tracks, of tracks across the countryside, became William Wilgus's central theme and defining metaphor. In the unpublished memoirs he wrote near the end of a long life frustrated by unfulfilled visions, he wrote of flows of his ancestors' blood across the mid-Atlantic and New England states as the "rivers of [his] parentage" intermingled. He wrote of his own life's trajectory as a westward flow and eastward ebb. He characterized the central challenges and obsessions of his career as the smooth movement of millions of people and tons of freight in and out of the New York metropolitan region, the passage of millions of men and their materiel across France to win the First World War and across the rest of the continent to win the Second, and the creation of institutional structures to manage the rational coordination of these flows.

Looking back the aged Wilgus saw the moment that set his course. He was eleven years old. His father had just bought the acreage outside the city and moved his family there. The proud new estate owner wanted a surveyor's map of his property. The engineer he hired to draw it was Marsden Davey, who was known to the family because, as a young man, he had studied painting under the noted landscape artist who was Wilgus's uncle and namesake. "I trotted along with him," the old man recalled,

> holding the end of his surveyor's chain, peeking through the telescope of his theodolite, and watching him closely as he made a map after he had completed his outdoor labors. On the map he traced the sinuous path of the stream that traversed the property, tinted its margins with varying shades of blue to represent water, and on it inscribed the name, Smokes Creek, in shadow lettering, a name, by the way, harking back, it was said, to that of a chieftain who had ruled the Seneca Indians residing in that region. [The result was a] combination . . . of mathematical exactitude, lovely fields and forests alive with historic memories, and aesthetic charm. . . .

He, too, would be a civil engineer. His father, unable to pay for college, wanted him to go into business as a clerk in a friend's company. But Wilgus finally persuaded his father to "article" him to Marsden Davey, so that he could learn engineering the old-fashioned way. He received no pay for his first year of apprenticeship, for the second, a dollar a day—and a letter of recommendation.

Wilgus's plan to link New York to the mainland

The world beyond the railway industry learned of his genius soon after the turn of the century when he solved the problem of moving hundreds of thousands of people safely and efficiently into New York City, in the process helping to transform the center of Manhattan into its commercial heart. (Wall Street, until then the primary origin and destination for the nation's business travelers, suddenly seemed four inconvenient miles out of the way). And he did it with a bravura display of rationality and civic-minded planning that combined technological with financial innovation. The product of his vision, Grand Central Terminal, was a portal worthy of the center of the world.

Commodore Vanderbilt's line, which ran underground downtown from Ninety-sixth Street to Forty-ninth, then fanned out in an open cut crossed by high footbridges down to Forty-third, had long been an appalling nuisance. The huge track-filled hole cut off street traffic in all directions, while pedestrians crossing the walkways above the cut were assaulted by noise and soot. The coal gas in the tunnel was so thick it sometimes knocked out engineers at their throttles, while their firemen had to lay flat on the foot-plates to catch a breath of fresh air. Behind them their jam-packed passengers could only suffer the suffocating fumes in silence. In the impenetrable smoke the engineers, like moles, steered their trains by dead reckoning.

The accident waiting to happen finally occurred on January 8, 1902. In the midst of the morning rush hour a Central-Hudson train plowed into a New Haven train stopped at a signal. Fifteen commuters were killed at once in the telescoping cars; two more, scalded with steam, died soon after; forty-one others were injured.

The railroad refused to let reporters into the tunnel, which only made the public clamor wilder. The engineer of the second train was convicted of manslaughter and sent to jail. The New York Central was given another sort of sentence: steam trains would no longer be allowed to carry passengers into Manhattan.

George Westinghouse and Frank Sprague (the inventor of the electric trolley) were among those who said that electric engines could never power locomotives. The high voltage required, they said, and the dangers of short circuits and fires, made it impossible. But Wilgus had understood the severity of the steam problem two years before (soon after he had been made responsible for the Central's tracks), and soon after had drawn up a plan to solve them. *Before* the crash, the Central's board had merely been intrigued by Wilgus's cost-saving electric solution. Now, with the legislature's spur to immediate concentration, they asked Wilgus to carry out at once his plan to electrify the trains to Grand Central.

Historians of technology consider the locomotive that Wilgus and his subordinates developed one of the supreme achievements of twentieth-century design, an engineering enterprise of until then unparalleled managerial complexity. But the conversion from one form of motive power to another was just the first of the innovations that he went on to integrate into a seamless new whole, and though it was the basis upon which all the others depended, it was by no means the most daring. The rest of the idea came one afternoon eight months after the crash, when, staring out of his fourth-floor window at the crumpled fan of tracks leading into the station Wilgus began to sketch once more, in his precise, Marsden-influenced hand, the boundaries within which he was constrained (Forty-ninth Street to Forty-second, Vanderbilt Avenue to Lexington). He then began to rough out the office annex dictated by the railroad's desperate need for space. There was no way to squeeze a new tower into the available footprint in a way that made any operational or aesthetic sense. And then, "in a flash of light," he saw a solution that no one before had imagined: tracks, streets, buildings, all hung together in one steel-framed whole. He could bridge over the tracks to reconnect the streets that had been severed since the Commodore built the original Grand Central Station thirty-two years before, he could bridge the open rectangles between the streets to provide steel-plate floors for twelve blocks of new buildings, and below the street he could hang stacked layers of track. By layering the track fan he could expand its capacity many-fold, smooth its curves, and add new lines. And by tunneling under buildings, he could extend his fan as far as he wanted beyond the boundaries to which he had been confined, and could add turnaround loops that would vastly expand the efficiency of the whole system.

The cost would be enormous—34,360,000 dollars (Wilgus's estimate was accurate to within a few hundred dollars)—and would involve, among other things, tearing down the five-million-dollar station he had rebuilt only two years before. But Wilgus's calculations showed that his "air rights" invention—the notion of retaining ownership of the space below-ground and on the surface, while leasing the volume above (Wilgus envisioned it filled with grand hotels, giant office buildings, bustling shops and restaurants)—would pay for the whole scheme. Exactly three months later, Wilgus presented the detailed plan to William H. Newman, the company president, and then to a hastily called meeting of the board of directors. Newman raised objections: railroad hotels were always second-class, he said, and never made money. The reason for that, Wilgus said, was noise and smoke: electrification would eliminate these problems, while proximity to the station would increase a hotel's appeal. But cabbies will never stand there, Newman persisted, "Nothing could persuade them to leave the sunshine of Fifth Avenue. The horses need the sunshine, and the cabbies know it." Wilgus predicted that by the time the station was finished, there would be motor cabs all over the city. There were no other questions.

Under Wilgus's supervision, two million tons of granite were cut or blasted from beneath the streets—with the million tons of earth also removed, enough to fill a trench ten feet deep, ten feet wide, and 154 miles long. (It took an average of four hundred railcars working every day for ten years to haul them away.) He designed and built a system of portable bridges and trestles that allowed traffic to continue unimpeded while the old tracks and station were taken down and the new ones built. He managed to pry from the city every permit and approval he needed within six months of the board's authorization. He received architectural proposals from some of the most famous architects in the country—including Stanford White, who had built the Madison Square Garden in which he would soon be murdered, and Daniel Burnham, the father of the 1893 World's Fair, as well as from Wilgus's own brother-in-law, Charles Reed, who happened (perhaps with some suggestions from Wilgus) to submit the best proposal. Reed's design included the first ramps ever used for pedestrian traffic (like a barrel rolling downhill, a person or crowd entering any door would be pulled by a firm but gentle gravity straight to a ticket window); the revolutionary idea of tying together the severed ends of Park Avenue north and south of the terminal by pulling the roadway up and around the side of the building like a skirt (rather than running it through its legs—the two vast arches that Wilgus had envisioned at its base); and opening up a splendid civic court at the building's north face that would bring light and air and space to the grand gateway.

On September 30, 1906, Wilgus, trim, dapperly bearded, precise, drove the first electric locomotive into Grand Central Station. The smooth flow of engines that followed would soon make it the busiest, most profitable transportation facility in the world. With the problem of moving passengers into Manhattan solved, Wilgus turned his attention to freight.

The Central was the only one of the twelve trunk lines serving the city that actually rolled its freight into Manhattan. The Baltimore & Ohio entered Staten Island, and the New York, New Haven & Hartford ran into the Bronx, but the nine others deadheaded on the New Jersey side of the Hudson. From there, they had to load their barrels and bags onto the lighters that plied back and forth across the river, crowding the piers on either side of Manhattan, and, in their inexorably slow unloading, making the downtown streets all but impassable. But the Central's direct-rail freight system, which ran through the Bronx, across the Harlem River, and down the length of the West Side, was considered the worst of all, because, by cutting across every cross street in its path (as well as tearing through the center of Olmsted's Riverside Park) its murderous right-of-way had earned the name "Death Avenue."

Wilgus's solution cut to the heart of the problem. He proposed (shades of Egbert Viele) a narrow-gauge electric subway that would minimize handling costs and keep freight off the crowded surface of Manhattan by tunneling underground (as his passenger trains to Grand Central did), offloading its containers either at individual buildings or at dispersed terminals. (Closed containers into which freight could be easily loaded and unloaded, stored, or transferred to any other kind of conveyance were another of Wilgus's inventions.) In addition to bringing freight into the city, the narrow-gauge subway would haul the metropolis's refuse back out, an idea that would dramatically reduce the cost of waste disposal. Looking ahead, he also foresaw the need for a "belt line" to circumvent the congestion of the region's center, connect the splayed threads of the region's trunk lines as they crossed the Jersey waterfront, and, through a tunnel below the Narrows between Staten Island and Brooklyn— fulfilling an important piece of Andrew Green's vision for a Greater New York united around its port—connecting the city to the nation. It was a fine idea, the Central board said, but five years ahead of its time.

So Wilgus left the Central (the board's refusal to consider his freight plan—after it had vandalized his architectural design for Grand Central station—was the last straw) and formed a company to build the system on his own. In his elaborated plan, the tunnels for containerized freight would loop back and forth under the Hudson to connect with all the Jersey lines, since the cost of tunneling had been significantly reduced by an open-trench tunneling technique he had just invented while managing the construction of the Central's Detroit River tunnel to Canada. The first step was getting the New York City Public Service Commission's approval. Since the Death Avenue situation was at the top of their agenda, the commissioners were delighted with Wilgus's solution. After expressing their enthusiasm, they sent an emissary to cut a deal: the commission would be happy to approve the project, he said, in exchange for a piece of Wilgus's tunnel company, the Amsterdam Corporation. (Just the year before, after all, their colleagues on the Board of Aldermen had received a bribe worth four times the cost of excavating Pennsylvania Station in return for *their* approval of the

Pennsy's project.) But when the messenger delivered Wilgus's blunt response to their proposal the commission refused to take any action on the Amsterdam Corporation's application.

Like Andrew Green's frustrating attempts to control waterborne refuse from within the jurisdictional confines of a New York City that comprised only Manhattan, Wilgus's experience with New York City's Public Service Commission forcefully demonstrated that some more comprehensive institutional entity was necessary if the greater needs of all the entities surrounding the nation's premier harbor were to be met. When he drew the map for the Greater City, Green had included all the land that touched the harbor (including all the shores encircling Jamaica Bay). All the land, that is, whose institutional affiliations the voters of New York State could control. But this degree of coordination between the entities that depended on the harbor was not enough. An institutional mechanism had to be devised to bring New Jersey's shorefront communities into the picture, too. Wilgus did some research. He examined the charters for the metropolitan-scale park, sewage, and water boards that Frederick Law Olmsted had helped to establish in Boston. He studied the covenants creating the "Port Authorities" that London and Liverpool were using to manage their harbor operations. And then (without any prior legal or legislative experience) he drafted two bills that would allow the states of New York and New Jersey to join together to solve their mutual port-rail problems. In 1911, Governor Woodrow Wilson signed the bill the New Jersey legislature had passed without changing a comma, but six years dragged by before Governor Charles Whitman signed New York's version.

By the time both states were empowered to appoint representatives to a duly authorized bi-state harbor commission, the world was at war. When Wilson, now president, finally led his nation into the fight, Wilgus, then fifty-two years old—despite his age, the important projects with which he was engaged, his wife's frail health—enlisted. With the advance team of the Transport Division, he was one of the first five Americans to reach France. Commander-in-Chief Pershing appointed Wilgus director general of the division, but after a stateside error also sent W. W. Atterbury, Wilgus's former counterpart from the Penn Central, to France, Wilgus (to avoid anyone's embarrassment) offered to step aside to become Atterbury's deputy. No matter his title, Wilgus's contributions to their mission kept his colleagues amazed. "One day in September, 1918," one story goes,

> Pershing summoned Wilgus to a council of officers at general headquarters. Wilgus arrived two hours after the meeting began. Pershing had started in Wilgus's absence by announcing that the Americans were about to take over the San Mihiel sector, which until then they had been sharing with the British. The purpose of the council was to plan an immediate attack.
>
> Little progress had been made in the discussion when Wilgus arrived. In his typically abrupt way, Pershing told Wilgus the bare purpose of the council, then asked for his thoughts. Without knowing what any of the others had said already, without even waiting to remove his dripping raincoat, Wilgus began.
>
> He spoke for an hour and a half without stopping. He quickly outlined the whole situation at San Mihiel—the terrain, the obstacles, the troops, the guns, the whole state of readiness for an advance—even the names, the experience, and the reputation of the German regiments blocking the way. Each factor was carefully weighed, as if he were delivering a prepared lecture. He mapped out each step that would have to be taken in sequence, not as if they were part of a synthetic plan, but as if each in turn were dictated, as in fact they were, by elements inherent in the situation itself. He ended by predicting that the battle would be won in forty-eight hours.
>
> Then Wilgus sat down amidst the silence of men who had not the breath to speak. It was Pershing who broke the silence. They would do, he said, as Wilgus had made it plain they must do.
>
> The battle of San Mihiel began at midnight on September 11th/12th. It ended forty-eight hours later. It opened up the gap in the German line that enabled the Americans to launch the decisive Meuse-Argonne offensive.

Peace broke out two months later, before the War Department had had time to act on Pershing's request to make Colonel Wilgus a general.

In France, Wilgus and his colleagues (among them, Colonel Frederic Delano) came face to face with what Haussmann had built almost a hundred years earlier. Most striking was the *Grande Ceinture*, the belt of tracks that had kept troops and materiel flowing smoothly around Paris without getting clogged in the crowded spokes of the city itself, and without which the war could not have been won. More than ever aware of the pressing urgency for the parallel belt railway he had designed for the Port of New York, Wilgus wrote to a friend back in the states to ask him to present the plan to the War Department as soon as possible. The War Department staff agreed with Wilgus's proposal, and in turn, sent it to the New York/New Jersey Harbor Development Commission, the organization that, in Wilgus's absence, had begun to grow on the ground he had planted.

CHAPTER 6

Bridges and Tunnels

Like the Baron Haussmann he so much admired, whose rise to the pinnacle of administrative power depended entirely on the support of his quirky ruler the bohemian despot Napoléon III, Robert Moses's rise to power depended entirely on his relationship with one man, Al Smith, whose own political career embodied almost as many contradictions as Louis Napoléon's. Smith, born in Boss Tweed's Lower East Side neighborhood six weeks after Tweed was convicted of 204 out of 220 counts of criminal misconduct, was a self-described graduate of "FFM"—the Fulton Fish Market. His more traditional schooling ended at age thirteen, when he went to work to support his widowed mother and his sister, while meanwhile, in the evenings (when he was not rehearsing or performing in some neighborhood theatrical production) working his way up the Tammany pole by carrying out the ingratiating tasks that constituted a ward heeler's apprenticeship. In 1903 he was rewarded with an appointment to the state assembly, where he soon became, along with State Senator Robert Wagner (after Mayor McClellan's fall from grace), one of Boss Murphy's prize New Tammany exhibits.

After a stint in New York City government (as sheriff of New York County at the end of Mitchel's administration—his fond constituents gave the passionate amateur thespian a pearl-handled revolver for the part—and Board of Alderman president at the beginning of Hylan's), Smith returned to Albany in 1919 as governor. Swept over by the Harding landslide in 1920, Smith came home with his wife, five kids, two dogs, and a goat to Oliver Street. It was during this interregnum (he would return to the governor's mansion in 1923) that he came to know the young Bob Moses, then the director of a little reform group called the New York State Association. Their relationship—perhaps because of, rather than despite their differences in generation, class, and temperament—soon grew closer than the one between Olmsted and Vaux, Reynolds and Bailey, or Haussmann and Napoléon.

Besides putting on his trademark brown derby to step out in the evenings with Moses—the absence of convivial liquid refreshment was a problem for an unabashed wet like Smith, but nothing could prohibit the pleasure of wrapping his raspy honking *jolie-laide* voice around songs like "Danny by My Side"—serving as a commissioner of the new Port Authority that had grown out of the New York/New Jersey Harbor Development Commission was one of Smith's greatest interests during his brief exile from Albany. For Smith—unlike most of his fellow New Yorkers—the way freight moved was a subject of profound personal interest. His father, a small-time, self-employed trucker, had died from the backbreaking overwork of trying to push a horse and its crowded cartload through clogged city streets. Al's own first job was "chasing" such trucks—threading through narrow side-streets between rows of treacherous wheels, clambering across avenues by vaulting over the wagons themselves rather than taking the risk of slipping through the crack between the cart ahead and the horse behind—trying to get new assignments to the drivers before they wasted even more time trying to circle back to their office. As acting mayor (while Hylan was off on one of his Florida vacations with Hearst), he learned firsthand how chillingly fragile were the city's supply lines when the Hudson River clogged with ice and the thousands of tons of coal the city depended on to survive were stuck in New Jersey breakup yards. And while he waited until it was time to run again for governor, he supported his family in a style to which they quickly became accustomed by serving as president of a Canal Street trucking firm.

Among the advances the war brought in expanding the bounds of social and technological possibility were developments in the science of propaganda that Sigmund Freud's American nephew, Edward (Eddie) Bernays, had helped to promote. Doubly connected to Uncle Sigmund, who was his mother's brother as well as his father's sister's husband, Eddie grew up hearing Freud's latest work discussed along with the morning's news. Along with his colleagues in the US Committee for Public Information, Bernays—who had gotten his start in influencing opinion as the press agent for (among others) Enrico Caruso and Diaghelev's Ballet Russe—admixed peer pressure, ethnic hatred, and xenophobic panic to bolster enlistment and sell war bonds. After the war, Bernays and his partner, Doris Fleischman, (who soon would become his wife) set up shop in New York City as "public relations counselors." Another pioneer in the field—in fact, it was she rather than Bernays, her granddaughter claims, who coined the phrase—was a social-worker-turned-politician who one day would manage Al Smith's campaigns for president, Mrs. Henry (Belle) Moskowitz. While Bernays went on to use the insights and techniques of mass manipulation to support corporate ambitions, Moskowitz used his discoveries to influence public processes and political fortunes.

Belle Moskowitz had gotten into the public-relations game even before the war made propaganda something everyone was talking about. She was part of Eddie Bernays's first opinion-influencing adventure, when he first applied the family insights to achieve a practical crowd-related result, and succeeded so brilliantly that from then on neither of them did anything else. Bernays's first job was as assistant editor of two small journals, the *Dietetic and Hygienic Gazette* and the *Medical Review of Reviews*. In that capacity, he became aware of an actor's unsuccessful efforts to produce a play by Eugène Brieux that had recently been translated from the French—a play that, though it had earned Brieux's entrée to the French Academy for pursuing themes of which his spiritual forebear, Alexandre-Jean-Baptiste Parent-Duchatelet, would have been proud, his own contemporaries had banned from the Parisian stage. But George Bernard Shaw—in his preface to the English translation (coyly entitled *Damaged Goods*)—had called Brieux the greatest writer France had produced since Molière and his current subject "the most unmentionable" of all the taboos that he had violated in the name of truth and justice. To Sigmund Freud's nephew, assistant editor of the *Medical Review of Reviews*, shining the light of public attention on the mortal and moral dangers of venereal disease was an end too enticingly worthy to resist. He impulsively offered to sponsor the production.

On February 8, 1913, New Yorkers read that a private performance of Brieux's play was being organized "in aid of the eugenics movement" "under the auspices of the Sociological Fund of the Medical Review of Reviews.... The audience will be restricted to legislators, doctors, settlement workers, ministers, and others who may be in a position to help in the cause which led Brieux to write the play." After listing a number of eminently respectable New Yorkers who would be in attendance, the story concluded, "There will be no tickets sold at the theatre, and admission to the performance can be obtained only by becoming a member of the Sociological Fund of the Medical Review of Reviews."

There were updates in the weeks that followed. John D. Rockefeller, Jr. was helping to "choose" the audience for the play. Social worker Belle Israels (not yet become Moskowitz), well-known among women's society circles for her vigorous crusade to protect working girls from cheap dance halls where liquor might lead them astray, had discovered in the play an allied cause, and had agreed to help Mr. Rockefeller manage the Sociological Fund and distribute its largesse. The Belmonts, the Harrimans, and the Vanderbilts had ordered subscriptions. "The influence-leader technique" had just been invented.

The reviews from the play's "once-only" performance were uniformly respectful. Even the *Times*, which only days before had responded to the orchestrated appeals for public attention with dismay ("A certain morbid interest in the play has been aroused, which is not a healthy sign.... When the stage tries to teach, particularly when it tries to treat seriously of subjects generally considered too delicate for common conversation, it may accomplish some good, but it invariably causes harm, too, by its appeal to the merely curious and morbid minds"), found the performance "highly engrossing and impressive." But Bernays's opinion-engineering enterprise had just begun. He still had to transform the elite audience spectacle into the consciousness-raising vehicle for the masses for which it had been intended. His solution was another bit of psychological magic: he would have the nation's totemic fathers bless it as safe for their children. And so before "the most distinguished audience ever assembled in America" the play was performed again in Washington. When the Supreme Court justices, cabinet members, senators, congressmen, and diplomats emerged with due solemnity two hours later, their endorsements launched a run of performances into the middle of the New York summer, and then on across the country.

By making the disease that dared not speak its name the overnight subject of dignified concern and uplifting conversation, Eddie Bernays had launched a brilliant new career. And the future Belle Moskowitz had had a master class in learning how to "organize and effectuate" "the desires of the masses."

Mr. Potato

Making the way freight moved through the Port of New York into a topic everyone could care about was just another subject that could be packaged for sale by "influence-leaders." This was the assignment Al Smith gave Belle Moskowitz when he put her in charge of the Port and Harbor Commission's public relations campaign—in internal memoranda referred to as its "contact department"—and its two-hundred-thousand-dollar budget.

Moskowitz swung into action immediately, with Bernays's training showing through every stitch of her stilted prose. "The Port problem touches every home," she wrote in one of the first glossy pamphlets she produced.

> The people of the port district, 8,000,000 in all, are primarily concerned.
>
> This sociological aspect has never before been emphasized, and the Port Authority is now doing so.
>
> The Commissioners to the Port Authority, appreciating that the great public, so deeply affected, was not organized to promote its own benefits have asked prominent men and women to bring this phase of the problem to the attention of their respective communities, and these citizens have formed an Educational Council.
>
> This Educational Council, acting as an independent body [sic], is now engaged in an energetic campaign of enlightenment. It is divided into special groups and an appeal is being made to civic associations, schools, newspapers, the clergy, and all other individuals and agencies reaching the public to assist in making the people 'port-minded.'

Since there was no avant garde drama with which she could lure people to the theater, she used a new dramatic form—the public relations film. Even Bernays was impressed. The film opens with a wide angle aerial shot of the whole port region, then cuts to a funny little cartoon fellow standing on a railcar, his hand shading his eyes as he peers into the horizon. It is Mr. Potato, making his way from his farm in Michigan to the Terminal Market in the Bronx. The rest of the film follows the trials and tribulations of his journey. His eyes still bright, his skin still taut when he gets off the train in New Jersey, he finally reaches the family table in New York City four days later, withered, wrinkled, sixty-nine cents more expensive. Damaged Goods.

THE TERMINAL HANDLING OF FRESH PRODUCE A PORT PROBLEM

Mr. Potato is a much traveled gentleman
when he retires to rest in your electric oven

Hundreds of audiences saw the film over the course of the next year and a half, thousands of people attended meetings where the lessons it offered were discussed, millions of people read the press releases issued by the campaign which the editors of the region's dailies printed practically verbatim, all, as Port Authority Chairman Eugenius Outerbridge told the august members of his "Educational Council" at their first meeting, "to arouse this public opinion, which will bring the pressure necessary when the Legislatures convene."

One of the main reasons that Smith and his fellow Port and Harbor commissioners felt it so necessary to "arouse" the "pressure necessary" to affect the legislatures' deliberations was that William Wilgus had a better plan for uniting the two sides of the harbor—and a vision for an institutional structure to accomplish it that would be less susceptible to the machinations of political appointees. The route the Harbor commissioners were plotting for Mr. Potato (and his Irish cousin, the cabbage, who would be the new star when Al Smith performed the routine for the New York State legislature, equipped with the misleading maps and charts Mrs. Moskowitz provided) was a dead end.

Wilgus, who had been among the first to leave for France in 1916, was among the first to return as 1918 drew to a close. ("[A]s the emergency for which I entered the service is ended, and there appears to be no compelling reason why I should remain longer in the Army," he had written to General Pershing a week after the Armistice, "and also in view of . . . the urgent need, for personal reasons, of my presence at home"—it would have been unlike Wilgus to give the appearance of appealing for sympathy by admitting that he had just received the news that his wife had died—"I respectfully request that my resignation be accepted.") Since his return he had followed the Port and Harbor work closely. He had noted the similarities between the commission's plans (which were published in 1920) and his own design. The electric underground freight system that the commission proposed was almost exactly what he had envisioned. The belt to link the trunk lines outside the region's congested center was also his.

But amidst these similarities was a difference Wilgus felt undermined the logic of the whole endeavor. Rather than building the harbor tunnel upon which the rest of the network depended across the Narrows between Staten Island and Brooklyn, where nature and history dictated was the only rational place to put it, the Port and Harbor commissioners, for some reason, had dug in their heels and were insisting that it cut straight through the most congested part of the Jersey shore, through an area already so constrained for space that there was no room left to build the new rail-transfer yards that were the main objective of the enterprise (yards that would allow freight to be consolidated or dissassembled into larger or smaller units, and to be transferred between trains, ships, and trucks), across multiple shipping lanes that would have to be spanned by drawbridges whose opening and closing would constantly disrupt the smooth flow of freight, along a route that would leave a considerable portion of New York City's land area out of the loop. Rather than building a web that would treat all the railroads equally by connecting them with a belt around the region's rim, for some reason the commissioners were insisting that the tunnel be made twice as long and one-and-a-half times as expensive by running it straight through the Pennsylvania Railroad's yards.

There was an alternative. In addition to authorizing the temporary Port and Harbor Commission to develop a plan for rail lines connecting the two sides of the harbor, New York's state legislature had also passed a law that *required* the City of New York to fulfill the promises that had been made when the citizens of New York City had voted in favor of Andrew Green's consolidation plan. By 1923, the city was supposed to begin building its own rail tunnel under the Narrows. Wilgus volunteered to help Mayor Hylan develop a plan to meet this requirement in a way that would lead all twelve of the region's railroads to a more enlightened understanding of their own collective interests, so that a balanced regional economy of thriving manufacturing districts and healthy neighborhoods could be preserved. Within a week, Wilgus had drawn up plans to connect the western end of the tunnel with a rail line across Staten Island and the narrow Arthur Kill River to New Jersey, where it would link up with his proposed beltway around the region's core. By connecting the eastern end of the tunnel to the "marginal" railroad along Brooklyn's industrial waterfront (the land for which had recently passed through Billy Reynolds's scheming hands), the network would enable the development of the great Jamaica Bay port district that offered the city's greatest hope for a maritime and manufacturing future.

Mayor Hylan and Wilgus presented his plan—now the City of New York's plan—to a meeting of all the railroads' presidents. They agreed to consider the Narrows proposal. Over the following months, Wilgus and his engineering staff met with the railroads' engineers to discuss the details of his design. Then the presidents convened again. "From an engineering perspective," one admitted—his colleagues agreed—"there is nothing in the location of the tunnel that could be improved on." But the operational rationality of the integrated system was not the foremost objective of the most powerful line among them, the Pennsylvania Railroad. If Wilgus thought like General McClellan (another engineer), about maximizing an operation's effectiveness, the Pennsy thought like General Grant: it was perfectly willing to sacrifice revenues if it could make its rivals suffer as well. It was clear that the Harbor Commission's Pennsylvania Railroad-inspired plan (as Wilgus put it) was "a pig in a poke"—"not a plan in the true sense, but merely a picture" that would never materialize, and that the permanent Port Authority that the commissioners, under the legal guidance of the "oily" (as Mayor Hylan put it) corporate attorney Julius Henry Cohen was a far cry from the democratic entity Wilgus had envisioned. He denied Cohen's charge that he had "abandoned the baby which was born in your brain in 1910 on our doorstep." The proposed authority, as Cohen had framed it, he replied, "a group of non-expert political appointees, clothed with autocratic power and non-representative of the interests affected," is "a changeling which I have disowned from the start." The authority Cohen proposed, and that Al Smith and Belle Moskowitz were trying to ram down the throats of "an aroused public," followed "the name only, and not the substance of the successful port organizations of Great Britain which are really representative of the interests that in the last analysis foot the bills. One is tempted to rub his eyes to make sure that he is awake in viewing this reversal of traditions—autocracy in the new world, representative democracy in the old."

To be given permanent life, the changeling—and its peculiar plan for uniting the harbor by rail—had to be approved by the New York State legislature, a motley assemblage that Al Smith played like a fiddle. And so the steady stream of lies put out by Smith and Moskowitz's "contact" troops continued, with most of the region's editorial pages following suit (Bernays had been an excellent teacher), swallowing each preposterous new argument hook, line, and sinker.

The final showdown—the New York State legislature's vote on whether or not the Port Authority, as proposed by the Harbor commissioners, should become a permanent entity, and its plan a legally binding commitment—came in January 1922. Since Hearst was planning to run for the Senate (and expected Smith to be his gubernatorial running mate on the Democratic line), he sent Mayor Hylan to Florida to keep him out of harm's way in what otherwise promised to be a flagrantly public confrontation with Smith. The city's engineers were left to present the city's case alone. They used all of Wilgus's arguments in urging the legislature to adopt the city's version of a harbor-rail plan rather than the Harbor commissioners'. The costs the commissioners attributed to the city's plan were absurdly inflated. (Board of Alderman president Fiorello LaGuardia maintained that the malicious propaganda had "emanated" from George McAneny's Transit Commission "in the hope of killing the [city's] project.") The commissioners' claim that the authority could build its tunnel more cheaply because of cheaper interest on its bonds was spurious because the city's bonds would bear a *lower* interest rate and be paid off through the same user charges. Their charge that a Narrows tunnel could not support both subways and railcars was belied by the successful operating experience of several major railroads. Their assertion that the proposed grade in Wilgus's tunnel was too steep for freight was false—especially since the tunnel was to be electrified—and the grade in any event less than that for the Port Authority's proposed tube.

But the legislature seemed less interested in the truth of the message than in the magnetism of the messenger. Hearst had been quite right about the reception Smith would receive: he was a hero home from the wars. Even the cleaning ladies hanging from the balconies to welcome him roared with laughter as he described the tedious hypothetical journey Mr. Cabbage would have to make to wend its way from New Jersey through the city's tunnel to his Oliver Street dinner plate. (The map he used as the prop for this skit—showing absurdly circuitous routes on each side of the Narrows tunnel that bore no relation to the city's actual proposal—was another of Moskowitz's clever distortions.) Contrary to the city's claims, he said, the Board of Estimate staff were not only afforded full access to the Harbor Commission's data, but were treated with the utmost courtesy.

> Naturally we thought—we still think it, we always did think—that New York is the largest, the greatest city not only in the Port District, but in the world. (applause)...And, we invited her down, her Board of Estimate and Apportionment, had an arrangement made to treat them to lunch (laughter), and Corona Coronas (cigars), which was doing pretty well for the Port Authority with its limited funds and no salary, to provide for the entertainment of a guest that they felt they were directed by the State to confer with. Did they come down? They sent for eleven more copies of the Report; and we sent them up. (applause) And then they then sent down for all our statistics that we had in the Port Authority office, to back up the Report. Well, I voted for that resolution, to send that up, because I saw in it a trucking job which would be well worthwhile. (laughter and applause)

Swept along on the wit of influence-leader Al Smith and his Moskowitz-supplied propaganda, even the Tammany boys who had pledged their votes to the mayor swung to the other side and voted to create a Port Authority with full power to have its own way.

Watching with keen interest from the sidelines were two observers who would take the authoritarian lesson far. One was state senator Franklin Roosevelt, who would succeed Smith after his third term as governor, and then out-Bernays him in the 1932 campaign to become president; Roosevelt would use the Port Authority of New York and New Jersey as the model for the dozens of authorities he would call forth into being across the country as the way to channel his New Deal flows down to the Depression-parched ground. The other was Smith's protégé, Bob Moses (whose first mentor, before she introduced him to Al Smith, had been Belle Moskowitz), who would use more than his fair share of those authorities to have *his* own way.

CHAPTER 7

Parks and Parkways

When Frederick Olmsted and Calvert Vaux prepared their plan for Brooklyn's Prospect Park shortly after the Civil War (another job cut out from under Egbert Viele), they were impressed with the significance of recent advances in carriage construction. Narrower wheels and lighter, spring-hung frames made it possible to travel faster, which in turn increased the popularity of these vehicles, and created a demand for smoother road surfaces, particularly on the kinds of roads most likely to be used for family recreational trips. But beyond the mere surface of such roads, the increase in personal mobility offered by this technological advance suggested a new form for the urban roadway itself, a concept that the planners offered—while admitting that it fell outside their explicit sphere of jurisdiction—to the park's Board of Commissioners. Olmsted and his partner noted that city roads had evolved over time from the simple footpath that connected dwellings randomly arrayed, to wider tracks that allowed the use of wheeled conveyances, to streets in which pedestrians were separated from vehicles (and the mud and animal droppings left in their wake) on raised walkways along either side ("sidewalks"), to the formula sometimes used to link European palaces to parks, in which the roadway was bisected by a central mall between opposing directions of traffic. (The best example of this latest development was Haussmann's Avenue Foch, between the Place d'Étoile and the Bois de Boulogne, which Olmsted had inspected in 1859.) They now proposed a "fifth stage" of urban roadway, which improved upon the palace-to-park formula by bisecting the central mall with a road "prepared with express reference to pleasure-riding and driving." They dubbed this new form—with its six rows of trees separating sidewalks from ordinary roadways, roadways from mall, and mall from pleasure road, which produced a cross-sectional distance between house fronts of 260 feet, a gap sufficient to break the spread of fire and to provide enough light, air, and

The Parkway and Boulevards

```
                        L A N E .

85ft.

225 ft. 7 in.


                    Line of Houses.
                                          30 ft.
*  12¼  *    * Side * walk. *    *    *    *    *    *
   25
------------------------------------------------------------
    SIDE ROAD for the approach of vehicles to the adjoining Lots.
   7¼
*       *    *    *    *    *    *    *    *    *
   20
------------------------------------------------------------
   7¼            W A L K .
*       *    *    *    *    *    *    *    *    *
   55ft.
*       PARK-WAY.                                 *
   7¼
*       *    *    *    *    *    *    *    *    *
   20
------------------------------------------------------------
   7¼            W A L K .
*       *    *    *    *    *    *   *•   *    *
   25
------------------------------------------------------------
    SIDE ROAD for the approach of vehicles to the adjoining Lots.
*  12¼  *    * Side * walk. *    *    *    *    *    *
                                          30 ft.

225 ft. 7 in.        Line of Houses.


85ft.
                        L A N E .
```

greenery to support gracious living and commensurate property values—
"the park-way."

Although Olmsted's promotion would soon make such roads common-
place, the first ever built were Ocean and Eastern Parkways in Brooklyn,
one of which stretched from Prospect Park to Coney Island and the sea, the
second as far as the city line toward Long Island. Olmsted's parkway vision
also spread west, where he imagined a green ribbon crossing the East River
and snaking up Manhattan's west side (along his Riverside Drive and Riverside Park) and across the Hudson to the New Jersey palisades. On Staten

Island, Olmsted's plans (developed as recommendations to the Staten Island Improvement Commission for promoting public health) included a "high-road" down the central hilly spine to connect a series of "water preserves and public commons," and a "shore road" enwrapping it all around.

Despite his bias for personal forms of transportation, Olmsted also laid out the first plan for a rapid transit steam railroad *system* in the decade after the Civil War. After his descent into the senility and dementia that preceded his death, his son, Frederick Law Olmsted, Jr. ("Rick")—who would become perhaps the foremost planner of *his* day—took up where his father left off.

In 1902, Mayor Low's New York City Improvement Commission hired Rick Olmsted to help develop a comprehensive plan to guide the city's growth in the new century. The plan the commission devised was largely an elaboration of the senior Olmsted's work. Its foremost features were a series of parks connected by parkways, a network of parallel rail connections, and belts of road-and-rail routes along all the city's shores. As far as the future of Jamaica Bay was concerned—that vast sheltered waterbody that planners since Andrew Green had felt held the most important keys to the city's future—the Improvement Commission's report expressed some ambivalence. Rick Olmsted envisioned a necklace of parks around its perimeter, but the commissioners themselves foresaw commercial developments surrounding a port in its center. By the time the commissioners finally delivered their plan to the new city administration in 1907, however, Mayor McClellan had already committed the city to developing a Jamaica Bay Port nested within a seamless web of rail and roadway connections.

Jamaica Bay's port/rail future moved ahead with the help of the Brooklyn Committee on City Plan, which five years later took up the task of elaborating Brooklyn's role within the overall framework the City Improvement Commission had proposed. The Brooklyn Plan Commissioners turned to Daniel Burnham of Chicago, the eminence grise of city planning, who was best known for his role as the guiding spirit of the 1893 Columbian Exhibition that put Chicago on the world map, but who most recently—under the sponsorship of a group of businessmen that included Wabash Railroad president Frederic Delano—had framed the first complete plan for an entire metropolitan region. The central goal of Burnham's seminal Chicago plan was to replace the "chaos" (his term) of urban growth with an order derived from an understanding of the city as an organic entity in which the role of each part depended on its relation to the whole. (An ardent admirer of Haussmann—whose Paris plan Burnham kept constantly open on his drawing table—Burnham's sense of order also relied, as had Haussmann's and Napoléon's, on cutting broad swathes of streets through whatever anthropogenic impediments blocked their way.) Burnham managed to get to Brooklyn and to make a tour of the borough in an open-topped automobile to gather impressions, but died before he had a chance to get down to work.

It was left to Edward Bennett, Burnham's junior partner, to complete the project. Bennett, too, turned to Rick Olmsted for help. The plan they developed completed the roads Olmsted's father had begun to sketch to connect Brooklyn to the rest of the region, an armature of green ribbons strung between parks to provide a planning framework upon which the rest of a growing city could be hung. To complement his Ocean Parkway and Eastern Parkway, linking his Prospect Park to Coney Island and eastern Long Island, Olmsted Sr. had envisioned a shore road looping all along the borough's waterfront, which, by connecting with the Brooklyn Bridge (not yet built in Olmsted Sr.'s day) would link Long Island to the southern tip of Manhattan. To this romantic vision Bennett and Olmsted Jr. added an elaboration of Mayor McClellan's Jamaica Bay port scheme, with a "marginal" railroad rimming the waterfront to feed the planned commercial and industrial hub.

In 1916, the Bennett-Olmsted plan for Brooklyn was plugged into a larger context. Complaints from Fifth Avenue merchants about immigrant factory workers sitting on the curb of their exclusive boulevard to eat their lunches had produced a commission to create a plan for "zoning" the city. Mayor Mitchel put Board of Alderman president George McAneny—his fellow defendant in the latest Reynolds conspiracy trial—in charge. (Along with the city's comptroller, Mitchel and McAneny had been indicted for buying land for the Brooklyn marginal railroad at a price twice as high as Reynolds's dummy had paid only ten days before.) Though the McAneny commission produced the nation's first zoning plan, Charles Norton and Frederic Delano, who both meanwhile had moved from Chicago to New York, decided that it did not go far enough. As Andrew Green, Frederick Olmsted, and William Wilgus before them had realized the need for extending the framework for metropolitan plans over a larger base, they, too, felt the need to look beyond the bounds of the five counties that now made up New York City to encompass the whole region surrounding its harbor. What was needed, they believed, was a Burnham-style plan on a scale capable of controlling the chaos that threatened to engulf the region. Out of their vision the Regional Plan Association was born, and—with a million dollars of foundation money shaken down by Charles Norton—it produced the most exhaustively detailed plan ever produced in this country.

Although the Committee for the Regional Plan chose a Scotsman named Thomas Adams as its executive director (Thomas had become internationally known for his work planning two "new towns" in England), Rick Olmsted was one of the central figures in the (First) Regional Plan that the association released in 1929 two months before the stock market crash. William Wilgus, who had watched the Port Authority seeds he had planted grow into a sclerotic entity unwilling and unable to address the planning needs of the larger region, then seen his hopes for salvaging the situation dashed by the Pennsylvania Railroad legislation that Al Smith and George McAneny had foisted upon the port, was also drawn to the crusade. So, for very different reasons, was Robert Moses.

Moses had scrambled for two years to keep his New York State Association alive on a shoestring. Supporting his own young family on the frugal allowance his mother provided was another struggle. So as word of the new Regional Plan project got out, Moses wrote to its secretary to ask (somewhat indirectly) whether they needed someone in his line. A year later he was still dropping big hints to RPA chairman Delano. While it was all very well to produce "vague plans," he wrote, what the Regional Plan needed most was a "contact division" that could give the planning staff "the benefit of its practical experience." He himself had had plenty of such "contact experience." (The football image had been planted firmly in his mind through his work with Moskowitz. It would recur through his later career. "My job," he would say, "is to be the blocker for the engineers. I punch the hole in the line so they can get through.") On behalf of Mr. Delano, the group's assistant secretary thanked Moses politely for his interest—and the group hired Belle Moskowitz instead to do its initial tackling.

But while Moses stood knocking on the RPA door, unsuccessfully trying to get in, the Regional Plan staff kept asking Wilgus to join them. When, in 1924, Wilgus finally showed some interest in enlisting in the plan, Frederick Delano, his fellow officer in the Transport Division, who had become the plan's chairman, was delighted. He asked Wilgus to outline what he believed should be the plan's major objectives. It took only a few days for Wilgus's crisp response. "As I see it," he said,

> there are three elemental needs of mankind when grouped together in great cities—transportation, recreation and industry....Other elements, such as water-supply and sanitation, heat, light and power, small parks and playgrounds, civic centers, architectural treatment, financing and administration are truly essential to the rounding out of the plan, but it seems to me that their consideration should follow the determination of the basic structure on which they must rest.

The specific projects he therefore recommended, in order of priority were

> an outer belt railway and boulevard; twin inter-connected inner belt railways and boulevards; rapid transit systems suitably related to the belt railways and boulevards; an internal waterway system; parks, sea-side resorts, amusements and playgrounds; [and] industrial layouts, including port developments and manufacturing sites."

Delano and Olmsted enthusiastically agreed with these objectives (Olmsted called Wilgus's statement of the problems "clear, comprehensive, sane, and bold")—and asked Wilgus to become the plan's engineer. In just a few days he had begun to refine and elaborate for purposes of a humanely balanced plan the basic infrastructural elements he had long contemplated—the integrated inner and outer rail/road beltways designed to move people and freight quickly and efficiently from one part of the region to another without contributing to the congestion of the center, and park and parkway connections from the tip of Long Island across the Hudson up the Palisades and across the Harbor to the Jersey shore. But with a few weeks' more thinking, he produced the conceptual design for a completely new idea—one which, by bringing all the others into sharper focus—promised to heighten the benefits that his integrated vision for the region could achieve.

It was a 150-yard-wide causeway that swept in a breathtaking curve all the way across the harbor from Sandy Hook, New Jersey to the Rockaway Peninsula. A commodious marine channel would cut through it, the outer belt railway and boulevard would run over it. It would connect New York to the continent, bridge a north-south rail and road route up the Atlantic Seaboard from Washington to Boston that avoided the congestion in its densest center, and provide eight miles of stunning beachfront. Because it would be built from waste materials that otherwise would have to be towed out to sea for disposal (including the material bored from the Narrows Tunnel); would produce valuable recreational and commercial land; would increase the value of the New Jersey real estate by making it more convenient to New York; would generate tolls from the railroad and the boulevard; and would produce savings from the reduction in congestion at the Hudson and East River crossings, the project would quickly pay for itself. The causeway provided so many attractions and functions that its paramount purpose was not even evident at first glance: it would protect the inlet to Jamaica Bay from the shoaling that had pushed the sandy Rockaway Peninsula several miles to the west in the past century, keeping open the channel that was needed if Jamaica Bay were to become the world's greatest port. It was a career-capping project that had all the gentle splendor of Marsden Davey's graceful blue lines on a map.

Unfortunately for the causeway and the rest of the Regional Plan, Thomas Adams, its executive director, was scarcely a contact person. Delano and his staff could have used a Belle Moskowitz on their side when the next Narrows tunnel fight—for example—erupted in 1925. But she worked instead for the opposition. Once again Al Smith played the decisive role. Sitting impassively for five hours behind a hearing table, Smith listened as Transit Commission chairman George McAneny and Port Authority chairman Eugenius Outerbridge and counsel Julius Henry Cohen denounced the city's plan and insisted—to prevent any competition to the Pennsy's franchise—that any use of the Narrows tunnel be restricted to rapid transit. To placate Outerbridge and Cohen (who had threatened to resign from the Committee for the Regional Plan if it did not drop its support for a rail-freight Narrows Tunnel), Adams weaseled away from RPA's public position, ignoring the expert advice

of Wilgus and many of his engineering fellows that there was no technical justification for using the Narrows tunnel only for subway cars.

   After the farcical hearing was over, Smith took up his pen, and by signing
the Transit Commission-sponsored legislation, drove another nail into the
region's hopes for a rationally planned future. And the millions the city had
spent digging holes to build a rail crossing from New York to the mainland
were as wasted—Wilgus sadly acknowledged—"as so many autumn leaves
consumed in flame."

A Competing Vision

In 1925, Robert Moses, well schooled by the years he had spent at Al
Smith's and Belle Moskowitz's knees, was ready to begin building a power
base of his own. His means, largely learned through close observation of the
Port Authority, depended primarily on an ability to finance public works in
ways that were immune to the voters' control, through a stream of bond

issues whose force and velocity would have left the Baron Haussmann gasping with envy and admiration. Moses had first met Belle Moskowitz (and through her, Al Smith) when she hired him to work on Al Smith's "Reconstruction Commission." Thanks in large part to Moskowitz's propaganda work, New York's government was remodeled to match the commission's blueprint during Al Smith's second term, as duplicative administrative responsibilities and personnel were removed, new planning requirements added, and budgetary processes revamped.

For Robert Moses—whose imagination, like William Reynolds's, had long been fired by the beauties of Long Island's south shore—two changes wrought by the Reconstruction Commission stood out above all the others. The first of these was that spending was no longer limited by the tax revenues the state received every year: bonds could now be issued to pay for capital projects, and the bonds could be repaid over time through fees levied on the users of those facilities. The second was the replacement of the old ad hoc system for managing state parks with a centralized administration under the control of regional commissioners. The Long Island Park Commission, Moses told Smith, was the fief he wanted as reward for his years of vassalage.

There was little similarity between Moses's shorefront plans and William Reynolds's. Without the overarching conceptual elegance of Wilgus's causeway beach, the vision behind Jones Beach, Moses's first major work, as well as the architectural purity of its realization, were nonetheless more like Wilgus's imaginings than was the rough-and-ready speculative development (replete with brothels, gambling, and bootlegging) that Reynolds was erecting at Long Beach. But in one regard—the way they bankrolled the roads to their shores—there was an uncomfortable resemblance between the Moses and Reynolds projects. In June 1924, Reynolds found himself in jail for having required the contractors who were building his Long Beach projects to finance this construction themselves by buying the town's bonds. (The Town of Long Beach paid a premium for this unorthodox and uncompetitive approach because of a higher-than-necessary interest rate, but, for once, it appeared, this financial shortcut involved no influx to Reynolds's personal pockets.) Moses escaped a parallel fate for a comparably illegal expedience— appropriating the private lands he needed for his Jones Beach highway before the legislature had appropriated the funds to pay for them—with Smith's and

Moskowitz's help and a timely quarter-million-dollar donation from a super-annuated parks enthusiast. But he also did his best to help Reynolds out of his fix by urging Smith to appoint a more sympathetic magistrate for the next round of Reynolds's trial. (Reynolds's constituents, as usual, were equally untroubled by their mayor's behavior: on his release from jail he was swept up into a hundred-car motorcade and borne triumphantly through town amidst an explosion of banners, sirens, and fireworks.)

The lines Moses followed to connect Jones Beach to New York City were roughly those Olmsted and his son had put on the map beginning six decades before. The legal construct he used to wrest control over this massive public works project from the welter of competing state, county, and local highway and public works departments was also based on Olmsted's invention. Local supervisors had always been responsible for public roads, which, in the state's General Municipal Law were called *highways*. But that all changed when, with the artful insertion of the word *parkway* into the legislation establishing the Park Commission, Moses suddenly got sole responsibility not only for parks but for any road that could be made to touch one. And that was not all. Now, rather than having to squeeze the funds he needed from bare local budgets—usually by levying assessments on residents who might well not welcome the idea of paying for the privilege of living next to a new highway—the state park bond authorization he had pushed through with Al Smith's support and Belle Moskowitz's propaganda could be used to pay for them.

Pushing the main route back across the city line (the institutional barrier that had blocked Olmsted from extending his Eastern Parkway any farther along its intended trajectory), Moses tried to direct his course across the Queensborough Bridge toward Wilgus's Grand Central Terminal. To his disgust he discovered that the noncontact officials who had named the Grand Central Boulevard two decades before had done little more than that: they had bothered to acquire only a few thousand feet of the mapped right-of-way. Now it was too late to buy that strip even with the expansive purse provided by the state's new bond-issuing authority. So Moses instead turned his sights north, to where the senescent administration of Mayor Jimmy Walker was sinking pylons to build a bridge to span three boroughs.

Moses hoped to use an old railroad right-of-way that ran through northeast-ern Queens to get there, but soon discovered that a divided lane highway could not be squeezed into its narrow bed. And so, like water running downhill, or a horse being led to water, Moses eventually was led—as Queens politicians and other real estate speculators had known he would be—to follow the north-south course of the creek that Andrew Green, Egbert Viele, and William Wilgus had hoped would one day be a canal con-necting Long Island Sound and its northern and western tributaries with the great port in Jamaica Bay, but which Fishhooks McCarthy and his Brooklyn Ash Removal company had turned into the densest accumulation of ash and refuse since Rikers Island, Barren Island, and Montfaucon.

Brooklyn Ash had been trying to get rid of the sad ash-dump site for years. In 1922, when developers along the Bay and Sound shores were converting properties from recreational to industrial uses, Brooklyn Ash announced plans to build an "industrial colony" there—but after an unsuccessful meeting with the borough president, that idea was dropped. In 1924, when density pres-sures in other boroughs made it lucrative to convert vast swathes of Queens into cemetery—prompting an observer to call the borough the world's best argument for cremation—Brooklyn Ash proposed that use for its land, too. But because it had just been convicted of violating sanitary and penal codes—after a jury heard a witness testify that stoning had been useless against the hundreds of rats in his backyard, while tarring and feathering one before turn-ing it loose had worked wonders, and heard more testimony about the special traffic officers needed to direct motorists through dense smoke at the intersec-tion of Northern and Astoria Boulevards, and about odor complaints from as far as four miles away—"burying the survivors" (as a local alderman some-what incongruously put it) did not appear to be an acceptable solution. In 1925, when Moses and his colleagues in the Metropolitan Parks Conference tried to find and buy parkland in this fastest growing borough, Brooklyn Ash proposed this use as well, only to be told that Queens offered plenty of more practical sites. In 1927, when the city was trying to decide where to build its first municipal airport, and dozens were being proposed or developed in the city and neighboring region—three of which would be built on landfills of their own within a mile or two of the Corona Meadows—Brooklyn Ash offered it to the Walker administration for this purpose, but was again refused. A railroad center, an automobile raceway, and a giant boxing arena were proposed with equally fruitless results.

After another adverse court ruling in 1929 (and the stock market crash that must have dampened any further hopes for a sales opportunity), the company announced that it would create public amenities to compensate for its continued operations there. The first of these was a golf course that opened in 1931 with (Robert Moses thought) "all the pathetic beauty and frailty of a single rose in a dung heap."

But despite the company's increasing desperation (in 1933, Brooklyn Ash president Van Etten even offered to build there two grandiose "recreadions"—a term that Parks Association president Nathan Straus had coined to describe the playing fields the Nazis were building), prying the site away from the company when somebody else finally wanted it was not easy. It happened only because—after a twenty-eight-year reign—Brooklyn Ash was finally put out of business. During the years Fishhooks McCarthy and his partners had held a stranglehold on the rich offscourings of Brooklyn, they had seen their profits swell as they consistently charged a price twice that citizens in any other borough were paying. But Jimmy Walker's precipitous tumble from power (thanks to a high profile investigation presided over by Justice Samuel Seabury) left all the Tammany turtles stacked under him shaken loose from their positions. When Brooklyn Ash's contract came up for renewal in 1933, first one and then two competitors (from competing factions of the now shattered party) dared to breach what had once been the seamless wall of party unity.

One of these was Samuel Rosoff, one of the two contractors whose complaisance in Long Beach's bonding adventures had sent William Reynolds to jail nine years before. Rosoff first proposed using as his dump site a corner of the Corona meadows that Brooklyn Ash had already befouled, but when local protestors and politicians made that impossible, he took an option instead on a parcel in Staten Island, taking care this time to avert local opposition by keeping its location secret. No doubt the most dramatic moment in Rosoff's quest for the contract was his appearance at City Hall followed by two liveried retainers who carried between them a heavy trunk. They produced gasps among the hardened spectators in the Board of Estimate's chambers when they removed the trunk's cover to reveal a million dollars in cash (in all likelihood as naked a display of currency within the confines of City Hall as had been seen since Boss Tweed's day). This edifying spectacle, Rosoff assured his audience, should put to rest the vicious rumors that he was incapable of making good on his financial commitments.

Though his conduct was less theatrical, it must have been no less amusing for those who followed the affair to see the sanctimonious Samuel Seabury in the position of Brooklyn Ash's defender against its Democratic competitors. Seabury succeeded in having Rosoff's unanimously awarded contract enjoined after introducing evidence of the company's unusually brief and well-connected corporate history, and after making the argument that the apparent low bid was not the least expensive because it would require longer drives to the dump. (The firm had been organized only two weeks before the day the bids were due, which in turn was only four days before the contract was scheduled to go into effect; both the current Tammany head and the successor to Charlie Murphy's aldermanic seat were partners in the firm, though the latter had not yet paid for his shares, preferring to wait, as Rosoff's attorney explained, to be sure that they got the contract first.) Into the vacuum thus produced the second competitor sprang: following the ineluctable logic of the times, he was the second of the contractors in the bonding affair that had sent Reynolds to jail.

In the meantime, Walker's downfall had brought a new street-cleaning commissioner into office. Walker's friend, personal physician, and European traveling companion (whose administrative insouciance was matched only by his lavish attention to such details as the extravagant uniforms for the department's marching band) was replaced by George McAneny, who had succeeded Frederic Delano as president of the Regional Plan Association. Within a few months he would be called to assume the duties of city comptroller (just as Andrew Green, one of the city's most conspicuously honest men, had been called upon to assume the same duties following Boss Tweed's disgrace)—and within a year after that was asked to become chairman of Frank Bailey's Title Guarantee and Trust (another organization, if ever there was one, in desperate need of an honest man). But it was during his short stint as commissioner that the old way of getting rid of the city's waste fell apart, and the new one—which would last the next two-thirds of the century—began.

Brooklyn Ash's decades of depredation had convinced all but its apologists that municipal ownership of the means of destruction (the five incinerators Brooklyn Ash ran, along with the thirty barges, nine locomotives, and one-hundred-forty-five rail cars that brought the ash and refuse to the Corona Meadows) would save the city a prince's ransom. McAneny was equally convinced (as William Mills Ivins had established in his 1906 Brooklyn Ash investigation) that the real key to its value was the making of real estate. As president of the Regional Plan Association, McAneny was uniquely quali-fied to appreciate how and where newly created land could advance the city's long-term planning objectives. It was a waste of taxpayers' dollars to pay Fishhooks McCarthy and his men seventy cents *a cubic yard* to dispose of the city's waste when municipally controlled forces, he believed, could dis-pose of it for less than forty cents *a ton*. But it was even more a waste of tax-payers' resources to allow Fishhooks to pile up their refuse uselessly instead of using it to build the public works the city needed. Despite the regrettable role he had played in stopping the Narrows passenger-freight tunnel, McA-neny was one of those who believed that foremost among these was the long-anticipated Jamaica Bay industrial port. If paying Brooklyn Ash's price was the cost of securing the material needed to build the port, he would pay it—even if the figure they finally agreed upon left the usually tight-fisted Fishhooks in a position, at his death twenty years later, to leave eight million dollars to charity.

Building the proposed "West Island" in Jamaica Bay with city refuse was an integral part of the plan McAneny presented to the Board of Estimate for its approval of the deal to purchase Brooklyn Ash's empire. According to the City Committee on Plan and Survey (on which Wilgus had served, and which had issued its report a few years before), Jamaica Bay offered the only solution to the problem of the Port of New York's loss of business to its competitors; its development as an industrial port was "one of the most important improvements to which the City is committed at the present time" ("its geographical location and the almost perfect harbor provided by nature in Jamaica Bay, creates for New York City a solemn obligation to the entire nation that should be fully recognized and discharged"); and West Island itself was "the best location to be found anywhere in the country" for establishing the kind of duty-free trade zone that Congress was currently

[Entered at the Post Office of New York, N. Y., as Second Class Matter. Copyright, 1910, by Munn & Co., Inc.]

A POPULAR ILLUSTRATED WEEKLY OF THE WORLD'S PROGRESS

Vol. CIII.—No. 1.
Established 1845.

NEW YORK, JULY 2, 1910.

10 CENTS A COPY.
$3.00 A YEAR.

The city of New York in co-operation with the Federal government is about to begin at Jamaica Bay a scheme of construction of channels, bulkheads, and the reclamation of land which, when ultimately completed, will provide this port with 150 additional miles of water front.

THE JAMAICA BAY IMPROVEMENT.—[See page 9.]

Moses gave a slide show in 1936: "This is a rather uninspiring thing at the moment."

considering. A few Queens civic workers expressed some mild reservations about the enterprise—they were concerned about odors wafting off the bay—but with the assurance that all refuse that would be dropped in the water would be cooked first, they withdrew their objections and the Board of Estimate promptly gave its unanimous consent.

Robert Moses was pleased that the process—by city standards—had gone relatively swiftly: he was waiting to build his highway on Fishhooks's land. The name he gave the project revealed at least as much of the phrase maker's art as Reynolds's Dreamland or Metropolitan By-Products did. The Grand Central Parkway *Extension* no longer headed in anything like the direction of Grand Central, but pretending that it did made the federal and state budget agencies think that this work was necessary to complete a road for which they had already paid. *Parkway*, of course, not only gave Moses rather than any other entity control over the road, but allowed him to use the state parks-bond authorization to help pay for it. Since he had meanwhile usurped responsibility for building the Triborough Bridge, had created an authority to complete the job by issuing bonds against future tolls, and had gotten the federal Reconstruction Finance Commission to buy those bonds, he now

"We are going to make

"a World's Fair out of it."

was able to get approval to use these revenues for approach roads that stretched well away from the toll plaza itself. And then he had the job designated as a public-works project eligible to absorb WPA labor. But because these state and federal monies were eligible only for *construction*, it was essential that he get the *city* to scrape up the money to buy the Corona Meadows right-of-way. Getting George McAneny to pay for it from his sanitation budget—so that it would receive a higher priority than funds for playgrounds, schools, or hospitals—was the only expedient he could think of. How much McAneny had to pay was the least of his concerns.

Unfortunately, the end result of all his raids on these city, state, and federal budgets still left him too strapped to do much of anything but drill a ditch through the towering mounds, leaving the heaps on either side standing much as they had in F. Scott Fitgerald's day. His parkway was in danger of becoming his own solitary rose on the dung heap. So he was doubly, triply lucky when one day McAneny came to him with a plan to pay for transforming this lunar landscape into a more fitting surrounding for his cherished roadway. The idea, McAneny said, came from a twelve-year-old girl, the daughter of a Belgian immigrant who had thought that a world's fair would make a fitting tribute to the 150th anniversary of George Washington's inauguration, and that the Corona Meadows would be the most appropriate place to do it. (This touching story loses, perhaps, some of its ingenuous charm with the knowledge that the notion was transmitted to McAneny by Douglas Roosevelt, the president's cousin, who happened to be a real estate broker.)

Whatever its source, there was more than a touch of irony in the notion of offering the Corona Meadows as a tribute to the Founding Father, since Washington himself had considered the same site for the new capital he was planning. But before Fishhooks filled the swamp with ash and refuse, there were so many mosquitoes there that the new president jumped back on his barge and went off to found his eponymous city on another swamp. No matter: Moses, like Haussmann and Burnham before him, now had the excuse of a world exposition to carve his mark upon his city.

CHAPTER 8

Ports and Airports

As he bustled about moving refuse in the Corona Meadows to get his road built in time for the fair, leveling a lump of ashes here, using the material to fill a depression there, Robert Moses often bumped into the man who was building an airport out of refuse at the old North Beach amusement park next door. William Francis Carey, the burly president of the Curtiss-Wright Corporation, was the kind of man's man sportswriters adore. He lived hard, but spent easily. He read voraciously, yet loved boxing, a good cigar, and Dixieland jazz. Square-jawed, immaculately dressed, he was capable of throwing a world-champion wrestler on a five-dollar bet, or of taking a marshal come to arrest him on trumped-up charges out to lunch first. Even Moses—who outside of his old mentor, Al Smith, never expressed unqualified admiration for any contemporary—was clearly beguiled by Carey's mixture of competence, charisma, and gentle, good-humored machismo.

One of the things Moses found most amazing about Carey's airport operation was Carey's confidence that he could use garbage fill as a stable foundation for heavy construction. But he had to admit that Carey's self-confidence was well earned. Born in the little town of Hoosier Falls, New York, he had set off for Colorado at the age of sixteen to join a railroad construction gang. At twenty-two, he went to Panama to become a section hand on the Canal; three years later, he was the steam-shovel supervisor in charge of its Culebra cut, at the time the largest excavation on earth. From there he went on to build canals and railroads in Bolivia, China, Canada, and the United States, and with the companies he built or ran (he was simultaneously president of the Kennedy & Carey Construction Company and the William F. Carey Corporation, and first vice president of the International Cement and Southern Phosphate corporations) to mine coal, phosphates, and cement, and to build buildings and dams throughout North and South America. When he and two fellow ferry commuters from Long Island's North Shore thought of

Trucks being filled with refuse mined from the Rikers Island landfill

building a new airport on the point they passed every day—a former amusement park and beer garden which had been ravaged first by Prohibition, then
by fire—Carey was best known as the man who had built Madison Square
Garden, and after Tex Rickard's death, become its president. He kept this
position even after he was made president of the Curtiss-Wright Corporation
and handed the responsibility for building a new airport at North Beach.

Still, the airport enterprise was not a complete success. "I used to visit the
old North Beach Airport, now LaGuardia Airport, with one of its owners,
Bill Carey," Moses wrote in his memoirs,

> and one day as I listened to Carey expatiating on his filling operations
> and on the firm foundation underneath and . . . boasting that the Gates of
> Hell could not prevail against them, we were intrigued to see a sixteen-
> foot lamppost sink slowly into the sand, ooze and garbage and to spot
> rats large enough to wear saddles leaping out of the crevasses.

(The airport's settlement and rat problems never ceased. For years after
the initial Carey-run construction was completed the airport settled at such

Refuse-laden trucks crossing the causeway from Rikers Island to the airport being constructed at North Beach

a rate that by the late 1940s the main terminal building had all but collapsed. Even today runways have to be filled on a regular basis to be brought back to grade. Controlling the hordes of rats that nested underground, in buildings, anywhere they could, was a problem that also lasted for years; at least one flight was aborted soon after takeoff in the panic created by a stowaway scurrying down the aisles.)

It came as a considerable surprise to his friends and the informed public that a man as busy as Bill Carey had agreed to become LaGuardia's sanitation commissioner. Why Carey would accept yet another position (he gave up the Madison Square Garden and traded his presidency of Curtiss-Wright for a directorship, but kept his other posts even after he became sanitation commissioner) was an intriguing mystery. But Robert Moses—who himself had taken on another job when LaGuardia made him his parks commissioner—had lost all patience with LaGuardia's previous sanitation appointee. For one thing, this commissioner's men had left open a boom one night while they were dumping refuse to make Moses's Orchard Beach, leaving the coastline from the Bronx to Connecticut strewn with ketchup bottles and watermelon rinds. For another, he was doing little to get the landfilling stopped at Rikers Island and enough of its cached ash and refuse hauled away to fill in the remaining wetlands in the Corona Meadows in time for the World's Fair. Moses was almost certainly behind the decision.

Carey joined Moses as the only other of LaGuardia's commissioners whose personal aplomb and financial independence made him impervious to the Little Flower's rages. The mayor's tirades frequently reduced his secretaries to tears. His petulant treatment of his commissioners was even more legendary. If one of them did something the mayor found particularly stupid, he was summoned to a meeting of his peers and presented with a large bronze bone. But more often he used less jocular techniques to humiliate his underlings. Moses managed LaGuardia's ill-humors in his own way. After being kept waiting once too often for a meeting to which he had been summoned, he took to sending a potted plant in his place to the mayor's office. Among his own "muchachos" he called LaGuardia "Rigoletto," "the little organ grinder," or "that dago son-of-a-bitch." Moses so often threatened to resign that LaGuardia printed up a pad of notes that read "I, Robert Moses, do hereby resign as ___ effective ___." Carey's way was equally characteristic of the man: he watched the boss's "vaudeville stunts," Moses reported, "with a mixture of humor, friendly admiration, and amazed incredulity."

Though Moses's own vaudeville stunts far surpassed LaGuardia's, Carey managed almost always to take them, too, in his easy stride. The first sign of difficulty between the two appeared like a waft of smoke from Rikers Island. Since Colonel Waring's day a half-century before, the little island at the mouth of Long Island Sound—sheltered from the winter winds, and near the geographic heart of the city—was the sanitation department's favorite dumping spot. (The island, Moses said, "exercised an irresistible charm over the sanitary authorities.... [Their] barges swarmed to it.") As a result, Rikers had swollen from its original 87 acres to 130, and now tow-

Riker's Island, according to Moses, *"exercised an irresistible charm over the sanitary authorities. . . . Their barges swarmed to it."*

ered 140 feet above the water. The sight ("a cloud of smoke by day," he said, "and a pillar of fire by night") was scarcely what Moses had in mind as a backdrop for his fair just across the bay. In his view, Carey's sanitation department should have stopped dumping there the moment the fair was announced and immediately should have begun making penance for its past transgressions by building a screening berm and covering it with a forest of trees to hide the mess. Instead, in his first two years as commissioner, Carey not only did nothing to stop the dumping, he got LaGuardia to agree to ask the Corps of Engineers for permission to extend the landfill ninety-five acres farther into the Sound. As always, Moses managed to make his anger known—with a shouted tirade, several thinly veiled threats, and yet another insincere offer of resignation.

But the tension escalated quickly when Carey finally acquiesced to Moses's threats and began to prepare to leave the island. There should have been no mystery about where the sanitation department would go to begin its next landfill. Since Andrew Green and Mayor McClellan, William Wilgus

and George McAneny, it had been decided that the Jamaica Bay Port would
be built from refuse. Only five years earlier, in a very public decision in
which Moses himself had played a leading role, the Board of Estimate had
unanimously designated the as-yet-unbuilt "West Island" in Jamaica Bay as
the place the city would dump its waste after these spoils had been wrested
from Brooklyn Ash. But that was not the impression Robert Moses gave
when one day in April 1938, Carey announced that he was moving his
refuse-disposal operations from Rikers Island to Jamaica Bay.

In a friendly seeming note to Carey (which Carey must have been among
the last New Yorkers to read since he was on vacation in Brazil when it was
sent, while Moses's c.c. list included fifteen city hall reporters, and the "Chief
Editorial Writers of all Metropolitan dailies, including Brooklyn and
Queens"), Moses admitted that he was "aware of the fact that you have a serious problem and we have no doubt contributed to it to some extent by eliminating Rikers Island," and then posed a series of rhetorical questions to which
the answers were irrelevant. ("I should like to know just what area you have
in mind, how the work will be done, whether the scows can get under the
Marine Parkway Bridge or whether it will have to be lifted continually for this
purpose, what the island you propose to make would be used for eventually,
what steps would be taken to prevent garbage, rubbish and ashes from dropping off the scows as they go in and out, what would be done toward preventing fires, smell and other objectionable features ordinarily associated with
dumping, what procedure would be followed to level off the dumps, what
the ultimate elevation would be?") From what the newspapers said he said—
for instance, that placing refuse in Jamaica Bay would be a "tragic mistake"—
anyone would have thought that he was opposed to landfills.

That, however, was hardly the case. Starting at the top of the city, there
was Orchard Beach—a crescent moon whose golden sand covered the
garbage with which it was made. Heading south, there was Ferry Point,
where Moses had begun to build a refuse peninsula around the footings for
the Whitestone Bridge. There was of course Corona Meadows, and the
parkland he was building to make two islands into one beneath his Triborough Bridge. In northern Manhattan—thanks in large measure to the seventy thousand men William Wilgus had given him (LaGuardia had
recruited Wilgus out of retirement in Vermont to take charge of the

In April 1938, Carey announced that he was moving the city's refuse-disposal operations from Rikers Island to Jamaica Bay.

foundering Works Progress Administration)—Moses had spread tens of acres with refuse to build a dozen parks. In Olmsted's Riverside Park alone, he had laid down well over a hundred thousand cubic yards of refuse to fill the space out to General McClellan's bulkhead and to cover the tunnel that was finally being built to hide the New York Central's Death Avenue trains. There were twelve spots across Brooklyn, and another nineteen in Queens that Moses's Parks crews had landfilled in 1934 alone, while on Staten Island he was pushing full-speed ahead to finish building the 274-acre landfill park at Great Kills that he had been working on in one capacity or another since 1925.

Nor was it the case that there was something unique about Jamaica Bay that he was trying to protect. Just as Haussmann had once scattered the last inhabitants of Montfaucon to build his Buttes-Chaumont park, in March 1936 Moses served the remaining denizens of Barren Island with thirty-day eviction notices. Jane Shaw, who had played guardian angel to a whole generation of Island children as principal of P.S. 120 begged for a reprieve.

I find this little settlement almost in a panic since we received the notice to leave the Island.

Poor Mr. Gunyon, seventy-four years, born here, seldom leaving the Island comes to me with a pathetic 'What shall we do, can you help us?'

John and Walter Horodoski, boys eighteen and twenty, who have made a brave fight to keep themselves and the four little brothers together since their parents died three years ago also came. The four boys are in James Madison High School. What can they do?

Mrs. Helinski and Mrs. Liacabucco who have lived here over forty-one years and have beautiful flower gardens, plants that they have worked years to raise, sit sadly looking at the buds just coming up. The children ask, 'What can Mrs. Kishkill do with her two cows?'

There are fifteen children under a year old, how will they stand the tenement house air? The school children cannot smile; their pets must be killed.

. . . 'The Exile of the Acadians' always seemed a fairy tale to me, but here it is being brought home to us in such a cruel way!

"[T]hese people . . . are actually obstructing a contract which is under way," Moses complained. "[T]hose responsible for large enterprises of this kind cannot conciliate everyone and meet every request." He grudgingly allowed Ms. Shaw's students to finish their school year and then immediately began to dump refuse all around their island. Within a matter of months, the old Reynolds-Cranford-White estate had been joined to the rest of Brooklyn, making Barren Island—and for the same reason—as much an oxymoron as Coney Island.

And then he built Marine Park—a perfect name because there had been nothing there but seawater until he dumped nearly five hundred acres of refuse into it. And then, at the very moment he was fighting Carey's proposal to build a "West Island" a stone's throw away, he was a complaisant accomplice in landfilling the marsh next to the site that he would soon fill with refuse to make Idlewild Airport. "Fifty embattled housewives, many with babies in their arms"—according to the *Times*'s lead—"joined hands and flung their battle line across the path of the [incoming garbage] trucks." After an hour or so, after jeering at the borough sanitation commissioner, they reluctantly succumbed to their attorney's argument "that judicial proceedings were preferable to a mass blockade," cast a last defiant look at the stalled trucks, and went home. Their protest was futile. To build the Belt Parkway, the land beneath many new residential developments, the two towering mounds that would one day become national parks, and virtually all the rest of the northern shore of Jamaica Bay, dumping continued all through the next five decades despite repeated "judicial proceedings" (including the indictment of both Commissioner Carey and Commissioner Moses for their respective roles), the personal intervention of the US Surgeon General, the marching of children's protest brigades (perhaps some of those same "babies in arms" grown up enough to walk), and the spreading of hundreds of thousands of pounds of hypochloride (under the supervision of the health commissioner, Dr. Mustard) to quell the sulfur dioxide stench that—as the Rikers Island landfill had proved in Colonel Waring's time— was quite capable of turning white houses black.

Clearly, something else was going on.

The Bridge

The *real* reason Moses wanted to keep Carey out of Jamaica Bay was that he wanted him instead to dump his refuse on the lonely spot where Reynolds and Bailey had built their ill-fated plant on the tide-washed salt meadows of Staten Island. And the reason he wanted to do *that* was to put an end, once and for all, to William Wilgus's dream of a rationally planned, seamlessly integrated metropolitan region, the fulfillment of which depended on yoking New York City and the rest of Long Island to the continent via a rail tunnel at its Narrows fulcrum. Moses did not want trains or tunnels. He wanted only cars. And he wanted them to cross the Narrows (to reach the beltway he was building in Brooklyn) on a bridge.

Moses wanted to cover Reynolds's old Staten Island salt meadows with refuse for the same reasons he had made the sanitation department acquire the Triborough Bridge access route through the Corona Meadows. He wanted someone else to pay for the real estate he needed for his access road. And since this was not a purchase that the Depression-strapped city could afford to make from its normal discretionary budget, he wanted to be sure that this purchase was classified as a top priority.

In 1937, with the Triborough Bridge and its connections east to Long Island behind him, Moses had begun to assemble the pieces for his next projects. One of the most difficult problems he faced—since it depended exclusively on the *city's* spare budget—was getting the rights-of-way he needed to build his roads. He had learned an important lesson when he discovered that the long-mapped Grand Central Boulevard was in fact only a line on a piece of paper. When he had bent his Triborough route up the barren Flushing River valley, he had had to pay a premium for each parcel—even though he enjoyed a cozy relationship with the judge who handled the condemnations. Now, as he was trying to acquire approaches for his new Whitestone Bridge, he was bumping into some of the same political speculators (including the ubiquitous Queens Commissioner of Public Works) who had driven up the prior awards. If it was slightly easier to assemble the lots he needed for the lower loop of the Brooklyn-Queens "circumferential" along the top of Jamaica Bay, it was only because he had been able to convince many of the owners to accept new shorefront property (which he would make with Carey's refuse) in return for allowing him to build on their now inland plots. In the Bronx, even *he* was getting "cold feet" (he told an aide) about the possibility of actually getting the land he needed to connect the Bronx River Parkway to the Triborough Bridge; he therefore proposed the temporary expedient of widening an existing boulevard, deferring the extension of the north-south route, and postponing indefinitely the construction of an east-west shoreline route between the Triborough and Whitestone bridges.

The plans for Staten Island, in view of the city's more pressing priorities, were even more problematic. Perhaps because it was an election year (and without any regular party ties LaGuardia needed the support of as many borough presidents as he could get), the mayor revived the plans for a Brooklyn-Staten Island crossing (it should definitely be a tunnel, he said, a bridge would do too much damage to a fine residential neighborhood). Moses, meanwhile, had begun to map out a system of parkways that could carry cars from the Narrows across the island to New Jersey, roughly along the routes that Olmsted had conceived half a century before and that he himself had been contemplating for almost a decade. The difficulty, he discovered, was that it was politically impractical to levy either local or citywide assessments to pay for the Staten Island roads until the city was firmly committed to a schedule for building the crossing, while on the other hand the longer the acquisitions were postponed, the higher the costs would be—and it would be impossible to secure funding (either through bond sales or state or federal grants) until the land was in hand.

It was a problem that seemed to leave even Moses a bit perplexed, until he hit upon the expedient that had helped to pay for the Corona Meadows: a "Sanitation, Reclamation and Recreation Project." In the middle of the route he had drawn to connect the crossing to the New Jersey bridge at the other end of the island lay the uninhabited Fresh Kills marsh that Reynolds and company two decades earlier had chosen as the site for their reduction plant. If this land were filled, he could extend two nearby parks, build a base on which to build his road, reduce the cost of bridges to cross the creeks, and be able to tap funds from the priority budget reserved for only the most pressing civic needs. The icing on the cake was that it would even solve his Rikers Island problem.

Without divulging his motives—because he meant to build the Staten Island crossing himself (which he was not yet in a position to do because LaGuardia had refused to give him a seat on the new Tunnel Authority that had been given sole responsibility for building such crossings), and because he did not want to make the current authority's job any easier by allowing it to know that the Staten Island access road was getting underway—he approached Bill Carey with the suggestion that he move his disposal operations to the Fresh Kills marshes. Carey demurred. Because of the costs and logistical difficulties it would impose, he was loathe to leave Rikers Island. But just to make Moses happy he would take a look at the vast area on Staten Island's sparsely inhabited back shore anyway. When he came back he told Moses that he was not interested. Filling that wetland, he said, would be a waste because land built there would be in a place where it could "do no permanent good."

As 1938 began, the New Deal's stream of PWA dollars was trickling dry. But thanks to Senator Robert Wagner's efforts, another program was starting up that promised magnificent new cashflows. The Wagner-Steagall National Housing Act of September 1937 promised New York City hundreds of millions of dollars in loans for subsidized public housing. The fact that Robert

Moses had no prior experience, expertise, or most importantly, control of any authority in the field meant that gaining access to this funding source would be unusually difficult. To Moses's agile mind, however, it was a challenge worth the candle. He was in charge of all the parks in the city, as well as of all the (broadly defined) parkways that led to them. Parkways, of course, were for cars, but parks were for people, and city parks (as opposed to his Long Island ones) were for the people who lived there—in houses. "Housing and Recreation" was clearly as good a theme as "Sanitation, Reclamation, and Recreation" and promised an equally useful way to access already earmarked funds.

In deep secrecy, Moses's architects and engineers began drawing plans to build 180 million dollars' worth of new housing and 65 million dollars' worth of "recreation, streets, and other incidental public improvements" in four of the five boroughs. The place he chose for building the Bronx's portion of the plan was, to him, especially critical: it was just where he needed a big piece of land for the intersection of the two parkways he planned between his bridges. Unfortunately, most of this "land" (like "West Island") was under water, and the only kind of fill he could afford was refuse. But using refuse would also allow him to acquire the land with supplemental "Sanitation" funding. And it offered another way to solve his Rikers Island problem.

It would be awkward, of course, to mention his need for a new landfill before the secret housing projects were ready to be announced (or the referendum authorizing the necessary state bond issue even approved). So, for the moment—with the Fresh Kills offer still on the table as one solution to the Rikers problem—Moses had to keep the Sound View proposal to himself. But he began to set the stage for his Sound View announcement by increasing the pressure on Carey to get off Rikers Island before the fair.

This pressure backfired. It was not often that Robert Moses was caught completely off guard by another man's maneuvers, but he certainly was this time. Carey's response to the heightened campaign to get his landfilling operations off Rikers Island—his Jamaica Bay surprise—not only risked derailing both of Moses's bridge-and-parkway-and-park projects, it also threatened his vision for the future of the Long Island he was building. Like

Olmsted, Moses had always imagined that his parks and parkway ribbons would control the future of the space he had staked out as his own, that the armature of these routes would shape the empty space around them, and that the "green" lines would be as important for the land uses they precluded as for those they actually imposed. Despite all the bridges he had built and planned to build, Long Island, he said, was created by Nature as a residential and recreational cul-de-sac and should stay that way, undefiled by ships or rails or anything else that would put something besides houses, cars, and playgrounds there. And with his Marine Parkway Bridge to Barren Island, his Marine Park, and his Belt Parkway all well under way, Moses had thought that future safe.

Although landfilling *seemed* to be the main theme of the glossy broadside Moses produced to counterattack Carey's proposal—a triumph of World War I-style propaganda that showed two views of "The Future of Jamaica Bay," one an idealized vision of America at Peace, the other Belgium Sacked by the Hun—its real purpose was the final destruction (since it had not quite died of simple atrophy, inertia, and old age) of the prewar vision of a great industrial seaport tied by railway tunnels to the mainland, an alternative future Moses pictured as a flaming mountain in a haze of smoke but whose realization could have kept New York one of the premier shipping and manufacturing centers in the nation.

In the crucible of Moses' propaganda crusade (it was the usual barrage of meetings with editorial boards, orchestrated letter writing, and a flurry of pamphlets and press releases), Carey began to soften. In a private note Moses suggested that they "get together and discuss the Richmond matter again," and Carey told an intermediary that he was reconsidering Fresh Kills for his new dump site. As an added incentive to leaving Jamaica Bay alone, Moses decided in May 1938, that it was time to offer Carey the Sound View option as well.

By September, however, *only* Sound View was on Moses' mind. The reason for this was another dispute, not between Moses and Carey, but between Moses and his putative boss.

Moses and LaGuardia had long fought about how to pay for the massive interconnected highway project both wanted (a new crossing from Brooklyn to downtown Manhattan, a shorefront parkway wrapping around Brooklyn, and an elevated highway connecting the two). Moses was damned if he would give his Triborough Authority's money to his hated arch rival, the Tunnel Authority, to build its Brooklyn-Battery Tunnel, while LaGuardia had no intention of throwing all of his PWA appropriation—which he urgently needed to build schools and hospitals—into Moses' highway. But each needed the other's cash to do the project he wanted most. The compromise they finally reached was that Moses would agree to put Triborough funds into the tunnel project if LaGuardia would put the PWA money (and more city funds later) into his "circumferential."

LaGuardia was not happy about the deal. Capitulating to Moses' blackmail was hard enough to justify to himself, much less to his fusionist Board-of-Estimate allies whom he was forced to bully into going along with the decision—all the while telling the public (a barefaced lie) that the decision had not been his but the board's. For Moses, meanwhile, though the agreement gave him what he wanted (an immediate green light on the Belt Parkway and the promise of controlling the Tunnel Authority that he had tried to take over since its creation two years before), it also meant that anything on Staten Island would have to be postponed for several years at least. In light of the Belt Parkway's cost, it was inconceivable that any new money could be found in the near term for a connecting road across the Fresh Kills marshes, much less for the Narrows tunnel itself. And with the promise of controlling the Tunnel Authority, there was no longer any danger that the project would begin to proceed before he was ready. The need for a landfill at Sound View, however—with the referendum on the state housing bond issue just two months away and his planned surprise announcement immediately thereafter—was more urgent than ever. The day after the agreement was sealed, Bill Carey got a letter that ordered his disposal operations off Rikers Island and onto Sound View "Park" without any further discussion.

Carey complied with Moses' request that he ask the Board of Estimate to fund a Sound View unloading facility. But he was not happy about it. "I spent a good part of yesterday roaming around the Sound View section of the Bronx where you have requested our Department to fill in the low land, mud flats and waterfront," Carey told Moses in a private letter the day their budget request went to the board.

> I estimate that starting at almost the very edge and running back not more than six-tenths of a mile of this proposed fill, there are approximately 30,000 people residing. Shifting the very large operation from Rikers Island to this region will mean night and day activity for approximately two years, with many noisy tractors and other equipment. Then again,

because of continuous activity, some limited surface of garbage and ashes
will be exposed. There is always some odor in the immediate vicinity of
an uncovered fill, accentuated during the hot, sultry period of summer
weather,... and while we will endeavor to duplicate, in every practical
way possible, our present landfill operations, we will not, due to
continuous operation, be able to reach the state of perfection by complete
daily covering with which these landfills are now being treated. Neither
can we, during the hot summer period, adopt the procedures now in
effect on our landfills of temporarily shifting these activities, where
necessary, to a more remote section. The question arises, will these
objectionable features offset the highly desirable creation of a park, . . .
and if you receive concerted opposition, what do you propose to do
about it?... What I am attempting to guard against is an expensive setup
that might be disturbed by Court order or any other agency. Otherwise,
we could find ourselves in a very precarious situation without being able
to afford the time required to relocate this important operation.

For LaGuardia, the Sound View proposal was even harder to stomach.
No politician could relish creating a major public nuisance when two large
sites considerably more removed from voters were available. And
LaGuardia, who was more jealous of infringements on his "administrative
responsibilities" than were most mayors Moses would experience, was outraged that his parks commissioner would presume to tell his sanitation
department where to operate. But most importantly, in that dreadful month
when he had been forced to give all the money he had planned to spend on
schools and hospitals to Robert Moses' Belt Parkway: the city did not yet
own the "park" that Moses proposed to dump on. It was worse than that:
Moses purposely had understated its cost (it appeared to the mayor and his
corporation counsel) as less than an eighth of what the condemnation award
actually was turning out to be. And now, in addition to a bill more than
seven-hundred-thousand-dollars bigger than expected came evidence of
further deceit: the "two-year" landfill he had demanded that Carey dump on
was twice the size of the parcel they were about to acquire.

Rikers Island was still Carey's preferred dump site. His second choice,
Jamaica Bay, had been taken from him by Moses' rabble-rousing and media
manipulation. The Sound View site he was being forced onto was likely to

be an expensive headache and risked disrupting the city's entire waste collection and disposal system if a court order came out against it. And even if the courts did allow it to stay open, in two years he would have to start the trying process of finding a new landfill site all over again. With LaGuardia's blessing, he decided to resist.

On the day Hitler received Chamberlain, some Staten Islanders were surprised to discover the sanitation commissioner poking about their island; Carey refused to confirm or deny their fears that he had settled on the site of the old Reynolds reduction plant as an alternative to his controversial Jamaica Bay proposal. At the next Board of Estimate meeting, Moses, looking at the city hall reporters, demanded that the board pin Carey down about the location he had selected. At this, "the board members went into a huddle [the *Staten Island Advance* reported] and decided to have a show-down" behind closed doors. But when the doors opened again, neither of the two commissioners could refrain from letting the waiting journalists know just what he thought of the other. Calling Moses "a propagandist with no regard for the truth," who was "principally responsible for the anti-landfill attitude that now exists among the various civic organizations" (there had been no lawsuits when George McAneny had got the board's unanimous approval for dumping in Jamaica Bay five years before), and "a ruthless spender" whose projects served "no useful purpose other than a monument to himself," Carey revealed that "[a] few days ago he suggested to me that we might cooperate toward creating [additional] landfills around the edges of Jamaica Bay [in order to build the Belt Parkway]....It is exceedingly difficult for me to reconcile these private requests with his public opinion of landfills." Moses meanwhile claimed that the Fresh Kills proposal was "entirely new" to him; that he was going to oppose it as "harmful to the park system"; that there could be no comparison between his plan to "round out and complete a park in the Bronx" and Carey's plan to fill in the Fresh Kills meadows; and asked that the board "apply some common sense to this problem because the average fellow knows that the smoke, smell, flies, rats, mountains of undesirable materials go with most filling operations by water and barge and you are not going to make the average fellow, just on somebody's statement, I don't care how eloquent, earnest, or authoritative he is, believe that these objections don't exist."

And then with consummate disdain for consistency, the eloquent, earnest, and authoritative parks commissioner, playing to a crowd of angry Staten Islanders, told the Board of Estimate just a month later that if they would leave Staten Island alone he would "personally guarantee" that his plan to unload refuse barges at Sound View "will not be a nuisance." The mayor's representative and his allies on the board, angered by the opposition Moses was encouraging, closed the public hearing and voted to approve Carey's budget request for a new unloader—at a site that would be determined, the deputy mayor promised, only after a special hearing on the issue. But the mayor then made it clear that the site would *not* be Sound View: having been blackmailed for every PWA dollar in next year's capital budget for the Belt Parkway, he rescinded his prior approval of funds to landfill the part of Sound View that had just been acquired, as well as his approval for purchasing the second parcel upon which the plan depended.

The unveiling of Moses' surprise housing program the next week, a program that featured Sound View as the Bronx's flagship housing and recreation project, could hardly have encouraged the mayor to reconsider his decision. (Discovering the sneak attack a few hours before Moses went on the air to launch it, LaGuardia had the technicians from the municipal radio station pretend that their mikes were live in order to disguise the fact that he had ordered the channel turned off for the night.) The next month, in a chilling parallel to what Mayor Mitchel had done on behalf of his friend Reynolds, LaGuardia pulled an ambush of his own. At a special meeting of the Board of Estimate ostensibly called for other purposes a few days before Christmas, without any prior warning to the Staten Island borough president or anyone besides his allies on the board, its title hidden in a long list of unrelated measures, LaGuardia had his deputy introduce the dump-site resolution in direct violation of his solemn promise. The maneuver to create a Fresh Kills landfill was foiled, however, when Staten Island's representative recognized a sentence about a foundation for unloading equipment, and taking advantage of his prerogative, had the item "laid over" until the next meeting. A week later, LaGuardia called another special session and forced it through. The City Council countered by voting unanimously (with eight abstentions by the mayor's supporters) to rescind the appropriation for the new facility. But with the abstentions, the council's measure was two votes short of the two-thirds majority it needed.

Robert Moses, who had started the fight by raising opposition to landfilling to an unprecedented level, had failed to reach his objectives: he had not finished off the landfill-island port/rail plan upon which hopes for maintaining a viable manufacturing presence in New York City depended; and he had been unable to direct a necessary and expensive form of construction material from a place where he had no need of it to the place where he had to have it. The struggle had cost the mayor many political points (the *Staten Island Advance* compared him to "the European dictators"; the *New York Times* chided that the mayor's action set "a ticklish precedent" for the new charter), but LaGuardia had won the right to dump refuse anywhere he chose.

A month later, the mayor chose Sound View, and Moses got everything he wanted.

The mayor had made no secret of his anger with Moses. But just after the first of the new year, the ice began to crack. The deputy mayor told Moses "*very very* privately" that the mayor might be willing to reconsider another park project for which he had also rescinded funding, and Moses was so bold as to resubmit the Sound View funding request that had been so firmly rejected.

What had happened was that Moses had promised the mayor a new bridge: instead of just making a contribution that would supplement nonexistent other funds to dig a tunnel, Moses volunteered to have the Triborough Authority pay for a bridge from Brooklyn to the Battery all by itself, immediately.

It was a prize too tempting for LaGuardia to refuse. The Sound View appropriations were approved—though from then on LaGuardia had other officials check every one of Moses' figures (the mayor himself took a pencil to the back of each page to check the addition and multiplication) and the docks department, rather than the parks commissioner, was given lead responsibility. These were just pretenses, however, that did not conceal the reality of who was in control.

The mayor did have one small measure of revenge: he had Carey submit an application to the army for permission to extend Rikers Island far enough farther into the water to allow continued dumping there for several more years. Pleading with LaGuardia to withdraw the request, Moses promised that he would not (as usual) go behind his back to make his case directly to the federal officials (as he nonetheless did). Although federal permission to extend Rikers Island was denied, by the time the sanitation department finally left the island it was 1942, and the little girl's fair was long over.

After Pearl Harbor, parkways were no longer a national priority. The War Production Board wanted airports, however, as much as Major LaGuardia did. Following the money trail, as always, Moses began to expand Floyd Bennett Field on Barren Island with more refuse so that it could be sold to the Navy. With the proceeds, he bought (marsh)land to build a new airport at the opposite end of Jamaica Bay, then filled it too with garbage. While he was at it, he added more refuse fill to the Marine Park adjacent to Barren Island and began planning landfill parks near the new Idlewild Airport. In July 1942, he wrote to LaGuardia asking for seed money to begin work on another airport project.

> Dear Major,
> I have had occasion recently to make several more or less careful
> inspections of Staten Island in connection with rezoning, the tunnel,
> arterial improvements and Marine and other parks. There is an immense
> area of meadow land with tidal streams running through it, bordering
> on the Arthur Kill and on LaTourette and Springville Parks. It would be
> easy to fill this area by hydraulic dredging and to make land surrounded
> by usable canals and waterways. It looks like a natural location for a big
> future commercial and freight airport with industry and manufacturing
> immediately back of it, then a residential area and back of that the park
> system.... Some of the filling could also be done by the Sanitation
> Department after the completion of the work at Sound View in the
> Bronx and Marine Park, Staten Island.

By an astounding coincidence, the location he was referring to was the one Reynolds had selected for his reduction plant, and which Moses had proposed to Carey in 1937, and which Moses had opposed when Carey suggested it the following year as the site of the city's major refuse disposal facility. And although it appeared that the notion of filling in the Fresh Kills meadows had just come to him (again), the story of its re-emergence was apparently more complex.

Taking over the Tunnel Authority had taken somewhat longer than Moses had expected, because after he had outraged many of the city's most respected citizens and come but a hairsbreadth from building the Brooklyn-Battery bridge that he had dreamed of, Franklin and Eleanor Roosevelt stepped in behind the scenes to kill it with a word to the Army engineers about how to evaluate the military merits of tunnels versus bridges. Interior Secretary Ickes then decided to give the city the grant it needed to build the tunnel the Roosevelts said was safer, and the Tunnel Authority stayed intact.

The Staten Island borough president, who had watched his hopes for progress on a Narrows tunnel postponed in 1938 when the city could squeeze together only enough money to build the Belt Parkway, saw a new opening when Moses drafted the 1939 bill to enable the Triborough Authority to build the Battery Bridge. But to his request that a Brooklyn-Staten Island bridge be added to the enabling legislation, Moses responded, "You are moving too fast in the Staten Island bridge matter. We can't possibly include it in the Triborough Bill at this time, because it would simply sink the Bill. The Battery-Brooklyn Bridge is the next step in the program. These things have to be done piecemeal. As soon as the Belt Parkway and the new bridge are open the pressure for a connection with Staten Island at the Narrows will become irresistible. . . . All I can suggest Joe [Palma], is that you hold your horses and bide your time. It can't all be done at once. I have a hunch about the proper procedure which I will discuss with you some time later on."

The details of their discussion (assuming they had one) are not recorded. But what is known is that a year later Moses was saying publicly that "[a] start has already been made in laying out the future parkway and arterial road system on Staten Island," and was directly linking this with steps to be taken in the near term "toward a Brooklyn-Staten Island Tunnel from the Belt Parkway." It is also known that the north-south parkways planned to connect the Narrows to New Jersey, although they varied somewhat over time in their proposed alignments, always crossed the Fresh Kills marshes. Although he later denied it, Moses made another private visit to Borough President Palma in early 1943, after which Palma promptly had plans drawn up for filling in the Fresh Kills meadows and submitted them to the mayor with a formal request that they be adopted. These landfill plans were not

advanced or made public, however, until July 1945, when LaGuardia, tired
after twelve years as mayor and preparing to leave office, finally succumbed
to Moses' importunings and put him in charge of the Tunnel Authority, and
Moses immediately began to prepare the groundwork for building the Verrazano-Narrows Bridge.

After Palma chose not to run for re-election in 1945, Cornelius Hall, his
successor, also pressed Moses to help move the Narrows Crossing forward
and was satisfied with Moses' reply: "I have reached a point [Hall said]
where I agree with you completely that the matter from now on could be
better handled 'off the record.'" Two months later, at Hall's urging, the City
Planning Commission that Moses controlled announced that it would
resubmit the budget request for a Fresh Kills landfill that Borough Presi-
dent-elect Hall, sitting for his predecessor, had once gotten the Board of
Estimate to reject; despite his constituents' near unanimous opposition, Hall
said, he wanted the landfill so that he could get a shorefront road. Ignoring
the biggest demonstrations Staten Islanders had ever mounted at City Hall
(bigger than the protests against the Reynolds plant in Mitchel's day or
against Carey's 1938 proposal), the Fresh Kills measure passed on June 28,
1946 after Robert Moses, the hero of Staten Island's 1938 fight over Fresh
Kills, announced that he, too, had switched sides. The Fresh Kills landfill
would not be like others, he explained, because it would be done by scows
and because "only papers, refuse—clean fill" would be dumped there.
(Contrary to Moses' "guarantees," these other landfills had not gone as
smoothly as he had promised; to complaints about the nasty hydrogen sulfide odors at the Sound View scow-dump site, he had shrugged, "We can't
make an omelet without breaking some eggs and occasionally there will be a
bad egg.") Building incinerators was not an alternative, he said, because
they were too expensive and would take too long to build, and besides, it
would be impossible to get people to separate their refuse into combustible
and noncombustible fractions. He had considered filling in Jamaica Bay
instead, he added, but had concluded that it would be too hard to keep the
barge channels open in the winter ice.

If Bill Carey was still following Moses' pronouncements on the subject,
now that he had resumed full-time management of his continuing business
interests, this unabashed reversal of Moses' earlier public position might

Mayor LaGuardia (here being assisted by Al Jolson) *had enthusiastically taken up his patriotic duties as the local coordinator for salvaging the materials on which the War Production Board imposed manufacturing and use restrictions.*

have made him smile with the kind of indulgence he had once reserved for the antics of his former boss.

The neologism *re-cycling* would not be coined for another fourteen years; the idea that refuse materials might be reused in order to reduce the amount of incinerator capacity or landfill space needed occurred to no one. Mayor LaGuardia had enthusiastically taken up his patriotic duties as the local coordinator for salvaging the materials on which the War Production Board imposed manufacturing and use restrictions (rubber, paper, fats, and metals—"Save Some Scrap to Kill a Jap" was one of his slogans). But always eager to save the city money, he stopped the salvage collections the instant the War Production Board allowed him to, even before MacArthur had landed in Japan. "Trimmers" under their padrones continued the generations-old system of picking

Trimmers under the padrones continued the generations-old system of picking through the refuse at landfills and incinerators.

through the refuse at landfills and incinerators, a practice that the sanitation department had good reason to encourage since the franchise fees they paid went directly into the employees' pension system; this too, however, from the perspective of the economic logic then in place was inefficient (the Citizens Budget Commission pointed out) because the trimmers cut the department's productivity more than their pension contributions were worth. Incineration, all the experts agreed, was the only responsible solution, and the promise of full-speed ahead on the construction of enough incinerators to handle all of the city's combustible waste was the basis upon which the city's citizens were asked to accept for a short while longer the kind of sacrifice to which the war years had accustomed them.

Along with the city's new mayor (William O'Dwyer, who had made Moses the "coordinator" for all public works construction in the city), Moses promised Hall that "raw" garbage would only be landfilled at Fresh Kills for three years—the time it would take to build a large new incinerator in every borough, and coincidentally, as much time as it would take to fill in the right-of-way needed for the West Shore Expressway that would carry cars south from the Narrows. That this three-year promise was patently absurd everyone, including Moses, recognized (though this did not stop him from angrily attacking anyone in the administration who dared to not parrot this ridiculous party line). When three years had passed and only two new incinerators were finished, Moses revised the public schedule for closing Fresh Kills to raw waste, saying it would take four more years. Ten years after the original deadline (in 1961), five incinerators were completed, but six smaller ones had been closed down, so that the net increase in incinerator capacity was less than three thousand tons a day. At the end of Moses' years in power, New York City was incinerating only a third of its refuse; more than half of the rest of the city's refuse—some eight thousand tons a day—was going to Fresh Kills.

When the Verrazano-Narrows Bridge opened in 1964, travelers heading south to the Jersey shore or along the new interstate system that went all the way to Washington, DC passed on dry land through the former Fresh Kills meadows. The only part of the new landfill that was not actually refuse was the roadbed of the West Shore Expressway itself, because its engineers insisted that it be filled with solid material and that the refuse already in place be removed; they pointed out—as Carey had learned at North Beach—that refuse is not really a suitable construction material. The landfill had nonetheless contributed significantly to reducing the highway's expense. In addition to paying for the right-of-way, Moses also tried to make the sanitation department pay for a four-million-dollar bridge across Fresh Kills Creek. The watchdog Citizens Budget Commission complained that this was not a valid charge against the city's nondiscretionary budget, but Moses found a way to avoid that objection by filling in enough of the creek that another kind of bridge could be built at a fraction of the originally projected cost. (Dredging the creeks to make "usable waterways"—a concept that Moses apparently lost interest in after 1943—would no longer be possible.)

As the years passed travelers could see hills rising that dwarfed the Corona Meadows through which Jay Gatsby drove. Gatsby's creator had crossed the Corona Meadows by train, but this was a mode of transportation that had been excluded from the Narrows Crossing, as it had been from all of Moses' other works. With its rezoning as parkland, Jamaica Bay (and, by extension, most of the remaining cul-de-sac of Long Island) was saved from being a home to industry. While Brooklyn's population continued to decline after the bridge was opened, Staten Island's over the next twenty years increased by 60 percent; most of these newcomers settled in sprawling developments with a character quite different from the residential districts Olmsted had hoped his planned parkways would assure.

Due to the opposition his road-building methods had finally generated by the early 1960s, the "Richmond Parkway" Moses had planned along the old Olmsted route down Staten Island's spine and across a corner of the Fresh Kills meadows was never built. Nor was the planned airport, although Moses himself seems to have lost interest in that idea as soon as LaGuardia left office. Neither was Sound View completed as a park, although eventually, after O'Dwyer finally granted Moses' long-standing wish to run the City Housing Authority, Moses turned the adjacent neighborhood, not into the new development he had originally intended, but into one of his "slum-clearance" projects, since that was what the postwar federal housing grants were for (even though there were no discernable slums among its rows of neat frame houses). The project involved a 100 percent, half-million dollar profit for the political insiders who had just bought the property. This Sound View scandal in 1959 was the beginning of the end of Moses' iron hold on all the city's public works. Like the Baron Haussmann, Moses eventually "fell by his finances."

By the time Moses lost his authorities William Wilgus had been dead for a dozen years, his dream of a crossing to the continent that would allow the region to achieve a humane and rational balance between housing, recreation, commerce, and industry apparently dead with him. Called once out of retirement to bring order to the city's massive, ill-managed public works

The Fresh Kills Landfill, West Shore Expressway, 1987

program during the crisis of the Great Depression, Wilgus had to leave his beloved Green Mountains again when World War II broke out to spend a month wracked with rheumatic pain in a Washington hotel bed, drafting the War Department's top-secret strategy for moving troops across Europe's central sectors. Apart from these trying interludes, he lived a mellow old age filled with historical reminiscences (a biography of a Revolutionary War ancestor, railroad histories, a memoir) and civic good works (donating his Connecticut riverfront property to the state for a park, attempting to create a Green Mountain park and parkway to promote economic development for his depressed adopted countryside). Though he lived to be eighty-three, his life was too short to see the railroads' consolidation and nationalization, which he had long advocated and predicted, nor their adoption of the containerized technology he had designed, which finally spurred their revival.

Moses' predictions were not so neatly fulfilled. Fifty years after he promised that the Fresh Kills landfill would be closed to raw garbage, it remained the city's main repository for refuse, receiving over thirteen thousand tons of material a day, none of it cooked. But even his sense of irony (which was never known to be directed at himself) might have been struck by the fact that the man who had been so proud of cleaning up Mount Corona's "valley of ashes" would be responsible for creating refuse mountains several times higher on a base ten times greater, and that of all the public works he ever built—probably even combined—the Fresh Kills landfill had become the largest—had become, in fact, the biggest man-made object on the planet.

PART IV

Landscape Sculpture

CHAPTER 9

Citizens and Scientists

In the spring and summer months of 1951, Joseph Mitchell, a forty-three-year-old reporter originally from Fairmont, North Carolina, who loved to hang around anyone who had anything to do with the waterfront or the edible swimming or burrowing creatures found there, spent some time with Andrew E. ("Happy") Zimmer, a shellfish protector for the Bureau of Marine Fisheries of the state conservation department. Mitchell described Zimmer as a bald, barrel-chested man with incipient jowls and an habitually preoccupied expression that suggested he had outgrown his childhood nickname. His father had been a vaudeville ventriloquist who ran a saloon cum German-home-cooking restaurant on his Staten Island truck farm. As a boy, Zimmer had speared eels and collected soft-shell clams for the restaurant from the nearby marshes and mud flats. As a young man, he ran the restaurant himself for a few years, then gave it up to work for the conservation department. His job required him to spend most of his time on his twenty-eight-foot sea skiff, checking that net fishermen were keeping only the species they were licensed for and that lobstermen were putting back lobsters that were too small, and chasing clam poachers in Chris Crafts from New Jersey back up the shallow tide creeks they came out of. But

> Once in a while, Mr. Zimmer spends a day patrolling the Staten Island tide marshes on foot. He feels drawn to the marshes and enjoys this part of his job most of all. A good many people wander about in the marshes and in the meadows and little woods with which they are studded. He is acquainted with scores of marsh wanderers. In the fall, old Italians come and get down on all fours and scrabble in the leaves and rot beneath the blackjack oaks, hunting for mushrooms. In the spring, they come again and pick dandelion sprouts for salads. In midsummer, they come again, this time with scap nets, and scoop tiny mud shrimp out of the tide ditches; they use them in a fried fish-and-shellfish dish called *frittura di*

The photographer was Staten Island naturalist Howard H. Cleaves. The note he typed on this photograph was: "Claypit Ponds, Round Pond, Judy Horn and Gertrude Burggraff on shore, 8-22-52."

pesce. On summer afternoons, old women from the south-shore villages come to the fringes of the marshes. They pick herbs, they pick wild flowers, they pick wild grapes for jelly, and in the fresh-water creeks that empty into the salt-water creeks they pick watercress. In the fall, truck farmers come with scythes and cut salt hay. When the hay dries, they pack it around their cold frames to keep the frost out. Bird watchers and Indian-relic collectors come in all seasons. The relic collectors sift the mud on the banks of the tide ditches. Mr. Zimmer himself sometimes finds arrowheads and stone net-sinkers on the ditchbanks. Once, he found several old English coins. In September or October, the rabbis and elders come. On Hoshanna Rabbah, the seventh day of the Festival of Succoth, an ancient fertility rite is still observed in a number of orthodox synagogues in the city. The worshipers who take part in the

Cleaves's caption: "Negroes fishing, Summer, 1950, Greenridge, SI"

rite are given bunches of willow twigs; each bunch has seven twigs and each twig has seven leaves. After marching in procession seven times around the altar, chanting a litany, the worshipers shake the bunches or strike them against the altar until the leaves fall to the floor. The twigs must be cut from willows that grow beside water, the buds on the ends of the twigs must be unblemished, and the leaves must be green and flawless. For generations, most of the willow bunches have come from black willows and weeping willows in the Staten Island tide marshes. In the two or three days preceding Hoshanna Rabbah—it usually falls in the last week of September or the first or second week of October— rabbis and trusted elders go up and down the ditchbanks, most often in pairs, the rabbi scrutinizing twigs and cutting those that pass the test, and the elder trimming and bunching them and stowing them gently in brown-paper shopping bags.

Cleaves: "Frank Hauber looks at the wall of advancing putridity with which the
Sanitation Department of the City of New York is smothering all five of the once
lovely Claypit Ponds at Greenridge, Staten Island, New York. This is Long Pond,
largest pond of the group once promised as a rustic park for the people by Robert
Moses, who later betrayed the people of Staten Island in this matter. 10-31-53."

There is much resident and migratory wildlife in the marshes. The
most plentiful resident species are pheasants, crows, marsh hawks, black
snakes, muskrats, opossums, rabbits, rats, and field mice. There is no open
season on the pheasants, and they have become so bold that the truck
farmers look upon them as pests. One can walk through the pokeweed
and sumac and blue-bent grass on any of the meadow islands at any time
and put up pair after pair of pheasants. At the head of a snaky creek in
one of the loneliest of the marshes, there is an old rickamarack of a dock
that was built by rum-runners during prohibition. One morning, hiding
behind this dock, waiting for some soft-shell-clam poachers to appear,
Mr. Zimmer saw a hen pheasant walk across a strip of tide flat, followed
by a brood of seventeen. At times, out in the marshes, Mr. Zimmer
becomes depressed. The marshes are doomed. The city has begun to

dump garbage on them. It has already filled hundreds of acres with garbage. Eventually, it will fill in the whole area, and then the Department of Parks will undoubtedly build some proper parks out there, and put in some concrete highways and scatter some concrete benches about. The old south-shore secessionists—they want Staten Island to secede from New York and join New Jersey, and there are many of them—can sit on these benches and meditate and store up bile.

Talk of Staten Island's secession from Andrew Green's Greater New York figured on the city's political agenda any number of times between 1951 and 1993, and the usual instigating factor was the Fresh Kills landfill. In 1993, however, after permission was granted by the state legislature the preceding year, a popular referendum on the secession question finally was held. One of the tricky political issues was whether or not residents of the other boroughs should be allowed to vote on the question of Staten Island's future; the governor and legislature finally agreed that they should. The referendum did not pass because a resounding majority of New Yorkers did not want to let Staten Island go. But the Islanders themselves voted in favor of secession by nearly two to one—a margin approaching that in 1897 when their forebears had agreed to join New York City on the strength of promises that consolidation would bring a Narrows Tunnel.

Although the referendum did not achieve the end for which secession supporters were hoping, it did bring an unprecedented number of Staten Islanders to the polls. Since Tammany days, New Yorkers have overwhelmingly been registered as Democrats. Staten Island is the only borough in which the number of registered Republicans even begins to approach parity with the Democratic rolls. Although the Island's elected officials, like most of those elsewhere across the city, have generally been Democrats, it has sent a trickle of Republicans to Albany and Washington. For several years in the 1980s, it sent the only Republican to the fifty-one-member New York City Council. In 1989, Staten Islanders elected a Republican borough president. He was former Congressman Guy Molinari, the son of former Assemblyman Robert Molinari, and the father of Susan Molinari, who was the city council's Republican before taking her father's seat in Congress. The Staten Islanders who came to the polls in 1993 voted five to one in favor of the

The *New York Times,* October 18, 1989: "No election issue this year moves the Satmar Hasidic community of the Williamsburg section of Brooklyn more than the incinerator the city proposes to put in the nearby Brooklyn Navy Yard. That was why on Monday night in the middle of the Succoth holidays, David N. Dinkins—who has called for a moratorium on incinerators—found himself enveloped in the community's warm, almost crushing embrace."

Republican challenger for the New York mayoralty. The 115,000 votes they provided were the margin of victory for Rudolph W. Giuliani, a former US prosecutor who thereby became only the second Republican mayor of New York City since Fiorello LaGuardia sixty years before.

Four years earlier, Giuliani had lost the race to the man he later beat, David N. Dinkins, whose one term in office was the first for any African-American in the city's history. One of the issues with which Giuliani had scored points against Dinkins in that first race was Dinkins's position on the prior administration's proposal to build a refuse incinerator in the former Brooklyn Navy Yard. Following the advice of his campaign advisers, Dinkins had promised that, if elected, he would impose a five-year moratorium on the project. This position was embraced by the Satmar Hasidim, a sect of ultra-orthodox Jews from a Rumanian city called, in honor of the Virgin Mary, Satu-Mare, who had fled to Brooklyn after the outbreak of World War II. As a more general strategy, however, the position was not very helpful. The editorial boards of the city's daily newspapers—all of whom generally supported pro-development public works—were uniformly opposed to a moratorium. Since it was not a commitment sought by the city's more established environmental groups, who were prepared to give him their endorsement anyway, it is unlikely that the pledge was helpful in the Democratic primary, which Dinkins won by a nine-point margin. It was even less useful in the general election campaign, since it provided Giuliani with an illustration of the types of leadership decisions he accused Dinkins of wanting to avoid.

One of the advisers who had recommended that Dinkins pledge a moratorium on the Navy Yard incinerator was Barry Commoner, a Brooklyn-born biologist who had run for president of the United States nine years earlier at the head of a new and short-lived political organization called the Citizens Party. The party's central goal, as Commoner put it, was to "[break] the grip of the corporations in this country." "Behind every one of our crises," he told his campaign audiences,

> the environment, the economy, the drift toward war, is the fundamental fault in the systems. The country is now being run by the managers of a few big corporations and not in the national interest, but in the interest of maximizing profits.

The only solution, he said, was replacing corporate control with "social governance of the systems of production."

Saul Alinsky, the leading practitioner and theoretician of American-style grassroots political organizing in the second half of the twentieth century, taught that environmental degradation can be useful. "Remember: once you organize people around something as commonly agreed upon as pollution, then an organized people is on the move. From there it's a short and natural step to political pollution, to Pentagon pollution." His advice recapitulated the principle that had animated the "citizens' associations" of 1864, 1870, and 1888, when handfuls of elite New Yorkers used a common terror of sanitary hazards to spur not just the environmental engineering around which the first urban infrastructural planning took place (to produce water supply and sewer systems, parks, roads, and "sanitary" housing), but sweeping political reforms as well. The school of environmental organizing Saul Alinsky invented in a poor, ethnic neighborhood behind the infamous Chicago stockyards varied from its predecessors, however, in several crucial respects.

Despite their democratic-sounding names, the citizens' associations of the nineteenth century were scarcely open to all, and their fundamental goal was to exert a benevolent social control over the unruly lower classes. Alinsky's Back of the Yards Association, on the other hand, was created to embrace precisely these lowest and least enfranchised classes: its primary purpose was to "change the life" of the community by "rubbing raw [its] resentments" and "fan[ning] the latent hostilities of the people to the point of overt expression" by "search[ing] out controversy and issues." And although both types of citizens' associations depended for their motivating impulse on common perceptions and fears of environmental degradation, the causalities of this degradation were very differently understood. While the nineteenth-century sanitary reformer's basic fear was ultimately of the lower classes and the natural, unwashed organic circumstances in which they often found themselves, the late-twentieth-century environmental reformer was frightened by the toxicity of synthetic poisons injected into the environment by corporate oligarchs for economic gain. By the end of the nineteenth century, the contagionists with their theories of disease transmission from person to person had won the battle for public opinion. By the second half of the twentieth century, the miasmists—this time with a theory of cancer causation related to atom bombs, insecticides, and all their petrochemical cousins—had won it back again. And if the nineteenth-century environmental reformers were literally the captains of capitalist industry, the Morgans, Vanderbilts, and Graces, in the late twentieth century their corporate fellows (as Ralph Nader points out) had become the most useful targets of environmental activism.

While the sanitary movement of the nineteenth century engineered technological solutions to the problems of organic pollution (George Waring's sewers and incinerators were the culminating extension of Jeremy Bentham's Panopticon and Edwin Chadwick's skyscraping fresh air tubes), technology was the animating terror of its twentieth-century successor, the international environmental movement begun by a shy Bureau of Fish and Wildlife biologist named Rachel Carson. Carson's best-selling book, *The Silent Spring,* published while its author was dying of lung cancer, awakened Americans to the dangers of the synthetic pesticide dichlorodiphenyltrichloroethane, known universally as DDT. Like Chevreul's discovery of the "sweet oil" glycerin (which was considered useless until Alfred Nobel found a way to harness its explosive energy), DDT, first isolated in Germany in 1874, had no utility until 1939, when the Swiss chemist Paul Müller, who was trying to make new agents for chemical warfare, discovered its devastating effects on the nervous systems of flying insects. In World War II, as carpet bombing was used to soften up enemy emplacements before ground troops were landed, pre-invasion bombardments of DDT were used in the malarial climes to eliminate native insects. After the war, many more thousands of tons were used to control epidemics of typhus and malaria. For his discovery, Müller received the 1948 Nobel Prize for Physiology and Medicine.

One of the young soldiers involved in testing DDT on this side of the Atlantic was Lieutenant Barry Commoner, then a twenty-five-year-old navy officer. His crew's job was to spray the compound on New Jersey beaches to test its effects on the kinds of creatures so admired by Joe Mitchell and Happy Zimmer. Like Mr. Zimmer, he was profoundly disturbed by what he saw. After the war, the Columbia- and Harvard-trained biologist got his first job teaching at Queens College and worked briefly as an associate editor at a science magazine before joining the faculty at Washington University in St. Louis, where he spent the next thirty-four years. This post put him in the epicenter of the nuclear fallout then irradiating much of the western and central United States as a result of the Pentagon's testing program in the deserts of the Southwest. Again Commoner was disturbed by what he saw. With a handful of university colleagues, he organized a group called the St. Louis Scientists' Committee for Nuclear Information that conducted a mail-in campaign to collect children's milk teeth after the tooth fairy was finished with them. The radionucleide strontium 90 is a telltale marker of atomic weapons testing. Strontium 90 moves through the environment bound to calcium, with which it shares a similar chemical structure. It enters the food chain through grass eaten by cows that produce milk drunk by children—causing (along with the other isotopes associated with weapons testing, according to the latest estimates) tens of thousands of cases of cancer among those who were children living in the

ECOLOGIST BARRY COMMONER
The Emerging Science of Survival

United States in the 1950s. Because the strontium ingested by children eventually lodges in their bones, sampling the levels in teeth that are grown and fall out within the span of just a few years is one of the easiest ways to document strontium levels in the environment at any given moment. The nuclear contamination so vividly demonstrated by the two hundred thousand baby teeth in the St. Louis group's collection played an important part in achieving the 1963 ban on above-ground bomb tests.

These and related efforts (such as his subsequent work on the effects of petroleum-derived fertilizers on riverine ecosystems) brought him the signal recognition, in February 1970, of appearing on the cover of *Time* magazine— part of *Time*'s coverage of the upcoming first Earth Day—as "the Paul Revere of Ecology,...a professor with a class of millions." If Rachel Carson was the mother of the environmental movement, Barry Commoner was its father.

While Commoner's St. Louis group was evolving into the New York-based Scientists Institute for Public Information, others also were at work. On Long Island, a naturalist named Dennis Puleston had noticed that songbirds were not the only ones disappearing. Ospreys, commonly known as fish hawks, are magnificent brown and white raptors with wingspreads of up to six feet that soar high above the sea, then curl themselves into streamlined bullets for a headfirst dive from which they pull up at the last moment to extend their feet to stab fish. The population of ospreys on Gardiners Island, Puleston noted, had declined from three hundred nests during the late 1940s to just fifty-five by the mid-1960s. His observation of these pairs showed that though they had eggs in their nests, no chicks were hatching. The shells were too brittle. He sent some fragments of these damaged goods to a laboratory and discovered that they were riddled with DDT. DDT in a bird's plasma, British scientists had already discovered, increases the production of liver enzymes that in turn metabolize steroidal hormones that break down the estrogen required to mobilize the calcium needed for sturdy shells. Like baby teeth, ospreys' place at the top of the food chain demonstrated the prevalence and persistence of DDT in the environment.

When one morning in the spring of 1966 Mrs. Carol Yannacone of Patchogue, Long Island, learned of a fish kill at a nearby lake that appeared to be the result of DDT sprayed by the Suffolk County Mosquito Commission, she told her husband Victor. The next morning, he filed the nation's first environmental lawsuit to stop the spraying of DDT on Long Island. Puleston and two colleagues, Charles Wurster and Arthur Cooley, were standing by with the scientific research they had conducted, ready to provide technical support. After consulting a dictionary to find the meaning of *ecology*—a word the plaintiffs were tossing about—the judge granted a temporary injunction. Though ultimately they lost the case on technical grounds (the court determined that only the legislature could permanently ban the use of DDT), from a practical standpoint they had gotten what they wanted: an end to the use of DDT in Suffolk County. To replicate their local success as broadly as possible, the four incorporated the Environmental Defense Fund in the fall of 1967 and took their campaign on the road. Five years later, their efforts were crowned with federal regulations banning the production or sale of DDT anywhere in the United States. By 1994, the US population of ospreys had climbed to 14,246 pairs.

Although Barry Commoner had never been involved with the management of urban wastes, it was a subject he found of considerable interest. When his friend Norman Cousins, publisher of the *Saturday Review,* with whom he had worked on the test ban campaign, urged him to bring his environmental expertise to New York on behalf of Mayor John Lindsay's administration, Commoner was intrigued. Cousins duly arranged a meeting with Lindsay to discuss the possibility of Commoner's taking a position as environmental adviser to the mayor. But after Commoner told Lindsay that the two issues he would be most interested in were refuse management and union relations, a firm job offer never materialized.

It is unlikely that Lindsay's (in)decision had to do with his fear of Commoner's socialist politics or of his outspokenness, since the new administrator he had just hired for his environmental protection agency was a thirty-six-year-old lawyer named Jerry Kretchmer, who in four terms in the state assembly had acquired a reputation as "probably the most radical elected official east of Oakland," and who was almost as well-known for the pugnacity with which his views were advanced. His most pugnacious moment as the city's EPA administrator came one day in the rotunda of City Hall when he exchanged blows with a councilman who objected to his proposal to build a garbage-dumping pier in the Bronx (where Robert Moses' landfills were nearly full) to fill barges bound for Fresh Kills. (The councilman threw the first punch after Kretchmer grabbed him by the lapels and tore his suit; Kretchmer denied striking his opponent, but the police security detail—assisted by reporters who rushed out of the adjacent newsroom—had to pull the pair apart.) Despite the fervor of its proponent, the planned pier was never built. Nor was Kretchmer able to implement his proposal to replace non-returnable bottles with degradable cans. The most significant plan he failed to carry forward, however, concerned a six-thousand-ton-per-day refuse-to-energy incinerator proposed to be built atop a sewage treatment plant in the former Brooklyn Navy Yard, a proposal whose planning had already cost the city eight million dollars and one of his predecessors his job. (Sanitation Commissioner Sam Kearing, in his own way as brash as Kretchmer, had made the mistake of announcing the project while the mayor was still trying to convince the Navy to let the city have the yard so that poor people could be put to work there.) Kretchmer decided to end the expensive, soot-emitting project's misery after watching its continuing struggles under his stewardship. When he announced the decision, he noted that some new technology for managing the city's wastes was likely to lie just around the corner, and that, for the time being, the city could make do through the expedient of "mounding" the refuse at Fresh Kills—an idea his engineers had recently come up with, as had Fishhooks McCarthy's before them. They called it "landscape-sculpture."

H. R. FOOTE.
Furnace for Cremating Garbage.

No. 211,503.   Patented Jan. 21, 1879.

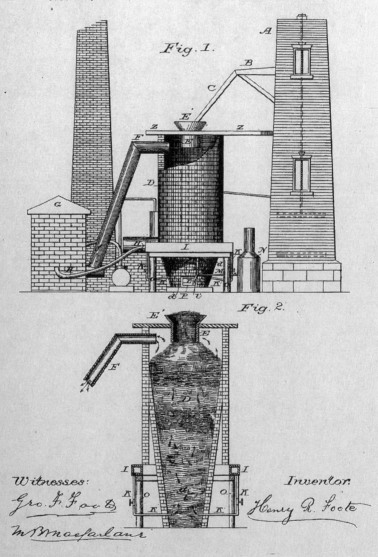

Fig. 1.

Fig. 2.

Witnesses: Inventor:

Geo. F. Foot   Henry R. Foote

M B Macfarlane

CHAPTER 10

Taking Heat

In the summer of 1874 an English inventor named Alfred Fryer produced a device to arrest the spread of cholera in his native Leeds. Reflecting the medical profession's growing conviction that diseases were transmitted in unsanitary circumstances from person to person, Fryer's device—in his patent application he called it a "Destructor"—was designed to purify the organic materials (such as infected bedding, putrefying meat, and household refuse) in which disease fomites or other animacules might be found. According to a description that appeared a few years later in the *New York Times,*

> The destructor consists of six cells or compartments, formed of ordinary brick, and lined with fire-bricks. It covers an area of 22 feet by 24 feet, and it is 12 feet in height. Each of the six cells is capable of destroying seven tons of refuse in 24 hours, and has a sloping furnace with hearth, and fire-grate covered in by a reverberatory arch of fire-brick, with one opening for the admission of the refuse, another for the escape of gases into the flue, and a furnace frame and doors for the removal of clinkers. ... The result is that everything is consumed, or converted into clinkers or fine ash.... The cremation is carried on without being in any way a nuisance. No fuel is employed, and the heat of the furnace is used to produce steam to drive an engine working two mortar mills, which grind the clinkers removed from the destructor and mixed with lime, into a strong mortar, which is readily sold at 5s. a ton.

By 1893, Fryer and his growing field of competitors had built destructors in fifty-six English cities and towns. Most of them were equipped with boiler tubes so that the furnaces' heat could be turned to steam. A number used this steam to generate electricity or run machinery. By 1912, there were three hundred English incinerators, seventy-six of which generated power. Although the performance of these plants was not uniformly flawless (there were some complaints about soot), they generally appeared to fulfill their sponsors' claims to reduce refuse to an inoffensive, biologically inert aggregate that occupied just a third of its original volume. Despite the occasional malfunctions of a few recalcitrant facilities, the first few generations of English destructors generally burned refuse at dependably high temperatures, while producing relatively little smoke and without the need for any supplements of coal or oil to keep their fires stoked.

In this country, American entrepreneurial ingenuity took the destructor along a somewhat different course. In 1877, in the ruins of a former sugar refinery at the foot of New York City's Front Street, an inventor from Stamford, Connecticut, named Colonel Henry R. Foote demonstrated for a select audience of potential investors, municipal officials, and at least two reporters ("gentlemen, including Generals, a Colonel and a Major") a "refuse cremator" of his own design that had two chambers: one for burning garbage, a second for destroying the off-gases thus released. (An observer noted that it reduced the waste volume by 88 percent, gave off no offensive smell, and left "a residuum unobjectionable in character and of great utility for filling and roofing material," "road-making and ship ballast.") For this he received the first US patent for refuse incineration in 1879. In 1885, the first permanent incinerator in the country was built on Governor's Island off the tip of lower Manhattan by Frederic Morse, a relative of the inventor of the telegraph, Samuel F.B. Morse. By 1892, there were more than a dozen incinerators operating in the country. A decade later, 15 percent of the largest American cities were using incineration (while only 10 percent were using any form of Barren Island-style "reduction.") By 1924, that proportion had nearly doubled. But unlike the English destructors—because of the problems of competing with private utilities for the production and sale of power—only a few American incinerators ever generated useful power, and none of these operated for more than a couple of years. Another difference was that while the English destructors were designed and built under the sponsorship of municipal entities to last for at least several decades, American plants typically were built by private interests concerned with short-term profits. The combination of the lack of power production (since functioning as a utility generator imposes a useful discipline on an incinerator's operators) and the relatively short-term private sector contracts under which American facilities were typically constructed and operated meant that, while the English destructors generally provided many years of reliable, nuisance-free service, the American cremators, reflecting the shortcuts taken in their design and construction, usually burned at lower temperatures that produced more smoke and odors and left much of the refuse unburned. The operational problems that ensued meant that the plants were often out of service, were costly to operate, and frequently annoyed the neighbors.

In New York, city officials repeatedly considered the pros and cons of incineration without ever quite making up their minds. In 1880, when the Fryer company tried to interest "his Worship the Mayor" in its patented process of destruction, the street-cleaning commissioner felt that his own way—dumping the refuse in the ocean—despite the cost of hauling it seventeen miles from shore in a near-futile attempt to reduce beach-wash-up complaints, was cheaper. In 1894, after the federal government had tried to end the wash-up problem for good by outlawing ocean dumping, the expert commission appointed by the mayor to select the city's new waste disposal system chose "reduction" (the Barren Island arrangement) over incineration as the solution to the city's refuse disposal problem, on the grounds that combustion technology was less dependable, never mind too expensive. When Colonel Waring entered office, he encouraged his brother-in-law's attempts to run an incinerator (on East Twenty-second Street near the East River) as a dry-refuse adjunct to the wet-garbage Barren Island contract. (Waring's incineration interests, of course, were more utilitarian than sanitary, since he went to his death unconvinced that germs killed.) His bacteriologist successor, Major John Woodbury (who monitored the concentration of airborne microbes in various spots around the city as a measure of his troops' effectiveness) was a fervent incineration enthusiast, but his citywide incineration/electricity-generation plans (power from one of his incinerators lit the Williamsburg Bridge) were squelched by Mayor McClellan, to whom the refuse-to-energy plants were just a chip to be played in a game of bluff with the utility companies.

By the end of the first World War, the only incinerators left in the city were either private (the five that Brooklyn Ash used to improve the quality of its real estate building material while also powering its electric trains) or in

Refuse-to-energy plants were just a chip to be played in a game of bluff with the utility companies.

the boroughs (Queens and Staten Island) where the 1898 amalgamation had left local officials in control of street cleaning. Though these plants seemed to produce few complaints, no one believed that city-run incinerators would be so benign, as Mayor Hylan's street-cleaning commissioner discovered when he tried to staunch the flow of garbage into the ocean after closing the Barren Island and Metropolitan By-Products plants. "The Street Cleaning department [with its incinerator plans] is like a waif whom nobody wants," he sighed. When the Supreme Court (at New Jersey's behest) finally ordered New York to comply with the 1888 law against dumping garbage in the ocean, Jimmy Walker too tried to build incinerators to take the place of barges and found that "everybody is in favor of incinerators, but nobody desires them as neighbors." Robert Moses maintained throughout his public life that "incineration is the only way to solve" the garbage problem. But though he promised that, within three years' of the opening of the Fresh Kills landfill, every ton of New York's refuse would be burned, he instead presided over the decline of incineration as a socially acceptable waste disposal technique.

For once, it was not just Moses' honesty that was at issue: the forces behind incineration's fall were felt in cities all across the country. In the decades after World War II the number of incinerators in the United States plummeted from a high of over 300 to a low of 67 in 1979. Expensive labor, cheap fuel, and abundant land were three of the main reasons. Another was the growing awareness that smokestacks were not simply the signs of a healthy economy (as the billowing plumes in the pictures of grade school social studies readers once taught). In five days in 1952, four thousand Londoners died of choking smoke and fog—smog: more than had died during any comparable period of the German blitz. These mortalities once again reminded city dwellers (since Chadwick's Fresh Air Company had never gotten its tubes off the ground, since "lungs" like the Bois de Boulogne were not quite up to the task) that chimneys could be dangerous. In New York, a new city agency, the Bureau of Smoke Abatement, revealed that refuse incinerators were responsible for 30 percent of all the life-threatening smoke in the city. Its director led the fight to overturn the city law that had required each building with at least twelve apartments to have its own incinerator; the new law (enacted in 1967) instead made all apartment-house incinerators—unless their owners chose to install certified air pollution control devices—illegal.

While the number of incinerators across the country was decreasing, the number of landfills went up. By 1970, there were about twenty thousand landfills in the United States (virtually all of which would one day be classified as "open dumps") leaking a steady stream of contaminants into the groundwater, and emitting, on a per-ton-of-garbage basis, more than a dozen pounds per year of pollutants into the air. When Robert Moses was finally turned out of the parks department office from which he had commanded the flow of every ton of refuse disposed of in New York City for over three decades, there were eleven landfills spread across every borough but Manhattan, which, as their filling continued, each year emitted some fifty thousand more tons of greenhouse gases (methane and carbon dioxide combined), thousands of additional tons of nonmethane polyaromatic hydrocarbons such as benzene, styrene, and toluene, and hundreds of additional tons of chlorinated organics such as vinyl chloride and trichloroethane.

In 1977, in the aftermath of the world-jarring power shifts that had taken place recently in the Mideast, which for the first time had given many Americans an acute awareness of their vulnerable dependence on imported oil, a cardiganned Jimmy Carter gave his country a cozy fireside talking-to. Like Roosevelt and Churchill a generation before, he tried to stiffen his nation's resolve—though this time, for only the paler "moral equivalent" of war. In World War II, some of the material resources to meet the national crisis had been supplied by efforts like LaGuardia's scrap drive to conserve scarce materials and by the "victory gardens" many patriots planted to expand the country's food supply. But while gardening provided a virile link to the nation's agricultural past, there was something vaguely un-American about scrimping to save a pile of old papers or a load of broken pots and pans, and the extra expense it added to the city's war-straitened budget made LaGuardia and his constituents eager to drop their scrap campaign as soon as they could. Like the homefront efforts, President Carter's campaign to reduce the country's dependence on foreign oil also had two components. One, like the cardigan he was wearing with the White House thermometer set at sixty-eight degrees, was not at all sexy. The other, calling forth as it did all the primal elements of American mechanical and entrepreneurial ingenuity in the drive to develop "alternative fuels," decidedly was.

Among the first Americans to sit up and pay attention to the president's call to moral action were the bond traders and investment bankers who saw in the program to jump-start an alternative energy economy a means to grease their own wheels of fortune. Among this group perhaps the foremost exemplar—its Paul Revere: the subsidies are coming, the subsidies are coming—was Robert Randol, of Smith Barney, who embarked on a cross-country crusade to ensure that local officials knew of the potential opportunities. The object of Randol's missionary zeal was a generic set of technologies known as "resource recovery," which embraced a range of devices that varied from the tried-and-tested to the frankly experimental, but all of which (like Barren Island's bubbling vats) were designed to distill marketable commodities from "urban ore." The price of a single resource recovery plant might run to several hundred million dollars. After a few plants, even a few percent of that—a broker's fee for selling the tax exempt bonds needed to finance construction, debt service, and a capital reserve fund—could become serious money. Dozens of these plants would be needed across the country to meet the big cities' need for waste disposal—at least half-a-dozen could be used in New York City alone, which boasted the biggest, densest, richest supply of refuse in the world, the Persian Gulf of Garbage.

While Randol was serving as a dollar-a-year adviser to Ed Koch, New York's voluble new mayor, the city secured several million dollars in grants from the EPA and the Department of Energy. With these seed funds in hand, he helped structure a deal to leverage enough tax-exempt industrial-development funds and private equity to begin building some plants. All the city had to do was promise to supply enough garbage to feed them. The man who could make this promise was the thirty-six-year-old sanitation commissioner whom Koch had just appointed.

Like Barry Commoner (whose father was a tailor), Norman Steisel had grown up in Brooklyn, the brilliant only son of a Polish baker. After finishing high school and college in the neighborhood, he went off to Yale to study systems design and administration. He returned to New York to become an analyst in Mayor Lindsay's highly regarded Budget Bureau, where his brash self-confidence, snarling charm, and impatient acuity quickly brought him to the attention of his superiors, and a string of rapid promotions. When Ed Koch needed someone to fix his badly broken sanitation department (which could get only half of its seventeen hundred trucks on the street on any given day), his first-deputy budget director (which Steisel had by then become) sprang to mind (a colleague said) as perhaps the only one in his administration arrogant enough to get the job done.

Steisel approached his new job as commissioner in charge of twelve thousand uniformed men with vigor. Not all his hours were spent at the office—the baby-faced bachelor's evenings contained such a succession of fashionable restaurants, power parties, downtown galleries, and elegant women that his friends began to call him "Mr. Taste and Mr. Waste"—but his days were still impressively productive. Within months he had substituted computerized tracking systems for the old pencil-and-ledger systems upon which the agency had always depended; shipped a batch of promising mid-level managers up to the Harvard Business School for polishing; reorganized truck maintenance methods to achieve a 100 percent reduction in unscheduled fleet downtime; hired a systems analyst to devise more efficient collection routes; and launched a wave of garage renovations so that the men would no longer have to install snowplows in the driving snow, could take lunch breaks somewhere other than on the curb, and no longer had to change their clothes in locker rooms whose broken windows and rusting pipes seemed not to have been repaired since Waring's time. Among his other efforts to lift his department's abysmal morale—a situation aggravated by a recent series in the Daily News that depicted "sanmen" shirking their duties by sleeping in their trucks as the garbage piled up around them—he even installed a performance-artist-in-residence who spent the better part of a year making the rounds of section stations six days a week at dawn to shake the hand of every man on the force while telling him "Thank you for keeping New York clean." While the introduction of female firefighters and police officers into other all-male departments during the same period was marked by hazing and other forms of turmoil, the integration of female workers into the historically all-male sanitation force that Steisel presided over was graceful and incidentless. His most important and dramatic innovation, however, was the introduction of a new collection truck with a steering wheel on each side. The dual steering allowed a worker to jump on from either side to drive the truck ahead while a second worker picked up the refuse on the other side of the street. It eliminated the need for a third worker to serve as driver. Since labor costs ate the lion's share of his department's 386-million-dollar budget, this radical reform—which he got the uniformed sanitation workers' union to accept by distributing a portion of the savings to the workers—saved the city some thirty-seven million dollars a year.

When Steisel could turn his attention from the immediate problems of rationalizing the way the garbage was picked up, Bob Randol was waiting with a suggestion for what to do with it when it was unloaded again. For a commissioner as interested in system mechanics and the art of a deal as Steisel was, Randol's message—hot new technology, other people's money—worked like an elixir.

Had it been necessary, there would have been no shortage of encouragement from other parties. Steisel's predecessor had claimed to have received a
hundred offers to take some or all of the city's waste off his hands, and there
were still plenty of people clamoring for the chance to put their own "urban
ore" plans into operation. Nor did there seem to be any naysayers. Politicians
from Bronx Borough President Robert Abrams (the city should pursue
resource recovery more "aggressively") to Congresswoman Bella Abzug
("We're sitting on an urban metal mine") were complaining that once again
New York City's hidebound bureaucrats were too slow to board the gravy
train. The Port Authority's executive director, Peter Goldmark, announced
that, to fuel industrial parks that in turn would power economic development, he intended to corner all the garbage within twenty-five miles of the
Statue of Liberty. The Power Authority's executive director, John Dyson,
meanwhile pleaded for refuse to fire his utility's plants in Staten Island and the
Bronx. And seven years after Earth Day, most environmental groups still had
not made any distinction between "energy recovery" and what later came to
be seen as more worthy, more ecologically uplifting forms of "recycling."

The economics were as apparently straightforward as the politics: provided the deal were structured correctly, there could be no doubt that the
city would come out ahead. The single interesting financial issue, it seemed,
was constructing a contract (unlike Fishhooks's) that would give the city a
proportionate return for its lucrative waste.

The technology end of things, however, was a bit more complicated. For
a start, "resource recovery" facilities came in a bewildering variety of mod-
els and styles, ranging from the giant hydropulper that Town Supervisor
Alphonse D'Amato had just bought in neighboring Hempstead, Long
Island, to the charcoal-dust factory that was going up in a big hurry in
nearby Bridgeport, Connecticut. The hydropulper worked on the principle
of a giant kitchen blender: just add garbage, water, and stir. What came out
was a slurry that after a squeeze through a set of rollers became a sheet of
garbage felt that was supposed to burn beautifully in a custom built furnace.
The charcoal was made by heating and drying garbage before shredding it
and adding a sulphuric embrittling agent to make a fluffy dust ("Eco-Fuel")
that could be sprinkled on coal in a utility boiler. But the Hempstead plant's
sweet stench (it was said) sickened horses at the racetrack across the road,

and the Eco-people went backrupt after an explosion at their first plant blew up one of their employees and their Bridgeport plant injured three more.

To convince themselves that reliable waste-to-energy technologies really existed, Steisel and his deputy went to Europe to see what their counterparts there had accomplished. In Parent-Duchatelet's Paris they found the biggest refuse plant ever built burning some three thousand tons of garbage a day to produce steam for the municipal heating system. In Germany they met with the venerable Walter Martin, the debonair chairman of his family's corporation, whose "reverse-reciprocating stoker-grates" of the finest German steel tossed and tumbled the garbage as it burned. In Switzerland they found a spic-and-span plant that fed its garbage-made steam to the chocolate factory next door.

Thus encouraged, Steisel and his staff followed Randol's blueprint for a business deal that, to protect both the bankers and the city, made the contractor fully responsible for the performance of the facility. The winner of the bidding process they structured for the first of what they envisioned as an eventual network of perhaps a dozen plants was a company that combined respected American business credentials (even its name, Wheelabrator-Frye, connoted a sturdy nineteenth-century sort of Yankee rectitude) with the clockwork precision of Swiss engineered technology As for the location of this first, this flagship plant, Steisel and his staff selected—an ill-auguring coincidence?—the same site in the historic Brooklyn Navy Yard that had cost his predecessor his job.

Barry Commoner and Norman Steisel first met in the spring of 1982 at a conference in the Hilton Hotel in midtown Manhattan. The famous professor, recently returned to New York from St. Louis, was giving the keynote address on "urban energy strategies"—a topic about which he had been speaking and writing since his 1980 presidential campaign to "return power to the people." The subject also happened to be the current focus of his Center for the Biology of Natural Systems, an institute he had established in 1966 at Washington University and brought back in his suitcase from St. Louis. His plan was to create a set of small energy cooperatives that could deliver heat and electricity to blocks of rowhouses through a common pipe between their interconnecting walls. This power would be produced by small-scale local generators fueled by methane made from garbage. This notion (though not made explicit) was at the center of the speech he gave at the end of the day, after the other speakers—including Steisel, who described his plan to build a steam-generating incinerator in the Brooklyn Navy Yard-—had finished. Commoner began his remarks by recapitulating some basic thermodynamic principles.

The cost of the energy required to make our economy function, he said, is constantly increasing because it comes from nonrenewable sources. The current energy system therefore "cannibaliz[es] the economic system it is supposed to support," diverting more and more resources from other critical needs, and increasing the disparity between rich and poor. "By suitably reorganizing the city's energy system," he went on, the situation could be reversed, and New York's control over a renewable energy supply could be used to expand its economy. This could be done through a decentralized cogeneration system fired by natural gas made from "biomass."

Since New York does not contain enough space to grow the biomass it would need to meet its natural gas production needs, Commoner continued, at least half would have to be imported into the city. Fortunately, however— though very little of it is now converted into useful forms—the city already imports organic matter (food and paper, mostly) which the city's "collective metabolism" converts to trash, garbage, and sewage. As Steisel listened intently, Commoner reached his conclusion: "[P]resent plans for recovering energy from trash are centered around directly burning it to produce electricity. It seems to me that is a move in the wrong direction. Apart from the likelihood of encountering intractable problems due to toxic emissions arising from the thermal conversion of the synthetic organic materials that are bound to occur in the city's trash collections"—dioxin had recently been detected in the smelly Hempstead hydropulper—"a trash-to-electricity system clashes with the requirements of the proposed cogenerator system. The latter requires an expanded supply of methane and obviates the need for centrally-produced electricity. A system of converting trash into methane for inclusion in the city's natural gas supply...would make a good deal more sense than further expanding the present, inherently inefficient, central power system."

Soon after, Steisel invited Commoner to his office to discuss their divergent views. Commoner repeated the argument he had made against incineration and mentioned that he also had concerns about the dioxin emissions that had been detected in Hempstead. He spent most of the meeting, however, describing a study of the flow of organic materials into and out of the city that he wanted his institute to undertake. He ended by asking Steisel to fund it. Steisel understood Commoner to suggest that there would be no more public attacks on the Navy Yard proposal, either as an obstacle to developing a more-rational energy system, or as a potential source of dioxins, if he agreed to pay for the mass balance analysis. This Steisel would not agree to do. By the end of the year it seemed that dioxin was the only waste management issue worth talking about.

Dioxin is the common name for a family of chlorinated organic compounds that are never produced intentionally, but are synthesized when volatilized benzene rings (compounds that form the basic building blocks of materials such as wood and paper as well as petrochemical products) combine with chlorine (which is found in nature as a salt in plants, water, and soil, and in manufactured products such as bleached paper, pesticides, and chlorinated plastics). Dioxins were first identified as a by-product of the manufacture of pesticides and herbicides such as DDT and Agent Orange. Their international reputation grew as a result of an explosion at a pharmaceutical plant in Seveso, Italy, in 1977 (the Italian government appointed Commoner to its commission to investigate the issue), and as a result of the discovery of dioxins in waste oils that had been used to suppress dust on a horse arena and roads in Times Beach, Missouri, in 1971 (not far from the university where Commoner then taught). In 1978, dioxins were detected in emissions from an incinerator in Sweden. When the Hempstead incinerator's angry neighbors called the EPA in to investigate their odor complaints, dioxins were discovered there, too. Once alerted to their presence in the environment, researchers began looking for dioxins in various industrial processes (including paper making, pesticide and herbicide manufacturing, and cement production); in combustion processes that ranged from cigarettes, charcoal grills, and forest fires, to trucks and cars, to medical waste incinerators; and in background air, water, food, and human fat. Everywhere they looked they found them.

The central element of the dioxin argument Commoner came to develop after his meeting with Steisel was that "mass-burn" incinerators—and only mass-burn incinerators—synthesize dioxin inside the very devices that are designed to control other harmful emissions. (The cooling effect of the "scrubbers" on the exhaust gases, according to Commoner, makes the volatilized lignins released from burning paper and the chlorine released from chlorinated plastics combine on the surface of fly ash.) If these toxic substances were to be released to the atmosphere, he said (using his own highly idiosyncratic risk assessment method) they would produce a chilling body count: up to 421 New Yorkers could be expected to sicken or die as the result of the Navy Yard plant's operation. These lives, Commoner suggested, would be part of the price paid by the city to the same companies that had built the nation's nuclear reactors, but because of the Three Mile Island incident and other market limiting factors had had to go into another business.

That significant portions of Commoner's claims would have been difficult to substantiate (for instance, the amount of chlorine needed to produce dioxin in an incinerator is so small that dioxin can be produced even when chlorinated plastics are largely removed from the waste stream, and nobody multiplies the cancer risk per million of seventy years' exposure at the point of maximum impact by the number of people in New York City to assess a facility's potential health effects) did not appear to temper his enthusiastic repetition of them. And the assertions proved effective in attracting not only the attention of the lay public, but of two of the most important national environmental organizations, who decided that the proposed Brooklyn Navy Yard facility was an issue with which they, too, should become involved.

While it seemed to help spur their interest, dioxin was not the issue of greatest concern to the Environmental Defense Fund or the Natural Resources Defense Council. As was also apparently Commoner's case, their primary objective was developing an alternative for managing the city's waste. Commoner's proposed alternative was a Bridgeport-style mechanical one, a plant (which, to increase its political attractiveness, he proposed be built on an island) where the city's refuse would be separated into its constituent elements, a sort of "Modern Times" assembly line in reverse, where some of the commingled products of the urban waste stream—especially the chlorinated plastics—would be removed before the remainder would be turned into a fuel product and burned. EDF and NRDC wanted to replace the city's proposal for centralized incineration with a system in which the city's citizens would be called upon to participate in managing their own wastes. The alternative they advocated was called "source-separation recycling."

The week before the Board of Estimate's final vote on the Navy Yard project, Norman Steisel convened another meeting in his dark-paneled office. He sat at one end of his polished table, the mayor's representative to the Board of Estimate at the other. In between were a Wheelabrator-Frye-fielded team of lobbyists in its own way as distinguished as any combination of Choates, Roots, or Seaburys ever hired by the New York Sanitary Utilization Company, Metropolitan By-Products, or Brooklyn Ash. To Steisel's left was Howard Rubinstein, eminence grise of the New York public relations industry, Eddie Bernays's undisputed heir. Next to him, trimly tailored, be-ringed fingers as smoothly manicured as his silver hair, was Samuel ("Sandy") Lindenbaum, who held a parallel place in the arcane, politically connected field of zoning and land use law. Beside him, in ample pinstripes, sat Andrew Fisher, whose massive father filled the place of honor to Steisel's right. With his little brother Kenny (on Andy's left), they were "the Fishers of Brooklyn," who together played a role in that borough's life not unlike the one Patrick Henry McCarren had played with such panache eighty years before. Across the table sat Sid Davidoff, the Ramboesque lawyer-lobbyist who had begun his career (after a stint managing rock bands and selling DDT in Harlem) as John Lindsay's campaign-chauffeur and political patronage dispenser, a cowlick of black hair sticking up in an unruly spike, his dark business suit somehow tugged over bulging shoulders an incongruous contrast to the wrestler's neck and sturdy face above it. Like his host (who was one of the few others at the table not running his father's business), he gave the impression that, beneath his poker face, he was having fun—that the deal they were so meticulously plotting was a gloriously amusing, Spaldeen-bouncing, broomstick-swinging, elbows-flying, three-sewer-cover game.

The rules by which Board of Estimate politics had been played since Andrew Green's time were intended to protect the interests of the little boroughs against any mayor's brute fiat. The "citywide" members (the mayor, comptroller, and city council president) each held two of the board's eleven votes; the remainder were distributed evenly among the presidents of the five formerly independent (and demographically unequal) boroughs. (This demographic inequality—a violation of the Constitution's "one man one vote" principal—was the reason the Supreme Court finally abolished the board five years later, ninety-two years after Green's creation had been adopted.) To outweigh a position taken by any one of the five borough presidents—since they usually circled their wagons in mutual support any time one of them was challenged—all three citywide officials had to agree. But in the case of the Brooklyn Navy Yard, there was no such disinterested consensus.

Ed Koch had lost his customary iron grip on the board three years before, when, with a hubris in part inspired by the most uninhibited newspaper presence in New York since William Randolph Hearst, he ran for governor just three months after collecting the greatest re-election plurality since Fiorello LaGuardia's. "Don't worry about my power. I've got plenty of power," he had told Steisel and his deputy when the Board of Estimate's role in decisions concerning the Navy Yard incinerator had first come up. "If they want to vote [on the Request for Proposals], *let* 'em. They're *pishers.*" But after he returned from an eight-day vacation to Spain to find reporters from Rupert Murdoch's Post waving a "Draft Koch" banner headline that produced 14,047 signed clip-out coupons urging him to run for governor against his old nemesis Mario Cuomo—and then lost—it was another story. Within days of his defeat, his two citywide colleagues on the Board of Estimate had begun to run for his job.

What would be the board's final vote on the incinerator was further complicated by the fact that the proposed site had been moved from the south end of the Navy Yard (where the chimerical facility had floated in Lindsay's time like an ominous mirage) to the north—directly across a hooker-lined truck route from a densely populated neighborhood composed of equal numbers of usually feuding Hispanics and Hasidic Jews, the latter of whom were known for voting as their rebbe instructed. When Koch had tried to get the Board of Estimate's approval to hire legal and financial advisers for the incinerator project after his defeat in the race for governor, for the first time since his re-election as mayor a resolution of his was defeated. He retaliated by accusing the comptroller, Harrison ("Jay") Goldin, of pandering to the Hasids. To defend his vote, Goldin commissioned a series of project critiques, one of which (written by a chemist who worked with Commoner's Center for the Biology of Natural Systems) focused on the threat posed by the plant's potential for emitting dioxin.

Attempting to play his challengers off against each other, Koch promised the city council president, Carol Bellamy, a special dioxin study in her honor so that her vote—unlike the comptroller's—could be ascribed to a reasoned evaluation of public health effects. Though the report's findings of negligible public health impacts due to dioxin were endorsed by an impressively credentialed body of peer reviewers, it evidently was not quite enough—since, as her spokesman pointed out, enough other members of the board were voting in favor of the project to make her vote unnecessary—to make her surrender a block of votes to her Democratic-primary opponent simply for the luxury of having taken, for the record, a statesmanlike course. (Commoner—though he dismissed the report as unduly optimistic about the levels of projected emissions—appeared to take a statesmanlike course by promising that he, "for one, would be prepared to withdraw my objections" if the city would only accept his challenge to promise that the dioxin emissions predicted in the report would not be exceeded. For the record, when the city committed to considerably lower dioxin emissions as a condition of its legal permit for the facility, Commoner appeared to have lost all memory of any such offer.) But though the result of the board's deliberation was not blessed with Bellamy's consent, her spokesman was quite right. Astonishingly, for the first time in living memory—all three of the board's citywide officials simultaneously campaigning to be the next mayor—the mayor had prevailed without the votes of either of his two citywide colleagues, and four of the five borough presidents had sided against one of their own.

Eight months after the vote to provide legal and financial advisers for negotiating the terms of the incinerator contract, the Department of Sanitation was to approach the Board of Estimate for its final approval of the project, a vote on the proposed contract itself. The strategy for getting the votes to vault this last political hurdle was to keep the historically anomalous, paper-thin coalition that had approved the prior proposal in place for one more session. And so, as the meeting at Steisel's table broke up, each man got his assignment: delivering—or at least stage-managing—at least one vote.

Lindenbaum got the Manhattan borough president, Andy Stein, who

The Fishers were detached to keep the lid on Howard Golden, whose unhappy constituents would receive the despised facility in their teeming midst. A particular target of the Hasids' ire was Andrew Stein, whose vote on the project (according to the Hasidic leadership) violated a pledge he made when courting votes for his maiden citywide race. His name was heard often during this protest march (in which police barriers help to guard the ritual separation between women [clothed in white] and men [clothed in black]).

was for professional reasons keenly interested in the cash flows produced by Manhattan's booming real estate business. (Part of the lobbying package was an agreement that the sharp-tongued mayor would cast no further aspersions on Stein's intelligence during the remainder of his campaign to become the new city council president; a more important concession—the one that could be discussed publicly—was that Stein could take credit for having forced the administration into its first steps to develop a source-separation recycling program to reduce the city's need for both incineration and landfill capacity.) Davidoff would use his muscle through the machines of Queens and the Bronx to reach Donald Manes (who in less than a year would be dead, a kitchen knife through his chest, the gory end to his leading role in a municipal contracting scandal) and Stanley Simon (who would soon join the Bronx Democratic leader in jail for his parallel role in a related case). The Fishers were detached to keep the lid on Howard Golden, the Brooklyn borough president, whose constituents would receive the despised facility in their teeming midst. As his campaign treasurer, Andrew was in a position to see that Golden would take the assault on the borough presidents' all-for-one mutual protection pact lying down. Rubinstein would guard the end zone, coordinating, with the help of David Rockefeller, New York Partnership president; real estate mogul Lew Rudin; and financier Felix Rohatyn, the final layer of the lobbyists' exhortatory strokes and enough media support (all four dailies gave helpful supporting plugs) to put the game away.

While the business sector proponents of the Navy Yard incinerator sat coordinating their strategy around a single table, there was no such unanimity in the environmentalists' camp. As the mainstream groups' leaders were saying things like "We would like to be able to support this facility," and "We don't want to be seen as opponents, or trying to slow up the process," Barry Commoner fumed that they were "unwilling to confront the fundamental political and economic issues and as a result are falling into the pocket of the establishment." It was a classic example of the "two paths" Commoner saw in the environmental movement. "There is in fact a 'hard path' and a 'soft path' in environmental politics," he would write a few years later. "The soft path is the easy one; it accepts the private corporate governance of produc-

tion decisions and seeks only to regulate the resultant environmental impact.
...In environmental politics, the hard path is the difficult one; it would
confront the real source of environmental degradation—the technology
choice—and debate who should govern it, and for what purpose. The hard
path is the only workable route to the soft environmental path." Legislative
and regulatory reforms and negotiated compromises on pollution controls,
he said, were just "palliatives."

Ten days before the board's final vote, echoing Hamlet, the Environmental Defense Fund released a slim report entitled "To Burn or Not to Burn."
In the trademark market-driven EDF way, the report stuck to the economics
(leaving aside any discussion of "environmental impacts") and purported to
demonstrate that recycling could absorb more of the city's waste at less cost
than could incineration. The surprise assault achieved a prominent story in
the *Times* that succeeded immediately in catching Steisel's full attention. (He
reacted with all the surprise and pained indignation of a hunting dog who,
thinking that he is just keeping his nose down and doing his job suddenly
finds that a porcupine has found it a convenient place to park a quill.) After a
brief but furious exchange of visits and correspondence, the quill was
extracted by his agreement to commit the city to establishing recycling programs "on a full equivalent basis" (the legalistic phrase upon which the fund's
negotiators insisted) with his waste-to-energy plans. In return, the fund
agreed to provide public support of the Navy Yard project before the coming vote. Taking a similar (but more diplomatic) tack, the Natural Resources
Defense Council many months earlier had focused its negotiating demands
on a commitment that devices to capture acid gases before they escaped from
the stack be grafted to the plant's design, a condition to which Steisel—after
protracted bargaining (so as to reduce the odds that NRDC would load more
demands onto the negotiating table)—had agreed just in time to allow the
revised calculations of emissions impacts, which I (as the sanitation department's manager for the environmental and public review process for the project) was responsible for marshaling.

In the stately public pavan that followed, NRDC and EDF kept their vows
and pronounced the project consistent with sound environmental practice.
This stance on the part of his wretchedly pragmatic offspring brought down
Barry Commoner's scorn. "Here in New York, the Natural Resources

Norman Steisel being questioned about the proposed Brooklyn Navy Yard incinerator by the Board of Estimate, 1984. Author in background center, in white shirt. *New York Times*

Defense Council and the Environmental Defense Fund worked with the Sanitation Department in promoting incineration," leaving "the New York Public Interest Research Group and the local community" (and, he was too modest to add—himself) to lead ("at great cost") the fight against it.

The day the Board of Estimate gave its final approval for the Navy Yard project the temperature was the same steamy ninety-five degrees it had been the day James Reyburn came down with the cholera. To my disgruntlement, an historical mini-pageant I had arranged to set the public stage for the next phase of waste management planning—a series of speakers briefly describing the decline in the city's waste management capacity since Moses' day, in which each in some way had presided or participated (as sanitation commissioner, EPA administrator, state legislator, authority head) while dozens of plans for new waste management facilities had gone unbuilt—was interrupted by a flurry of TV cameras rushing in, on schedule, to record the council president's "no" vote. (Fortunately the comptroller, whose cam-

Robert Moses, forty years earlier

paign financing in large part derived from the city's development-hungry bankers, had orchestrated no such fanfare for his.) The rest of the votes were cast, and then every light and air conditioner went out, keeping Lower Manhattan black and hot well into the night.

Two Paths

One element of the environmental movement was not ready to accept the Navy Yard incinerator as a fait accompli. But if the New York Public Interest Group was alone in refusing to accept defeat, there were compelling institutional reasons for its insistence on continuing to fight. Unlike its soft counterparts, NYPIRG had no incentive to compromise.

While the organizers of Earth Day were working to expand the movement out of which mainstream membership-based, foundation-supported environmental groups like NRDC and EDF were growing, consumer-advocate Ralph Nader was traveling the country with an idea that would have different but comparably far-reaching effects. Nader, who had come to national prominence four years before with an exposé of the purposely concealed safety hazards in a General Motors sports car, had come up with an ingenious plan for putting organizers to work. Because there were few permanent jobs for young lawyers and other professionals who wanted to change society instead of defending it from change as the hired servants of state and corporate interests, the idealism that he found on Vietnam-era campuses around the country was being squandered at graduation.

What was needed was a way to tap the financial resources of the nation's campuses while also creating the kind of institutional continuity that a disciplined agenda-for-change required. Fundraising events like dances and concerts produced too sporadic an income to provide an adequate promise of employment. So too did anything so quixotic as a voluntary check-off campaign that would require an affirmative act on the part of contributing students, particularly when they would not yet be indoctrinated in a particular campus's mores (putting "incoming freshmen and transfer students in a particularly bad position"). A mandatory fee levied at registration would be "shamelessly coercive," and yet, if rhetorically transformed into a "voluntary" fee by allowing whatever minority of students who so chose to seek a refund weeks later, could produce a year-in-year-out income on which full-time organizers could depend. As liberating as a perpetual income in return for a modest upfront investment of organizing capital (an organizer's version of the coupon-clipper's annuity) was another aspect of a campus power base. Saul Alinsky taught that organizers have to work with what they have, turning weaknesses into strengths that can be used to fight the established order. The fact that a student body turns over every four years—a major reason the natives themselves found it so hard to establish the institutional continuity necessary to rearrange the off-campus world—also meant that any effective constituent oversight of the professional staff's efforts would be unlikely to develop, further enhancing the enthusiasm-harnessing moral authority lent the "Public Interest Research Group" staff by their technical credentials and one-track focus. Let other groups worry about staying within paths prescribed by their boards of directors, let others compete for short-term grants from fickle foundations: like a hydro-powered turbine, the PIRG's professionals would use the clean, renewable energy of an endlessly changing, constantly flowing stream of students.

The sanitary reformers of the nineteenth century had demonstrated the effectiveness of political campaigns based on fears of mysterious, invisible, airborne threats to the public health, threats made more chilling by their nexus in class antagonism. Rachel Carson had proved the power of the purifying moral fervor that could be generated by a single-minded focus on a particular corporation-built pollutant. Barry Commoner had showed the usefulness of tying "the most toxic" (and, parenthetically, synthetic and therefore unnatural) compound known to man to a particular—perforce unnatural—practice. And so, sparing no pains to rub as raw as possible the resentment of tens of thousands of readily identifiable New Yorkers, the local embodiment of Nader's platonic paternity, the New York Public Interest Research Group ("Nigh-Purg"), found in New York's garbage its single greatest organizing opportunity, and the hiring of a full-time "toxics coordinator" its most productive strategic decision.

Though Norman Steisel was no longer around to manipulate it—amidst a flurry of rising eyebrows he had left the sanitation department three months after the final Board of Estimate vote to join a bond firm that counted

Wheelabrator among its clients—the split between "hard" and "soft" paths continued to divide New York's professional environmentalists. But despite their sectarian discord over means and ends, they held in common a delicious opportunity. Though Wheelabrator's five years' of patience and well-paid lobbyists had achieved the final political approval from the city's governing body, one last hurdle remained before the Navy Yard plant could be built. The New York State Department of Environmental Conservation— an early product of the post-Earth Day environmental movement—needed to issue the permits that would be required to construct and operate the plant. And in this court—the adjudicatory hearing process—the wiles that had worked so smoothly in the political arena were distanced by at least one remove. This was the field that the lawyerly Environmental Defense Fund and Natural Resources Defense Council had built. And in it they got everything they sought. Following the same regulatory inclinations that had produced the federal Clean Air Act, they sought and got permit conditions to guarantee that the plant would be closed if specified levels of a range of airborne pollutants were exceeded. These conditions would add several millions to the cost of the plant's construction, and a couple of percentage points to its operating costs—to the profit of the waste-to-energy corporations that would supply the additional layers of air pollution control equipment. And then with an assist from the city council, they got another concession worth hundreds of millions more.

Because of a protracted series of negotiations—the new sanitation commissioner's ineffectual attempt to blunt or at least soften its budgetary impact—Local Law 19 (of 1989) took three months longer to gestate than a human embryo. When it was finished, all of the thousands of businesses and millions of inhabitants of New York City were required to separate their garbage into different piles for recycling—or be handed a summons by a gun-toting, garbage-bin-poking enforcement agent. But how many piles there would be, what would be in each of them, how often trucks would come by to pick them up, where they would take them, how the mangled materials would be processed for marketing, or who would buy them were all unanswered questions. The only specificity the law contained was the tonnage requirement—the product of the environmentalists' dissatisfaction with the city's lackadaisical response to the recycling promise they had

exacted from Steisel. If 25 percent of the city's waste stream was not recycled by 1994, the city would be subject to legal sanctions. But all the argu-
ing, pleading, and haggling stopped soon after the two primary representatives from EDF and NRDC went to Albany to pay a visit to the state conservation commissioner, who then sent a telegram to the council saying that
it would have to pass the environmentalists' version of the bill if the city was
to have any hope of getting a Navy Yard permit out of his department.

Achieving incremental change through the leveraged bargaining of a legislative or regulatory process was not, however, what every environmental
group wanted. NYPIRG went on the offensive against the mandatory recycling law sponsored by their soft-path colleagues. (It was NYPIRG who
spread the word about the conservation commissioner's threat, since it
proved that recycling would be just the first step along the road toward
incineration.) Instead of alternative legislation, NYPIRG began to shape the
kind of locally based coalition that could block any waste management
compromise that the city, its corporate allies, or the soft-path environmentalists could devise. To do this it would need to bypass the institutions
through which these matters customarily were discussed, and the media and
organizations through which environmental information typically was pur-
veyed. To take the hard path, NYPIRG would go straight to the kid on the
corner, the shopper in the mall, the homeowner at the barbecue grill.

It began one spring day in 1987. NYPIRG's toxics coordinator showed
his newest organizer into his little cubicle of an office and pointed to a map
of Staten Island hanging on the wall. Indicating Fresh Kills at its center, he
said, "there is your objective."

Just as there had been nothing really "wrong" with the *Mobro*'s contents—
though NYPIRG never admitted this, nothing was found that would have distinguished the barge's cargo from the contents of a wastebasket in any home or
made it more difficult to manage than any normal waste—there was nothing
particularly dangerous about the ash that remained on the grate after it was
incinerated. But by the time the *Mobro*'s most famous load had gone up in
smoke, NYPIRG's new toxics organizer, a graduate of the Oberlin Conserva-
tory of Music named Arthur Kell, whose full-time assignment was stopping the

Brooklyn Navy Yard project, with the help of his colleagues and hundreds of student volunteers, had made the words "toxic" and "ash" as tightly linked in the popular imagination as "orange juice" or "Love Canal."

When any solid fuel is burned, a residue composed largely of inorganic substances remains. While most of the organic compounds in refuse (paper, plastic, wood, vegetable matter) are oxidized during the combustion process (as the bonds linking their carbon, hydrogen, oxygen, and nitrogen atoms are broken by high temperature, allowing these now gaseous elements to re-combine with oxygen to produce carbon dioxide, nitrogen oxide, and water vapor), depending on the efficiency of the process some fraction—about a twentieth by weight, much less by volume—remains on the grate along with the noncombustible glass and metals that are also in the waste. In addition, in new incinerator systems, there is another kind of "ash": the solids condensed from the exhaust gases by a sprayed lime slurry that cools the hot fumes and provides an attractive surface onto which volatilized metals, acid gases, and newly synthesized organic compounds (such as, respectively, mercury, sulfur dioxide, and dioxin) can adsorb before most of the reagent particles are removed by fabric filtration (like a sneeze into a handkerchief) or electrical attraction (like dust onto a computer screen). Thus while most of the refuse's former mass escapes into the atmosphere—primarily as carbon dioxide and water vapor (adding about as much atmospheric carbon to the greenhouse effect as would burning coal or oil or the disposal of the refuse by landfilling)—the ash is the refuse that remains, purged of the biologically active ingredients that otherwise would have made it a medium for producing odors, transmitting disease, and attracting animals and insects.

The "toxicity" of ash is determined for regulatory purposes by laboratory tests that measure the amount of metals and organics that can be extracted when a sample is soaked in reagents considerably stronger than the slightly acidic rainwater likely to fall on a landfill. The concentration of heavy metals and harmful organics in "bottom ash," the material remaining on the grate, is usually less than in the fly ash on which these materials tend to be concentrated. If the two kinds of ash are combined, the concentration of metals typically is only a few times greater than the amount in normal household waste, and dioxin concentrations are generally below the level recommended by the federal government as a concentration in soil—about as high, in fact, as

A sanman hoses down an ash truck near the beginning of Moses' waste management rule.

the levels that the EPA thinks are in a typical American's fat. Fly ash that is not combined with bottom ash—because it contains all the material removed from the exhaust gases by high-efficiency air pollution control devices—contains higher amounts of metals and dioxins. The proportionately greater alkalinity of fly ash (which is made more alkaline by the addition of lime or other compounds to capture the acid gases), however, decreases the potential for most of these compounds to leach out, although it somewhat increases the solubility of hydrophilic metals such as lead.

Because the "toxic" constituents of incinerator ash are *less* likely to escape from a landfill than are the solvents and metals in raw refuse, state and federal requirements for controlling leachate from ash-only landfills are less stringent than those for refuse-only or refuse-and-ash landfills (provided that the ash passes the screening test for hazardous materials, as does the ash from all the incinerators operating in New York State).

The ash from Moses's incinerators had gone to Fresh Kills since it opened in 1948. Because ash was clearly less of a nuisance than raw refuse, Moses had in fact promised the Staten Island borough president (to whom he had "traded" Staten Island's West Shore Expressway for the right to build the landfill) that the landfill would receive only ash after 1951. But after NYPIRG's campaign on Staten Island, the decades-old accepted wisdom—as well as the contemporary analytical findings—became politically irrelevant.

No excuse for delay was too slight to suit the ends of the NYPIRG anti-incineration campaign. Arthur Kell thus won his first tactical victory with a legal maneuver that the soft path environmentalists had deemed beneath consideration. Having spared no expense on its teams of lawyer-lobbyists and other supporting players to get this far, Wheelabrator had offered to pay for a freelance administrative law judge rather than waiting in line until a hearing officer on the Environmental Conservation department's own small staff became available. Biding his time, Kell waited until the hearing process had begun, and then in the spring of 1986, on the last possible day, filed a lawsuit charging that a conflict of interest was produced by having a permit applicant pay hearing costs. His tactic was rewarded with unimagined success when an appellate court found that although an applicant's hiring of an outside lawyer when an agency's hearing officers were otherwise occupied did not in itself pose a conflict of interest, this outside lawyer (whose energy-development company was hired for technical advice both by the environmental agency and by private developers) might indeed "derive a benefit from his decision," and he was therefore disqualified.

By the time an agency adjudicator had become available and the hearing process was ready to begin again, more than a year had passed, a year during which dozens of waste-to-energy plants had been built or planned elsewhere in the country, sixteen of the state's landfills had closed (within another seven years, nine out of ten of the state's remaining landfills would be shut down), and waste disposal prices had risen steeply (quadrupling in a number of the region's cities), while meanwhile the waste-to-energy industry had lost access to important federal tax benefits, Clean Air Act amendments had been introduced to make emission standards for waste-to-energy facilities significantly more stringent, and the price provisions established by Jimmy Carter's Public Utilities Regulatory Policy Act been seriously weakened—a year, in short, in which the need for new waste management options apparently had increased while the window of opportunity for building new waste-to-energy plants had grown smaller.

When the hearing finally reconvened, the participants hunkered down in earnest. Sixteen months later, after seventy days of testimony and cross-examination, dozens of witnesses, and more than twelve thousand pages of transcript, it concluded. But while the parties waited patiently for the conservation commissioner's decision, NYPIRG's Fresh Kills strategy came to full bloom. Early in 1988, Governor Mario Cuomo began to receive a stream of letters from Staten Islanders begging him not to allow any ash to be sent to their giant landfill straddling the meadows where the Fresh Kills emptied into the Arthur Kill; at the end of November, ten thousand anti-ash signatures were stapled to a rope hung across three garbage trucks parked in front of the landfill. In the face of such unequivocal evidence of the opinions of Island voters (whose ranks were filled with a higher proportion of fellow Italian-Americans than any other portion of the state),Governor Mario Cuomo's office appeared to have little interest in what the environmental conservation agency's scientists were telling their commissioner, nor in the degree of environmental hazard that might be avoided through a significant increase in costs to the taxpayer, nor in the dampening effect this precedent might have on the development of solutions to reduce the state's dependence on landfilling raw waste.

Was it someone in the governor's office who instructed environmental commissioner Thomas Jorling to reject the city's proposal for placing the ash in a dedicated portion of the landfill that substantively met the requirements of the state's new regulations for ash disposal? In any event, the commissioner's negative ruling came as a great surprise not only to city officials, in effect sending them back to the drawing board after it had appeared that all issues of any regulatory significance had been addressed, it "surprised the hell out of everyone" on Jorling's own staff (according to one of them). But no one seemed more surprised by this second successive unexpected victory than NYPIRG's Arthur Kell, protector of the Arthur Kill, who had feared the game was almost over.

Ten thousand signatures are on the petitions roped between two garbage trucks parked in front of the Fresh Kills landfill. Arthur Kell is in the center.

Three months later (in March 1989), having devised what seemed a foolproof solution to the Arthur Kell problem—a signed agreement to send the ash to a legal landfill outside the city—the city asked Commissioner Jorling to reconvene the Navy Yard permit hearing. Wheelabrator, which several years before had become a subsidiary of Waste Management, Inc., the world's largest refuse-handling corporation, recently had signed an "air-rights" agreement with Waste Management that gave it access to a third of the parent corporation's millions of cubic yards of space in landfills across the country. All were in compliance with all local permit regulations, Wheelabrator told the parties to the hearing; any one of them therefore would be a permissible disposal site according to the new state regulations.

Kell saw the last few feet of rope slipping from his hands. He quickly went back to read the regulations again and found a phrase everyone else had apparently missed: the applicant must identify "the landfill or landfills that will receive the residue." Not "could" or "might," Kell insisted in a phone call to the judge. Two weeks later, Wheelabrator identified the landfill where the Navy Yard ash would go, the new, ash-only Fairless facility in

Falls Township, Pennsylvania. Discouraged that Wheelabrator had over-come the technical flaw he had found and proposed a facility that apparently complied fully with the state's regulations, Kell could think of nothing else to do but to go have a look at it for himself. The next Saturday morning he found Falls on a map, got into his eleven-year-old van, drove across the Verrazano-Narrows Bridge, down the expressway through the former Fresh Kills meadows, across the Arthur Kill, past the giant landfills in the New Jersey meadowlands, and across the Delaware. On the other side he passed another huge landfill, aptly named GROWS, where Waste Management piled thousands of tons of waste a day from locations up to hundreds of miles away, but could not find its little sibling, the Fairless ashfill. As he circled the spot where it was supposed to be—somewhere behind the closed gate and chain-link fence surrounding a USX steel plant—he realized that there was nothing there: it did not yet exist. Before leaving, he picked up a copy of the local paper ("one of the first things any organizer does any-where"), then drove home, not yet aware of what he had.

The next week he called up the *Bucks County Courier Times*. The recep-tionist passed him to a reporter named J. D. Mullane. Kell told Mullane that New York City was planning to send his little town a thousand tons of toxic ash every day—a twenty-ton truck-worth rumbling down the two-lane road to the steel plant every ten minutes every hour of every business day. He faxed him the hearing papers that Wheelabrator had filed, along with some information about toxic ash. Then he sat back and waited. And waited. Three weeks later, the story finally hit. The front page of the *Courier Times* announced that none of Falls Township's elected officials, who had just concluded negotiations giving Waste Management permission to build the ashfill, had ever heard of Waste Management's agreement with Wheel-abrator and New York City. Nor had any state environmental officials—who had yet to receive a final permit application for the facility. The fact that the town supervisors had approved the landfill as the place to put their own ash when their new Wheelabrator-built incinerator started operations in 1994—ash that would be indistinguishable from the Navy Yard's—did not mean that they would accept toxic ash from New York City, they hotly told Waste Management. One of the supervisors volunteered to go to New York "to tell Mayor Koch what he can do with his ash." Five days later,

Waste Management apologized for the "communication failure" and promised that it would never happen again.

With a strategic tug—one which simultaneously implied that Staten
Islanders should prefer the landfilling of raw garbage to the landfilling of ash,
and that reducing the volume of material deposited at Fresh Kills was an
insufficient cause to justify shipping New York's waste out of the city—Kell
had pulled back a lot of rope. Now it was Wheelabrator and the city who
were down to their last two hopes—either that the state environmental
commissioner would reconsider the city's request to use a section of Fresh
Kills that had not received fresh refuse for years, and under which lay a
leachate-inhibiting layer of glacial till and clay (new borings were being
done to support the city engineers' claim that there were at least ten feet of
clay under the whole area), or that the commissioner would grant a variance
from the requirement that the city provide a signed commitment letter from
a specified landfill (a letter that would no doubt be expensive to obtain)
before knowing whether he was even going to grant the facility a permit in
the first place.

In April, the results of the new borings were revealed: the bed of clay
which on the basis of previous borings taken only around the area's perimeter was predicted to be between ten and sixty feet thick across the site, on
closer examination, had "lenses" where the clay was only a few feet deep.
Only one hope now remained—a "conditional" permit. But since they had
been successful in demonstrating that the project complied with all other
regulatory requirements, city officials remained hopeful that the commissioner would allow the small exception from the rules that they sought, and
allow them to move ahead to seek financing for the project before they had
purchased a commitment to provide ashfill capacity. Again Commissioner
Jorling took his time making up his mind, and again he waited until the
election was safely past before announcing his decision. He would not, he
said, grant a variance from the requirement that the city purchase a commitment letter up front. Soon thereafter his agency would eliminate this
requirement for any other project, but by then it would be too late to have
any bearing on the case of the proposed Brooklyn Navy Yard incinerator.

All but single-handedly, Arthur Kell had made common currency the
magical belief that landfilled ash is more dangerous than raw garbage and

made politically correct the notion that exporting ash outside the city was not an acceptable alternative. Accepting these premises left no logical alternative but to recycle everything the city's 7.4 million citizens threw away. Despite the fact than no community in the country—from the smallest New Age commune in California to the most environmentally conscious suburb of Massachusetts—had ever managed to a recycle more than a third of its refuse, despite the fact that the softs thought the 25 percent target in their mandatory recycling law near the limit of what was realistically achievable for New York, NYPIRG's incinerator opponents unrolled their Panglossian new campaign slogan: "Total Recycling." Though Barry Commoner might have been able to support such a slogan with straight-faced enthusiasm, it left between the softs and the hards a distinct frost. It seemed that only an intellectual miracle could pull the distended wings of New York's environmental movement together.

CHAPTER 12

Waste Management

Ronald Reagan's inauguration as the country's fortieth president gave new impetus and direction to the national environmental movement. Basking in the cozy glow of the Carter administration's demonstrated concern not just for energy efficiency but for a whole range of renewable resources, the membership of the nation's leading environmental groups had grown somewhat complacent. But despite the hard-to-hate white-hatted actor at the center of the administration, there were around him more than enough bad guys to put a good, stiff sense of moral outrage back into the environmental movement. Interior Secretary James Watt, of course, in his seeming eagerness to strip federal lands of resources, renewable or not, who never met an oilman he did not like, who confessed to a belief in the polluting propensities of trees, was Villain Number One. But there were also the EPA's administrator, Anne Gorsuch Burford, the wicked step-mother who presided with frosty glee over the evisceration and dismembering of her own agency, and Rita LaValle, whose appetite for lunches with corporate polluters seemed boundless. Together, they were like a refreshing splash of cold water on a hive of sleeping bees. Contributions from NRDC members shot up by 54 percent in 1981, EDF's members gave 20 percent more. The surge continued over the following three years, too, as NRDC's membership increased by 25 percent (to fifty thousand) and its budget by another 44 percent (to 6.5 million dollars), while EDF's budget also went up by an additional 25 percent (to 3.5 million dollars).

Under the unifying influence of a common enemy, the tactics of the newly fortified environmental groups also changed. Putting aside the adversarial sectarian approaches of its formative years, the environmental movement entered a second phase characterized by greater pragmatism and broader coordination between its rivalrous denominations. With their greater strength and more influential role came a moderation in rhetoric, and a heightened focus on market mechanisms and incentives. Rather than campaigning against corporations, as Ralph Nader had done, or trying to "break [their] grip," as Barry Commoner had urged, the movement's current goal seemed simply to be producing laws and regulations that would "level the playing field" between the corporate exploitation of "virgin" and "secondary" resources. Rather than replacing corporate control with "social governance of the systems of production," the shared goal now appeared to be "re-engineering the corporation" and "reinventing government" to encourage investment in "sustainable" modes of production. And if an outgrowth of this was that more control became concentrated in fewer corporate hands—if, for instance, the new recycling laws and landfill regulations were helping a handful of strong-armed garbage-hauling firms to take over most of the nation's "recycling infrastructure" along with most of its landfills, just as they had already begun to gobble up most of the country's municipal collection forces and mom-and-pop carters—no one seemed to care.

A third phase of the national environmental movement (one in which activists would begin trying to fuse environmental justice and economic development) was already aborning by the time David Dinkins—the candidate who counted Barry Commoner among his close advisers and who had distinguished himself from the rest of the Democratic pack by pledging a moratorium on Norman Steisel's proposed Brooklyn Navy Yard incinerator—was elected mayor of New York City in 1989. Despite Dinkins's moratorium pledge, one of his first actions as mayor-elect was to delight his Wall Street supporters (while distressing many environmentalists) by announcing that Norman Steisel, of the Lazard Frères bond firm, who in his private-sector life had become perhaps the country's premier incineration lobbyist, would be his first-deputy mayor. What Jim Watt was to the national environmental movement Norman Steisel, waste-to-energy-industry operative, quickly became for New York City's environmental industry. He was a convenient solution to the Reaganesque problem of a soft and hard-to-hate chief executive—straight from central casting as a Thomas Nast vision of a 1990s municipal bureaucrat, the snarling, cigar-smoke-blowing personification of the Dark Side of the Force.

Steisel lost little time in convincing the leaders of the city's environmental

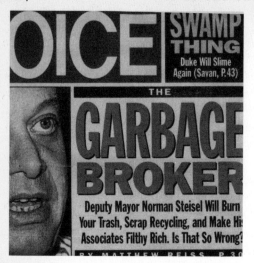

OICE **SWAMP THING** Duke Will Slime Again (Savan, P.43)

THE **GARBAGE BROKER**

Deputy Mayor Norman Steisel Will Burn Your Trash, Scrap Recycling, and Make His Associates Filthy Rich. Is That So Wrong?

groups that their suspicions had been well-founded. As the city's chief operating officer he had a great deal more to worry about than the performance of his old department, and yet sanitation's record under his successor, Brendan Sexton (who was still in office), rankled like a personal affront. The magnificent productivity gains Steisel had made with the two-man truck had been all but eradicated under the clumsy shackles Local Law 19 had thrown on the system. Instead of one productive truck rumbling down the street to pick up the waste, there were now three—a second to pick up newspapers and cardboard and a third for bottles and cans. With the local economy in a nosedive from Wall Street's recession, the incoming administration's first task was to shave an additional four hundred million dollars from the city's budget for the remaining six months of the fiscal year and find a way to close a billion-dollar budget gap for the coming fiscal year.Steisel found that the Department of Sanitation was spending over a hundred million dollars a year (a 10 percent increase over his old budget) just to recycle a paltry 6 percent of the city's waste. And to add insult to injury, some of the new garages he had built and equipped with modern furnishings, including televisions and exercise equipment, were being used as recreation halls, since—with three trucks running in the place of one—collection workers in districts with high recycling levels now finished their routes in just half a day. The obvious answer to this problem was to increase the length of collection routes to make up for the decreased tonnage they were collecting, but Sexton (whose father was a well-known union leader) had precluded this possibility by agreeing to a union contract that set a "floor" on the number of "truck shifts" that could be assigned to the collection of nonrecyclable refuse—effectively dictating that the number of refuse routes could only go up, never down, no matter how much waste was recycled.

Sexton had to go. To replace him, Steisel chose Steven M. Polan, who, as counsel to the Metropolitan Transportation Authority, had proved his skills as a tough labor negotiator. But when he came on board, the new sanitation commissioner found that he and his boss had very different views about how best to reach their mutual goal—the route extensions that might help to achieve the economic recycling rationality that was the soft-path environmentalists' objective.

In Polan's view, the most effective threat with which to chasten the union was the specter of privatization. Since the sanitation department's creation in 1881, New York City's refuse collectors—like most of those elsewhere around the country—had always been public employees. But even before the wave of governmental "reinvention" that swept the country in the wake of the 1987 stock market downturn, cities everywhere had begun experimenting with the benefits of "outsourcing" traditionally municipal functions. By 1990, two out of three American cities were using private sector employees to pick up the trash. In most of these cities, local governments were saving money. The threat of a little free-market competition, Polan reasoned—not for the whole city, of course, but perhaps for the collection of recyclable materials in some of the city's fifty-nine sanitation districts—might be just the way to get the union to be a bit more flexible.

But Steisel (whose own boss had been elected with active union support) preferred an approach that (though less obviously a threat to union hegemony) was even blunter. If the Sanitation Workers' Union would not agree to fewer collection routes, he would not privatize recycling collections: he would simply abolish them. Since NRDC (joined by two council members) had already filed a lawsuit charging that the city had violated the City Council's mandatory recycling law, Steisel's approach had the corollary benefit of giving the council a pretty fair idea of what he thought of their recycling law, and of how many concessions they should be prepared to extract from him in their ongoing efforts to strengthen it. And so, despite Polan's arguments—among them, the certainty that Conservation Commissioner Jorling would never release a permit to build Steisel's Navy Yard incinerator if the recycling law Jorling so admired was so conspicuously flaunted—the preliminary budget Steisel submitted for the council's review in May 1990, contained no funding at all for recycling for the fiscal year that began on the first of July.

As much as he had succeeded in raising the sanitation department's morale in his prior post, Steisel's new strategy lowered it. Within weeks, Polan had received the resignations of the first half-dozen analysts, planners, and managers on his formerly enthusiastic recycling staff[37] (the beginning of the brain drain that by the end of 1995 would have sucked thirty civilian recyclers from their jobs), and he had found himself having to address the tearful entreaties of their colleagues who remained. The effect on Polan's own morale was almost as devastating, since his goal had been to replicate for the recycling system the historic productivity gains Steisel had achieved on the garbage side. But the inflammatory effect on public opinion was ultimately the most significant of all. Citizens famous and obscure, all of whom believed (along with the editorialists who were misled to the same conclusion) that the city's *budget* problems were the reason the recycling program was about to end, made clear, as did the Christos of the West Village, future wrappers of the Reichstag, that they were "outraged!" Jerry Stiller and Anne Meara, the Upper West Side husband-and-wife comedy team, were not amused ("I [they wrote] know we are in a budget crisis, but expanding, rather than cutting, the city's recycling program would actually save a considerable amount of money."). Marian Heiskell, long influential in public life through her close relationship with the *New York Times,* told Steisel ("Dear Norman") "I cannot believe the rumor that the recycling program is about to be eliminated, but so many people are saying this that I am writing to urge you to help and change your mind." ("As always, Marian")

But even more dramatic was the galvanizing, fusionating effect the elimination of the recycling budget had on the city's warring environmentalists, who suddenly stood together, hard and soft on the steps of City Hall, arm-in-arm—shades of Eddie Bernays—with some of the city's most glamorous

Standing on City Hall's steps between Barry Commoner and Arthur Kell, actress Susan Sarandon holds up a giant postcard to Mayor Dinkins.

celebrities. Organizer Arthur Kell next to actress Susan Sarandon. Defender of the common man, Barry Commoner, next to Superman, Christopher Reeve. It was a twentieth-century equivalent of the fusion meetings once held by the sanitary reformers to waves of organ music and stamping feet in Cooper Union's Great Hall. But there was an important difference. The 1881 rallies had combined Republicans and Democrats, social workers and captains of industry, but everyone wore—or might as well have—the same top hats and tails, and white ties that matched their Caucasian complexions. On City Hall's steps not everyone wore a tie; many wore sneakers. And, reflecting the new slogan organizers everywhere were beginning to use— "environmental racism"—not all the complexions were Caucasian.

The historic coalition brought to life by Steisel's clumsy attempt to tame the sanitation union got a huge infusion of androgens the day Steve Polan held an exclusive interview with the *New York Times* that was meant (he later explained) to revivify his recycling program. If the coalition between the feuding environmentalists was an attempt from outside the administration's walls to rescue the recycling budget, Polan's exclusive interview was the work of the sapper within. But the charge backfired.

Watching from a safe distance (I was out of town on vacation), I had more than a passing interest in the page-one headline. An indirect result of the long-running brawl that the distended permit-hearing process for the Brooklyn Navy Yard incinerator had been was a state law requiring every locality to develop a long-term plan for managing all of the wastes generated within its borders. Without such a plan, adopted by the governing body of the locality and approved by the state department of environmental conservation, no permit could be granted for any type of waste management facility. As the director of policy planning for the Department of Sanitation, preparing this plan was my responsibility. The complexities of the enterprise were significant. The law specified that the plan had to provide for every type of waste generated over the next twenty years, reduce the amount of waste produced, and recycle as much waste as would be economically and environmentally practicable. Means were to be devised to recover energy from wastes that it was not feasible to "prevent" or recycle, and adequate landfill capacity was to be provided for wastes that could not be managed by any other means.

The problem before us was like assembling a three-dimensional jigsaw puzzle, in which one dimension represented the disparate waste materials generated by the many different sectors of New York City, the second the various interrelated technologies for collecting, transporting, processing, and disposing of these materials, and the third the economic and environmental effects of these alternative interconnected collection and processing and disposal systems.

Despite the howls of protest Robert Moses' operations often aroused—when the putrefying organics he dropped off the shore of Jamaica Bay produced enough rotten-egg-smelling sulfur dioxide to blacken the lead paint on nearby houses, or when the garbage he dropped on Marine Park, Staten Island, fed rat packs that terrified whole neighborhoods—Moses had it easy. If your trucks just dump into the water (perhaps after taking the precaution of hanging a chicken-wire screen offshore to keep the largest chunks from floating away), or into an incinerator pit, it does not much matter what the load is composed of, or how much it weighs: witness the exchange between the sanitation commissioner and his aides the day the last ceremonial barge-fuls of New York garbage were hauled off to sea in 1934.

> . . . [A] tugboat, hauling the three dumpers which had been singled out for this distinction, nosed laboriously upstream against the current. The load was headed upstream, so that it could turn and pass the commissioners en route for the high seas. No one paid any attention to the barges on their trip up the river. In fact some of the departmental officials pretended not to see them. But a half hour later when the garbage came swiftly downstream on the breast of the current, cameras clicked and there was a great waving of hats and hands.
>
> 'That load is rich in garbage,' Major Edward Bromberger, Deputy Commissioner, observed admiringly.
>
> 'Why, it looks rich in rubbish to me,' interjected Colonel H. C. Eastman, superintendent in charge of final disposition.
>
> 'The center dumper,' ruled Commissioner Hammond, 'seems to contain more ashes than anything else. In fact, I'd say there were a hell of a lot of ashes.'"

But to recover as cheaply and efficiently as possible specific materials to be made into new newspapers, bottles and cans, or plastic bags, you need to know more about the stuff you are starting with.

To figure out how best to collect, transport, process, and market the materials in our waste we needed to know, for example, how much of the paper in the residential waste stream was newspaper, how much was magazines, how much cardboard, paper bags, writing paper, and junk mail. We needed to know how refuse collections varied with the seasons; whether refuse from rich and poor neighborhoods, from high-rises and single-family houses, was different; whether there was enough metal and glass in particular types of private carter routes to justify collecting these materials separately. To answer these questions, we deployed teams of dozens of sorters over the course of a year to weigh each item in over three hundred seventy-five tons of waste collected from samples taken to represent the city's range of income classes and housing types, to carefully sort the "sharps" and "pathological" materials from the other ingredients of hospital waste, and to chase a carefully selected sample of green private carters' trucks on their midnight routes to weigh the bags they picked up at each stop.

Knowing what was in the refuse, and where it came from (and projecting how those variables were likely to change over time as population profiles shifted and production systems evolved) was just the first step. We also needed to know which discarded materials were marketable, in what form, to whom, and at what price, in order to assess the relative feasibility of alternative collection and processing systems. Balancing the associated costs of collecting and processing these materials, the effects on people's willingness to recycle and on the ultimate marketability of the material, into how many piles should the refuse be sorted? How many different trucks should be used to pick it up? What were the most effective combinations of processing equipment? Was there reliable equipment capable of opening plastic garbage bags filled with recyclable materials without damaging these materials, or would other types of containers need to be used? Balancing transportation costs, the capital and operating costs of variously sized processing facilities, the availability of suitably zoned parcels of land, and the associated impacts of traffic, noise, and air emissions, how many processing facilities should there be, and where might they be located? Could reliable, cost-effective, environmentally acceptable composting facilities operate in New York City? How much incineration capacity would be required for wastes that could not be recycled or composted? Would it be cost-effective to upgrade the city's three remaining Moses-era incinerators so that the heat they produced could be captured as usable energy, and so that they would comply with current regulatory standards? How many more years of disposal capacity could be expected from the Fresh Kills landfill, at what cost, and with what effects on the environment? What landfill capacity existed outside the city, how much would it cost to transport waste to those locations, and what would be the likely disposal costs and the associated environmental impacts? How much new landfill capacity was likely to be developed in the United States, at what distances from New York City? What combinations of waste prevention, recycling, composting, incineration, and landfilling—for which specific materials from which specific waste generating sectors—would provide the least overall cost to the city's environment and economy?

Naturally, this was an iterative process. It was also a very public one. On one level, it was hard enough to coordinate the mutually suspicious bureaus of the sprawling sanitation department, whose collection people and disposal people had never before agreed even about how much waste had been picked up and disposed of over any given period of time. Hammering out agreements between the various other agencies who were responsible for pieces of the problem—the Department of Environmental Protection (responsible for sludge disposal); the Health and Hospitals Corporation (medical waste); the other agencies that would have a role in how the city's waste-management system would be operated (the Department of City Planning; Office of Operations; the Budget Office; the Corporation Counsel; the Department of Ports & Trade)—added to the challenge. And then there were the myriad publics.

As we had assembled intra- and interagency working groups to sort out differences of opinion on tonnage, on demographic and economic projections, on environmental impacts, on logistical feasibility—and on how the technical expertise to perform each phase of the interrelated analyses should be procured and managed, and how the overall planning process should be structured—we (Jim Meyer and I)★ also convened a public committee composed of representatives of community boards, elected officials, environmental groups, civic groups, and business and real estate interests to advise us.

Given our respective histories, we entered the process with widely varying perspectives. NYPIRG's position was that "total recycling" made unnecessary any consideration of incineration or landfilling. Barry Commoner's position was not much different—he now claimed (with mystifying precision, based on a fourteen-week sample of ninety families in East Hampton) that 84.4 percent of the city's wastes could be recycled. EDF and NRDC were intent on establishing that enough of the waste stream could be recycled—perhaps a third—to allow offsetting economies in the collection and disposal of the remaining refuse. The business interests in the room were concerned with cutting costs. Clearly, the only way to forge a working consensus from such a group—an essential prerequisite if the plan was to survive the political and regulatory approval process ahead—not to mention

---

★As a bureaucratic technicality, Meyer was my deputy; substantively he was an equal partner in the enterprise.

the inevitable legal challenges—was to conduct our analyses in as transparent a fashion as possible, allowing everyone the opportunity to review and comment on each stage of preliminary results as they were produced, and allowing everyone a role in designing the next iteration of the system we would ultimately propose.

To accomplish this, we met for a morning every other week to review the results of the preceding two weeks' effort and to shape the work that would follow. Barry Commoner called this fishbowl process "a model of how a problem as serious and complex as trash disposal should be evaluated and solved." It produced, he said, "a common understanding of the rich store of data generated by the DOS [Department of Sanitation's] study—largely overcoming the differences that originally separated us. This is one of the great virtues of the DOS study; it has enabled all of us to test our opinions against the facts—which have a way of clearing up differences of opinion." And indeed, we were close to forging an agreement—NYPIRG alone was on the sidelines—as to how the city's wastes should be managed in the years ahead, about how much could be recycled and how this degree of recycling could be accomplished most effectively, that composting should be tested, that a significant portion of the waste should be incinerated, and that the city should take advantage of abundant landfill capacity outside the five boroughs through the use of barge and rail transfer systems while disposal prices were cheap in order to maximize the life of the Fresh Kills landfill, whose decades'-worth of remaining capacity were the city's only assurance of being able to control the disposal of the wastes that could only be landfilled.

This was the fragile entente that Polan's exclusive interview, played on the first page of the *Times*, above the fold, between historic events in the Soviet Union and South Africa—"NEW INCINERATORS TERMED ESSENTIAL. Recycling Called Inadequate." "68 percent" of the city's trash, according to "the administration," will "have to" be burned—sent to instant oblivion with all the rollicking force "of a good explosion.

There was jubilation the next morning at NYPIRG headquarters. Within an hour, dozens of youthful protestors had been assembled to demonstrate in front of the state office building where Polan was about to testify before a joint state legislative commission. Though Polan's testimony provided a more sober, less sensational account of the plan's preliminary findings, the second day's news coverage only magnified the effects of the first's. A joint statement issued by Barry Commoner, NYPIRG, EDF, NRDC, and other groups ("Contact: Barry Commoner") said that Polan's announcement "makes a mockery of the orderly process that the Department itself established to deal with the problem," and called it "a disrespectful affront to the deeply concerned citizens who have participated in the process." To a *Newsday* reporter Commoner was more succinct. "We were dissed," he said. The next day, every member of the advisory group resigned. It may well have been the first unanimous action ever taken by every major environmental group in the city.

Eddie Bernays would have been delighted with the slogan the now united environmentalists devised to sell the plan they produced to counter what Polan had hypostatized as "the administration's plan": RECYCLE FIRST. In a stroke of advertising genius as great as Dreamland or Metropolitan By-Products, it accurately and convincingly encapsulated the "counterplan's" central message: that the city should empirically establish the degree to which waste reduction, recycling, and composting programs could absorb its wastes before making the capital and political commitments necessary to build incineration plants. Apart from the schedule for building incinerators, the design of the plan embodied in Recycle First—the materials to be recycled and composted, the collection system, the processing network—was in every essential feature the same as the one my colleagues and I had developed in consultation with these groups. To sell it, NYPIRG organized "The Campaign for Recycle First," a door-to-door, sidewalk-tabling, community-meeting, demonstrating, radio-and-print-ad blitzkrieg that involved thousands of volunteer canvassers, tens of thousands of meeting participants, and film star spokespersons—no doubt the biggest grassroots movement focused on an environmental issue in the city's history.

Though Polan succeeded (if that was his intent) in forcing the mayor to restore his recycling budget while at the same time knocking him off the fence about incineration, he did not stick around long to enjoy the fruits of his effort. Even before the counterplan campaign was in full swing, he

Thirty-four councilmembers said they would not approve the administration's waste management plan.

resigned to be replaced by another Steisel first, the first woman—Emily Lloyd—ever to head a major New York City uniformed agency. But instead of taking advantage of her newcomer status to fashion a modified position that might have found favor with every environmental and civic activist in the city—their sudden unanimity offering an historic opportunity to produce an unshakeable political consensus behind a well-defined strategy to reduce reliance on the Fresh Kills landfill—she instead chose to make the immediate advance of "Norman Steisel's" Navy Yard incinerator the one irreducible element in her plan.

The former members of the advisory group lost no time, after Lloyd and the mayor had declined their requests for support, in enlisting the aid of the moribund city council—the only governing body left in the city after the dissolution of the Board of Estimate—in ratifying their counterplan. Though NYPIRG, at the helm, was deeply skeptical of the council's influence (one of its own members, after all, had been the first to observe that the defining difference between the council and a rubber stamp is that the latter leaves an impression), they "gave" (NYPIRG's chief organizer claimed) Walter McCaffrey, a droopy-mustached member from Queens whom they considered "the best politician in the council" a bill authorizing the council to veto any waste management plan its members did not like. (At the beginning, it appeared that NYPIRG's confidence in McCaffrey was well-placed, for soon afterwards he appeared on a platform with Barry Commoner, and, updating Patrick Henry's stirring call to arms against an earlier tyranny, thundered, "We have a choice: death or recycling.") After the bill passed, thirty-four of the council's fifty-one members stood on the steps of City Hall to announce that they would never approve the administration's plan. Some called it the city council's proudest moment.

But despite the fervor of its thousands of doorbell-ringing recruits (I got my own bell rung, as Emily Lloyd and Norman Steisel did, too), blowing holes in the ranks of the children's crusade was not as difficult as a count of relative numbers alone might have suggested. Following behind the contact troops assembled and funded by Waste Management, the refuse-industry behemoth that had sucked Wheelabrator-Frye into its giant maw, the whole "pro-growth coalition" (as NYPIRG's chief organizer characterized it with a wan smile)—"developers, unions, folks who generate income from consulting, [and] the capital side" leapt into the fray to help the Dinkins administration's own persuasion team. What followed was a display of wheedling, threatening, and horse trading perhaps unseen since the days of Boss Tweed's Black Horse cavalry. Ironically, Walter McCaffrey's resolve was among the first to go. After he was promised the closure of the Moses-built incinerator in his district (which the sanitation department had just spent twenty-five million dollars renovating) he switched sides with scarcely a look back. With little further ado, the rest of the Queens delegation followed.

From an economic perspective—not to mention the cost to any hope of salvaging any pretense of intellectual credibility the plan might have retained—the concessions made to get the Staten Islanders on board were pretty expensive, but there was nothing very elaborate about the stratagem employed. Lloyd simply promised not to put any ash from the Navy Yard plant at Fresh Kills—even though the city had already designed a regulatorily compliant lined "monofill" for a "virgin" section of the fill and Conservation

Commissioner Tom Jorling's department had already certified the permit application for it. The move reflected a studied ignorance of the costs and vulnerabilities associated with establishing ash-disposal contracts that Arthur Kell's successful search-and-destroy mission had been only the first to prove. (On September 6, 1986—six months before the *Mobro*—the *Khian Sea* had sailed from the Port of Philadelphia with a load of that city's incinerator ash in a Lowell Harrelson-like scheme for building a reef that Bahamian developers could put a resort on. Two years and three months later, after a voyage that made the *Mobro*'s appear insignificant—but which uncannily seemed to recapitulate many parts of it, including gunboat encounters with the navies of several nations,—after having changed its name successively to *Felicia, Pelicano,* and *San Antonio,* it turned up empty in Singapore. Four years later its owners were convicted of dumping the load in the Indian Ocean, thus ending a sort of modern Grecian tragedy in which Greenpeace played the Arthur Kell/chorus role.) And so the two votes Lloyd thus picked up made the cost of her prime objective, the Navy Yard incinerator, truly unknowable.

To capture a couple of Brooklyn votes, Lloyd promised to close the city's second-to-last incinerator (thus erasing two-thirds of the capacity her three-thousand-ton proposal would create). She promised another Brooklynite that a prime site in his district would never, through the end of time, be used for any type of waste management facility. A councilman on the Rockaway Peninsula was promised that the trauma center in his local hospital would not close, that a development project he favored would be approved, and, for good measure, that some boulders that had been dumped illegally on the shore of his cooperative's beachfront would be hauled away.

Council Speaker Peter Vallone also pitched in. To counter the claim that incinerators killed (an assertion repeated in many of the fifteen thousand letters that NYPIRG got sent to the speaker's office), Vallone solemnly declared from editorial page and podium that "every car is an incinerator." Money from his political action account flowed to the councilmembers who joined his team, along with promises of more support for their coming campaigns; those who did not were told to expect nothing.

And race, never far from the stage of New York politics, played its usual supporting role. Never forgetting that the city's first African-American mayor was elected by a coalition he called a "gorgeous mosaic"—and that his margin of victory had come from mixed ethnic and minority neighborhoods like those surrounding the Brooklyn Navy Yard (neighborhoods where his campaign moratorium promise had been understood as an anti-incinerator commitment)—NYPIRG organizers picked these (along with Speaker Vallone's home district) as their first targets. They found that Alinsky was right: talking about pollution was a good way to get former enemies to join hands. From their promptings came a new addition to the city's roster of environmental organizations, most of whom, like EDF and NRDC, had been homogeneously white. Called the Community Alliance for the Environment (or, more cozily, CAFÉ), its mission was uniting the formerly feuding Hispanics and Hasids in Williamsburg, along with African-Americans from nearby Fort Greene. Meanwhile, asserting that environmental racism had already caused disproportionate harm from the effects of pollution, some councilmembers from central Brooklyn (one of whom, courting her fellows' fury, was white) suggested that African-American incinerator supporters were traitors to their race. Declaring himself outraged by this argument, the mayor himself used the opposite tack, demanding ethnic solidarity of his African-American supporters to show the "boys downtown" that one of their own could do the tough work of governing.

The suspense continued to the last moment. The council committee hearing scheduled to begin at 10 AM the day of the deadline for the waste plan vote (a date the council had legislatively imposed on itself to avoid Conservation Commissioner Jorling's threat of withholding the state's reimbursement of a couple of the millions the plan had cost) finally began at 1 AM the next morning. The morning, afternoon, and evening had been consumed with last-minute threats and deals. The mayor agreed that the city would go back to the drawing board—and bring everything back before the council—before any incinerator other than the Navy Yard plant could ever be built. Lloyd agreed that Wheelabrator would not be allowed to sell bonds for the Navy Yard incinerator until a wide range of recyclable materials was being collected everywhere in the city. She also dropped six million more dollars through the meter of near-term city budget commitments, and annual millions more thereafter (in addition to the eight million that had been dropped in the previous weeks of negotiations), including four million to run the same pilot program in every borough to test the feasibility of recycling things from the mixed garbage pulled out of regular collection trucks (as the trimmers beneath the piers and the children at Barren Island had done a hundred years earlier). As the night wore on, councilmembers were seen huddling one-on-one with one deputy mayor or another in a corner, or slipping down to Norman Steisel's intimate office (ignoring the NYPIRG youth waving their placards and gas masks and chanting "Shame, shame!" and "We won't forget" loudly enough to bring twenty policemen running to quell the disturbance).

Shortly after dawn, when the votes were finally cast, only fifteen exemplars of "the new, independent council" had escaped the mayor's grasp. Of these, ironically, the only one of the original ringleaders who still held out was Williamsburg's representative, former Wheelabrator lobbyist Kenny Fisher. As the birds outside in City Hall park began to chirp, the rumpled deputy mayor for politics sat sprawled, exhausted, on the nearly empty council floor, amidst heaps of crumpled placards, empty takeout containers, and other emblematic remains of the recent battle, grinning like a cheshire cat.

CHAPTER 13

Hauling Biomass

The victory was Pyrrhic.

It was not the reason that David Dinkins lost his campaign for re-election to his old rival, Rudy Giuliani—his ineffectual management of the racially charged aftermath of a hit-and-run accident in Crown Heights, Brooklyn was generally considered the most decisive issue—but neither did it help. Once in office, Giuliani lost no time in dismantling the house of cards that had been slapped together in the hectic rush to buy off the City Council ("Clean, Courageous Politics," the *Times* had called it). In the new mayor's first executive budget, delivered to the City Council a month after his entry into office, few of the promises exacted in the final hours of the waste plan showdown ("one of the greatest victories this city has seen in a long time," David Dinkins had called it) remained. Gone were the millions that were to have been handed to the borough presidents to hire "public education coordinators" to exhort the citizenry to greater levels of recycling, to test the recycling of material from mixed-waste garbage trucks in all five boroughs, and to expand the advertising campaigns designed to prevent waste. Gone, too, were more important capital-budget commitments, such as the promise to build a pilot facility to compost food waste collected from institutional kitchens, and to build six materials-recovery plants to process the recyclable materials that were supposed to have been collected. Not that it much mattered any more: by the time the budget was finalized in June the basic recycling-collection budget itself had been cut, none of the additional materials identified in the waste management plan for recycling were being collected, and collection frequency had been reduced from an already lean once a week to twice a month.

Nor did the now infamous incinerator itself fare much better. Despite the pledge Emily Lloyd had made about waiting to build the Navy Yard plant until her department was running a full-scale recycling program everywhere in the city, just four days after the all-night fight she filed papers with Tom Jorling's Conservation Department to identify a landfill in Virginia as the recipient of its ash and asked that the permit hearing again be reopened. As he had before, Arthur Kell took a keen interest in the proceedings. His first observation was that Lloyd's initial contact with Jorling's department—a telephone call to the administrative law judge—violated the rules governing ex parte contacts between applicants and judges. After Lloyd apologized and promised not to do it again, Jorling agreed to let the hearing process proceed, but then committed a protocol breach of his own by announcing that he would close the hearing record and make the final permit decision himself (rather than, as usual, allowing the judge assigned to the case make a determination)—nor would he allow the customary opportunity to appeal his ruling—in order to meet a deadline imposed by recent amendments to the Clean Air Act. If the permit were not granted before the deadline (then just six weeks away), the city would be required to demonstrate that it had purchased or otherwise produced greater reductions in emissions of nitrogen dioxides than the Navy Yard incinerator itself would produce—a task that Jorling's staff believed impossible because of the paucity of such sources in the downstate region.

Kell, of course, was not about to let Jorling's legerdemain pass unchallenged. With his protegé, CAFÉ, he filed for a preliminary injunction on the grounds of bias. Jorling quickly backed down, but then announced that, on second thought, the deadline was irrelevant because the permit application had been filed six and a half years before, and the new rule applied only to new proceedings. Jorling stuck to this interpretation as the hearing reconvened once again, despite compelling arguments to the contrary from each of the environmental groups' attorneys, until, the following Fourth of July weekend, the state legislature passed a bill that explicitly revoked the exemption on which Jorling's excuse was based. But while it appeared to kill the Navy Yard incinerator with one hand, the legislature (in a last-minute compromise passed in the assembly after midnight and in the senate a few hours later) gave the plant one last loophole to squeak through: the city, it said, could use in its calculation of emissions credits the apartment house incinerators that, under pressure from NRDC, it had recently ordered closed, as well as the two Moses incinerators it had given away for solid waste management plan votes.

As if these difficulties were not enough, the course of the reopened permit proceedings was complicated further by the fortuitous discovery—just as the judge had decided once again to bring the hearing to a close on a slow news day (Christmas 1992)—that the bones of Revolutionary War heroes might be below the incinerator's intended foundation. Emily Lloyd cleared this new hurdle by pointing out that this possibility had already been identified in the environmental analysis for the project and promised to conduct additional field testing before the start of construction. But no sooner had she thus dashed project opponents' hopes for the same sort of delays that had recently affected Manhattan's new Federal Building when an African-American burial ground had been discovered there, than Arthur Kell was handed a better weapon by an anonymous source in Jorling's department.

The new issue was a leaked internal report about "toxics" beneath the site. When Kell set to work on it, unexpected good fortune once again came his way. It seemed that the sanitation department had found traces of PCBs and fuel oil in the site's soil—as they are almost everywhere along the city's shoreline—but had neglected to mention this discovery to the DEC. Kell's anonymous source had presented him with the politically delightful spectacle of a seemingly purposeful cover-up. Though the sanitation department had grounds to consider the findings insignificant—the concentrations, after all, were scarcely unusual, and cleaning the site would be the first step in preparing for construction (the purpose of the soil samples had in fact been to estimate those costs in advance)—the "scandal" led to a full-scale Department-of-Investigation investigation, got the site added to the state's list of Superfund hazardous waste sites, and formally put the incinerator project on hold until such time as negotiations between the city and state on how to clean up the site might one day be completed.

But the project's prior lack of progress (despite the debilitatingly expensive compromises that had been made in its sole behalf as the council's debate on the waste management plan drew to a close) paled to insignificance once the new mayor was in office. Despite his tough talk in his unsuccessful election campaign four years before, Rudy Giuliani seemed to have decided that the incinerator was a political liability he would just as soon not assume. After some mild initial statements that appeared to suggest that he might one day consider building it, his lack of stomach for any fight on behalf of incineration became increasingly apparent as first he agreed to close the city's last remaining incinerator, then agreed to prepare a new environmental impact statement before taking any further steps to proceed with the Navy Yard project, then deleted funding for its construction in the 1996 capital budget, delaying the appropriation until 1998, and then, on further thought, to 1999.

This was where things stood when one late winter day in 1996 Borough President Guy Molinari of Staten Island walked into City Hall. Molinari had been one of Giuliani's earliest supporters, but relations between the two had been severely frayed since the Republican mayor had supported Democrat Mario Cuomo's re-election for governor instead of former Hempstead supervisor Al D'Amato's candidate, state Senator George Pataki of Peekskill.

Guy Molinari was the pivot man in a three-generational vendetta against the Fresh Kills landfill. His father, "Fighting Bob," the one-term Democrat-turned-Republican assemblyman, had fought against the landfill since before its opening in 1948 (even though his real estate company, like his son's real estate law practice, presumably benefited from the boom brought by Moses's Verrazano-Narrows Bridge, which in turn was made possible in part by the Fresh Kills landfill). Guy's daughter, Susan (sometimes referred to, in Staten Island Republican circles, as "Guy's Doll"), had taken her fight against the landfill from the City Council, where she had held hearings about its odors, to Congress, where her most recent coup had been securing 1.25 million dollars to produce a study of its health impacts. But Guy himself, a mercurial former Marine with a reputation as a loose-lipped cannon, had carried the fight longer and further than either of his worthy kin.

Still, until recently, even Guy Molinari had not dared hope for an end to the Fresh Kills landfill. But now that George Pataki had been elected governor (another candidate who owed his margin of victory to the Republican voters of New York City's smallest borough)—and Republicans simultaneously occupied Staten Island's Borough Hall, New York's City Hall, and Albany's Governor's Mansion—it seemed that finally the stars might be favorably enough aligned to arrest the further expansion of the largest man-made object on the planet.

Only those in the room that day know what they said, and they are not telling. But the idea of closing Fresh Kills by a fixed date somehow must have come up (perhaps it was coincidence that, because of term limits, the day would be Rudy Giuliani's last in office), because not long afterwards the rumor spread that a deal had been cut, and, curiously, bills in the City Council and in Albany—the kind of bills that normally would have drawn immediate opposition from the chief executive of New York City, which called for the closure, in one fell, unplanned swoop, of the facility that absorbed nearly 40 percent of all the refuse generated every day in New York State—were starting, for the first time ever, to gain momentum with nary a hint of the opposition that even their sponsors had expected from the city's and state's executives. A few months later the mayor called a meeting in the "Committee of the Whole" room on the second floor of City Hall for some twenty senior officials from the Office of Management and Budget, the sanitation department, the law department, and his own staff. A legislative staffer told the assembled group about a bill in Albany that would require the imminent closure of the Fresh Kills landfill. Its prospects, he concluded (not dwelling on the fact that no opposition to it had been expressed by either of the officials who ultimately would bear responsibility for its implementation), were excellent. In fact, it appeared likely that it would pass in a matter of days. "Any reason I should not get out ahead of this?" the mayor asked. Not one of his senior advisers said a word. The meeting was over in fifteen minutes.

Two days later, standing at a podium in City Hall's Blue Room with Guy Molinari and Governor Pataki, Mayor Giuliani announced that he would close Fresh Kills forever. He did not draw attention to the fact that, since he would by then be out of office, someone else would be left to pick up the pieces. Neither the reporters in attendance, nor their editors back at their offices, appeared to consider the announcement particularly newsworthy. The story received considerably less play than Steve Polan's offhand interview on the possibilities of incineration a few years before, or than the coverage of the all-night fight in the City Council that the announcement made moot. Despite the fears the city's editorial pages had so often expressed about the harm a reliance on exporting its waste could wreak on the city's economy, the announcement that the city was about to enter into the biggest set of contracts it had ever let, contracts on which the city henceforth would be forever dependent, was almost beneath notice.

And so, without a shred of analysis—at least as far as has ever been shown or even alluded to in public—or any planning, or any consultation with knowledgeable advisers inside or outside the administration, without any consideration of the public health impacts, if any, or of environmental effects, or of financial consequences (again, as far as has ever been made public), a facility that by the administration's own figures (published in a permit application for the landfill filed with the Conservation Department the month before) had at least twenty years' of remaining capacity (although those one hundred million cubic yards of landfill space, if supplemented in any meaningful way by recycling, composting, or incineration might well have lasted for fifty years) was ordered closed.

The value of these one hundred million cubic yards of capacity (roughly one hundred million tons' worth), relative to average landfill disposal fees in the region, was at least six billion dollars in 1996. But since the increase in landfill disposal fees was projected to continue to increase by 7 percent a year nationally—before considering the effect of dropping a market-swamping additional thirteen thousand tons a day into the equation—even this amount was likely to be dwarfed by the effects of twenty or thirty years' inflation. For a mayor who prided himself on throwing more than 160,000 women and children off welfare in his first four years of office to save some eighty-nine million dollars per year, and who, since entering office had cut the Board of Education's annual budget by eighty million dollars, this was a puzzling prodigality, since the increased cost to the city's budget—by the administration's own understated estimate—was at least one hundred million dollars a year. The offhandedness of it all showed a fiscal arrogance on the scale of a Haussmann or Moses. But the most troubling aspect of the whole reckless business was that, by refusing to allow for the future use of Fresh Kills even in the event of dire economic necessity—that is, by taking away any bargaining leverage the city might have hoped to maintain—the Giuliani administration played right into the oligarchic hands of those who control the nation's waste management industry—the free-market monopolies so strengthened in the last decade by the environmental regulations advocated by groups like NRDC and EDF. With one political decision, Rudolph Giuliani made generations of New Yorkers yet-unborn vulnerable to the predations of Fishhooks McCarthy's kind.

Almost as an afterthought—no doubt it added to the Fresh Kills closure bill an additional frisson of political correctness—the measure outlawed the Navy Yard incinerator as well.★ Thus came to a formal, if anticlimactic end (a legislative footnote, like a minor-league player tacked onto a major-league trade), an unborn project grown frail with age in utero, "among the most carefully scrutinized...infrastructure project[s] in the country" (according to Conservation Commissioner Tom Jorling, who should know). And so it at least was spared the humiliation of simply being postponed further and further into the sunset of future capital appropriations, well into the no-man's land of the next fellow's term of office, until, like a ghost of legislative intentions past it had simply faded from the memories of the living.

And yet, it seemed that it almost had. The headline and editorial writers who had spilled so much ink over the years declaiming its necessity and posturing about how the city's future would not be secure without it, and about how its approval represented the pinnacle of political courage, when its end finally came, considered it just another detail in the follow-up to the Fresh Kills story that in itself was of little general interest. The Navy Yard incinerator was no longer on page one above the fold, between Gorbachev and DeKlerk, but was buried—in the *Times'* late city edition—in a one-sentence reference in the sixth paragraph on page seven of the second section, between "Roof Leaks and Winter Tied to Façade's Fall" and "Brooklyn Man Accused of Posing as Gynecologist." (But this one-sentence reference revealed the *Times'* editorial staff's news-sniffing ability at its crack best, since in the late edition story published an hour or two earlier there had been no mention of the Navy Yard incinerator at all.)

Strangely, the environmental groups that had been in the thick of the fray were almost as silent when its end finally came as the editorial writers were. Perhaps it was unsettling to see such an unexpected culmination of their years of impassioned engagement. Maybe it was difficult to resolve

★From a tactical perspective, the Navy Yard ban had the important advantage of inducing the speaker of the Democratically controlled assembly, whose district was just across the East River from the Navy Yard, to join the Staten Island-led Republicans in the senate.

the contradictions between their hopes for a purer environment and this unsatisfying denouement, which meant simply more landfilling, somewhere else, or the discrepancy between their demands for environmental justice and New York City's abandonment of responsibility for what became of its wastes, where they were sent, or what benefits (if any) the "host communities" (as they were so disingenuously called in the new waste management "plan"—talk about, as Commoner would say, "linguistic de-toxification") would get in return.

Mayor Rudolph Giuliani won his race for re-election the next year by 234,000 votes. But with what he had, effectively, spent to secure the votes of 86,000 Staten Islanders (23,000 fewer than he had received four years before, 54,000 fewer than he had received eight years before) he could have bought a new clean-burning methane-powered car for every man, woman, and child on the Island.

The other party to the deal won his next election, too, by a similarly lop-sided margin, but no one thought electoral politics had been Guy Molinari's primary motivation. He had a clear gain: "the same legal rights as the rest of the country to refuse [New York's trash]." Unfortunately, the borough president's legal analysis was not quite right. The rest of the country did not *yet* have the right to refuse New York's trash, but the law he had just had passed was making legislators in other states begin to think more seriously about passing some new legislation of their own. A House bill that mirrored the interstate waste transportation restrictions the Senate had passed the year before, which had been on hold while New York officials and those from other waste-exporting states were meeting to negotiate some accommodation with their waste-importing colleagues, received an instant jolt of fresh momentum. As of this writing, the book on federal waste-export restrictions is not closed. Many analysts expect that the initial reaction to the actuality of Fresh Kills's closure will be the most important factor in determining whether limitations ultimately are enacted. If the rest of the country *does* get the legal right to turn away New York trash, Guy Molinari might after all end up where he started.

A so-called end-use plan for the Fresh Kills landfill's next incarnation has not yet been developed, although the city's planners have begun to consider the possibilities. The hillsides will probably be seeded with native grasses, perhaps shrubs and trees will be planted along the ridge "to soften the angularity of the slopes." There may be paths to the top for a view of New Jersey. Perhaps some plateau expanses will be reserved for "passive recreation." Few other options will be available. Certainly it will not be possible to construct major buildings on the site, or to build anything that would be damaged by the steady settling that will occur for many decades to come. The cost of providing these modest "open space" amenities—along with the other things that will need to be done before it is safe for people to once again set foot there—will be somewhere on the order of a billion dollars, and it will probably be thirty years or so before all sections of the site will be accessible. When it is finished, the transformed, re-constituted landscape sculpture will be a far cry from the salt-marsh meadows Happy Zimmer knew. He no doubt would not be pleased to know that, despite the efforts invested in developing safeguards to protect other such places from a parallel despoliation, New York at the start of the twenty-first century is no more able—perhaps less able—to plan and implement solutions to such basic municipal functions as waste management than it has ever been, and therefore, in all likelihood, in the decades and centuries ahead, the hapless inhabitants of many more miles of meadows, in other once rural places like Pennsylvania, Kentucky, New Mexico, and Virginia—some in states that have seceded once already—will be sitting around storing up more bile.

Pee-Yew Choo Choo

Two weeks before the proudly independent members of New York's City Council posed on the steps of City Hall to declare that they would never approve the Dinkins administration's waste management plan, 2,200 tons of New York waste rolled out of the South Bronx on rail, headed for a landfill in Libory, Illinois, whose permit had just expired. When the eighty boxcars arrived, they were re-routed to Sauget, where they were prevented from being unloaded by a contract dispute between the company that owned the cars and the company that owned the trucks that were supposed to have hauled their contents to the landfill. From there they went to nearby Fairmont City, where the refuse sat on a siding for twelve days (considerably longer than Mr. Potato ever had to wait in the Greenville yards). Eventually, the cargo was reloaded into ninety-nine steel containers—but after a series of thunderstorms punctuated the ninety-degree heat, trickles of smelly leachate still dripped onto the tracks. On the grounds of endangerment to the public health, a county judge ordered the train out of Illinois. Two days later it arrived in Kansas City, Kansas, just across the border from a new landfill in Clinton, Missouri. Angry Clinton residents met the trucks that carried the containers from the train and blocked them from entering the landfill. Shortly after police officers had broken up the blockade, and the unloading began, a heavy rain began to fall. Only seven containers were emptied before the rising water and mud made it impossible to continue. After a judge ordered the remaining waste out of Kansas, the other containers were reloaded onto flatcars and sent to Medille, Missouri, then on to Fort Madison, Iowa, and then to Streator, Illinois, where the train sat for three more days before beginning its trip back east. On July 17, it arrived in Kearny, New Jersey, where the containers, their once straight sides now bulging from their heat-swollen loads, were lifted onto trucks. The trucks then drove across the Arthur Kill to the Fresh Kills landfill in Staten Island, where the refuse—no longer smelly, but "dried and mummified" and as "clean as a whistle," was buried the next day—containers and all.

Adding to the unfavorable attention in the weeks that followed were four more waste trains from New York, two of which pulled out of the same rail-yard from which the first had come (the sole surviving piece of Egbert Viele's dream of turning the South Bronx into a world-class port-and-rail hub), two of which came from Senator Patrick McCarren's old Greenpoint, Brooklyn, neighborhood. The first of these trains carried nine thousand tons in ninety-two boxcars. It, too, went to Sauget, Illinois, whose fire department was called in three times to extinguish blazes caused by spontaneous combustion in the summer sun. (On the bright side, according to the local fire chief, the fires seemed to be a good way of killing "disease carrying flies.") The local trucking contractor handling the unloading operation missed the court-mandated deadline for getting the train unloaded because local residents staged a sit-in that closed one of the landfills in which the refuse was being buried. "The people here have dictated they don't want any part of it," their mayor said. "If it was from Illinois, it might not be near as bad. But being from New York, they frown on that."

There were more frowns back in New York ("How offensive that when it comes to garbage, the train inevitably stops on Staten Island," Borough President Guy Molinari said. "Apparently our borough does not have the same legal rights as the rest of the country to refuse the trash train and send it on its way.")—even though, like the *Mobro*'s load, upon examination what the containers held turned out to be just ordinary waste from offices, restaurants, and bodegas in the Bronx.

Collectively, these incidents were referred to in full-sheet papers like the *Times* as "the trash trains." In tabloids, the electronic media, and the US Senate—where they occasioned days of impassioned debate—they were called "pee-yew" or "poo-poo choo choos." Like any number of other media-titillating events that bestow upon unlikely subjects their fifteen minutes of fame, the sudden newsworthiness of interstate waste transport provided opportunities for instant political gratification. Soon after the first train's departure from the Bronx, federal legislators began to trade graphic conjurations of the dangers the trains held for their constituents, jockeying to see who could express the most revulsion and concern. "While some of my colleagues had the opportunity of enjoying New York City, the Big Apple, over the recess, the state of Missouri was threatened with the apple cores," said Senator Christopher S. ("Kit") Bond, "—forty cars of rotting, maggot-filled trash. For two weeks it simmered and boiled in the hot sun with plenty of rain to moisten it up and keep it nice and juicy." The senators from New York and New Jersey were forced onto the defensive. Frank Lautenberg of New Jersey claimed that people from the rest of the country had a mistaken image of his state, which, despite the stereotypes, has "more horses per square mile than any state in the country." ("We may not have a lot of horses," he added by way of preemptory explanation, "but we do not have a lot of square miles either.") His Democratic colleague, Bill Bradley, was more blunt: "You stand there... in front of the television cameras and say, 'I stopped the garbage, elect me.' That is, until next year, of course, or the year after that, or the year after that, when you want to export the garbage because your state is filled up and now you need to export. But that will be down the road. 'I will not have to worry about that. I will be reelected.'" Before the end of July—a month before the final showdown vote on the New York City solid-waste-management plan—the Senate voted eighty-nine to two to allow states to limit the amount of out-of-state waste they would accept.

This development, of course, had a very direct and chilling effect back in New York. Just as New York trash had prodded Congress from lethargy into prompt action, the Congress's moves toward limiting the transport of inter-state waste added a new electricity to the City Council's deliberations over the solid-waste-management plan and lent an ominous urgency to the pro-growth lobbyists' and editorialists' predictions of dire consequences should the city fail to take the decisive steps needed to control its own destiny. After the dramatic all-night session was over, many in the city breathed a sigh of relief: New York had saved itself from the terrifying prospect of having to depend on the hope of finding a willing home somewhere else for its waste.

Though the federal debate on restricting the movement of waste between states was far from over when Rudolph Giuliani announced his decision to close the Fresh Kills landfill, by then somehow these fearsome prospects seemed to have been forgotten. The editorialists who four years before had been so fearful of committing the city to a dependence on waste export ("the cost of disposing of garbage could bury the city's economy") said nothing about the vulnerabilities that the *Garbarge* and the *Pew-Yew Choo Choos* suggested. The pro-growth lobby said nothing about the increased costs of doing business in New York that reliance on private long-distance-landfilling contracts with one of the nation's least competitive industries was sure to produce. Even Wheelabrator-Frye, which was losing its last hope for its Navy Yard incinerator, said nothing. Perhaps its managers anticipated that the parent company, Waste Management, Inc.—the world's largest owner of landfills—would make more money this way.

But not everyone was so sanguine. The governors of Pennsylvania, Virginia, and Ohio were among the first to make their "disappointed" feelings known. In Congress, hearings on the interstate waste transport bills started up again. And in New York City itself, residents of Brooklyn and the Bronx suddenly realized that the waste that was about to be diverted from Fresh Kills would probably make its first stop at the "transfer stations" in their neighborhoods into which hundreds of private garbage trucks were already rumbling every day, dropping their loads to be crushed, compacted, and reloaded into bigger trucks, trains, or barges. Building on the grassroots organizations that NYPIRG and the Campaign for Recycle First had spawned in their anti-incinerator fight, these neighbors began to make it clear that waste-transfer stations were another type of facility that could not be counted on as a solution to the city's waste management problems. A whole new wave of acronym-bearing groups—OWN (Organization of Waterfront Neighborhoods), BARGE (Boroughs Allied for Recycling and Garbage Equity), NAG (Neighbors Against Garbage), BRAG (Bay Ridge Against Garbage) and OUTRAGE (Organizations United for Trash Reduction and Garbage Equity), among others—was born, and along with it, a whole new series of lawsuits began.

In January 2000, the state's own attorney general joined in, filing a suit that pointed out that the additional trucks rumbling through the Holland and Lincoln Tunnels and across the George Washington Bridge to take garbage to New Jersey were exacerbating an already unhealthy level of air pollution. (There was a touch of irony in this, since the attorney general's immediate predecessor had meanwhile become president of one of the major beneficiaries of the city's waste-export contracts, the New York division of Waste

Management, Inc.) The portion of the 40,000 Jersey-bound semi-trailers and 148,000 packer trucks on Canal Street, for example, had increased the levels of dangerous fine particulates (PM2.5)—which were already double the federal standard—by 16 percent. Since the constituents of diesel exhaust are considered carcinogenic as well as asthma-inducing, these impacts—unlike any discovered in the EPA's 1.25 million-dollar-study of the potential health effects of emissions from the Fresh Kills landfill—*do* have a demonstrably adverse effect on human health.

The attorney general's suit focused only on the well-defined air-pollution issues that offered the strongest grounds for legal action: he did *not* mention the cost impacts of running all those trucks to New Jersey—the costs of extra wear and tear on city streets and bridges, of extra trucks and maintenance, of thousands of hours of overtime—which indirectly (as Moses' "sanitation" expenses did to LaGuardia's budget), by decreasing the funding available for hospitals and other forms of health- and social-services, have a health impact of their *own*. Just buying the extra trucks it took (eight hundred) to cover all those extra miles (well over ten thousand a day even before all the city's waste was diverted from Fresh Kills) cost the city 133 million dollars in 2000. And then there were the salaries of the extra 1,050 sanitation workers it took to run those trucks.

Nor did the attorney general's suit mention that the costs of *disposing* of the waste after it had finally been removed from the Sanitation Department's long-running white trucks had (predictably) exceeded the administration's predictions as well. Instead of the fifty-five dollars per ton upon which the budget had been based, the actual cost for the 1999-2000 contracts turned out to be sixty-two dollars a ton. So after the sanitation commissioner assured the City Council in October 1999 that his budget would cover the costs of the contracts the city was about to sign, he had to go back to the council three months later to request an additional twenty-eight million dollars to cover overruns from the Manhattan portion of the program (nine million dollars for the increased operational costs to the sanitation department itself, nineteen million more to pay the increased dumping fees their contractors were charging). Meanwhile the bids for the *next* fiscal year (beginning in July 2000) averaged seventy-two dollars a ton—which, when the additional transportation costs were included, totalled (by the administration's estimate) ninety-six dollars a ton (compared to the forty-two dollars it cost to dump refuse at Fresh Kills). By April 2000, the Giuliani administration had acknowledged that the long-term costs of exporting trash would be more than 323 million dollars a year—and accordingly had raised the budget for its export contracts by *127 million dollars more* than it had requested a mere *two months* before.

On April 30, 2000, the attorney general's case—which was still pending—became not *moot* (because the conditions it outlined presumably would continue for at least several more years), but moot*er*. The city administration took a major step toward placating its local critics (reversing its prior position that the city's old barge-dumping piers were hopelessly unsuited for the city's future needs) by announcing that its garbage trucks would go back to dumping their loads at their old barge-loading piers, and that the major site of new transfer operations (where the city's barges would be offloaded onto trains for shipment hundreds or thousands of miles away) would be in Linden, New Jersey, a blue-collar town of thirty-seven thousand just across the Arthur Kill from Fresh Kills. Apparently finding the annual "$4 million or $5 million" "host fee" it could reap from Browning-Ferris, Inc. too tempting to refuse (its deliberations may have been further eased by the fact that the site BFI happened to pick on which to build its proposed fifty-million-dollar transfer station would be on land leased to them by Mayor John T. Gregorio's son-in-law), the Linden town council had given its unanimous approval to allow the transfer station. (Gregorio's reaction: "This is going to put us in the butter tub.")

But the town's approval only raised the question of the differences between a "host town" (a geographic point designating the citizens who would be paid for their willingness to allow garbage nearby) and a "host route" (a geographic line composed of a continuous series of points on which a stream of trash travels past people's houses). Mayor Gregorio promised his Linden constituents (the nearest of whom lived 1.7 miles from the industrial transfer-station site that happened to fall within their township) that their taxes would not go up for years—and in fact might go down. Carteret's mayor noted that his constituents—many of whom lived fifty feet from the rails the mile-long train of garbage-bearing cars would roll down twice each day—would not get a cent.

Meanwhile dissatisfaction farther afield had not stopped spreading. When New York City Deputy Mayor Joseph Lhota announced that the city planned to keep 15 percent of its waste in New York State, some upstaters began to feel that their interests were being sacrificed to the city's need to demonstrate to the rest of the country—in the transparent hope of fending off national legislation to restrict the interstate transport of wastes—that the state was doing its fair share to manage the wastes of the nation's foremost city. There, too, semantic distinctions about the geographic definition of the term "host community" began to drive a wedge between neighbors who stood to reap vastly disproportionate returns. Gerard J. Fitzpatrick, chairman of the Cattaraugus County Legislature, wrote to Mayor Giuliani: "We have read newspaper reports that you have promised not to send New York City solid waste to any community that does not want it. . . . Cattaraugus County and the communities around the IWS site [the recommended landfill that Integrated Waste Systems proposed to double in size to accommodate New York City waste] do not want this landfill to be built. I request your written confirmation that New York City will not send any municipal solid waste to Cattaraugus County without the County's consent." Deputy Mayor Lhota's artful response—"The City of New York has adopted an unequivocal commitment of disposing its municipal waste at facilities in conjunction with signed 'Host Community Agreements.' New York City would never send its waste to a community that does not agree to receive it."—succeeded only in making it clearer that if the *town* of Farmersville (with its 350 voters) was willing to accept the landfill (with its host fees), there was little the Cattaraugus *County* (with its thousands of additional neighbors) could do about it. (Or, as The Concerned Citizens of Cattaraugus County put it, "New York City has now officially joined with private dump developers in a symbiotic relationship, at our expense.")

Lhota went on to add:

> The disposal of municipal waste is a business. It is an enterprise which creates numerous jobs, valuable economic activity and, when conducted in an environmentally sound manner, is profitable to both the private sector companies and local communities involved. So long as the processes recommended and utilized are safe, then the disposal of waste

should be a matter left to the decisions made by the local governments and private sector companies involved.

Robert Eisenbud, director of legislative affairs for Waste Management, Inc., explained one "private sector company's" simple decision-making process to the Senate Committee on Environment and Public Works, whose members were considering bills to restrict the interstate transfer of wastes.

My comments thus far have dealt with interstate waste shipments generically, because the bills before you are applicable throughout the Nation. Let me turn now to comment on the "Fresh Kills Issue" that has attracted so much attention and motivated, at least in part, some of the legislative proposals.

In doing so, I want to stress that it is New York, not Waste Management, that has decided to close Fresh Kills landfill, and to request proposals for disposal of its MSW [municipal solid waste] outside New York City. We are competing for that business. Our shareholders expect us to do so.

Fortunately for his shareholders, as Eisenbud also pointed out, with operations in all fifty states, more than three hundred landfills, fourteen waste-to-energy plants, twenty-three-thousand trucks, 1.6 million commercial and industrial customers, and 19 million residential customers, Waste Management, "the world's largest publicly held solid waste management company," was in an excellent position to compete. So too were three other firms, since the four of them together shared 85 percent of the sixty-five billion dollars (a conservative estimate) that flow into the country's waste industry coffers every year.

The kind of decisions these companies and local governments made had led to a doubling of the percentage of the nation's landfills in private hands over the fifteen-year period that ended in 1998, by which time 60 percent of all landfilled waste went to private facilities. Given the economics involved with filling what amounts to a hollow polyhedron (a flattened-off pyramid whose maximum height is fixed by the length and width of its base)—the bigger the base the more profit per acre—the landfills of the future are going to be huge. (Already landfills in Utah and Georgia have weighed in at twenty-four hundred acres apiece.) And since these mega-fills cost on the order of four-hundred to six-hundred-thousand dollars an acre to build, it is scarcely likely that many new players will be able to cut very far into this action.

It is not clear that such literally monumental decisions are—pace Messrs. Lhota and Eisenbud—the sort that from a rational public-policy perspective are necessarily best left to the free market to determine. Nor can there be much doubt that such unfettered trade—barring of course effective federal and international agreements to the contrary—eventually will result in an inexorable flow of metropolitan by-products from richer to poorer, as the cities and counties and countries whose citizens have the most give what they no longer want to the towns and counties and countries that have the least. This additional disquieting outcome of globalization—less a rising tide lifting all boats than an invisible hand letting waste run downhill—stretches even further the rationalized definitions some would make of "economic development."

But who knows what future millennia may bring? Perhaps, like the guano-piled Chinchas, these unprepossessing heaps may someday inspire another round of international jousting for the rights to mine these mother lodes.

The recent developments in New York City's waste management planning situation made me wonder what the figures whose energetic exploits are recounted in the preceding pages would think. If only it were possible to get Robert Moses's reaction! (Sorry, Bob. The railroads you thought you were helping to kill when you started to build that landfill—though they nearly *did* die—may, with the boost in freight impelled by Fresh Kills's closure, begin to bounce back.) . . . Or Bill Carey's. (Bill, you were right all along. Landfilling *is* the way of the future.) . . . Or William Wilgus (Colonel, the New York Central was wrong—you were not five years ahead of your time. It was a century. But now the tunnel you envisioned, which is back on the city's drawing boards, and the containers you designed to run through it, may finally be put to the uses you intended.) . . . George Waring. (Commissioner, New York's sewage sludge finally is being spread on fields across the country, just as you said it should be. But so is its garbage. In piles that are going to make your little Rikers Island look like a quaint reminder of the "breath of feudal days coming modified through the long tempestuous ages.") . . . Fishhooks! (Stop grinning! Maybe Waste Management too will manage to give a few millions to charity.) . . . Inspector White. (Remember your Barren Island solution?)...Parent. (You're the one who said that, like prostitution, there would always be a Montfaucon.)

Since none of them was around to talk to, I rang up Lowell Harrelson instead. I was surprised to hear that he had not been following the national press coverage of the city's latest waste-export dilemma ("I tell you, Mr. Miller," he explained, "after my experience with that doggone barge, you know I've not had a lot of appetite for waste—you can probably imagine that....I feel a lot like the lady that just gave birth to triplets—I'm not quite interested in sex right now.") But when I told him what had happened, and that from now on it seemed that *all* of New York's waste would be loaded onto barges or trains and hauled somewhere out of town to places not-yet determined, his reaction was just one word. It burst out like a sort of sudden soft explosion.

"Wowwwwwww!"

Notes

PROLOGUE

First story: Search of national newspapers in Vu-Text. *Observer*, p. 2B.

4-8-87 article: Thomas J. Maier, *Newsday*.

4-18-87, covered by most papers: based on survey of all indexes of national daily newspapers in the New York Public Library.

Harrelson's house: Richard C. Firstman, *Newsday*, 6-11-87.

"Not shyster": Former US Senator Maryon Allen, quoted by Michael Brumas in *Staten Island Advance*, 5-14-87.

"Does not know...people": Carole Agus, *Newsday*, 5-17-87, p. 4.

Methane for milking: Philip S. Gutis, *New York Times*, 5-6-87, p. B2.

Shipping price: NYS Legislative Commission on Solid Waste Management (hereafter, LCSWM), "Where Will the Garbage Go? New York's Looming Crisis in Disposal Capacity," May 1986, p. 12.

Long Island tons and distances: LCSWM, May 1986, p. 36. Hempstead and Oyster Bay were already shipping their waste at least a hundred miles away, paying over sixty dollars per ton for transport and disposal.

Long Island mafia: LCSWM, 1986, 1987.

Hroncich's mob ties: Mark McIntyre, *Newsday*, 2-17-87, p. 7; *Staten Island Advance*, 8-14-87; Chris Franz, *Staten Island Register*, 8-20-87 (reporting on statements made by Assemblyman Maurice Hinchey).

Corrigan: Joshua Quittner, *Newsday*, 9-2-87; *New York Times*, 11-28-90, p. B1:2.

No landfill: LCSWM, "Where Will the Garbage Go," June 1987. Complicating matters even further, Hroncich and associates had no bond (as the abandoned RFP and state law required).

Bar scene: All of these details are from Firstman, *Newsday*, 6-11-87.

Byrd not interested: Agus, *Newsday*, 5-17-87, p. 4.

Hroncich's economics: LCSWM, June 1987. The economics for the private carters who delivered waste to Hroncich were also relatively straight-forward: no Islip or state officials prevented them from charging their customers whatever price they wanted, or did anything to check the accuracy of the carters' weights and measures.

Jones County information: from Firstman, *Newsday,* 6-11-87.

Tonnage origins: Newsday, 5-13-87.

Sonny Lane quote: Charlotte Observer, 4-6-87, p. 2B.

Louisiana his original destination: Firstman, *Newsday*, 6-11-87.

Edwards quote: Gutis, *New York Times*, 4-18-87.

Philadelphia v. NJ: 437 US 617, 1978; see also: *Harvey & Harvey v. Delaware Solid Waste Authority (600 F. Supp. 1369, 1985); Hybud Equipment Corp. v. City of Akron, Ohio (654 F.2d 1187, 1981); and Glenwillow Landfill v. City of Akron, Ohio (485 F. Supp. 671, 1979).*

Harrelson threatened to sue: Shirley E. Perlman, "Trash Odyssey: The Next Move," *Newsday*, 4-17-87.

Carson routine: Quittner, *Newsday*, 4-26-87.

Environmental Commissioner had indirectly caused: LCSWM, June 1987. DEC's most direct contribution to the barge had been signing an agreement allowing Hroncich's firm to set up a transfer station for Islip's waste, thus tacitly allowing the town to bypass any competitive procurement process (in violation of state law), without producing any bond or evidence of a commitment for a disposal location.

Jones's appointment: Catherine Woodard, *Newsday*, 9-2-87.

"Laughingstock": Gutis, *New York Times*, 5-3-87, Long Island section p. 11; Robert Braile, *New York Times*, 5-17-87. *Jones trying to get name recognition:* Nicholas Garaufis, *Newsday*, 6-10-87, Peter Marks, *Newsday*, 6-25-87, II, 18.

Governor's involvement: Jones quoted by Miriam Pawel, *Newsday*, 5-11-87, and in *Newsday*, 5-13-87; Braile, *New York Times*, 5-17-87. A *Newsday* editorial, 5-18-87: "Gov. Mario Cuomo's chief aide on environmental issues insists that the garbage voyage did not precipitate the agreement with Islip. That's hard to believe. Both the state and the town were embarrassed by the publicity given to the wandering barge, and they deserved to be. Every point in the agreement could—and should—have been negotiated years ago."

Islip consent order not mentioning barge: Robert Weddle, *New York Post*, 5-13-87. Other quotes from 5-13-87 *Newsday* story.

Hroncich quote: Edward Kirkman and Tony Marcano, *Daily News*, 5-13-87.

Harrelson's "No sir": Eric Schmitt, *New York Times*, 5-13-87.

Harrelson's expenses: e.g., Lawrence Neumeister, Associated Press, in *Staten Island Advance*, 5-21-87, p. A27.

Harrelson's "foolish": Gutis, *New York Times*, 5-15-87.

"Gunboats": Perlman, *Newsday*, 5-17-87, p. 3.

Stopped by police boats: Perlman, *Newsday*, 5-17-87, p. 4.

"Lenin": e.g., Robert D. McFadden, *New York Times*, 5-18-87, p. A1; Marty Lipp, *Staten Island Advance*, 5-18-87.

Shulman quote: Marks, *Newsday*, 5-20-87.

Sayville Fats: Marks, *Newsday*, 6-25-87, II, p. 4.

First Jones quote: Marks, *Newsday*, 5-20-87; *second:* Perlman and Sandra Peddie, *Newsday*, 5-18-87, p. 2.

Susan Molinari's age: Ed McCormack, *Daily News Magazine*, 2-15-87.

The Henley group offered to burn the trash in Peekskill, Andrew O'Rourke vetoed the deal: e.g.: *Daily News*, 5-28-87, p. 17.

Columbus offer: e.g., *New York Post*, *Staten Island Advance*, 6-13-87.

Luken quote: *Staten Island Advance*, 6-16-87, p. A6.

Koch quote: Kim I. Mills, Associated Press, in *Staten Island Advance*, 6-19-87, p. A20.

Golden quote: Chuck Scarborough, Channel 4 News, 7-13-87.

Commoner's dioxin arguments: Howard Golden et al. v. Edward I. Koch, et al., *Supreme Court of the State of New York, County of Kings: IAS Part 13, Index No. 18196/87*, pp. 30-31, 76-78.

Mobro cargo should be landfilled at Fresh Kills: ibid., p. 36, and passim.

Scientists work for incinerator companies: ibid., p. 80.

Novelty company: Pat Smith, *New York Post*, 8-25-87.

Cost of processing Mobro waste: William Kleinknecht, *Staten Island Advance*, 8-29-87.

PART I

Mental unease leads to cholera: e.g., Board of Health public notice printed in, for example, *Evening Post*, 12-9-1848, p. 2:3.

Temperature: New York City Inspector, *Annual Report, 1847-51*, document #28, p. 526.

Almost a Panic: Herald, 7-17-1849, p. 2:1.

"Knocked down with an axe": John Stearns to the New York City Board of Health, July 19, 1832, Filed Papers of the Common Council, File Drawer T-592, NYC Municipal Archives, quoted in Charles E. Rosenberg, *The Cholera Years* (Chicago: University of Chicago Press, 1962), p. 3.

"One often thought of the Laocoön": Edward H. Dixon, *Scenes in the Practice of a New York Surgeon* (New York, 1855), quoted in Rosenberg, loc. cit.

Syphilis exacerbated by wading in sewers: A.-J.-B. Parent-Duchatelet, *Hygiène Publique, ou Mémoires sur Les Questions Les Plus Importantes de l'Hygiène Appliquée aux Professions et aux Travaux d'Utilité Publique* (Paris: J.-B. Baillière; 1836), pp. x; 256-7.

Conflict institutionalized in two organizations: Nelson Manfred Blake, *Water for the Cities. A History of the Urban Water Supply Problem in the United States* (Syracuse, NY: Syracuse University Press, 1956), chapter 1.

Paris, London populations: B. R. Mitchell, *International Historical Statistics: Europe, 1750-1980*, Third edition (New York: Stockton Press, 1992), table A4, pp. 73-74. Less-rounded, the London increase was 1.6 million, or 140 percent.

"Smell is disease": S. E. Finer, *The Life and Times of Sir Edwin Chadwick* (London: Methuen & Co., 1952), p. 298.

Yellow fever characteristics: More than one physician with conflicting cholera evidence on his hands consciously ignored it in the interest of promoting—if not health—at least sobriety (Rosenberg, p. 97). With similar reasoning, the official body of Parisian physicians had recently proscribed as immoral the sale of any product said to *prevent*—as opposed to *curing*—the scourge of syphilis.

"Evolved from seething mass of corruption": A History, Chronological and Circumstantial, of the Visitation of Yellow Fever at New York (originally printed in *American Medical Monthly,* February 1858) (New York: 1858), pp. 7-8.

"Congregation of animal and vegetable matters": John H. Griscom, *The Sanitary Condition of the Laboring Population of New York* (New York: Harper & Bros., 1845), p. 4.

"Swept from office": Anthony Brundage, *England's 'Prussian Minister.' Edwin Chadwick and the Politics of Government Growth, 1832-1854* (University Park: Penn State University Press, 1988), p. 102.

"No one can rise": Griscom, p. 5.

Political economy needed rationalizing: Like "statistics"—the new study of measures related to the power of the state—"political economy" was a new discipline designed to maximize the overall efficiency of governmental institutions.

Fathers are taken: Griscom, p. 4.

"The greatest happiness": Maurice Marston, *Sir Edwin Chadwick (1800-1890)* (London: Leonard Parsons, 1925), p. 35.

Smith's tasks: Brundage, p. 1.

Skeleton was dressed in his own clothes: Gertrude Himmelfarb, *Victorian Minds* (New York: Knopf, 1968), p. 81.

Bentham's obsession: Himmelfarb, 1968, p. 33.

Panopticon idea: Himmelfarb, 1968, p. 72.

Subsidized by Ireland: Himmelfarb, 1968, p. 45.

"Morals reformed": John Bowring, ed., *Bentham's Collected Works* (London, 1843), pp. x, 39, quoted by Himmelfarb, 1968, p. 33.

250 Panopticons: Himmelfarb, *The Idea of Poverty: England in the Early Industrial Age* (New York: Knopf, 1984), p. 79. By the end of two decades, the numbers were to have doubled.

16 1/2 hours a day: Himmelfarb, *The Idea of Poverty*, p. 79; Himmelfarb, *Victorian Minds*, p. 62.

Panopticon company's particulars: Himmelfarb, *The Idea of Poverty*, pp. 62, 64-72, 80-82.

Poor Law Commission and sanitary problem: Finer, chapter 4. Quotation: pp. 155-6. The commissioner was Frankland Lewis.

"Wherever animal and vegetable": Health of Towns Association Report on Lord Lincoln's Bill, 1846, pp. 72-3, quoted in Finer, pp. 297-8.

Chadwick and Nightingale: Brundage, p. 164.

"I was brought up": René J. Dubos, *Louis Pasteur, Free Lance of Science* (Boston: Little, Brown and Co., 1950), p. 249.

Liebig's theories: Justus von Liebig, *The Natural Laws of Husbandry* (New York: D. Appleton and Co., 1863).

Liebig's company: R. A. Lewis, *Edwin Chadwick and the Public Health Movement, 1832-1854* (London: Longmans, Green and Co., 1952), p. 353.

Duchatelet métier: Parent-Duchatelet, 1836, pp. viii-ix.

"He loved them": ibid., p. xii.

Marât's skin disease: David P. Jordan, *Transforming Paris, The Life and Labors of Baron Haussmann* (New York: Free Press, 1995), p. 267.

"As often as I would have wished": Parent-Duchatelet, 1836, p. 113.

"Very good and savory": ibid., p. 175.

Cat carcasses: ibid., p. 241.

"Insisted on coming along": ibid., pp. 541-2.

"Wheel à l'Anglaise": ibid., p. 141.

"Prostitution is inevitable": Parent-Duchatelet, *De La Prostitution dans la ville de Paris, considérée sous le rapport de l'hygiène publique, de la morale et de l'ad-*

ministration; ouvrage appuyé de documents statistiques puisés dans les archives de la Préfecture de police, 3rd edition, vol. 2 (Paris: J.-B. Baillière et fils, 1857), pp. 337–8.

Liebig quote: Dubos, p. 122.

Description of White: Testimony of Gaspar Goldstein, Board of Aldermen Documents, vol. 2l, pt. l, no. 43 (6-5-1854), p.834.

"Dr. White": There is no way to be certain of White's credentials. He listed himself as a druggist in city directories until his appointment as city inspector, when he first began to use the title *Dr.* There were no formal certifications for physicians in New York City in 1849, nor records of medical school graduates until several decades later.

White quote: City Inspector, Annual Report, 1849 (Board of Aldermen Documents, doc. no. 28, 1850), p. 507.

Common Council committee: A.W. White to the Common Council, 7-16, Municipal Archives, City Inspector, 1849, folder #473; Proceedings and Documents of Board of Assistant Aldermen, vol. 17, p. 246.

Floating with tides: City Inspector, Annual Report, ibid.

Lent quote: deposition of William C. Lent by Francis R. Tillou, recorder of the City of New York, May 1853, Board of Aldermen Documents, vol. 21, pt. 1, no. 43, pp. 792ff.

White's powers: He was referring to the extraordinary, post-cholera powers given the city inspector in Chapter 275 of Laws of 1850, passed 4-10-1850.

Meeting with Baxter: deposition of William L. Baxter, 6-23-1853, Board of Aldermen Documents, vol. 21, pt. 1, doc. no. 43, pp. 796-7.

"That is the way we do things up here": ibid., p. 798.

Brother Island cost: 3,250 dollars, Baxter testimony, Board of Aldermen Documents, vol. 21, pt. 1, doc. no. 43, p.798; Baxter receipt, pt. 2, doc. no. 45, p.885.

Bone black for sugar: L. P. Brockett in Henry Stiles, *History of Kings County* (New York: Munsell, 1884), vol. 2, p.671.

Marrow: Leebert Lloyd Lamborn, *Modern Soaps, Candles and Glycerin: A*

*Practical Manual of Modern Methods of Utilization of Fats and Oils in the Man-
ufacture of Soap and Candles, and of the Recovery of Glycerin* (New York: D.
Van Nostrand Co., 1906), p. 34.

Kitchen-waste contracts, e.g., Astor house, for 250 dollars/year: R. B. Coleman
testimony, Board of Aldermen Documents, ibid., p. 839.

Price of bones: Francis Munret testimony, Board of Aldermen Documents,
vol. 21, pt. 1, doc. no. 43, p. 837.

Plunkitt on opportunity: Plunkitt's most famous remark, along with many
of his others, is memorialized in William L. Riordon, *Plunkitt of Tammany
Hall* (New York: McClure, Phillips & Co., 1905). The following year
(1906), during the course of the Ivins investigation of the Department of
Street-Cleaning, it was discovered that Plunkitt was leasing a string of stables to the department for profits on the order of 600 percent.

White's contract manipulations: Board of Aldermen Documents, vol. 19, pt.
1, no. 20, p. 521. *Poaching penalties:* Board of Aldermen Documents, vol.
21, pt. 1, no. 38, p. 602.

Sand, sedge, cedar: Stiles, vol. 1, p. 77.

Reynolds's factory: Stiles, ibid. *two-to-three thousand hogs:* Green testimony
in Comptroller's investigation, Board of Aldermen Documents, 6-5-
1854, p. 791.

Other qualified proposers: Board of Aldermen Documents, vol. 22, no. 41
(10-11-1855), p. 15; see also Board of Aldermen Documents, vol. 21, pt.
1, doc. no. 43, p. 787. Twenty thousand dollars comes from Board of
Aldermen Documents, vol. 21, pt. 1, no. 32, p. 596. The other offers for
the city's refuse were serious. One proposer, Leffert Cornell, had an
island just east of Reynold's plant, and later had a plant on Barren Island
that had the exclusive contract for the city's refuse; Cornell offered a
fifty-thousand-dollar bond to support his offer.

Goldstein, etc.: All this is documented in the records of the comptroller's
investigation, Board of Aldermen Documents, vol. 21, pt. 1, no. 43 (6-5-
1854), pp. 757ff. See also nos. 16 and 38, and pt. 2, no. 45, and vol. 19, pt.
1, no. 13 (2-4-1852), and vol. 22, no. 27 (8-6-1855) and no. 41 (10-22-
1855).

Names for Barren Island: e.g., Frederick Van Wyck, *Keskachauge, or the First White Settlement on Long Island* (New York: G. P. Putnam's Sons, 1924), p.13 [Van Wyck cites *Memoirs of the Long Island Historical Society*, vol. 1, 1867]. The derivation of *coney* from the Dutch word for rabbits seems less clear-cut than the derivation of Barren from Beeren. Eugene L. Armbruster quotes Judge Egbert Bensen's 1816 address to the New York Historical Society, in which Benson states that it derives from Conyn, a Dutch surname still found in New York at that time. Armbruster, on the other hand, notes that Konoh was the Lenape word for bear, so bears may have been everywhere. Armbruster: *Coney Island* (New York: np, 1924), pp. 5, 7-8.

Leblanc: For a discussion of Leblanc's contribution (and life), see Archibald and Nan L. Clow, *Chemical Revolution* (London: Batchwork Press, 1952), pp. 91-109.

Soap: The impetus for the commercial production of soap had little to do with personal hygiene and much to do with the demands of the textile industry. Clow, chapter 5.

Glycerin uses: S. W. Koppe, *Glycerine. Its Production, Uses and Examination.* Trans. from German, 2nd ed. (London: Scott, Greenwood & Son, 1915), pp. 3-4; Leebert Lloyd Lamborn, *Modern Soaps, Candles and Glycerin* (New York: D. Van Nostrand Co., 1906), pp. 618-9.

Glycerin production: William Lant Carpenter, *A Treatise on the Manufacture of Soap and Candles, Lubricants and Glycerin,* 2nd ed. (New York: Spon & Chamberlain, 1895), p. 421. Its value is given at .25F/lb; the franc in 1878 was worth 19.3 cents. *New York Times,* 1-6-1878, p. 2:7.

Glycerin price: US War Industries Board, Price Bulletins, no. 49, *Prices of Soaps and Glycerin* (Washington, DC: Government Printing Office) pp. 18-19.

Glycerin in World War I: James Wright Lawrie, *Glycerol and the Glycols* (New York: The Chemical Catalog Company, 1928), p. 321.

Propelling President Millard Fillmore's administration to the brink of military adventures off the coast of Peru: Richard A. Wines, *Fertilizer in America: From Waste Recycling to Resource in Exploitation* (Philadelphia: Temple University Press, 1985), pp. 56-7.

A hundred bushels of potatoes from an acre if he fertilized it, but only sixty if he did not: Wines, p. 154.

Queens hay, manure: ibid., p. 11.

Mapes and Cooper sponsored the 1844 Sanitary Report: Griscom, preface.

Waring lectures: Dr. Albert Shaw, *The Life of Colonel George E. Waring, Jr., The Greatest Apostle of Cleanliness* (New York: The Patriotic League, 1899), pp. 13, 21.

Dirt mixed with street manure: e.g., James Coleman, Commissioner, Department of Street-Cleaning to Abraham Hewitt, Mayor, 7-11-1887, Municipal Archives, 87-HAS-42.

St. Leger's discovery: e.g., *Working Farmer* 1 (1849), p. 41. *French bone-buyers:* ibid., p. 26.

Native Americans: Wines, pp. 33-4.

European discovery: ibid.

Chincha: ibid., pp. 35, 42.

Whaling captain found island (Ichaboe) off Africa: ibid., p. 55.

Lobos affair: ibid., pp. 56-7.

Guano Island Act: ibid., pp. 61-5.

Grace: New York Times, 6-29-1880, p. 1:1; 6-30-1880, p. 1:1; J. Peter Grace, Jr., *W. R. Grace (1832-1904) And The Enterprises He Created* (np, nd, in New York Public Library).

Cornell's material shipped to fertilizer plant in London: Stiles, vol. 2, p. 756.

Reynolds's partnership with Pratt, and Pratt leaving for petroleum: Brockett, p. 674.

Patent history: F. J. Machalske, *The Progress of the Fertilizer Industry. A History of Progress in the Manufacture of Fertilizer in America. A Resume of United States Patents Relating to Fertilizers to the End of the Year 1910* (Philadelphia: Ware Brothers Co., 1912).

Swearing around women: Roy Rosenzweig and Elizabeth Blackmar, *The Park and the People: A History of Central Park* (Ithaca, NY: Cornell University Press, 1992), pp. 102, 374; John McNamara, *History in Asphalt. The Origin of Bronx Street and Place Names* (Harrison, New York: Harbor Hill Books, 1978), p. 236.

Waring's body: New York Times, 10-30-1898, p. 1:7; *Sun,* 10-30-1898.

Viele on Waring: Tribune, 3-21-1895, p. 8:1; 3-24-1895, p. 6:2 (ed).

"No one who has": Frederick Law Olmsted, *Public Parks and the Enlargement of Towns* (New York: Arno, 1970), p. 34 (originally published by American Social Science Association, Cambridge, MA: Riverside Press, 1870.)

Olmsted and Chadwick on population density: Irving D. Fisher, *Frederick Law Olmsted and the City Planning Movement in the United States* (Ann Arbor: University of Michigan Research Press, 1976), p. 183.

Pure Air Company: Edwin Chadwick, *The Health of Nations, A Review of the Works of Edwin Chadwick, with a Biographical Dissertation by Benjamin Ward Richardson, in 2 Volumes* (London: Longmans, Green, & Co., 1887), vol. 2, p. 316.

Baron Haussmann: Although it was characteristic of him to claim it, Haussmann was not actually a baron, since French law at the time did not allow the use of a maternal grandfather's title.

"If heaven had given me": Jordan, p. 159.

Haussmann improvements: Jordan, pp. 227, 282.

Olmsted's first Central Park tour: Albert Fein, ed., *Landscape Into Cityscape; Frederick Law Olmsted's Plans for a Greater New York City* (Ithaca, New York: Cornell University Press, 1967), pp. 57–61.

Viele's railway: Egbert Ludovickus Viele, *The Arcade Under-Ground Railway. Report of Egbert L. Viele, Engineer in Chief* (np, nd) (New-York Historical Society, *F128* TF847/Box 2).

"The Harlem River": Viele, *The Transval of the City of New York* (New York: Johnson & Co., 1880), p. 23.

Viele convinced the federal government to blow up Hell Gate: New York Times, 4-23-02, p. 9:1.

Central Park proposed as the solution to a sanitary problem: This would provide (as Bryant's rival James Gordon Bennett put it in another editorial), "an occasional ventilation of the lungs of our industrial classes." Eric Homberger, *Scenes from the Life of a City: Corruption and Conscience in Old New York* (New Haven: Yale University Press, 1994), p. 248.

Viele on the Central Park site: Viele, *The Topography and Hydrology of New York* (New York: Robert Craighead, Printer, 1865), p. 4.

Viele's relations with Waring: Tribune, 4-21-1895, p. 8:1.

"It is a pleasant thing": George E. Waring, Jr., *Whip and Spur* (Boston: James R. Osgood and Co.; 1875), pp. 67-8.

New York's death rate: Report of the Council of Hygiene and Public Health of the Citizens Association of New York Upon the Sanitary Condition of the City, 2nd edition (New York: D. Appleton and Company, 1866), pp. x-xi (first edition was 1864); Seymour J. Mandelbaum, *Boss Tweed's New York* (New York: John Wiley, 1965), p. 8.

Before the month was out: John Duffy, *A History of Public Health in New York City 1625-1866* (New York: Russell Sage Foundation, 1968), vol. 2, p. xxi.

"Fatal connection between physical uncleanness and moral pollution": Here the committee quoted the *Edinburgh Review* (vol. xci, 1850).

"The mobs that held fearful sway"; "Exposed themselves to repulsive and nauseous scenes": Report of the Council of Hygiene and Public Health of the Citizens Association of New York Upon the Sanitary Condition of the City, pp. xi-xviii.

Pulling quote: ibid., pp. 60-61.

Furman quote: ibid., p. 196.

"Builded better than they knew": Egbert L. Viele, "Topography of New York and its Park System," in James Grant Watson, ed., *The Memorial History of the City of New York* (New York: New-York Historical Co., 1893), vol. 4, p. 556.

Boole's arguments: In the Matter of the Charges Presented to his Excellency Reuben E. Fenton Governor of the State of New York, Against Francis I. A.

Boole, City Inspector of the City of New York, Impleaded with others, as a member of the Commission, to award the Street-Cleaning Contract. Arguments of John Graham, Esq., on the Motion to Dismiss the Charges.

Boole's demise: New York Times, 9-3-1869, p. 5:2.

"The mayor's politics": Tribune, 4-7-1881, p. 5:2

Roosevelt on spoils: New York Times, 4-9-1881, p. 1:7.

Andrews's career: Tribune, 7-22-1893, p. 2:5.

Andrews's misconduct: Tribune, 6-9-1906, p. 9:3; *The Triumph of Reform. A History of the Great Political Revolution, November Sixth, Eighteen Hundred and Ninety-Four* (New York: The Souvenir Publishing Company, 1895), p. 121.

Budget had more-than-doubled: Triumph of Reform, pp. 15-16.

"Height of folly": Viele, *The Topography and Hydrology of New York,* pp. 4-7.

"It smells as horrible": Sam Kaufman to Gilroy, 7-1-1894; Frederick Theodore Howe to Gilroy, 7-1-1894; Bigelow to Dr. William O'Byrne, 6-22-1894; Anonymous, 7-1-1894 (Municipal Archives, 89-GTF-17).

"At the dumpage": meeting no. 11, 9-14-1894 (Municipal Archives, 89-GTF-17).

Timing of recommendations: The commission's report to the mayor is dated 11-19-1894 (Municipal Archives, 88-GHJ-51, Street-Cleaning, 1891 [misfiled]).

Committee of Seventy: The Triumph of Reform, pp. 12, 20ff.

Waring's dressing-down: Tribune, 2-28-1895, p. 4:1.

Bell bill hearing: "Public Hearing No. 2," 2-15-1895, Municipal Archives, 90-SWL-49; Rogers quote, p. 4.

"He attempted to argue": 2-16-1895, p. 9:4. The reporter no doubt knew that the paper had often carried stories about Rogers in the past. The tall, good-looking, Princeton-educated Civil War veteran dabbled in good-government politics, had run for office on his own, and been an effective stump speaker in Strong's recent mayoral campaign. He had also flirted

with alcoholism and insanity, and the *Times* had carried accounts of his escapades in bars and cabs and hotels, and of his repeated institutionalizations at the Bloomingdale, Ward's Island, and Bellevue Asylums. From his frequent court appearances, the *Times*'s readers knew, among other things, that the Bloomingdale doctors had deprived him of his most precious possessions, including a top hat he had worn to President Cleveland's inaugural ball, a book of Irish ballads that had been of great solace, and notebooks filled with notes and sketches of his fellow inmates and their attendants, and that he had recently created a disturbance in a restaurant by ordering three thousand gallons of milk delivered to his house. After the hearing on the Bell bill, Rogers's life, if possible, got worse. At the end of the year, he begged a judge to release him from Ward's Island, where he was being held against his will, living in soiled linens on bread and water and being injected with "deadly drugs." (*New York Times*, 6-5-1885, p. 2:3; 6-6-1885, p. 5:4; 1-27-1886, p. 8:2; 10-10-1889, p. 2:6; 10-13-1889, p. 13:6; 10-19-1889, p. 5:3; 2-18-1890, p. 9:2; 2-25-1890, p. 9:1; 5-27-1890, p. 2:5; 7-16-1890, p. 8:2; 7-22-1890, p. 8:6; 11-25-1895, p. 9:7; 12-3-1895, p. 14:1; 12-4-1895, p. 14:3; 12-5-1895, p. 14:4.) In 1902, Rogers would escape from an asylum in Flushing—where, among his other hallucinations, he believed that he was campaigning for the state senate against one of his street-cleaning predecessors, Senator George Washington Plunkitt—presumably to Canada, never to be seen again.) (*New York Times*, 8-21-1902, p. 3:6; 8-26-1902, p. 14:2; 8-27-1902, p. 14:3; 10-1-1902, p. 16:1.)

"Now as to the men": T. P. Tuwitt, Bell Bill hearing, pp. 12-13.

Hall quote: ibid., pp. 17-19.

Queens County Board of Health: New York Times, 6-30-1894, p. 2:4; 7-17; 8-1; H.B. Hollins & Co. to Gilroy, 4-3-1894; G. Pauly, president, Village of College Point and E.H. Biederlindess, to Gilroy, 4-7-1894; Charles Roberts, M.D., to General Emmons Clark, secretary, Health Department, 7-19-1894; Andrews to Gilroy, 7-20-1894 (all correspondence cited in Municipal Archives, 89-GTF-17).

Woolf's Electrozone: New York Times, 7-7-1893, p. 9:5; 8-15-1915, II, p. 12:8; 8-19-1915, p. 8:6; 9-21-1915, p. 10:8.

Thirty thousand dollars: Woolf to Andrews, 4-13-1894 (Municipal Archives, 89-GTF-17); *New York Times*, 8-8-1895.

Charles Bell quote: Bell bill hearing, p. 48.

"The Evil One": Charles N. Glaab and A. Theodore Brown, *A History of Urban America* (New York: MacMillan, 1967), p. 165.

Waring on bacteria: Waring, "Garbage and Bacteria," *Living Age*, 2-12-1898, 216, p. 484.

"Coast defense rifles": William W. Locke and Joseph B. Taylor, "I. Garbage Disposal in the Outlying Wards. II. History of the Garbage Contract. III. Refuse Disposal of Cities," in *Brooklyn Health Department Report for 1896*, App. F1.

Viele's charge: Tribune, 3-21-1895, p. 8:1; 3-24, p. 6:2 (ed).

"Never had a subordinate": Tribune, 4-14-1896, p. 4:4; *New York Times*, p. 9:3.

Herbert Tate's interests: e.g., *Tribune*, 10-17-1897, p. 4:3; Richard Stephen Skolnick: *The Crystallization of Reform in New York City, 1890-1917* (Ph.D. dissertation, Yale University)(Ann Arbor: University Microfilms International, 1964), p. 195.

Reduction bids: The bids were a game of musical chairs. The New-York Sanitary Utilization Company's present bid undercut Merz's previous 90,000 dollars a year bid by 10 dollars, while in its second bid Merz tied New-York Sanitary's previous bid of 144,000 dollars. Merz's first bid was for 90,000 dollars (90 cents a ton for the city's estimated eight hundred tons), while Arnold's was 1 dollar and 44 cents (144,000 dollars); Merz's second bid was 144,000 dollars; Root and Clarke's letter of 4-29-1896 saying that the city had accepted a 144,000-dollar bid; N-Y's second bid was 89,990 dollars. e.g., *Engineering News*, 2-20-1896 (no page, clipping in Municipal Archives, 90-SWL-50).

Board of Estimate: The other members of the Board of Estimate at the time were the president of the Department of Taxes and Assessments and the corporation counsel. Waring, *Annual Report of the Department of Street Cleaning*, 1898.

The children of Philadelphia cry for this: Choate's joke was based on the well-known slogan for Castoria, a senna-colored root-beer-flavored laxative for children. Daniel B. Schneider, *New York Times,* 1-30-00, CY2:4.

Board of Estimate description: New York Times, 6-3-1896, p.9:5.

Only plant in Philadelphia: Engineering News, 2-20-1896 (no page, clipping in Municipal Archives, 90-SWL-50).

"Dave" Martin: Lincoln Steffens, *Shame of the Cities* (New York: Peter Smith, 1948), p.203 (originally published 1903).

Cranford contracts: Many sources document the Cranfords public works contracts, including: *Eagle,* 10-26-1916 and 12-10-36, p. 16:2. The Cranfords had built much of the borough's surface and underground rail system, among other things.

Network of investors: The partners are listed in many sources, e.g., *New York Times,* 8-2-1901.

Andy White and Docks Department: NYS Special Committee to Investigate the Police Department ("Lexow Committee"). N.Y.C. Report and proceedings, vol. 4, Oct. 18-Dec. 11, 1894, pp.4417ff. *Details on White's dubious performance as Docks Commissioner: New York Evening Post,* "Tammany Biographies," October 1894, p.13. He was removed from the post by Mayor Strong: *New York Times,* 1-24-1900, p.7:5. For more details on White's political career, see: *New York. The Metropolis* (New York: The New York Recorder, 1893), p.34; NYC Docks Department: *Annual Report, 1894,* p.59; ibid., 1895, pp.443, 451; *New York Times,* 10-13-1885, p.1:3.

Barren Island population: New York Times, 9-27-1896, p.14; Stiles.

Mixed population: Tribune, 9-5-1897 (Supplement, p.10).

Barren Island products: Frederick R. Black, *Jamaica Bay: A History. Historical Resource Study, Gateway National Recreation Area. Cultural Resource Management Study No. 3* (Washington, DC: US Department of Interior, 1981), p.34. (He cites Charles B. Law, "Speech of Charles B. Law in the House of Representatives, 6-29-1906," Washington, DC, 1906, p.7.)

Grease and fertilizer prices: William Francis Morse, *The Collection and Dis-*

posal of Municipal Waste (New York: The Municipal Journal and Engineer, 1908), p. 416.

Brooklyn contract: Annual Report of the Department of Street-Cleaning, p. 14.

Nagle: There are many references for Nagle's nefarious career and close ties to Croker, e.g., *Tribune*, 10-13-1901, (supplement) p. 2:3; 10-18-1901, p. 3:2; 10-27-1901, p. 2:4 and II, p. 5:4; Morse, "The Street-Cleaning Department of New York City Under Tammany Administration," in *The New-York Vigilant*, 10-10-1901. James McCartney, Waring's deputy, was his immediate successor, but died in office in 1899.

Celebratory picnic: Tribune, 8-4-1901, p. 6:5.

Barren Island description: Tribune, 9-5-1897 (supplement) p. 10.

Salt pork: New York Times, 8-6-1897; *school closings:* e.g., *New York Times*, 9-17-1897; *chlorine gas: New York Times*, 3-8-1899, p. 7:3. Their method, if perhaps no more effective, was at least safer than the then accepted medical practice—to which they were also subjected—of administering chlorine gas by inhalation.

Principal demented: New York Times, 3-8-1899, *Tribune*, 6-23-1899, p. 5:2.

Children picked through garbage: e.g., *Staten Island Advance*, 5-17-1916, letter to ed.

Wrote to Mayor: Shaw to Hylan, 11-17-1918, Municipal Archives, Hylan #191, shelf 2623.

Prospect Park: Eagle, 4-23-1921, p. 24:3. Later in the century, Brooklyn children would be taken to the "Gateway National Recreation Area on Jamaica Bay"—the former Barren Island—for camping trips that would provide *their* first exposure to a pastoral landscape.

Miss Shaw succeeded: New York Times, 9-6-39, p. 23:4.

Ethel Croker's marriages: New York Times, 3-5-1916, p. 21:4; *Eagle*, 3-4-1916, p. 2:7; *Tribune*, p. 3; clipping from *Eagle* morgue, (nd)-4-1916, p. 4:16. Questioned by surprised reporters as to why he had officiated at the wedding of a divorced person, the priest said that he had been given orders to do so by "somebody higher in the Church." The Whites' proclivity for intermarriage with the family's business partners seems to have begun the previous generation: Thomas's widow was named Katherine Swift White; Francis Swift was the business partner of Patrick White, their father.

Glencairn Castle: Once there, he extensively remodeled it "so that it became a mixture of Baronial and American Colonial; with a veranda of granite columns running round it and an Irish-battlemented tower. Here he had his famous stud, where his horses included Orby, winner of both the English and the Irish Derbys 1907. Glencairn is now the British Embassy." Mark Bence-Jones, *A Guide to Irish Country Houses* (London: Constable, 1978).

Bula Edmonson: New York Times, 1-9-1956, p. 25:1.; Morris R. Werner, *Tammany Hall* (Garden City, New York: Doubleday, Doran & Co., 1928), p. 478.

Suit over Croker's will: New York Times, 7-11-1922, p. 8:1.

T. White's death: Eagle, 4-11-1904, p. 3:2; *his estate: Eagle*, 3-4-1916, p. 2:7.

Thomas White, Jr.: Eagle, 9-6-1945, p. 11:3; Black, p. 36.

A. White's death: New York Times, 1-24-1900, p. 7:5.

Emily Waring's bad luck: Shaw, p. 29.

PART II

Reynolds's traits: Frank Bailey, *It Can't Happen Here Again* (New York: Knopf, 1944), p. 119.

Reynolds's businesses: National Cyclopaedia of American Biography (Clifton, NJ: James T. White & Co.), vol. 25, p. 352; *Eagle* clippings in the Brooklyn Historical Society, vol. 142, p. 48.

Reynolds's actresses: His use of actresses for the entertainment of his friends is illustrated, for instance, in the claim quoted in Hearst's *New York American* that Reynolds had taken Mayor Mitchel and others on a cruise to Europe with "a certain well-known actress... one who doesn't come cheap." (10-24-1917, p. 4:1)

Reynolds's friends' amusements: Edo McCullough, *Good Old Coney Island* (New York: Charles Scribner's Sons, 1957), p. 192.

Bailey's background: Bailey, p. 69.

"Wherever Reynolds is": ibid., p. 118.

Reynolds-Bailey partnership: ibid., pp. 71, 118-25.

City of Churches: In 1855, the City of Brooklyn had one church for every 1,600 people, compared to one church for every 2,500 people in Manhattan. Ira Rosenwaike, *Population History of New York City* (Syracuse, NY: Syracuse University Press, 1972), tables on pp. 31, 36, and 53.

Population figures: Rosenwaike, table 2, p. 16; Anna Mary Lanahan, *Brooklyn's Political Life, 1898-1916*, Ph. D Dissertation, St. John's University, 1977, pp. 5-6 and appendix I.

Fulton ferry: Regular ferries had crossed the river at Fulton street since 1642; Fulton's steamboat service started in 1814. Carol von Pressentin Wright, *Blue Guide New York* (New York: W.W. Norton, 1983), p. 518; *WPA Guide to New York City* (New York: Pantheon, 1982 [1939]), p. 441.

"People began coming out": Bailey, p. 121.

Dreamland and Freud: There are many descriptions of Dreamland. A particularly useful source is Edo McCullough's *Good Old Coney Island. Coney Island*, a documentary by Ric Burns/Steeplechase Films, mentions the Freud visit.

Dreamland details: McCullough, p. 193. Eric J. Ierardi, *Gravesend: The Home of Coney Island* (New York: Vantage, 1975), pp. 124-32.

Dreamland sale: There are a number of contemporary newspaper and public proceeding sources concerning this transaction, but the issues are reliably summarized (although without citations) in Henry Klein's *Save New York from the Greed of the Money Gang*, p. 4 (no publisher or publishing date given).

Venice-on-the-Bay: Eagle, 6-29-1902, magazine, p. 5.

Green death: New York Times, 11-14-1903, p. 1:5.

Hints on Green's sexuality: John Foord, *The Life and Public Services of Andrew Haswell Green* (Garden City, NY: Doubleday, 1913), pp. 12-13. I am not alone in this supposition: see Gore Vidal, *1876* (New York: Random House, 1976, pp. 112ff).

Green on Olmsted's street proposal: Fein, p. 158.

"We cannot parcel out the air": Green 1868 report, reprinted in Foord, p. 299.

"The waterfront of no municipality here": ibid., p. 296.

"Great is the activity": ibid., p. 233.

Port of New York losing market share: David C. Hammack, *Power and Society: Greater New York at the Turn of the Century* (New York: Russell Sage Foundation, 1982), pp. 37-8.

Narrows Tunnel proposal: Triborough Bridge and Tunnel Authority, *Spanning the Narrows*, 1964.

New York's "imperial destiny": Hammack, p. 193.

Equal assessment on real estate: Hammack, p. 360, n77. (Green, to keep the support of Manhattan developers, thwarted Reynolds's equal assessment efforts.)

Green agrees with Reynolds: Hammack, p. 204.

Steffens preferred his Tammany unvarnished: Lincoln Steffens, *Shame of the Cities* (New York: Sagamore Press; 1957 [1902-4]), p. 213.

Gaffney's blackmail: e.g., *New York Times*, 6-22-1904.

New York energy prices: New Yorkers paid 20 to 40 percent more for light than did residents of other US cities. Samuel Seabury, *Municipal Ownership and Operation of Public Utilities in New York City* (New York: Municipal Ownership Publishing Co., 1905), p. 42; Robert Grier Monroe, Commissioner of Water Supply, Gas and Electricity: *Report Submitted to the Hon. Seth Low, Mayor, on Municipal Lighting*, March 1903.

Gaffney's wife: *New York Times*, 6-26-1904, II, p. 2:1-2, also 6-22. Mrs. Murphy was also a member of the firm (Seabury, p. 33).

When Edison began to set up his electric-supply system, he had not yet invented many of the components on which it would depend: Harold Clarence Passer, *The Electric Manufacturers, 1875-1900*, (New York: Arno Press, 1972 [Harvard University Press, 1953]), pp. 88-92.

Edison used Ohm's law: Passer, pp. 80-2.

Edison's Pearl Street demonstration: Thomas P. Hughes, *Networks of Power* (Baltimore: Johns Hopkins University Press, 1983), pp. 30-42.

Edison companies: Milo R. Maltbie, *Franchises of Electrical Corporations in Greater New York, A Report Submitted to the Public Service Commission for the First District* (New York: 1911), pp. 30ff; Leonora Arent, *Electric Franchises in New York City* (New York: [privately printed], 1919), pp. 24, 54; Robert Grier Monroe, "The Gas, Electric Light, Water and Street Railway Services in New York City," *Annals of the American Academy*, 27:111-9 (10-1906).

Els: Clifton Hood, *722 Miles. The Building of the Subways and How They Transformed New York* (New York: Simon and Schuster, 1993), p. 25 (Trams traveled at five to six miles an hour).

Electric trams: Passer, chapters 15 and 16; *Jay Gould's experience:* p. 42.

Evolution of transit/utility links: This understanding was explicitly used in corporate maneuvers at the time (e.g., testimony of Col. T.S. Williams, vice president of the B.R.T., State of New York, Public Service Commission, First District: *Investigation of Interborough-Metropolitan Company and Brooklyn Rapid Transit Company, Aldermanic Chamber, New York, 8-1-07*, pp. 2236ff).

Interlocking control of transit and utility corporations: There are many sources on the networks who controlled these conglomerates, and on the centrality of Brady's role. Among them are several of Klein's books; The Merchants' Association of New York, "The Public Service Commissions Bill: Suggestions for its Modification," 4-22-1907; State of New York: *Testimony Taken Before the Joint Committee of the Senate and Assembly of the State of New York, To Investigate the Gas and Electric Light Situation in the City of New York*, vol. 1, testimony of Charles F. Lacomb, Engineer of Surface Construction, p. 2118.

The Yellow Kid: Roy Everett Littlefield, III, *William Randolph Hearst: His Role in American Progressivism* (Lanaham, MD: University Press of America, 1980), pp. 16, 75.

Street-Cleaning Scandal: Tribune, 1-24-06, p. 8:3; 2-6-06, p. 7:5; 2-7-06,

p. 9:1, 2-22-06, p. 8:3, 3-1-06, p. 10:1, 3-6-06, p. 8:1, 3-9-06, p. 11:3, 3-16-06, p. 4:3, 3-17-06, p, 10:5, 3-18-06, p. 4:5 and (IV), p. 6:3, 3-25-06 (IV), p. 6:5, 3-27-06, p. 5:5; *World*, 2-23-06, p. 10:5, 3-1-06, p. 1:7, 3-2-06, p. 3:1-2; Klein, *My First Fifty Years* (New York: Isaac Goldman Co., 1935), p. 17.

Ivins and Roosevelt: The National Cyclopaedia of American Biography, xxx: 10-11, "Ivins, William Mills."

"Loved an investigation": Milton MacKaye, *The Tin Box Parade, A Handbook for Larceny* (New York: Robt. M. McBride & Co., 1934), p. 177-8.

Barren Island made Nagle rich: New York City Board of Aldermen, *Report on the Administration of the Department of Street-Cleaning of the City of New York. Adopted by the Board of Aldermen, 7-10-1906* (Hereafter, *Ivins Investigation*), vol. III, p. 210.

Woodbury helped White-Cranford crew: Ivins Investigation, vol. III, p. 212; vol. IV, pp. 77-95.

Kennedy contract: Department of Street-Cleaning, *Annual Report*, 1906, pp. 75-6; *Tribune*, 3-18-06 (IV), p. 6:3.

Kennedy bid: Department of Street-Cleaning, op. cit., passim; *New York Times*, 5-12-06, p. 16:2.

Brady blackmail: World, 3-1-06, p. 1:7.

"I am glad you got out all right": New York Times, 5-10-06, p. 1:1.

Brady ran open cars: Ivins Investigation, passim and *World*, 3-2-06, p. 3:1-2.

McCarren demanded twenty-five thousand dollars: New York Times, 5-10-06, p. 1:1; 5-11, p. 6:2; *Ivins Investigation*, vol. I., pp. 1220ff.

Ivins's examination of witnesses: Governor Tim Woodruff and Judge Beardsleys are cited in the *Ivins Investigation*, vol. II, p. 1619; under examination by Ivins, Edward C.M. Fitzgerald, secretary of the Harway Company, also identifies "Senator McNulty." (ibid., pp. 1671-2); former Governor Roswell Flowers was with Brady when they were both approached by Kennedy for the original financing.

Contract cost: Ivins Investigation and *New York Times*, 5-10-06, p. 1:1.

City payments: The Public Service Commission in 1907 reported a net profit of only a few thousand dollars a year on the operation from all direct income sources (not including the value of real estate assets owned through shares in the Harway company and other holdings) [NYS Public Service Commission, loc. cit.], but this calculation included all "interest" payments for stock and equipment; since the stock was typical of the watered shares that the Brady conglomerate controlled, this accounting can scarcely be taken literally. Moreover, the income figures from private contracts given to the commission (as opposed to the more publicly accessible payments made by the city)—judging by the Morrone payments reported—are clearly at least an order of magnitude too low. (The Morrone contract figure given to the commission was a total of 60,819.61 dollars for a three-year-four-month period, while the *Tribune* [3-18-06, (IV), p. 6:3] reports an admittedly undocumented 750,000 dollars per year; this latter figure, however, is much closer to what the city was receiving on a volumetric basis, which, as the Ivins investigation showed, was less than a fair market value—and it is highly unlikely that the BRT company would handle its end of the negotiations as badly as did the city.)

Money from refuse: Ivins Investigation, vol. II, p. 1619.

Laborers: There are many accounts of Morrone's workers (and other trimmers) subsisting on food fragments salvaged from the refuse. An example is the testimony of Dr. Bayles, consulting engineer and former president of the Board of Health, as brought out by Ivins's examination. *Ivins Investigation,* vol. I., p. 939.

Marrone paid Brooklyn Ash: Ivins Investigation, passim; *Tribune,* 3-18-06 (IV), p. 6:3; 4-8, p. 10:4; State of New York, Public Service Commission, First District, p. 2685.

Brooklyn Ash's steam: State of New York, ibid.; Brooklyn Rapid Transit, Annual Report, 1906.

Brooklyn Ash real estate: Board of Aldermen, Special Committee on the Administration of the Street-Cleaning Department, *Testimony and Records in Preparation for Hearings. 1906* (hereafter, *Ivins Preliminary Investigation*). Testimony of Superintendent A. DeWilde, vol. III, p. 66, 220ff, 907, 1198,; vol. II, pp. 1600ff, 1619, 1671ff. *Ivins Investigation,* testimony of

Edward C.M. Fitzgerald, secretary of the Harway Improvement Company, p. 1672. *Tribune*, 3-15-06 (IV), p. 6:5; 3-18, (IV), p. 6:3; 3-28, p. 8:3.

Cost of Woodbury's plant: This calculation is based on the 45.22 dollars per day that Woodbury said was the cost, plus a portion of the 520 dollars per week that Ivins claimed was paid for labor to Marrone, the trimming contractor (Woodbury said that the trimming revenues received from Marrone offset these costs) and the cost of the coal used as an auxiliary fuel. Ivins's calculations, however, did not account for the "avoided" cost that would have been paid to dispose of the refuse at sea or on a landfill, and when these costs are included, the city came out *ahead* (by Woodbury's calculations and those of the *Engineering News Record*, by 34.20 dollars—not counting the value of the electricity that the city was able to use itself, which Woodbury claimed was worth about 50 dollars). NYC Department of Street-Cleaning, Annual Reports, 1902-11, pp. 82-5; *Ivins Investigation*, p. 79.

Plunkett contracts: Ivins Preliminary Investigation, vol. I., p. 190; *Tribune*, 2-22-1906, p. 8:3.

Franchises awarded below value: Ivins Investigation, passim; *Tribune*, 4-8-06, p. 10:4; *New York Times*, 4-20-06, p. 10:7.

Vote to remove Woodbury: New York Times, 6-27-06, p. 5:4; 7-3, p. 16:1; *Tribune*, 7-11-06, p. 2:5.

"An illiterate body of rum-soaked bums": New York Times, 5-25-1904, p. 16:2.

"The first necessary move": George B. McClellan, Jr., *The Gentleman and the Tiger: The Autobiography of George Brinton McClellan, Jr.* (New York: Lippincott, 1956), pp. 248-9. Used with permission by HarperCollins Publishers Inc.

Green's Jamaica Bay vision: Joseph Caccavajo, "The Development of Brooklyn and Queens," a lecture delivered before the Allied Boards of Trade and Taxpayers' Associations at the Johnstone Building, Brooklyn, 5-20-1909.

Jamaica Bay plan: The Report of the New York City Improvement Commission to the Hon. George B. McClellan, Mayor of the City of New York and to the

Hon. Board of Aldermen of the City of New York, 1907. (The preliminary report of the commission was issued in 1905.)

Municipal ownership of the shoreline of Jamaica Bay: Edward M. Grout, comptroller of the City of New York, *Improvement and Development of Jamaica Bay*, 11-17-1905.

"The syndicate thought that it had a stranglehold": McClellan, loc. cit.

"If McClellan is not using the army": Lincoln, 4-9-1862, *Bartlett's Familiar Quotations*, 16th edition (Boston: Little, Brown, 1992).

McClellan intended to avenge father's defeat: Harold C. Syrett, introduction to McClellan's *The Gentleman and the Tiger*, pp. 15-16 (citing the "Reminiscences" of William Prendergast in the Columbia Oral History Collection, II, p. 207.)

McClellan felt that he had to restore his reputation: McClellan, p. 221.

McClellan's career plans: McClellan, p. 285.

Woodbury resignation threat: McClellan, pp. 241-2.

Woodbury resignation accepted: Tribune, 10-2-06, p. 1:3; 12-27, p. 2:1; *Eagle*, 10-13, p. 1:3; *Sun*, 10-14, p. 1.

McCarren death: Lanahan, p. 68 (cites *Standard Union*, 10-14-09); McClellan admits this in his autobiography.

Brady and McCarren will: New York Times, 7-3-15, p. 7:5.

Wrote about Napoléon and Mussolini: Modern Italy: A Short History (Princeton: Princeton University Press, 1933) (see especially pp. 228-end); *Venice and Bonaparte* (Princeton, 1931). *Commander of the Order of the Crown of Italy: The Gentleman and the Tiger*, p. 369.

Woodbury at GE: New York Times, 9-25-14, p. 11:7.

Mitchel background: Dudley Field Malone, "John Purroy Mitchel," *World's Work*, 27, pp. 391-7 (February 1914).

McClellan asked Mitchel to investigate Bronx borough president: McClellan, p. 291.

Four borough presidents left office: The Manhattan and Bronx borough presidents were removed by Governor Hughes, who elected not to remove the Brooklyn borough president because his term of office was about to end (Lanahan); the Queens borough president fled to Europe rather than face charges.

Mitchel refused to appoint Mrs. Hearst: George McAneny, Columbia Oral History Collection, interviewed by Allan Nevins and Dean Albertson, January/February 1949, p.7; Ferdinand Lundberg, *Imperial Hearst: A Social Biography* (New York: Equinox Cooperative Press, 1936), p.120; Edwin R. Lewinson, *John Purroy Mitchel, The Boy Mayor of New York* (New York: Astra Books; 1965), pp.213.

Mitchel knew Reynolds: Lewinson, p.239.

Mitchel shot Reynolds: New York Times, 6-25-14, p.1:6; 6-26-14, p.22:3.

Reynolds offers Mitchel partnership: There are many sources for this, including *New York Times,* 9-15-17, p.9:1.

Reynolds and Bailey indicted: Bailey, p.128.

Bill killed: The bill failed in two consecutive Tammany controlled sessions of the legislature. In 1915, when the Republicans gained the majority, the bill passed, but Wagner succeeded in obtaining a veto from Republican Governor Whitman, using the theme that contracts on this scale (a nine-million-dollar citywide incinerator construction program under a fifteen-year contract) would allow enormous latitude for corruption.

Brooklyn Ash cost the city twice as much as it was paying in any other borough: e.g., J. T. Fetherston, commissioner of Street-Cleaning, "Memorandum Regarding the Proposed Amendment of Section 542 of the Charter . . ." 3-1-15, Municipal Archives, Mitchel papers, box 43, #13.

Reynolds and Bailey influenced Board of Estimate specifications: Board of Estimate Minutes, 1-31-19; Board of Aldermen Proceedings, 2-23-16, 3-7-16; "Memorandum in Re. Garbage Contracts," Hylan papers, #30-2.

"There is no veiled reason": New York Times, 10-22-17, p.4:1.

Citizen Doyle: The official accounts make no mention of a gun, but how else could Doyle have single-handedly rounded up and hauled off a gang of thugs?

Doyle's last hurrah: Doyle's exploits became, naturally enough, exaggerated in later Staten Islanders' accounts (e.g., *Staten Island Advance*, 10-21-38). My account is based on a contemporary clipping attached to an anonymous threat mailed to Mayor Mitchel on 5-31-16 (Mitchel papers), and on a letter to the editor of the *Staten Island Advance* by Doyle in 1938, correcting the exaggerations of its 10-21-38 story (11-17-38, p. 3).

Manhattan borough president found the lack of advance notice unsporting: Marcus M. Marks, borough president of Manhattan, to Joseph D. Holmes, 5-1-16, Municipal Archives, Hylan #30-4.

Hearing denouement: Staten Islander, 4-12-16, p. 1:1; 4-15-16, p. 1:1.

Metropolitan By-Products operations: "Memorandum in Re. Garbage Contracts. The Contract Between the City of New York and the Metropolitan By-Products Company, Inc.," n. d., based on affidavits filed by Commissioner MacStay in November, 1918 (Municipal Archives, Hylan Papers, #30-2). *Brooklyn Chamber of Commerce Bulletin,* vol. II, no. 2 (9-25-20), p. 5.

Metropolitan By-Product odors: Hylan files, letters and petitions, 6-25-18 to 7-30-18, from signatories living, among other places, in St. George (seven and one-half miles downwind—"nauseating"), W. New Brighton (over six miles, "odor unbearable", "awakened at 1-2 AM") and Tompkinsville (over seven miles).

"A corner in Arcady": Letter from Markham to Hylan, Hylan papers, #191, shelf 2623.

Hearst's perfect puppet: e.g., William Bullock, "Hylan," *American Mercury,* 4-24-18, pp. 444-450, Klein, *My Last Fifty Years,* p. 151.

"The next Health Commissioner of this city": American, 10-28-19, p. 7:1; also quoted in *New York Times,* I, p. 5:6, and *Eagle,* 12-3-18 and nd, Brooklyn Public Library, Brooklyn History Collection, vertical files, "Barren Island."

Mitchel's counterattack: Staten Islander, 4-22-16, p.1. After the mayoral election the indictments against Greve, Reynolds, and Bailey were dismissed and were not re-introduced.

Mitchel's death: There are many sources on the circumstances of Mitchel's death, including *Dictionary of American Biography,* VII, pp. 37-8.

Over the protests of Herbert Hoover: Eagle, 10-31-18, p. 1:5.

Barren Island re-opened: The contractual history of the Barren Island re-opening, as well as the protests over it, are documented, among other places, in the Hylan papers (Municipal Archives, box 191, shelf 2623).

Barren Island closed: It closed on 2-15-19 (*Eagle,* 2-14-19, p. 2:3 and 1-15-19, p. 2:3).

Whalen a Brooklyn Ash heir: This is according to Robert Moses, in his *Public Works: A Dangerous Trade* (New York: McGraw-Hill, 1970). Whalen's autobiography mentions only that his father was in the trucking business. (No obituary or other source on Whalen's father has been located.) A contemporary, Milton MacKaye, in *The Tin-Cup Parade,* also refers to Whalen having inherited "a small ash-trucking business," and George Walsh, in *Gentleman Jimmy Walker* (New York: Praeger, 1974), refers to Samuel Untermeyer reducing Whalen to tears during a cross-examination, getting him to admit that his company's ash trucks illegally dumped on city property.

McCarthy one of the mayor's strongest supporters: Grover Whalen, *Mr. New York: The Autobiography of Grover Whalen* (New York: G. P. Putnam's Sons, 1955), chapter 3. (It was Fishhooks who had originally scouted Hearst's candidate for Charlie Murphy, reporting back with a favorable verdict.)

Corona Meadows: New York Times, 7-21-23, p. 12:8; 9-26-23, p. 3:3.

Among the Ash-Heaps and Millionaires: Charles Scribner III, introduction to the Scribner Classics edition of *The Great Gatsby* (New York: 1980), pp. ix, xii ff.

"A valley of ashes": F. Scott Fitzgerald, *The Great Gatsby* (New York: Charles Scribner's Sons, 1925), p. 23.

Reynolds and Long Beach: New York Times, 5-2-24, p. 1:4; 6-17-24, p. 21:5; 6-18-24, p. 21:8; 6-20-24, p. 1:3; 6-21-24, pp. 12:5 and 28:2; 6-27-24, p. 21:2; 7-6-24, II, p. 1:8. Although he was convicted of one charge, and spent a brief amount of time in jail, that conviction was overturned on appeal.

Reynolds's funeral: Eagle, 10-14-31, p. 1:3.

Reynolds's monument: Long Beach Life, 9-4-38, Brooklyn Historical Society clip file, vol. 35, p. 35.

PART III

"Leave the son of a bitch off": Robert Caro, *The Power Broker: Robert Moses and the Fall of New York* (New York: Vintage, 1975 [Knopf, 1974]) p. 607.

Triborough putsch: Triborough Bridge and Tunnel Authority (hereafter, TBTA), Tunnel Authority files, cabinet #186, top drawer, back: diaries.

Moses and Haussmann: Moses's fascination with Haussmann is also noted by one of Haussmann's more recent biographers. David P. Jordan, *Transforming Paris, The Life and Labors of Baron Haussmann* (New York: Free Press, 1995), e.g., fn, p. 227. Caro also points out the Moses self-identification with Haussmann (p. 1062).

Haussmann dossier: TBTA, coordinator's files, cabinet #1123, 3rd drawer, file: "Baron Haussmann, Memo, etc. Prepared for Robert Moses by S.T. Herrick, 6-26-41."

Morizet: Du vieux Paris au Paris moderne; Haussmann et ses prédécesseurs, 1932.

1939 Fair losses: Caro, p. 1085.

Wilgus rides rails: William J. Wilgus, *Milestones in the Life of a Civil Engineer* (unpublished typescript, 1947, formerly in the Engineering Societies Library, New York City), p. 20.

"I trotted along with him": ibid., p. 18.

Vision of Grand Central Terminal: The section that follows owes much to David Marshall's *Grand Central Terminal* (New York: McGraw-Hill, 1946). (Near the end of his life, Wilgus and his closest friend, Oswald Garrison Villard, discussed the possibility of having Marshall write his biography.)

Accident January 8, 1902: Carl W. Condit, *The Port of New York. A History of the Rail and Terminal System from the Grand Central Electrification to the Present* (Chicago: University of Chicago Press, 1980-1), p. 6.

New York Central sentence: This sentence was handed down in the form of a newly enacted state law.

They asked Wilgus to carry out his plan: Condit, pp. 8-9; Marshall, p. 237.

One of the supreme achievements of twentieth-century design: Condit, p. 11: "The process by which the design concepts were translated into a practical working machine is perhaps the supreme example in technological history of technique carried to the level of a highly complex, multi-dimensional scientific enterprise. In the technological revolution that produced electrified mass transportation, the creation of the New York Central's pioneer class of electric locomotives constituted one of the most decisive steps."

Grand Central start: This and the preceding paragraph is based on Marshall, pp. 237-45.

Grand Central excavation: Marshall, p. 255: a pit 40 feet deep, 770 feet wide, half a mile long.

Original Grand Central design: Marshall, pp. 237-66.

The busiest, most profitable transportation facility: Condit, p. 95: "The full urbanistic role of Grand Central Terminal—the place, function, life, and meaning of this civic monument in the circulation and architectural ambience of New York—far transcends internal rail traffic and the lively commerce of the numerous shops and restaurants that make it the greatest microcity in America. With respect to urban movement the terminal is one of the primary nodes in the whole New York pattern of interrelated circulatory systems, not only by virtue of the traffic within the body of the station complex, but also through the interaction of that complex with the surrounding arteries. The many entrances, exits, internal passages, and ramps, and the principle of gravitational flow for pedestrians serve not only to tie all the parts of the terminal together into a working unity, like a living organism, but equally to interconnect the complex with the arterial pattern around it...."

Wilgus invented containerization: As Condit points out (p. 122), Wilgus readily acknowledged that he did not originate the concept of the underground freight tunnel itself: "it was derived from the narrow-gauge freight-carrying tunnels built in Chicago in 1901-09 by the Illinois Telephone and Telegraph Company and the Illinois Tunnel Co." But Wilgus's proposed tunnel was longer, and originated the idea of containerized freight handling, and of rail-to-truck transfer.

The Central board said the idea was five years ahead of its time: This was how Wilgus originally reported the exchange. In later years, he changed first to "ten years," then to "twenty." (Wilgus papers, New York Public Library, box 48, 3-24-33 introduction to his 1913 belt line proposal.)

Wilgus invented an open-trench tunneling technique: The work was done as a consulting engineer for the Central's subsidiary, the Michigan Central. The invention involved not only a trench-digging method, but watertight tunnel sections that could be assembled underwater. The Institute of Civil Engineers of Great Britain awarded him the Telford Gold Medal for the achievement. *New York Times*, 10-15-49, p. 27:1 (obit.).

The commissioners were delighted with Wilgus's solution: Actually, the commission had hired the newly independent Wilgus to solve this problem and enthusiastically accepted his solution. But since the commissioners told Wilgus that only a private company could implement the plan, Wilgus returned the fee they had paid him, made the plans public, and formed his own company to build it.

Wilgus rejects the commission's blackmail: papers, box 45, 5-20-14 memo in bound volume, "Proposed Solution of Manhattan's Freight Problem." Josef Konvitz, in his seminal "William J Wilgus and Engineering Projects to Improve the Port of New York" (*Technology and Culture* 30 [1989], pp. 398-425), notes Wilgus's cryptic reference to this situation in his unpublished memoirs, but says that he was unable to discover any clues in his papers that would explain his allusion. I believe that this memo describing the bribe request is what Konvitz was looking for. The technical reason the commission gave for not approving the proposal was that Wilgus's corporation would have to enter into a contract with the Central for freight service before the proposal would be considered: since the Central was in litigation with the city at the time—litigation that would drag on for more than a decade more—the Central refused to enter into negotiations. It appears that the position the city took (as Wilgus's papers suggest) was a convenient excuse rather than a necessity.

Wilgus's research: Wilgus papers, box 56, file 55: 12-30-09, "A Suggestion for an INTERSTATE METROPOLITAN DISTRICT Embracing The Territory Tributary To The Port of New York."

"One day in September, 1918": This episode is closely paraphrased from David Marshall (pp. 245-6), who interviewed at least one of Wilgus's World War I colleagues, as well as Wilgus himself.

"FFM": e.g., Caro, p. 88.

During this interregnum he came to know Moses: Smith had been introduced to Moses in 1919 by Belle Moskowitz, but the two did not become close until 1921. Caro, p. 112.

Rows of treacherous wheels: For accident statistics and traffic volumes, see Clay McShane, *Down the Asphalt Path* (New York: Columbia University Press, 1994), pp. 48-9.

Smith's first job: Caro, p. 115.

Hylan in Florida with Hearst: New York Times, 2-23-18, p. 13:1.

Coal problem: Alfred E. Smith, *Up to Now. An Autobiography* (Garden City, NY: Garden City Publishing Co., 1929), p. 158.

He waited to run again: In his autobiography, Smith claims that he had not planned to run for governor again, and did not want to run, but was prevailed upon by the party to stop Hearst from running. I do not find Smith's claim convincing.

Bernay's memoirs: Caruso to Bernays at 1.30 one morning in Pittsburgh: "eighteen pillows and three mattresses—or no concert tomorrow." Bernays on the Ballet Russe: "they behaved like inmates of a rabbit hutch." Edward L. Bernays, *Biography of an Idea: Memoirs of Public Relations Counsel Edward L. Bernays*, (New York: Simon and Schuster, 1965), pp. 141 and 113.

The war: Bernays and his famous uncle had very different views of Wilson and the war. See Freud's monograph on Wilson's psyche (*Thomas Woodrow Wilson, Twenty-Eighth President of the United States; A Psychological Study*).

Moskowitz coined the phrase: Elizabeth Israels Perry, *Belle Moskowitz: Feminine Politics and the Exercise of Power in the Age of Alfred E. Smith* (New York: Oxford University Press, 1987), p. 141.

Brieux's play was banned: After a performance in Switzerland sponsored by a clergyman, the Parisian ban on *Les Avariés* eventually was lifted. George Bernard Shaw, preface to *Three Plays by Eugene Brieux* (New York: Brentano's, 1913).

The greatest French writer since Molière: ibid., pp. vii and xlvi.

New Yorkers read that a private performance of Brieux's play was being organized: New York Times, 2-8-13, p. 13:2.

John D. Rockefeller was helping to choose the audience: New York Times, 2-28-13, III, p. 13:1.

"A certain morbid interest": New York Times, 3-2-13, IV, p. 6:3 (ed.)

"Highly engrossing": New York Times, 3-15-13, p. 13:2.

"The most distinguished audience ever assembled in America": Upton Sinclair, preface to his novelization of *Damaged Goods* (Philadelphia: John C. Winston Co., 1913), p. 7.

Al Smith, Belle Moskowitz, and the Port and Harbor Commission's public relations campaign: Perry, p. 142; passim; Erwin Wilkie Bard, *The Port of New York Authority* (New York: Columbia University Press, 1942), pp. 48-9. The "contact department" phrase was used in a speech by Julius Henry Cohen to the Educational Council, Wilgus papers, box 56, folder #55, "The New York Port Problem in its Relation to the Public," p. 14. (In this speech, by the way—as Outerbridge did on the same occasion—he denied that any money was being spent on "publicity," which was a very lawyerly distinction.)

Moskowitz wrote: (Or her staff: the brochure is unsigned.) "The New York Port Problem in its Relation to the Public."

The public relations film: Moskowitz had invented the idea of the public relations film the year before, in her work on behalf of Smith's Reconstruction Commission.

"To arouse this public opinion": Outerbridge speech, ibid., p. 4.

"As the emergency for which I entered the service is ended": Wilgus to General John J. Pershing, 11-17-18, copy in appendix to *Milestones*. It was in char-

acter that Wilgus did not mention his wife's death to Pershing. The only indication of her death is in a footnote on p. 313.

Wilgus's proposed rail network: All twelve trunklines serving the city would have unimpeded access to this highly profitable route. To manage the coordinated operations, Wilgus proposed the formation of three corporations, "1. The New Jersey Belt Line Railroad Company, to be organized in the interest of the trunk lines, and the necessary capital therefor to be raised by them or under the auspices of the National Railway Service Corp, with a view to building and equipping a belt line on the route suggested in my letter of August 9th, from the Hudson River on the north to the Arthur Kills on the south. 2. The New York Belt Line Railroad Company...3. The Metropolitan Belt Line Railroad Company, to be organized, if possible, under a Federal charter, and with a comparatively small capitalization, of which 51 percent of the stock would be owned by the City of New York or a trustee acting in its behalf . . ." (Wilgus papers, box 55, folder #222: "Tunnel Beneath New York Bay Between Brooklyn and Staten Island," memo, 8-10-21, to Arthur Tuttle, chief engineer, Board of Estimate and Apportionment.) Just as the notion of a beltway that coordinated the flows of different railways had been demonstrated in several places (e.g., Buffalo), as Wilgus pointed out, so too had the successful operation of inter-railway corporations for managing such an enterprise (e.g., St. Louis). Wilgus papers, box 53, folder: "Minutes of the Meeting of the Engineering Committee," transcript of meeting held on 10-21-21, p. 25.

The "oily" Julius Henry Cohen: New York Post, 5-5-25 (Wilgus papers, loc. cit.); John J. Desmond's (Wilgus's secretary) notes from meeting on 5-4-25 (box 55, unlabeled folder).

Hylan went to Florida: New York Post, 1-31-22 (in Wilgus papers, box 55, Scrapbook, "Narrows Tunnel, Vol. XVII.") That Hearst was the one who instructed Hylan not to appear in Albany was the common presumption at the time.

LaGuardia maintained that the propaganda emanated from the Transit Commission: New York Times, 12-30-21 (in Wilgus papers, loc. cit.).

"Naturally we thought": extract from hearing transcript, quoted by Julius

Henry Cohen in letter to Wilgus of 8-7-25 (p. 19), in Wilgus papers, box 56, folder: "Regional Plan of New York...., vol. III.," and by *New York Times* of 2-1-22. The Cohen version gives the last sentence as ". . . because I saw in it a trucking job. (Laughter and applause.) I regarded it as well being worth while."

Avenue Foch: In Haussmann's day it was called l'Avenue de l'Impératrice.

They now proposed a fifth stage of urban roadway: F. L. Olmsted and C. Vaux, "Report of the Landscape Architects and Superintendents to the President of the Board of Commissioners of Prospect Park, Brooklyn," 1868, in Fein, pp. 158-59.

Olmsted's bias for personal forms of transportation: He so firmly believed in the physical and mental-health benefits of riding and driving that he planned parkways even alongside railroads to give commuting businessmen the option to take some healthful exercise instead of sitting back and reading the newspaper (see his uncompleted plan for Riverside, IL). He was decades ahead of his time in predicting that travelers would soon begin to abandon rail-based mass transportation and instead drive their own horseless carriages over roads—by 1871 he had begun to plan his road grades and surfaces with such steam-powered vehicles in mind. "Report to the Staten Island Improvement Commission of a Preliminary Scheme of Improvements," appendix "Steam on Common Roads," reprinted in Fein, pp. 173ff.

Olmsted laid out the first plan for a rapid transit steam railroad system: NYC Board of Estimate and Apportionment, Committee on the City Plan, *Development and Present Status of City Planning in NYC*, 12-31-14, p. 16.

The plan was largely an elaboration of the senior Olmsted's work: NYC Improvement Commission, Report,... p. 190.; Fein; David Alan Johnson, *The Emergence of Metropolitan Regionalism: An Analysis of the 1929 Regional Plan of New York and Its Environs* (Dissertation, Cornell University, 1974), pp. 61-5; Johnson, "Regional Planning for the Great American Metropolis: New York Between the World Wars," in ed. Daniel Schaffer, *Two Centuries of American Planning* (London: Mansell Publishing, Ltd., 1988), pp. 168, 170.

Wabash president Delano: Delano's interest in regional planning began with his Wilgus-like attempt, as president of the Wabash Railroad, to consolidate Chicago's widely scattered railroad terminals. His failure in this led him to support the Burnham effort. Mark Gelfand, *A Nation of Cities: The Federal Government and Urban America* (New York: Oxford University Press, 1975), p. 83.

Burnham had recently completed the first complete plan for an entire metropolitan region: Mario Manieri-Elia, "Toward an 'Imperial City:' Daniel H. Burnham and the City Beautiful Movement," in Giorgio Ciucci, Francesco Dal Co, Mario Manieri-Elia, and Manfredo Tafuri, *The American City From the Civil War to the New Deal,* trans. from Italian by Barbara Luigia La Penta (Cambridge, MA: MIT Press, 1979 [Ital. 1973), pp. 89ff.

Burnham's role: Paul Barrett, *The Automobile and Urban Transit: The Formation of Public Policy in Chicago, 1900-1930* (Philadelphia: Temple University Press, 1983), p. 73.

Mitchel and McAneny were indicted: e.g., *New York Times,* 3-25-15, p. 6:4; 3-31-15, p. 7:2; 7-20-16, p. 12:1; 7-21-16, p. 9:1; 11-3-17, p. 4:1. William Bullock, director, Bureau of City Inquiry, New York, *Mitchel-Prendergast-Reynolds, and Rockaway Park. How the City of New York Paid 2,400 Per Cent* (New York, 2-17-17), p. 3. (This imbroglio was going on at the same time that Reynolds and his friends, on the one hand, and Mitchel and McAneny, on the other, were under indictment for the Dreamland deal, and Reynolds et. al were meanwhile beginning to plan the Metropolitan By-Products affair.)

Out of their vision the Regional Plan Association was born: Robert Fishman, "The Regional Plan and the Transformation of the Industrial Metropolis," in eds. David Ward and Olivier Zunz, *The Landscape of Modernity: Essays on New York City, 1900-1940* (New York: Russell Sage Foundation, 1992), p. 106.

Supporting his own young family: Caro, pp. 87, 131, passim.

Moses wrote to its secretary: Moses to Agar, 4-13-22, papers, box 7, folder: "Metropolitan Park Plan, Russell Sage Foundation."

"Vague plans": loc. cit., 4-9-23.

The group hired Belle Moskowitz instead: Perry, p. 162. (The file strippers who would one day tear much of the meat out of "the Chief's" files left the brittle, yellowed evidence of Moses's consolation prize from the Sage Foundation: a checkstub showing a five-hundred-dollar contribution to the New York State Association.)

The Regional Plan staff kept asking Wilgus to join them: Wilgus papers, box 56, folder 55.4: "Sage Foundation Plan of New York."

"An outer belt railway": 8-28-24, in Wilgus papers, box 56, bound folder: "Regional Plan of New York. Projects Proposed by W.J. Wilgus, vol. 1."

"Clear, comprehensive, sane, and bold": This is Adams's paraphrase of Olmsted's views. Adams to Wilgus, 11-3-25, Wilgus papers, box 56, folder: "Regional Plan of New York. Projects Proposed by W.J. Wilgus, vol. 1."

He produced the conceptual design for a completely new idea: "Proposed Causeway Between Rockaway Beach and Sandy Hook," in Wilgus papers, box 56, folder: "Regional Plan of New York…Causeway, vol. 2."

Smith listened: New York Times, 4-21-25, Wilgus papers, loc. cit.

Adams weaseled away from RPA's public position: To Wilgus, on vacation in Vermont, he wheedled, "I agree with you as expressed in your telegram that we should not weaken on points of principle or be stampeded by political expediency. I hope that you will pardon me if I have failed to meet a difficult situation in the best way." Adams to Smith and to Wilgus, 4-17-25. Wilgus papers, box 55 (unlabeled folder).

Adams, ever the coward, shortly after begged Wilgus not to do anything more to rock the boat. "The fact that the issue is dead for the time makes it particularly desirable that the Committee's relations with the Port of New York Authority and Mr. Outerbridge should not be strained more than is necessary." Wilgus did not respond. He underlined Adams's word *dead* in pencil, and in the margin next to it drew an *x*. Adams to Wilgus, 5-2-25, loc. cit.

There was no technical justification for eliminating freight and passenger rail service: Johnson, p. 408.

"So many autumn leaves": Wilgus, *Milestones,* p. 216.

Largely learned through close observation of the Port Authority: e.g. (one example of Moses' close attention to the details of Port Authority financing
from Day One) Moses' 1-25-22 letter, as Secretary of the NYS Association to Port Authority Chairman E. H. Outerbridge inquiring about
financial details, such as how the self-supporting bonds would be sold.
Quoted in Bard, footnote, p. 226.

The transaction involved no influx to Reynolds's pockets: e.g., *New York Times,*
6-21-24, p. 12:5.

Moses escaped a parallel fate: Perry, p. 173; Caro, pp. 202-3.

Moses did his best to help Reynolds out of his fix: Moses to George Graves,
Secretary to the Governor, 12-23-25, Moses papers, box 2, folder: "Long
Beach Reynolds Case."

Reynolds's constituents were untroubled by their mayor's behavior: New York
Times, 7-6-24, II, p. 1:8.

The artful use of the word "parkway": Architectural Forum, "Pattern for
Parks," December, 1936, p. 494; Caro, pp. 174-5.

State bond authorizations could be used: Perry, pp. 166, 171. Even better, if
the seller of the underlying land did not want to accept the offered price,
the state could skip the expensive and time-consuming condemnation
process simply by "appropriating" the lands Moses needed.

They had bothered to acquire only a few thousand feet of the mapped right-of-way:
Moses to Raymond V. Ingersoll, 5-28-37, Moses papers, box 97, folder:
"Parks, 1937."

Moses hoped to use an old railroad right-of-way: The rail line was the abandoned "Stewart right-of-way." The proposed parkway is first discussed in
the Metropolitan Conference on Parks's "Program for Extension of Parks
and Parkways in the Metropolitan Region," 2-25-30, p. 10. The pursuit
of this option is discussed in various documents in the Moses papers.

Brooklyn Ash announced plans to build an "industrial colony": Long Island
Daily Press, 4-29-39 (clippings in Queens Public Library, Long Island
Room, vertical files, folder: "Waste Disposal, Queens County, 1926-69,
Envelopes 1 and 2").

The world's best argument for cremation: MacKaye, p. 186.

"Burying the survivors": Long Island Daily Press, loc. cit.

Brooklyn Ash proposed this use as well: Flushing Evening Journal, 1-5-25, p. 1 and *Newtown Register,* 1-6-25 (clippings loc. cit.); *New York Times,* 1-6-25, p. 16:2.

Dozens were being proposed or developed: forty-six existing or proposed airports are listed in the Regional Plan Association's *Graphic Regional Plan* (pp. 374-5).

Brooklyn Ash offered it to the Walker administration for this purpose: New York Times, 10-3-27, p. 25:1.

A railroad center, an automobile raceway, and a giant boxing arena: Moses, *The Flushing Meadow Improvement,* vol. 2, March-August, 1937, p. 18.

"All the pathetic beauty": ibid.; Moses, "From Dump to Glory," *Saturday Evening Post,* 1-15-38 (Municipal Reference Center, vertical files).

Recreadions: New York Times, 3-30-33. Although Brooklyn Ash was offering to fund these recreadions on its own, Nathan Strauss was working with Lewis L. Delafield, Jr. (the lawyer who handled Moses's authority work) to develop legislation to create a state "Recreadion Authority." (Moses, needless to say, was adamantly opposed to another authority encroaching on his turf.) Moses to Lehman, 8-19-33, Moses papers, box 89, file: "N.Y. State Recreadion Authority."

They consistently charged a price twice that the citizens in any other borough were paying: e.g., *New York Times,* 1-26-33, p. 24:6.

This edifying spectacle should put to rest the vicious rumors: Brooklyn Ash's attorneys alleged that Rosoff had missed payments on a sizeable loan for over a year. *New York Times,* 4-5-33, p. 40:1; 5-3-33, p. 7:1.

The firm had been organized only two weeks before the bids were due: New York Times, 5-2-33, p. 38:2.

Brooklyn Ash's apologists: These included such interested investors as Standard Oil chairman Herbert Pratt. Municipal Archives, McKee papers, Pratt to McKee, 10-3-32.

Municipally controlled forces, he believed, could dispose of it for less than forty cents a ton: New York Times, 1-26-33, p. 24:6.

In a position to leave eight million dollars to charity: McCarthy left his home and five hundred thousand dollars to his spinster sister, fifty thousand dollars in trusts for each of his three nieces and his nephew, five thousand dollars to the Church of the Blessed Sacrament, ten thousand dollars to the Roman Catholic Archbishop of New York to be distributed among the ten neediest Catholic churches in the city, and the remainder to the Catholic Charities of the Archdiocese of New York. *New York Times,* 2-4-55, p. 27:5.

Jamaica Bay offered the only solution to the problem of the Port of New York's loss of business to its competitors: Report of the City Committee on Plan and Survey, released to the press 6-6-28, Wilgus papers, box 57, pp. 74-76.

Pretending that it did made the federal and state budget agencies think that this work was necessary: Moses was explicit about this naming game in correspondence with a variety of influential people who questioned him on the mundane names he gave his roads. e.g., to Myron Taylor, chairman, United States Steel Corporation, 10-24-35, Moses papers, box 97, file: "1935."

Building the Triborough Bridge: The hapless Walker administration had begun construction on Black Friday—October 25, 1929, the day the stock market crashed—and had run out of funds for the project before Walker himself was forced from office, leaving only the concrete pylons standing there like the bleak reminders of a former civilization. Wright, p. 386.

It was essential that he get the city to buy the Corona Meadows right-of-way: He had had the more southerly "Flushing Meadows" portion included in the city's parks-bond authorization.

McAneny came to him with a plan to pay for transforming this lunar landscape: e.g., Herald Tribune, 5-22-49, Moses, "Flushing Meadow Park, 10th Anniversary" (offprint in Municipal Reference Center vertical file: "Flushing Meadow").

The new president jumped back on his barge: David Oats, "The World in a

Park: History of Flushing Meadow," *Queens Tribune*, a series that ran from 7-26-80 to 11-6-80 (Queens Public Library vertical files).

The kind of man's man sportswriters adore: e.g., *World-Telegram*, 5-18-36, p. 3:6; *Herald Tribune*, 5-17-36, p. 7:1; *Eagle*, 4-2-39 (ed) (in Municipal Reference Center notebooks).

Carey's self-confidence was well-earned: New York Times, 7-12-38, p. 27:7; *Herald-Tribune*, 2-24-51 (obituary) in Municipal Reference Center vertical file; *Who's Who in America*, 1940-1, 1950-1.

Carey became president of Madison Square Garden: The directors of Madison Square Gardens selected Carey over such other well-known candidates as Jack Dempsey and Jimmy Walker. *New York Times*, 3-19-29, p. 26:1

"I used to visit the old North Beach Airport": Moses, *Public Works: A Dangerous Trade*, p. 329.

Even today, runways have to be filled on a regular basis: Wilfredo Guzman, P. E., Port Authority of New York and New Jersey, personal communication, 1994. At that time, Mr. Guzman was the construction supervisor in charge of LaGuardia Airport's renovation.

At least one flight was aborted: LaGuardia papers, 1933-45, box 3374, file 9: "Subject: Airports (North Beach), Rodent Problem, NYC Department of Health, 9-18-42," p. 5.

His men left open a boom one night: e.g., *New York Times*, 6-2-35, II, p. 1:2.

Moses was champing with impatience to get the landfilling stopped at Rikers Island: Moses's disgust with Sanitation Commissioner Thomas W. Hammond on this issue is clearly documented in a series of memoranda in the Moses papers, box 97, folder: "Department of Parks, 1935-," e.g., Moses to LaGuardia 11-1-35, Moses to Hammond, 10-31-35 and 10-26-35. See also Department of Parks, City of New York, *Report to the World's Fair Committee of the Board of Estimate and Apportionment on the Acquisition and Development of the World's Fair Site*, 12-18-35 (Municipal Reference Center), and *New York Times*, 12-20-35, p. 27:6.

He was presented with a large bronze bone: Caro, p. 445.

"That dago son-of-a-bitch": Caro, p. 447.

LaGuardia had printed up a pad of notes: Caro, p. 448.

He watched the boss's "vaudeville stunts": Moses, "LaGuardia: A Salute . . .", quoted in August Hecksher, *When LaGuardia Was Mayor* (New York: Norton, 1978), p. 156.

The island "exercised an irresistible charm": Moses, "From Dump to Glory."

Rikers's original eighty-seven acres: Kenneth T. Jackson, ed., *The Encyclopedia of New York City,* "Rikers Island."

"A cloud of smoke by day": Moses, "Flushing Meadow Park," (*Herald Tribune,* 5-22-49, reprinted by Parks Department). Moses was not engaging in hyperbole: Thomas DeLisa, a sanitation department employee who worked there for eighteen years, said "The rats became so numerous and so large that the department imported dogs in an effort to eliminate the rats. When I left, there were more than one hundred dogs on the island, dogs which were never fed by authorities, but lived solely on these rates. Despite this the rats, some of them as big as cats, continued to multiply. It was nothing to see as many as one hundred rats in a walk across the land-fill at night. . . . Although the department maintained a large fire-fighting force on Rikers Island, it could not eliminate the fires. Gases . . . were constantly exploding, erupting through the soil covering and bursting into flames. There was never a day in the summertime when fires were not breaking out and the stench from these fires gave off the most noxious odor imaginable. . . . [W]hen a hot spell would come along in the summer the ground resembled a sea of small volcanoes, all breathing smoke and flames." Quoted in *Staten Island Advance,* 6-12-46, p. 1.

In Moses's view, Carey's Sanitation Department should have stopped dumping there the moment the fair was announced: New York Times, 8-8-36, p. 15:4.

Carey got LaGuardia to ask the Corps of Engineers for permission to extend the landfill further into the Sound: The permit was eventually granted; still another extension request was filed in 1939 (see below) and rejected.

"I should like to know just what area you have in mind": Moses papers, box 97, Moses to Carey, 4-18-38.

A "tragic mistake": New York Times, 4-20-38; also, *Herald Tribune,* p. 9:1; *Eagle,* p. 1:3.

He laid down well over a hundred thousand cubic yards of refuse in Riverside Park: e.g., *Memorandum to the Mayor on Park Department Revised Plan for West Side Improvement in Riverside Park,* 6-10-35 (Municipal Reference Center); *Annual Report of the Department of Sanitation, 1934,* appendix no. 1, p. 48.

Haussmann scattered the last inhabitants of Montfaucon: Hervé Maneglier, *Paris Impérial. La vie quotidiene sous le Second Empire* (Paris: Armand Colin, 1990), p. 147.

Jane Shaw begged for a reprieve: Jane Shaw to Raymond V. Ingersoll, 3-22-36; Ingersoll to Moses, 3-25; Moses to Ingersoll, 3-26. Moses papers, box 97.

"Fifty embattled housewives": New York Times, 8-20-38.

The dumping continued despite repeated protests: The New York newspapers for the years after 1938 are replete with stories about landfill nuisances and judicial proceedings. Just one example: the *Eagle*'s coverage of "The Battle of the Big Stench"—about dumping in Marine Park, Brooklyn, in 1949. The articles were reprinted as a pamphlet with that title, which can be found in the vertical files of the Brooklyn Public Library (where the *Eagle* morgue is also located).

Wilgus's dream of a seamlessly integrated metropolitan region: Though the dream of a Narrows rail-freight tunnel had now been deferred for the two decades since Wilgus had first come back from the war to fight for it against the propaganda assault Al Smith and George McAneny led from their respective quarters, Wilgus had not entirely given it up. "I may say," he told the Regional Plan's engineer in 1931 (refusing his request for more detailed comment "on the Jamaica Bay project") "that I have always considered that it offered an opportunity for creating a great port on noble lines, free from the limitations that dwarf and hamper a proper development on the Upper Bay; and, above all, with suitable rail connections with the continent. The latter I have long championed (for twenty years), but my voice has been as of one in the wilderness.... It seems to me that the Regional Plan must become militant...if it expects to see its projects be adopted." Wilgus papers, box 56, folder 55.4: "Sage Foundation Plan of New York," 2-13-31, J. J. Desmond [Wilgus's secretary, quoting Wilgus] to Harold M. Lewis, executive engineer, Regional Plan of New York.

He enjoyed a cozy relationship with the judge who handled the condemnations: Charles G. Lockwood was a member of the Parks Association, and he and Moses frequently corresponded in friendly fashion concerning issues of mutual interest—including the condemnation proceedings that Lockwood was handling. e.g.: Moses papers, box 98, file 1940; box 97, file 1936.

He was bumping into some of the same political speculators: New York Times, 4-28-38, p. 25:5.

Even he was getting "cold feet": Moses to Allyn Jennings, 7-6-37, Moses papers, box 97, file: "Parks, 1937."

It should definitely be a tunnel, he said: LaGuardia press release, LaGuardia papers, subject file, roll 1, folder: "Tunnels, Staten Island, 1934-7," document 1700.

He had been contemplating for almost a decade: e.g., Metropolitan Conference on Parks, 2-25-30, p. 13.

It was politically impractical to levy assessments: Moses to Mrs. Alice F. Cogan, 7-27-37 and to Joseph W. Wanty, 10-13, Moses papers, box 97, folder: "Parks, 1937."

Filling that wetland would be a waste: Ingersoll to Moses, 5-4-38, Moses papers, box 97. Carey acknowledged that the original idea of landfilling Fresh Kills was Moses's and that he had asked Carey in 1937 to landfill there (*Staten Island Advance*, 10-19-38, p. 1:1).

Moses's architects and engineers began drawing plans: New York Times, 11-23-38, p. 1:4.

It was just where he needed a big piece of land for the intersection of two parkways: The two planned parkways were the Bronx River Parkway, for which he had begun seeking final authorization, and the planned shorefront road between the Triborough and the Whitestone bridges, which for the moment—in order not to muddle the progress of his more immediate plans—he was keeping under his hat.

Using any kind of material other than refuse would have cost a couple of million dollars—as much as he had budgeted for extending the Bronx River Parkway itself. Moses projected that the park would take fifteen million cubic yards of refuse (Moses and Carey to Board of Estimate, 5-5-39, LaGuardia papers, box 3217, folder #04); since refuse would settle over time, it was assumed to equal about a third the volume of soil fill. Delivered clean fill cost on the order of fifty cents per cubic yard. (*Eagle*, 3-28-38, np, [Queens Public Library, folder: "Waste Disposal, Queens County, 1926-69," envelope 1].) The state budget for the Bronx River Parkway Extension in 1939 was 2,200,000 dollars. (Moses to LaGuardia, 2-4, LaGuardia papers, loc. cit.) Accepting "cellar dirt" from construction excavation was a way of obtaining free soil, but it was not available on a scale that would have met any reasonable schedule requirements.

Moses' propaganda crusade: To Raymond Ingersoll, his old acquaintance the Brooklyn borough president, Moses wrote (5-3-38): "I know that you agree with me that the future of the greater part of this area is residential and recreational and that the plan to which the City has been more or less committed to devote most of this area to shipping and industry should definitely be abandoned excepting along the railroads leading to the Bay and along some of the creeks and basins on the north side," and asked for his help in re-zoning it. Ingersoll wrote back reassuringly (5-4-38), expressed his support for Moses's vision, and said that he had already discussed the dump proposal with Carey. Carey, he said, had mentioned another place, the [Fresh] Kills section of Staten Island, that he might be willing to use instead. Moses papers, box 97.

Moses decided to offer Carey the Sound View option: The offer was conveyed through Moses' trusted parks superintendent Allyn Jennings, to whom Moses wrote in disgust after Carey turned it down: "Your memorandum about the conference with Commissioner Carey is not very responsive.... [A]ssuming that Carey is unwilling to go along with us [on providing fill for the Sound View project], we cannot 'forget the bulkheading entirely.' After all, we still have the problem. How do you propose to solve it? I never know of anything to be solved by forgetting it, and this particular little problem cannot be swept under the sofa." If getting fill was the Parks Department's problem, getting rid of refuse was the Sanitation Department's, Moses continued. "As to Commissioner Carey's problem, what does he say about building additional incinerators?... [Carey was not only shelving plans the WPA had already funded for building incinerators to produce the ash that Moses preferred as fill, but, to shave operating costs, was in the process of closing half the incinerators he already had.] I wish you would see Mrs. Sulzberger [the Parks Association chairwoman whose ties to the *Times* made her one of his most important supporters] and explain the whole situation to her. Don't do it, however, unless you are prepared to represent our point of view. If you feel that you must be sympathetic to Bill Carey, I shall have to ask someone else to represent us in this matter. Let Bill roll his own! He can take care of himself, and he will have a lot more respect for us if we don't swallow the guff he is handing out to the public." To Carey himself he wrote, "Allyn Jennings has reported to me about the talk he had with you.... Where will you go [when you leave Rikers Island]? I tell you, Bill, Jamaica Bay is out and we might as well proceed on that basis. Why can't we get together and discuss the Richmond matter again?" Moses to Jennings, 5-25-38, and to Carey, 5-26-38, Moses papers, box 97.

(In spite of being one of Moses' most trusted assistants, Jennings's sympathies with Carey were long evident, but never more obviously than when he went to work for Carey instead of Moses when he was released from the Coast Guard at the end of World War II. A bit of Coast Guard business during the war, when Commander Jennings represented the US government's interests rather than Moses', may have been the immediate cause of Jennings's change in postwar employers. [Jennings, Superintendent of Landfills, to Moses, 7-2-45, Moses papers, box 73, folder: "AS3-1945 & 1946"; Caro, p. 833].)

Moses continued his suasion campaign all summer and into the fall. His own devices comprised a kind of carrot-and-stick game with Carey: a stream of letters to editors (e.g., a press release to fifteen City Hall reporters and the "Chief Editorial Writers of all Metropolitan Dailies, including Brooklyn and Queens," 4-18-38; to editor, *Herald-Tribune*, 4-25-38; to Iphigene Sulzberger, 5-25-38; to F. E. Schmitt, editor, *Engineering News-Record*, 9-7-38 and 9-15-38 [papers, box 97]), lobbying of Board of Estimate members (Moses to Ingersoll, 12-29-38 [Moses papers, box 97]), sympathetic support for civic associations' suits, and friendly personal notes. "You will no doubt have seen my report on Jamaica Bay," he wrote after the brochure had been front page news in most of the city's papers. [*Eagle*, 7-18-38, p. 1:6; *Herald-Tribune* (Municipal Reference Center vertical file, no page); *New York Times*, p. 1:2.] "Of course, you know there is nothing personal about it and I am sure that you will not take it in this way. . . . Why not take this off your plans and the issue will then narrow down to a scrap between the residential and recreational interests and the industrial boys and speculators?" [7-20-38, Moses papers, box 97.] Upon hearing that Carey was in the hospital: "Yesterday evening I heard . . . [the] very bad news ["that they had stuffed you into a hospital"] and I am hastening to write to tell you that I hope you will be back in the ring in the shortest possible time and that if we have to have any more battles they will always be on a friendly basis," and again, "Hurry up and get well because several rounds are being fought in your absence by means of shadow boxing." 11-3-38 and 11-9-38, Moses papers, box 11.

All the while telling the public that the decision had not been his but the board's: LaGuardia press release/letter to the Board of Estimate, 11-14-38, LaGuardia papers, departmental correspondence, box 3217, folder: "Parks, 11/12-38."

The promise of controlling the Tunnel Authority: With the mayor on his hook, wriggling angrily but nonetheless caught, Moses lost no time in cracking the whip on the agencies over which he had just gained influence. The general manager and chief engineer of the Tunnel Authority were called into LaGuardia's office the afternoon the agreement was sealed to find Robert Moses and some of his men already there, as described at the beginning of this chapter. TBTA warehouse, cabinet #186, top drawer, Tunnel Authority Diary.

The day after the agreement was sealed, Bill Carey got a letter: Moses to Carey, 9-9-38, Moses papers, box 97, file: "Parks '38."

"I spent a good part of yesterday roaming around the Sound View section of the Bronx": LaGuardia papers, departmental correspondence, box 3217, file: "Parks, '38, Circumferential Parkway." A copy of this letter was sent by Carey to LaGuardia only the next year, when the Sound View matter was finally going ahead, with the curt cover note, "Please find attached hereto a copy of my letter to Commissioner Moses of September 16th which is self-explanatory." 2-1-39, LaGuardia papers, departmental correspondence, box 3217, folder: "1938-40, Parks, Department of, Sound View Park."

LaGuardia was outraged about the infringement on his "administrative responsibilities": (as an ally on the Board of Estimate, Newbold Morris, phrased it for him) *Staten Island Advance*, 12–29–38, p. 9:1.

Moses purposely had understated its cost: Moses to LaGuardia, 10–27–38; William C. Chanler, corporation counsel, to LaGuardia, 11–21–38; LaGuardia to Moses, 11–26–38. LaGuardia papers, departmental correspondence, box 3217, folder: "Parks, 1938, Circumferential Parkway."

Moses's rabble-rousing and media manipulation: Though Carey knew better than anyone else how disingenuous Moses's opposition was, he remained unruffled by it. "[O]f course, my dear Bob," he wrote, "I don't believe I am advancing your knowledge of this particular situation one iota by mentioning that any one who takes the popular side of the question where ashes, garbage and rubbish are concerned is already eight up and ten to go, but I cannot blame you for that." Carey to Moses, 7–22–38, Moses papers, box 97.

Some Staten Islanders were surprised to discover the sanitation commissioner poking about their island: *Staten Island Advance*, 9–15–38.

"The board members went into a huddle": *Staten Island Advance*, 10–7–38, p. 1:1.

"A propagandist with no regard for the truth": *Staten Island Advance*, 10–11–38, p. 1:1.

Moses meanwhile claimed that the Fresh Kills proposal was "entirely new" to him: *Staten Island Advance*, 10–12–38, p. 1:1. Moses breached Board of Estimate etiquette for its closed sessions by releasing a stenographic transcript of his remarks the following day.

Moses said he would "personally guarantee" that his plan "will not be a nuisance": *Staten Island Advance*, 11–18–38, p. 1:1.

LaGuardia had the technicians pretend that their mikes were live: Caro, pp. 611–612; *New York Times*, 11–23–38, p. 1:2.

LaGuardia pulled an ambush of his own: The mayor had been driven to such measures by the City Council's action two days before, when it rescinded the following year's appropriation for the new unloading facility; if he wanted a new unloading facility before 1940, LaGuardia had to get the board to release its 1938 appropriation before the year ended. So, technically LaGuardia's Board of Estimate resolution vetoed the council's budget recission, and the council's subsequent action was an attempted rejection of the mayor's veto.

LaGuardia called another special session and forced it through: The "layover" perquisite could be used just once. For good measure, LaGuardia also vetoed the City Council's rescission of the 1939 appropriation.

"European dictators": Staten Island Advance, 12-28-38, p. 4:1.

The New York Times *chided that the mayor's veto set "a ticklish precedent":* 12-30-38.

The deputy mayor told Moses "very very privately": Henry H. Curran to Moses, 1-4-39, LaGuardia papers, box 3239, folder 9.

Moses had promised the mayor a new bridge: Caro, pp. 639ff; 657.

The docks department was given lead responsibility: John McKenzie, commissioner of docks, to Moses, 6-16-39, Parks papers, box 102443, folder: "Sound View Park, #1."

Moses promised that he would not go behind his back: 6-16-39, LaGuardia papers, departmental correspondence, box 3239, folder: "Parks, 6/7-1939."

(As he nonetheless did): Moses to George Spargo, 10-9-39, Parks papers, box 102443, folder 3.

While he was at it, he added more refuse fill to the Marine Park adjacent to Barren Island: The connection between the continued filling of Marine Park and the sale of Floyd Bennett Field is documented in Moses to Joseph D. McGoldrick, comptroller, 1-21-42, Moses papers, box 98, folder 42.

"I have had occasion recently to make several more or less careful inspections of Staten Island": 7-24-42 (draft), 7-27-42 (final), Moses papers, box 98.

Franklin and Eleanor Roosevelt stepped in behind the scenes to kill it: Caro, pp. 671-3.

"You are moving too fast in the Staten Island bridge matter": Moses to Joseph Palma, 2-18-39, Moses papers, box 98, file 40.

"A start has already been made in laying out the future parkway and arterial road system on Staten Island": New York City Department of Parks, "Improvement of Marine Park," 5-20-40, p. 3.

The parkways planned to connect the Narrows to New Jersey always crossed the Fresh Kills marshes: The Richmond Parkway was Moses' priority—he thought that it would be 'the most beautiful parkway in the city'—and always included it on planning maps. The West Shore Expressway sometimes appeared on his public planning maps, but at other times was left off. The Richmond Parkway was always planned to cross LaTourette Park at Richmond Creek. The extension to the park there, as well as along its eastern border, where the parkway would intercept land then outside the park, were to be added as part of the Fresh Kills acquisition. Moses later modified his originally proposed alignment of the Richmond Parkway in relation to the West Shore Expressway, which was being built first. Howard, Needles, Tammen & Bergendoff, Consulting Engineers, *Engineering Report on the Proposed West Shore Expressway,* 9-15-52.

He later denied it: Staten Island Advance, 7-18-46.

After Moses made another private visit to him in early 1943 Borough President Palma promptly had plans drawn up for filling in the Fresh Kills meadows and submitted them to the mayor with a formal request that they be adopted: Staten Island Advance, 7-16-46, p. 1:2; Palma to LaGuardia, 12-30-43, and Moses to LaGuardia, 2-11-44, Moses papers, box 98.

LaGuardia finally succumbed to Moses's importunings: e.g., a series of continued aspersions on the Tunnel Authority's planning of the Verrazano Narrows approaches, some of which are in LaGuardia papers, subject files: "Tunnels, SI, 1940-3."

Moses immediately began to prepare the groundwork for building the Verrazano-Narrows Bridge: e.g., Moses to Miss Mary J. Collins, nd [but, from context, prior to 7-11-45], admits that the authority is making application to the War Department for a permit for the Verrazano crossing, although at the same time he is telling others (e.g., Congressman Donald L. O'Toole, 8-3-45) that "[y]ou need have no fear that the Tunnel Authority as presently constituted will do anything for many years toward the actual construction of this project." TBTA papers, coordinator, cabinet 1122, drawer 4, file: "Narrows Tunnel or Bridge, 1945."

"I have reached a point [Hall said] where I agree with you completely that the matter from now on could be better handled 'off the record'": Moses to Hall, 4-1-46, Hall to Moses, 4-2-46, Parks papers, box 102739, folder: "Narrows Bridge."

He wanted the landfill, Hall said, so that he could get a shorefront road: Staten Island Advance, 6-7-46, p. 1; 6-8-46, p. 1; 6-27-46, p. 1; Hall to Edwin Salmon, chairman, City Planning Commission, 6-11, Parks papers, box 102739, folder: "Landfill: parks."

The biggest demonstrations Staten Islanders had ever mounted at City Hall: A hundred fifty Staten Islanders showed up at City Hall the day the Board of Estimate approved the project (*Staten Island Advance*, 6-28-46, p. 1); five hundred Staten Islanders were expected for the 7-9-46 hearing (*Staten Island Advance*, p. 1:4) preceding the City Council's approval; thousands of Islanders rallied on Staten Island in 1938, but smaller crowds came to City Hall; thousands demonstrated on Staten Island in April 1916 and crowds came to City Hall, but as in 1938 the surprise scheduling tactics of the administration prevented full mobilization of a Staten Island's delegation.

The Fresh Kills measure passed on June 28, 1946 after Robert Moses announced that he too had switched sides: When Fresh Kills had come to a vote in the Board of Estimate in November 1945, Moses had been conspicuously absent (although behind the scenes he was doing everything he could to pave the way for it), limiting his public comments in the affair to denunciations of the Sanitation Department's shoddy handling of the existing landfill on Staten Island at Great Kills, which was by all accounts a considerable nuisance.

"We can't make an omelet without breaking some eggs and occasionally there will be a bad egg": To the Editor of the *Bronx Home News*, 9-16-42, Moses papers, box 98.

He had considered Jamaica Bay instead, but had concluded that it would be too hard to keep the barge channels open in the winter ice: Staten Island Advance, 6-12-46, p. 1.

If Bill Carey was still following Moses' pronouncements on the subject, this unabashed reversal of Moses' earlier public position might have made him smile with the kind of indulgence he had once reserved for the vaudevillian antics of his former boss: Moses, meanwhile, tried to give the impression that Carey's views over time had become more like his; he told the editor of a Bronx newspaper that was criticizing the Sound View landfill: "Bill isn't so bad as a park man.... Before you know it, we will have the big ash and rubbish man looking like a landscape architect. If you know Bill you will realize that no such transformation has been wrought since Saul of Tarsus became Saint Paul." Moses to the editor, *Bronx Home News*, 9-16-42, in Moses papers, box 98; also in Parks papers, box 107864.

The neologism re-cycling *would not be coined for another fourteen years: 3rd* Barnhart Dictionary of New English (H.W. Wilson Co., 1990).

"Save Some Scrap to Kill a Jap": photograph of LaGuardia during a scrap metal drive, 10-3-42, Municipal Archives, Department of Sanitation photos.

He stopped the salvage collections the instant the War Production Board allowed him to: The cost of collecting these materials was considerably more than the revenues the city received from their sale—an unwarranted subsidy of private industry according to LaGuardia. *New York Times*, 8-29-45, p. 13:7; on costs also see 8-27-45, p. 1:1; on LaGuardia's views on subsidizing scrap dealers: 8-30-45, p. 16:6.

The trimmers cut the department's productivity more than their pension contributions were worth: Citizens' Budget Commission, *A Better Government for a Better City. A Study of Five Departments of the City of New York*, 1-20-48, chapters 13 and 18.

Along with the city's new mayor, Moses promised Borough President Hall that "raw" garbage would only be landfilled at Fresh Kills for three years: The three-year promise was made in a variety of places and was formally embodied in the resolution adopted by the Board of Estimate on August 19, 1948.

That this three-year promise was patently absurd everyone, including Moses, recognized (though this did not stop him from angrily attacking anyone in the administration who dared to not parrot the party line that the construction deadline would indeed be met): Frederick H. Zurmuhlen, commissioner of Public Works, to O'Dwyer, 8-19-48; Moses to O'Dwyer, 8-26-48; Thomas J. Patterson, director of the budget, to John J. Bennett, deputy mayor, 9-27-48, enclosing memorandum from Thomas F. O'Connell, mechanical engineer. All in O'Dwyer papers.

Moses revised the public schedule for closing Fresh Kills to raw waste, saying it would take four more years: New York Times, 5-21-51, p. 1:2.

The net increase in incinerator capacity was less than three thousand tons a day: The incinerators at Gansevoort Street in Manhattan and at Betts Avenue in Queens were completed in 1950; the South Shore Incinerator at Wortman Avenue in Brooklyn was completed in 1954, and those at Hamilton Avenue and Bay Forty-first Street in Brooklyn in 1961. All except Betts Avenue (at 800 tpd) were designed for a capacity of 1,000 tons per day (Betts was later upgraded to 1,000 tpd). An incinerator originally planned for Clifton in Staten Island was never built.

The incinerators that closed between 1946 and 1961 were at East Seventy-third Street in Manhattan (320 tpd); College Point (300 tpd), Ravenswood (150 tpd), and the prior facility at Betts Avenue (800 tpd) in Queens; at Paerdegat Basin (500 tpd) in Brooklyn; and at Richmond Terrace (100 tpd) in Staten Island.

The only part of the new landfill that was not actually refuse was the roadbed of the West Shore Expressway itself, because its engineers insisted that it be filled with solid material and that the refuse already in place be removed: Howard, Needles, Tammen & Bergendoff, consulting engineers, *Engineering Report on the Proposed West Shore Expressway,* 9-15-52, p. 20.

Moses also tried to make the sanitation department pay for a four-million-dollar bridge across Fresh Kills Creek: Moses to O'Dwyer, 8-12-48, O'Dwyer papers. This was the figure that was presented to the City Planning Commission.

The Citizens Budget Commission complained that this was not a valid charge against the city's nondiscretionary budget: Robert W. Dowling, president, Citizens' Budget Commission to O'Dwyer, 8-18-48, pp. 1, 5. O'Dwyer papers, box 41.

Moses found a way to avoid that objection by filling in enough of the creek that another kind of bridge could be built at a fraction of the originally projected cost: George Spargo to Deputy Mayor Charles Horowitz, 2-3-53, Moses papers, box 90; City of New York, "Fresh Kills Landfill," 11-51-53, p. 8; Moses, *Public Works, A Dangerous Trade,* p. 32.

The project involved a 100-percent, half-million-dollar profit for the political insiders who had just bought the property: Caro, p. 1046.

Wilgus drafted the War Department's strategy for moving troops across Europe's central sectors: The last copies of his book on the American Transport Division's work in World War I in France had been snapped up at the beginning of the war for distribution to the command staff abroad.

Thirteen thousand tons a day: City of New York, Department of Sanitation, *Comprehensive Solid Waste Management Plan Draft Update and Plan Modification,* 6-1-95, pp. 2-33 and 4-21.

Moses had been proud of cleaning up Mount Corona: Moses' pride in this particular accomplishment is discussed in Marshall Berman's *All That Is Solid Melts Into Air* (New York: Simon and Schuster, 1982), pp. 303-4.

Fresh Kills had become the biggest man-made object on the planet: William Rathje, presentation at New York State Legislative Commission on Solid Waste Management, 2-2-90, NYC: in 1991, Fresh Kills would pass the Great Wall of China to become the largest man-made object in the world.

PART IV

In addition to the documents and archival sources cited in the notes below, this section is based on the author's experience as the director of policy planning for the New York City Department of Sanitation (in which capacity I was responsible for developing the city's Comprehensive Long-Term Solid-Waste-Management Plan and its primary author), and on interviews with the following people:

Carol Ash, former regional director, NYS Department of Environmental Conservation;

John Banks, NYC Council, finance staff;

John Beckman, former press officer, mayor's office;

Martin Brennan, former campaigns coordinator, NYPIRG;

Anne Canty, former assistant commissioner, public affairs, NYC Department of Sanitation;

Paul D. Casowitz, former deputy commissioner, NYC Department of Sanitation;

Kendall Christiansen, former chair, Solid Waste Advisory Board;

Barry Commoner, Center for the Biology of Natural Systems;

Marilyn Dahl, former governmental liaison, New York Chamber of Commerce;

Ben Esner, former environmental adviser, Brooklyn borough president;

Barbara Fife, former deputy mayor;

Kenneth Fisher, NYC Council;

Michel Gelobter, former environmental adviser, Dinkins for Mayor;

Eric A. Goldstein, NRDC;

Jeffrey Haberman, former counsel, Environmental Protection Committee, NYC Council;

Arthur Kell, NYPIRG;

Carolyn Konheim, consultant to Brooklyn Navy Yard Citizens Advisory Committee; president, Konheim & Ketcham;

Emily Lloyd, former commissioner, NYC Department of Sanitation;

Langdon Marsh, former executive deputy commissioner, NYS Department of Environmental Conservation.

Dan Master, counsel to the Staten Island borough president;

Thomas McMahon, former finance director, NYC Council;

Stanley Michels, chairman, Environmental Protection Committee, NYC Council;

Frank New, former director of Intergovernmental Affairs, NYC;

Robert Baird Paterson, president, Wallabout Partners Associated;

Ross Patten, former vice-president, Wheelabrator Environmental Systems;

Steven Polan, former commissioner, NYC Department of Sanitation;

Pamela Ransom, former environmental assistant to the deputy mayor for policy and planning

Steven Romalewski, NYPIRG

Brendan Sexton, former commissioner, NYC Department of Sanitation;

Norman Steisel, former deputy mayor;

Joseph Strasburg, former chief of staff to the Speaker of the NYC Council; and

James T. B. Tripp, general counsel, EDF.

I also benefited from conversations with Albert Appleton, former commissioner, NYC Department of Environmental Protection; Chris Boyd, environmental adviser to the Brooklyn borough president; Nevin Cohen, former legislative aide to Councilman Sheldon Leffler; Michael Herz, former staff attorney, EDF; Joe Martens, former environmental aide to Governor Mario Cuomo; Douglas Martin, reporter, *New York Times*; Meir Ribalow, cochair of the Creative Coalition's Environmental Committee; Larry Shapiro, executive director, NYPIRG; Salvatore Ervolina, former solid waste engineer, Region 2, and Glen Milstrey, Municipal Waste Section, NYS Department of Environmental Conservation; Rob Sacks, former chair, Citywide Recycling Advisory Board; Sarah Dolinar, associate counsel, Philip Gleason, director of Landfill Engineering, Jane Levine, former deputy commissioner, Legal Affairs, and Harry Szarpanski, director of Project Management, NYC Department of Sanitation; Barbara Warren, Staten Islanders for Clean Air; and with present and former Giuliani administration staff who preferred not to be identified here.

Once in a while, Mr. Zimmer spends a day patrolling the Staten Island tide marshes on foot: Mitchell, Joseph, *Up in the Old Hotel* (New York: Pantheon, 1992), "The Bottom of the Harbor," [1951] pp. 482–3.

The Staten Islanders who came to the polls in 1993 voted five to one in favor of the Republican challenger for the New York mayoralty: Jackson, p. 743.

New York Times quote: Celestine Bohlen, p. B5:1.

The editorial boards of the city's daily newspapers—all of whom generally supported pro-development public works—were uniformly opposed to a moratorium: New York Times, 10-25-89, I, p. 30:1; *New York Post*, 10-14-89; *Daily News*, 10-23-89; and also, *Crain's New York Business*, 10-23-89, p. 8.

It was not a commitment sought by the city's more established environmental groups: e.g., Bill Hewitt, DEC Region 2 to Pamela Ransom (Dinkins staffer), 5-23-89, and Skip Hartman and Allan Hershkowitz (NRDC) to David Dinkins et al., 7-21-89 (Municipal Archives, papers of Deputy Mayor Barbara Fife, box 1, "Campaign.")

It is unlikely that the pledge was helpful in the Democratic primary: New York Times, 9-13-89, I, p. 1:6. The moratorium did not even get the Hasids' primary endorsement, since the political arm of the Satmarer community, the United Jewish Organization of Williamsburg, gave its endorsement to the mayor who had proposed the project. *New York Times,* 9-6-89, II, 2:4.

It provided Giuliani with an illustration of the types of leadership decisions he accused Dinkins of wanting to avoid: e.g., Bob Liff, *Newsday,* 10-18-89.

One of the advisers who had recommended that Dinkins pledge a moratorium on the Navy Yard incinerator was Barry Commoner: Commoner was not the only adviser calling for a moratorium, nor the most vociferous proponent of this position.

The only solution, he said, was replacing corporate control with "social governance of the systems of production": New York Times, 10-30-80, p. B19:1.

"Remember: once you organize people around something as commonly agreed upon as pollution, then an organized people is on the move": Saul Alinsky, *Rules for Radicals* (New York: Random House, 1971), p. xxii.

Alinsky's Back of the Yards Association, on the other hand, was created to embrace precisely these lowest and least enfranchised classes: ibid., p. 116.

Corporations had become the most useful targets of environmental activism: Ralph Nader, Ronald Brownstein, John Richard, eds., *Who's Poisoning America. Corporate Polluters and Their Victims in the Chemical Age* (San Francisco: Sierra Club Books), 1981, passim.

Müller was trying to make new agents for chemical warfare: Rachel Carson, *Silent Spring* (Boston: Houghton Mifflin, 1962), p. 16.

One of the young soldiers involved in testing DDT on this side of the Atlantic was Lieutenant Barry Commoner : Barry Commoner, *Science and Survival* (New York: Viking, 1966), p. 22; Commoner C.V.; Thomas Vinciguerra,

"Barry Commoner '37: Prophet of the Environmental Movement," *Columbia College Today*, Winter 1989, p.28.

Tens of thousands of cases of cancer: On 8-1-97 the National Cancer Institute released a study that estimated that between ten thousand and seventy-five thousand cases of thyroid cancer might be associated with Iodine 131, another isotope associated with weapons testing. The NCI study did not examine the effects of other isotopes, such as Strontium 90, which can cause leukemia and other cancers. (J. Truman, director, Downwinders, www.downwinders.org/nci.html, August 1997)

The St. Louis group's collection played an important part in achieving the 1963 ban on above-ground bomb tests: Commoner, *Science and Survival*, pp. 53, 112, 120; *The Closing Circle* (New York: Knopf, 1972), pp. 51-6.

"The Paul Revere of Ecology": 2-5-70, p. 58.

On Long Island, a naturalist named Dennis Puleston had noticed that songbirds were not the only ones disappearing: Dennis Puleston, *The Gull's Way: A Sailor/Naturalist's Yarn* (New York: Vantage Press, 1995), pp. 172-3.

When one morning in the spring of 1966 Mrs. Carol Yannacone of Patchogue, Long Island, learned of a fish kill at a nearby lake that appeared to be the result of DDT sprayed by the Suffolk County Mosquito Commission, she told her husband Victor: e.g., Frank Graham, Jr., *Since Silent Spring* (Boston: Houghton Mifflin, 1970), pp. 126-9, 251-6; www.edf.org: "Where It All Began."

By 1994, the US population of ospreys had climbed back to 14,246 pairs: www.edf.org, 6-13-97, "EDF's Campaign Against DDT."

"Probably the most radical elected official east of Oakland": David Chanin, *Village Voice*, 1-29-70.

The councilman threw the first punch: Max H. Seigel, *New York Times*, 7-7-72. The councilman, "Fightin' Mike" DeMarco—presumably not for his fighting abilities—would one day be elevated to the bench.

Kretchmer proposed to replace nonreturnable bottles with degradable cans: Chanin, loc. cit.

The planning of the proposed Brooklyn Navy Yard incinerator had already cost eight million dollars: David Bird, *New York Times*, 8-6-71, p. 1:5.

Kearing announced the project while the mayor was still trying to convince the navy to let the city have the yard so that poor people could be put to work there: Bird, *New York Times*, 1-11-67; Seth S. King, *New York Times*, 11-17-67.

"Landscape sculpture": e.g., Kretchmer to Policy Planning Council, 3-17-71, to which is attached "Solid Waste Disposal in New York City," 3-12-71; and New York City Environmental Protection Administration Press Release, 8-5-71. *Sculpturing:* Jacob Friedlander, executive assistant, to Merril Eisenbud, administrator, EPA, minutes of 12-5-68 meeting to discuss "use of landfill for topographical alterations of New York City." (All in Municipal Archives, Lindsay Subject Files, EPA).

Soon thereafter, Kretchmer had an apparent change of heart after visiting some incinerators in Japan. The Japanese incinerators looked clean, and, after waiting three months, the new technology that he had hoped for had not yet appeared. Bird, *New York Times*, 11-16-71.

"The destructor consists of six cells or compartments": 12-19-1880.

By 1893, Fryer and his growing field of competitors had built in fifty-six English towns and cities: Robert W. Shortridge, *Solid Waste & Power*, April 1990, "We've Come a Long Way... [sic]", p. 47.

By 1912, there were three hundred English incinerators: J. Petts, "Incineration as a Waste Management Option," in R. E. Hester and R. M. Harrison, eds., *Waste Incineration and the Environment* (Cambridge, England: Royal Society of Chemistry, 1994), p. 1.

In 1877, Colonel Henry R. Foote demonstrated a "refuse cremator" of his own design: New York Times, 9-9-1877, p. 12:5; 10-10-1877, p. 8:2; *Tribune*, 9-10-1877 and 10-10-1877. No "offensive smells" were noted during the September demonstration; during the October demonstration one reporter found "a somewhat pungent odor in the neighborhood of the furnace yesterday afternoon," but pronounced it "not nearly so offensive as the scent which is brought over by the easterly breezes from Hunters Point [where there were manure handling, rendering, coal gasification, and chemical plants], or the foul smell around Harlem Flats [where land-filling took place]."

He received the first US patent for refuse incineration in 1879: Robert H. Brickner, Gershman, Brickner & Bratton, Inc., "Historical Overview of Air

Pollution Control Equipment for Municipal Incineration Systems," presented at Acid Gas and Dioxin Control Conference for Waste-to-Energy Facilities, Washington, DC, 11-25/26-1985, p. 1.

By 1892, there were more than a dozen incinerators operating in the country; a decade later, 15 percent of the largest American cities were using incineration (while only 10 percent were using any form of "reduction"): William Francis Morse, "The Collection and Disposal of Municipal Waste," *Municipal Journal and Engineer*, 1908, cited by E.S. Savas, *The Organization and Efficiency of Solid Waste Collection*, (Lexington, MA: Lexington), p. 22.

By 1924, that proportion had nearly doubled: New York Times, 7-8-1924.

Because of the problems of competing with private utilities for the production and sale of power, only a few American incinerators ever generated useful power. . . . : W. Francis Goodrich, *The Economic Disposal of Towns' Refuse* (London: P.S. King & Son, 1901), pp. 7, 207, 208-9; Goodrich, *Refuse Disposal and Power Production* (New York: E.P. Dutton [nd; 1904?]), p. 335 and passim; Joseph G. Branch, *Heat and Light from Municipal and Other Waste* (St. Louis: William H. O'Brien Printing and Publishing Company, 1906), passim; National Bureau of Municipal Research, *Making Money Out of Garbage* (Johnstown, PA, 1910), pp. 7, 20.

Seventeen miles from shore: Chapter 463 of the Laws of 1880, passed on May 27, set the dump site at a location triangulated five miles from Coney Island and four miles from Sandy Hook. The nearest dumping pier, on the Lower East Side, was about twelve miles by water from Coney Island.

"The Street Cleaning department [with its incinerator plans] is like a waif whom nobody wants": New York Times, 8-28-23, p. 7:1.

"Everybody is in favor of incinerators, but nobody desires them as neighbors": New York Times, 12-16-1931, p. 14:4.

"Incineration is the only way to solve" the garbage problem: e.g., Moses to Iphigene Sulzberger, 5-25-38, in NYPL Moses papers, box 97.

The number of incinerators in the United States plummeted from a high of over 300 to a low of 67 in 1979: Brickner, Exhibit 5. The estimate of 300 is based on the fact that 289 North American incinerators were built or rebuilt between 1945-1965, during which time at least some existing incinerators must have continued in operation. In 1960, 30 percent of the municipal solid waste in the United States was incinerated; by 1980, that figure was 10 percent (*Waste Age*, November 1995, p. 44).

More than had died during any comparable period of the German blitz: Most of those who died from the pollution created by domestic coal fires that December had pre-existing heart and lung disease. "ARIC Briefing Note: Air Pollution & Asthma," Manchester Metropolitan University, Atmospheric Research & Information Centre (www.doc.mmu.ac.uk/aric/applied_research/briefing/bn22.htm). London mortalities from the Blitz were 13,596 for all of 1940; 6,487 for all of 1941; 27 for 1942. Tom Harrisson, *Living Through the Blitz* (London: Collins, 1976), p. 265.

The Bureau of Smoke Abatement, revealed that refuse incinerators were responsible for 30 percent of all the life-threatening smoke in the city: New York Times, 1-16-52, p. 23:5. The director of the bureau was Admiral Austin Heller.

The new law (enacted in 1967) instead made all apartment-house incinerators (unless their owners chose to install certified air-pollution-control devices) illegal: Bird, *New York Times,* 6-19-67, "Kearing Sees a Crisis in Garbage Disposal."

By 1970, there were about twenty thousand landfills in the United States: Edward W. Repa and Allen Blakey, "Municipal Solid Waste Disposal Trends, 1996 Update," *Waste Age*, p. 43. As Repa and Blakey point out, it is difficult to assess the accuracy of this estimate, which may be on the high side. Nonetheless, it is clearly of the right order of magnitude.

Some fifty thousand more tons of greenhouse gases . . . : The emissions calculations are based on Radian Corporation, *Determination of Landfill Gas Composition and Pollutant Emission Rates at Fresh Kills Landfill, Revised Final Report, EPA Contract No. 68-D3-033,* 11-10-95, table 5-19. Based on an extensive review of historical waste-disposal records, landfilled tonnage for NYC in 1965 is estimated at four million tons.

Some of the material resources to meet the national crisis had been supplied by efforts like LaGuardia's scrap drive: But recycling during the war did not play the role it could have had a recycling infrastructure been in place. A lot of the paper collected, for example, was simply warehoused, and later landfilled.

The subsidies are coming: The package the Carter Administration put together to support the resource-recovery industry included a variety of interacting components: direct development grants from the Department of Energy and the Environmental Protection Administration, opportunities for the use of tax-exempt bond financing, and, through the Public Utilities Regulatory Policy Act, guaranteed energy markets at guaranteed prices.

Perhaps the foremost exemplar was Robert Randol: "Managing Director Robert Randol of Smith Barney said he personally has arranged $5 billion in financing for solid waste. . . ." *Integrated Waste Management,* 3-29-95, p. 1.

The Persian Gulf of Garbage: This phrase is from Paul D. Casowitz, former deputy commissioner for Resource Recovery and Waste Disposal Planning, NYC Department of Sanitation.

Randol served as a dollar-a-year adviser to Ed Koch: James P. Sterba, *New York Times,* 5-16-78, p. 37:1.

He helped structure a deal to leverage enough tax-exempt industrial-development funds: According to Carolyn Konheim, an environmental consultant and former city and state official who was active in the resource recovery field in the early 1970s, it was Randol who first proposed the idea of financing waste-to-energy facilities with industrial revenue bonds. "I always thought and think that he's the father of a lot of the whole waste-to-energy movement." (Konheim interview, 5-9-95.)

Only half the sanitation department's seventeen hundred trucks could run on any given day: Charles Kaiser, *New York Times,* 4-27-78, p. B13:1; 5-9-78, p. 43:6.

Steisel was perhaps the only one in his administration arrogant enough to get the job done: Soho Weekly News, 9-28-78, clip in Municipal Reference and Research Center Vertical File, "Norman Steisel."

Twelve thousand uniformed men: Within a few years of taking office, Steisel presided over the introduction of women to the formerly all male agency.

"Mr. Taste and Mr. Waste": Deirdre Carmody, *New York Times,* 4-7-82, p. B4:5.

A 100 percent reduction in unscheduled fleet downtime: 0 percent of "required" collection trucks were out of service in the first four months of Fiscal Year '81, down from 3.1 percent in Fiscal Year '80 (*Mayor's Management Report,* January 1981, p. 51).

The sanitation department's abysmal morale was aggravated by a recent series in the Daily News*:* The series, by Alex Michelini, ran in July 1979.

Two-man trucks saved the city thirty-seven million dollars a year: Mayor's Management Report, September 1994, pp. 90, 98.

Steisel's predecessor had claimed to have received a hundred offers to take some or all of the city's waste off his hands: James P. Sterba, *New York Times,* 5-16-78, p. 37:1.

Bronx Borough President Robert Abrams: the city should pursue resource recovery more "aggressively": Dena Kleiman, *New York Times,* 5-20-78, p. 48:1.

Congresswoman Bella Abzug: "We're sitting on an urban metal mine": New York Times, 8-21-77, p. 29:5.

Port Authority Executive Director Peter Goldmark intended to corner all the garbage within twenty-five miles of the Statue of Liberty: Sterba, ibid.; Steve Goldstein, *Daily News,* 2-4-78, p. 7.

Most environmental groups still had not made any distinction between "energy recovery" and what later came to be seen as more worthy, more ecologically uplifting forms of "recycling": e.g., Walther A. Rosenbaum, *The Politics of Environmental Concern* (New York: Praeger, 1977), p. 262. Rosenbaum argues that we need both "resource recycling" (materials) and "energy recycling" (incineration and pyrolysis/"garbage gasification").

The Hempstead plant's sweet stench (it was said) sickened horses at the racetrack across the road, and the Eco-people went backrupt after an explosion at their first plant blew up one of their employees and their Bridgeport plant injured three more: Claire Poole, *Forbes,* 4-25-88, p. 116. The Brockton worker died in an explosion on 11-15-77 (David G. Santry, *Business Week,* 1-30-78, p. 77.) The Bridgeport accident: *Business Week,* 12-1-80, p. 50.

The winner of the bidding process: The original bid was won by a company called UOP, Inc. Within months of the award, UOP was bought by the Signal Companies and merged into Wheelabrator, its former competitor.

The site that had cost his predecessor his job: Steisel's *immediate* predecessor was Anthony Vacarrello; Samuel Kearing had been one of Vacarrello's predecessors.

"Return power to the people": Loren Stell, Suburbia Today, Gannett Westchester Rockland Newspaper, 5-10-81: "Commoner's ideas could, in short, truly return power to the people, as he explains."

The initial mission of his "Center for the Biology of Natural Systems": Samuel Weiss, "Commoner Takes on City's Environment," *New York Times,* 4-8-80, III, 1:1; Jeffrey Gale, *Bullshit: The Media as Power Brokers in Presidential Elections* (Palm Springs, CA: Bold Hawk Press, 1988), pp. 48; 118-9; 122.

Commoner began his remarks by recapitulating some basic thermodynamic principles: "New York City's Energy Future," Address before the Conference on Urban Energy Strategies, New York City, 2-3-82.

Steisel understood Commoner to suggest that there would be no more attacks: Steisel interview, 4-12-95.

The argument Commoner developed was that only mass-burn incinerators synthesize dioxin: e.g., "Why is dioxin the key problem? The answer's very simple. That is the distinction between burning trash and burning anything else. …Dioxin, the chlorinated compounds, raises a whole new class of problems that are distinctively connected with the burning of mixed trash. That is the thing you have to focus on. Now, the other reason why it's so important is that by understanding the origin of the dioxin problem, you can see what alternatives are important. I'll say flat out, no point talking about landfills any more. That's finished… We have to ask now, are we going to burn without separating, or are we going to separate?… As long as we can separate out the paper, we can burn it without any fear of dioxin production." (Transcript of the Brooklyn Lung Association's Annual Meeting, 10-25-83, pp. 106-7.) Among the other examples of Commoner's repetition of this argument is: Center for the Biology of Natural Systems (hereafter, CBNS), "Barry Commoner, Summary of Remarks Before the Public Forum on the Resource Recovery Plant in Northern Brooklyn," 2-28-83, p. 5.

A chilling body count: CBNS, *Environmental and Economic Analysis of Alter-*

native Municipal Solid Waste Disposal Technologies. vol. 1: An Assessment of the Risks Due to Emissions of Chlorinated Dioxins and Dibenzofurans from Proposed New York City Incinerators, 5-1-84.

These lives would be part of the price paid to the same companies that had built the nation's nuclear reactors: There was some truth to the charge that certain incinerator companies had connections with firms that supplied equipment and construction services to nuclear power plants.

Reducing the volume of chlorinated plastics in waste may not affect dioxin production: e.g., Walter Shaub, presentation to the special dioxin panel convened by the New York Academy of Sciences, 12-18-84; Floyd Hasselriis, P.E., "Controlling Dioxins from Municipal Waste Combustion," *Solid Waste Technologies,* July 1995, pp. 32-33; Randall T. Curlee, et al, *Waste-to-Energy in the United States: A Social and Economic Assessment* (Westport, CT: Quorum Books, 1994), p. 12.

That significant portions of Commoner's claims would have been difficult to substantiate did not appear to temper his enthusiastic repetition of them: e.g., Steisel interview; David C. Locke (chairman, Ph.D. program in chemistry, The Graduate School, City University of New York) to the Citizens Advisory Committee for Resource Recovery, 6-5-84 and 9-27-84; Carolyn S. Konheim to Citizens Advisory Committee on the Proposed Brooklyn Navy Yard Resource Recovery Facility, 5-7-84 (revised 5-21-84 and 6-8-84) and 11-2-84. CBNS issued a response to the first round of Konheim and Locke comments on 8-1-84, which were responded to by the second round of comments by Locke and Konheim cited above.

Commoner's proposed alternative was a Bridgeport-style mechanical one: Testimony Before the New York City Board of Estimate, 12-20-84. Despite his insistence that the Italian Sorrain-Cecchini technology was what should be used in New York, when he finally saw it in operation in Rome (a plant that Steisel and I had also visited), he realized that it was a less than ideal solution—"it was very messy." (interview, 7-12-95.) He did not, however, ever provide a public retraction of his view. The licensees of the Cecchini technology never won a bid in this country and went bankrupt. The parent company also suffered some operating and financial difficulties.

After a stint managing rock bands and selling DDT in Harlem: New York
Times, 11-22-67 (clipping in Municipal Reference Center Vertical File).

"Don't worry about my power": interviews with Paul D. Casowitz (4-12-95) and Norman Steisel (4-12-95).

The Post's *"Draft Koch" headline:* Charles Carillo and Richard Johnson,
New York Post, 2-11-82, p. 3, and New York Post, 1-25-82 through 2-8-82,
passim.

He accused "Jay" Goldin of pandering to the Hasids: Joyce Purnick, New York
Times, 12-20-82, p. B2:5.

To defend his vote: "[An engineer on Goldin's staff] told me right after-wards that Jay calls [the engineer] up, and says 'Get me an issue, so I can
explain it [his negative vote].' And [the engineer] says, 'I read in a maga-zine—dioxin.'" (Casowitz interview, 4-24-95).

An impressively credentialed body of peer reviewers: The members of the peer
review panel were nine nationally prominent scientists, physicians, and
engineers. Dr. Arthur Upton, Dr. Thomas Chalmers, and Dr. Otto
Hutzinger were among the panel members.

*As her spokesman pointed out, enough other members of the board were voting in
favor of the project to make her vote unnecessary:* Edward C. Wallace quoted
by Josh Barbanel, New York Times, 12-21-84, p. A1:2.

"I, for one, would be prepared to withdraw my objections": Barry Commoner,
Testimony Before the New York City Board of Estimate, 12-20-84; Bar-banel, ibid.; Commoner, New York Times, 1-5-85, p. A20; Steisel, New
York Times, 1-15-85.

Commoner appeared to have lost all memory of any such offer: In any event,
there was no decrease in his public opposition to the project. When I
asked him about it in 1995, his response was: "Did I say that [about the
Chicago NW emissions levels]? [The] only thing I ever said was that if he
[Steisel] would guarantee that there was no dioxin emitted. . . . That's in a
letter to the *Times?*—You'd better send me that." (Commoner interview,
7-12-95; his letter to the *New York Times* appeared on 1-5-85, p. 20:2)

A vote on the proposed contract itself: The vote approved the terms of the contract, which the department could then finalize and sign without going back to the board.

Personal communication with a former Koch administration official, 1995.

The final layer of the lobbyists' exhortatory strokes; media support: David Rockefeller to Edward I. Koch, 11-11-82; Norman Steisel to Felix Rohatyn, 8-21-85; Koch to Max Frankel (of the *New York Times*), to Michael Pakenham (of the *Daily News*), to Roger Wood (of the *New York Post*), and to Bob Hollingsworth (of *Newsday*) (all 9-26-85).

"We would like to be able to support this facility": Eric Goldstein, staff attorney, Natural Resources Defense Council, quoted by Matthew L. Wald, *New York Times*, 9-26-84, p. A1:3.

"We don't want to be seen as opponents": Adam Stern, science associate, Environmental Defense Fund, ibid.

"Unwilling to confront the fundamental political and economic issues": Quoted by Philip Shabecoff (with reference to the national conservation groups in general), *New York Times*, 11-29-85, p. D28:1.

"There is in fact a 'hard path' and a 'soft path' in environmental politics": *Making Peace with the Planet* (New York: Pantheon, 1990), p. 174.

Legislative and regulatory reforms and negotiated compromises on pollution-controls, Commoner said, were just "palliatives": Quoted by Philip Shabecoff, *New York Times*, 10-30-80, p. B19:1.

The surprise assault achieved a prominent story in the Times: 8-4-85, I, p. 39:4.

After a brief but furious exchange of visits and correspondence: Norman Steisel to Michael Oppenheimer, Environmental Defense Fund, 8-2-84; Oppenheimer to Steisel, 8-6-84. (Municipal Archives, Brezenoff papers, 1984-4, B1/3, file: resource recovery.)

"Here in New York, the Natural Resources Defense Council and the Environmental Defense Fund worked with the Sanitation Department in promoting incineration": Commoner, "Environmental Democracy is the Planet's Best Hope," *Utne Reader,* July 1990. (See also the response to this from Richard A. Denison, senior scientist, Environmental Defense Fund, September 1990, pp. 15-18.)

Ralph Nader was traveling around the country with an idea that would have far-reaching effects: Ralph Nader and Donald Ross, *A Student's Manual for Public Interest Organizing* (New York: Grossman, 1971), chapter 1.

A mandatory fee levied at registration would be "shamelessly coercive": Nader and Ross, pp. 35-6.

Alinsky taught that organizers have to work with what they have: Alinsky, pp. 36-45; 138-48.

NYPIRG's most productive ever decision: In 1992 (the year when NYPIRG led the organizing effort against the city's solid waste management plan), it received revenues of 4.2 million dollars. The following year, revenues dropped to 1.6 million, and 1.4 in 1994. (New York State Department of State, Charities, Financial Report Summary.)

Amidst a flurry of rising eyebrows: After a nine-month inquiry by the city's corporation counsel, Steisel was cleared of wrongdoing in joining Lazard Frères, although (the committee appointed to handle the investigation wrote) "We believe... that Steisel could have, and should have, taken further steps before accepting the job with Lazard to address possible questions, fair or unfair, about an appearance of impropriety which he himself foresaw." (New York City corporation counsel, *Committee Report: Impact of Norman Steisel's Employment by Lazard Frères on the Brooklyn Navy Yard Resource Recovery Project*, 12-1-86, p. 53.)

The conservation commissioner said they would have to pass the environmentalists' version of the bill if the city was to have any hope of getting a Navy Yard permit out of his department: Jorling sent a telegram with this message to the council speaker. It was not a politic move, however, since several councilmembers delightedly waved it in front of their colleagues' (and reporters') noses as proof of their claims about the administration's real objective in getting the bill passed. (Reginald Patrick, *Staten Island Advance*, 3-29-89, p. A17:1. Re the Environmental Defense Fund/Natural Resources Defense Council visit to Jorling, interview with Jim Tripp).

There was nothing particularly dangerous about the ash: In six samples from one truckload of ash analyzed by an independent state certified lab for *Newsday*, cadmium levels ranged from 0 to 22.42 parts per million (averaging 13.71 ppm), and lead levels ranged from 32.40ppm to 44.00 (averaging 37.28 ppm). By comparison, ash residue from six municipal solid waste incinerators tested by the DEC in 1990 showed cadmium levels ranging from 15.6 to 202.2 ppm and lead levels from 369.0 ppm to 4680.0 ppm (NYS DEC, *Ash Residue Characterization Project*, 3-92, pp. 51-2; Robert Fresco, *Newsday*, 9-6-87).

About a twentieth by weight: NYC Department of Sanitation, *Comprehensive Solid Waste Management Plan for New York City and Final Generic Environmental Impact Statement, appendix volume 4.2, appendix 4-E*, p. 66.

A lime slurry: Other types of caustic reagents are sometimes used. One is a special industrial-strength baking soda made by Arm & Hammer (*Solid Waste Technologies*, May 1995, p. 49).

Incineration adds about as much atmospheric carbon to the greenhouse effect as would burning coal or oil or the disposal of the refuse by landfilling: Net greenhouse gas emissions from a landfill compared to those from an equivalently sized waste-to-energy facility, measured in carbon-dioxide equivalents, are well over two to one (Kay H. Jones, "Comparing Air Emissions from Landfills and WTE Plants," *Solid Waste Technologies*, 3/4-94, p. 36). Per-ton emissions of volatile organic compounds (VOCs) from a mass-burn waste-to-energy facility are on the order of 1.17E-02 pounds, while from an MSW landfill they are 2.38E-02 pounds, and a landfill also emits 1.30E-02 pounds of methane. (NYC DS, *Comprehensive Solid Waste Management Plan*, appendix 5-B, table 1.) VOCs from burning oil at a utility plant are on the order of six times higher than from burning refuse on an energy-equivalent basis (ibid., [main volume], table 21.2.3-3). Landfill methane is the largest source of anthropogenic greenhouse gases in the United States; on a unit basis, methane produces twenty-five times the global-warming effect of carbon dioxide (Cindy Jacobs, *MSW Management*, November 1995, p. LMOP-4). In general, landfill-gas emissions (including dioxin emissions from landfill-gas-control devices) are comparable in their environmental and public-health effects to those from waste-to-energy facilities (e.g., Jones, op. cit.; Donald L. Gill, Ph.D., "Landfill Gas Emissions: A Study of Two Landfills in Price George's County, Maryland," Department of Biological Chemistry, University of

Maryland School of Medicine, Baltimore, MD 21201 [unpublished ms., n. d.]; Roger W. Powers, "Curbside Recycling: Energy & Environmental Considerations," *Solid Waste Technologies*, 9/10-95, p. 38).

If bottom ash and fly ash are combined, the concentration of metals is typically only a few times greater than the amount in normal household waste. . . : An ultimate analysis of NYC residential waste conducted in 1990 is presented in NYC Department of Sanitation, *Comprehensive Solid Waste Management Plan*, appendix 1-J, and ash data in appendix 4-E.

. . . and dioxin concentrations are about as high as in a typical American's fat: The EPA found 2,3,7,8-TCDD levels in the ash it tested from five newer incinerators to range from 10 to 35 parts per trillion (averaging 19 ppt); the EPA considers 2,3,7,8-TCDD concentrations in adipose tissue of 5 to 7 ppt to be typical. (*Characterization of Municipal Waste Combustion Ash, Ash Extracts, and Leachates*, March 1990, table ES-3; *Science Advisory Board Review of EPA's Dioxin Reassessment, Executive Committee Review Draft, Final Revision*, 9-19-95, p. 33.)

Ash from all the incinerators operating in New York State passes the screening test for hazardous materials: NYS Assembly, Legislative Commission on Solid Waste Management, *Where Will the Garbage Go?*, April 1995, p. 14.

A legal maneuver that the soft path environmentalists had deemed beneath consideration: "Don't do it," an attorney for one of the other opposing parties had advised—"you've got no grounds and you'll just make them angry." Kell interview, 7-17-75. Jim Tripp and Michael Herz of the Environmental Defense Fund deny giving this advice (conversations on 8-22-95 and 8-24-95, respectively). Eric Goldstein of the Natural Resources Defense Council (8-28-95) does not remember whether he did or did not give such advice.

An appellate court found that this outside lawyer might indeed "derive a benefit from his decision": appeal no. 28817, New York Public Interest Research Group, Inc. against Henry G. Williams, etc. This appellate decision largely overturned the Supreme Court decision in *NYPIRG v. Williams*, IA Part 32.

Within another seven years, nine-tenths of the state's remaining landfills would be shut down: NYS Legislative Commission on Solid Waste Management, *Where Will the Garbage Go?*, April 1995, p. 11 (257 of 294 landfills closed between 1986 and April 1995).

Waste disposal prices had risen steeply: e.g., Essex County rates increased from 25.28 dollars per ton to 102.50 dollars, as haulers had to travel to Pennsylvania, Michigan, and Ohio after the Kearny landfill closed. (*New York Times,* 8-4-87, II, p. 2:1.)

When the hearing finally reconvened, the participants hunkered down in earnest: By the end of 1989, the hearing record had produced approximately fifteen thousand pages of expert witness testimony, nearly four hundred documentary exhibits, thousands of pages of post-hearing briefs and reply briefs from at least half a dozen active intervenors, as well as from the city and SES (New York City Law Department, *Memorandum of Law in Opposition to Plaintiffs' Motion for a Preliminary Injunction . . . Community Alliance for the Environment, et al. v. Thomas C. Jorling, et al.,* pp. 3-4).

A higher proportion of Italian-Americans than any other portion of the state: In 1990, 35.2 percent of Staten Islanders listed "Italian" as their first ancestry. The next three highest New York State counties were Putnam (26.4 percent), Suffolk (23.5 percent), and Westchester (21.4 percent). (US Census, summary tape file 3A, table P033.)

Was it someone in the governor's office who instructed the environmental commissioner to reject the city's proposal?: Jorling did not respond to a request for an interview.

The parent corporation's millions of cubic yards of space in landfills: In 1990, WMI had at least one hundred twenty-eight landfills in at least thirty-six states. Charlie Cray, *Waste Management, Inc.: An Encyclopedia of Environmental Crimes & Other Misdeeds* (Greenpeace, 1991), p. 5.

"The landfill or landfills that will receive the residue": 6 NYCRR § 360-3.2(e)(1).

Kell insisted in a phone call to the judge: The conference call also included attorneys for Wheelabrator, the city, the Environmental Defense Fund, and the Natural Resources Defense Council.

Kell realized that there was nothing there: In its permit filings, Wheelabrator had clearly disclosed the fact that the facility was not yet in operation, but Kell apparently had not focused on this fact until visiting the site. John T. Dowd, vice-president, Wheelabrator Environmental Systems, to Robert O'Connor, 3-13-89.

Three weeks later, the story finally hit: J. D. Mullane, *Bucks County Courier Times,* 4-5-89, p. 1; 4-7-89, p. 1; Patricia Wandling, ibid., 4-12-89, p. 1; Waste Management Inc, 4-11-89, press release.

No community in the country had ever managed to recycle more than a third of their refuse: Commoner's pilot study of recycling in affluent East Hampton, NY, the poster child of the Total Recycling campaign, involved only a few dozen families and lasted only a few months. In late 1999, Virginia Beach, VA, claimed to have achieved a 75 percent recycling rate in a program started two years before. *Solid Waste Report,* 11-4-99, p. 340.

Natural Resources Defense Council and Environmental Defense Fund contributions and members shot up: In 1982, the Natural Resources Defense Council had forty thousand members who gave 4.5 million dollars, and the Environmental Defense Fund's fifty thousand members gave 2.8 million dollars (William Symonds, *Fortune,* 10-4-82, pp. 136ff); in 1985, these respective figures were fifty thousand and 6.5 million dollars for the Natural Resources Defense Council; fifty thousand and 3.5 million dollars for the Environmental Defense Fund. *National Journal,* 6-8-85, p. 1352; William H. Miller, *Industry Week,* 7-11-83, pp. 46ff; Nancy Shute, *National Review,* 8-5-83, pp. 924ff.

The environmental movement's current goal seemed simply to be producing laws and regulations that would "level the playing field" between the exploitation of "virgin" and "secondary" resources: e.g., E. Bruce Harrison, *Public Relations Journal,* October 1983, pp. 44ff; Patrick P. McCurdy, *Chemical Week,* 9-12-84, pp. 3ff; David McKay Wilson, *New York Times,* 9-16-84, 6:6; Patrick Crow, *Oil & Gas Journal,* 5-6-85, pp. 99ff; Neal R. Peirce, *National Journal,* 8-3-85, pp. 1808ff; Philip Shabecoff, *New York Times,* 11-29-85, p. D28:1.

The new laws and regulations were helping a handful of strong-armed garbage-hauling firms to take over most of the nation's "recycling infrastructure" along with most of its landfills: Wayne Huizenga, co-founder of Waste Management, Inc. (now WMX Industries, Inc.), the largest of the four global waste management monopolies, and current owner of Republic [USA Waste], another of the biggest conglomerates, on these regulations: "At Waste Management, we always took the position that regulations were good, not bad. [Republic] is not against regulations. In some industries, being over-regulated is not good. In this industry, regulations are a positive, not a negative." (*Waste Age*, March 1996, p. 82.)

On ownership of recycling infrastructure: Browning-Ferris Industries, Inc., for example, (as of November 1995) according to its CEO, owned "'the largest recycling company…in the world,'" while Waste Management opened seventy new recycling facilities in 1995 alone. John T. Aquino, "Recycling and Internal Growth are Key to Profits, Says Alex. Brown," *Waste Age*, November 1995, pp. 26, 28.

David Dinkins pledged a moratorium on the proposed Brooklyn Navy Yard incinerator: This five-year commitment apparently was made verbally, as reported in conversations and press reports. The Dinkins campaign appears not to have put it in writing, except, perhaps, in a response to a questionnaire submitted to the Sierra Club.

The incoming administration's first task was to shave four hundred million dollars from the city's budget for the remaining six months of the fiscal year: This amount was in addition to the 640 million dollars the outgoing mayor had already cut. *New York Times*, 1-6-90, I, p. 27:6; 1-9-90, p. B3:1; 1-13-90, I, p. 30:6.

A billion-dollar budget gap: New York Times, 2-6-90, p. B1:5. By March, the budget gap for the coming fiscal year had grown to 1.8 billion dollars (*New York Times*, 3-22-90, p. B2:3).

By 1990, two out of three American cities were using private sector employees to pick up the trash: John T. Aquino, "MSW Collection: A History," *Waste Age*, February 1999, p. 26.

The threat of a little free-market competition, Polan reasoned, might be just the way to get the union to be a bit more flexible: Polan to Steisel, 5-3-91 (Municipal Archives, Steisel papers, B16795,37/47, file: '91 Sanitation).

Polan argued that Jorling would never release a permit to built the Navy Yard incinerator if the recycling law was so conspicuously flaunted: ibid.

Within weeks, Polan had received the resignations of the first half-dozen of his formerly enthusiastic recycling staff: In addition, twenty uniformed sanitation workers who had been assigned to public-education and similar activities were transferred to other bureaus. Anthony Solomita, former director of Institutional Recycling, NYC DS, personal communication, 10-17-95.

The brain drain: Some of this downsizing was due to citywide and agency-wide reductions, but it is unlikely that any other bureau had a head-count reduction approximating 50 percent (from a staffing level of sixty-one in January 1991 to thirty-four in July 1995). Personal communications, Eric Zimiles, director of administration, Bureau of Waste Prevention, Re-use and Recycling, 10-10-96 and 10-17-96.

The editorialists who were misled to the same conclusion: e.g., New York Times, 6-10-91, p. A16:1.

Citizens famous and obscure: Christos to Dinkins, 5-6-91; Stiller and Meara to Steisel, 6-10-91; Heiskell to Steisel, 5-8-91 (Municipal Archives, Steisel papers, loc. cit.) The former two letters were apparently written in response to a Creative Coalition campaign organized by Blythe Danner and Meir Ribalow (conversation with Ribalow, 8-28-95.)

Commoner's original family name was Commenar: Vinciguerra, loc. cit.

Polan meant to revivify his recycling program: e.g., interview with James T. B. Tripp, 4-13-95.

Without such a plan no permit could be granted for any type of waste-management facility: Private facilities that handled only waste from private entities were excluded from this stricture.

The exchange between the sanitation commissioner and his aides: Herald Tribune, 6-29-34, p. 1:2.

To figure out how best to collect, transport, process, and market the materials in our waste: Most of the waste produced by New York City's 7.4 million inhabitants and tens of thousands of businesses is the kind of refuse picked up in "garbage" trucks. (Construction and demolition debris and dredge spoils each make up about of the fifth of the load, while sewage sludge, medical waste, and "harbor debris"—the flotsam and jetsam scooped from the surface waters surrounding the city, or washed up on the shores—add only a couple of percent to the overall pile.)

We deployed teams of dozens of sorters: SWMP, 1.1, p. ES-1.

Commoner claimed that 84.4 percent of the city's waste stream could be recycled: Testimony Presented Before the New York City Council Committee on Environmental Protection, 3-18-92, p. 6

"A model of how a problem as serious and complex as trash disposal should be evaluated and solved": CBNS, EAC, Environmental Defense Fund, Natural Resources Defense Council, NYPIRG, Sierra Club, 9-5-91, Contact: B. Commoner, L. Shapiro, "Statement From The Environmental Community Regarding Incineration In New York City."

"A common understanding of the rich store of data": Commoner continued: "For months,... the Department has asked [a range of public and environmental representatives] to help design the Plan. It has cost the City and the State at least two million dollars to hire consultants [the actual cost for consultants was well over four million dollars].... Meeting with Department representatives, environmentalists have reviewed the information as it has been gradually supplied by the consultants, have pointed out its inadequacies, and have debated alternative interpretations—a model of how a problem as serious and complex as trash disposal should be solved." Testimony to City Council Committee on Environmental Protection, 3-18-92.

Polan's interview: Allan R. Gold, *New York Times,* 9-5-91, p. A1.

"Contact: Barry Commoner": NYPIRG executive director Larry Shapiro was listed as a second contact.

"We were dissed": Michael H. Cottman, 9-6-91.

Film star spokespersons: Blythe Danner, Susan Sarandon, and Christopher Reeve were among the celebrities involved in the campaign. Documents provided by Martin Brennan, phone conversation with Meir Ribalow, 8-28-95.

NYPIRG organized "The Campaign for Recycle First": Information on the campaign was provided from his files by Martin Brennan of NYPIRG, who organized it brilliantly.

A major New York City uniformed agency: That is, the police, fire, or sanitation departments.

Lloyd chose to make the immediate advance of the Navy Yard incinerator the one irreducible element in her plan: After initially favoring the former course [Lloyd to Steisel, Barbara Fife, Bill Lynch, Lee Jones, 3-23-92 (Municipal Archives, Lynch papers, box 37, file: sanitation)], which promised an enthusiastic response from almost everyone [e.g., Ruth Messinger, Manhattan borough president to Stanley Michels, chair, City Council Committee on Environmental Protection, "I believe these changes ("a deferral of decisions on the need for new incineration capacity until after the full city-wide recycling program has operated for at least two years") will not only build a city-wide consensus favoring the Plan, but will actually create *enthusiasm* for it" (emphasis in original) (Municipal Archives, Steisel papers, loc. cit.)], she chose the latter, which assured the opposite.

It was a mystery to me why she should change her mind. Eventually, after talking to almost everyone who had had access to the decision-making circle, I discovered who Lloyd's adviser was. It turned out to have been Tom Jorling, the environmental commissioner who had been responsible for blocking approval of the project in the first place, who now thought it his responsibility to make amends by ramming it down the city's throat at the moment it would be hardest to swallow. Do it now, he had told Lloyd, taking advantage of her complete unfamiliarity with her new position, or I will make you start all over again the hearing process that has thus far consumed six years. Do it now, he said, or your environmental impact assessment will be judicially "stale." (The "staleness" issue, I later discovered, had been another one of Arthur Kell's ideas, raised among many others during the earlier hearings [Carol Ash interview, 8-3-95]. But when I told him that it had been the primary motive Emily Lloyd had given to explain her decision [Emily Lloyd interview, 5-4-95], his face wrinkled with pained disbelief. "I find that hard to believe," he said to me dubiously. "That's pro*found*ly naive.") [This judgement on the triviality of the "staleness" issue is shared by, among others, Wheelabrator Environmental Systems and its legal counsel (Jennifer Cutschall, personal communication, 10-5-95), and Benjamin Cardozo Law School Environmental Law Professor Michael Herz, who in his former role as an attorney with Environmental Defense Fund played a prominent role in the Navy Yard hearings (personal communication, 8-24-95). Among other informed parties, they understood the "staleness" threat as a "political/policy stick."] Do it now, or you will never be able to comply with the Clean Air Act requirements that, after the coming November 15, will require nitrogen-oxide emitters to decrease air pollution from another source. Do it now, or I'll close the Fresh Kills landfill.

Although hollower threats would be difficult to imagine —the commissioner clearly had discretion to leave a hearing record open for a couple of years if circumstances justified so doing, just as he had during the last three years while the Dinkins moratorium had been in effect; the issues that had absorbed six years' of hearings could scarcely crop up in those forms again; the work to "freshen" the environmental impact statement, if that were ever necessary, would be a drop in the bucket compared to the efforts expended on the waste management plan; a variety of low cost ways of addressing the need to provide nitrogen oxide "offsets" presented themselves as soon as the November 15 deadline was missed; closing Fresh Kills would leave half the state's refuse without a home—she bought them. (Of course Jorling's arguments also provided a rationale for going along with what she had to imagine her boss, the strong-willed Norman Steisel, wanted [even though both deny that he ever gave her any explicit instructions on the Navy Yard project, and though he apparently had had no objection to her original Recycle-First postponement course].)

The defining difference between the council and a rubber stamp is that the latter leaves an impression: an observation by one of its members: former Manhattan Councilman-at-Large (Liberal) Henry J. Stern.

"The best politician in the council": interview with Martin Brennan, chief organizer, NYPIRG, June 1995.

"Death or recycling": Michael Efthimiades, *Long Island City Journal*, 5-7-92, p. 10, "Queens Residents Voice Outrage Over Incinerators."

The city council's proudest moment: James C. McKinley, Jr., *New York Times,* 9-1-92.

"Pro-growth coalition": Brennan, ibid.

The Moses-built incinerator (which the sanitation department had just spent twenty-five million dollars renovating): Polan to Steisel, 4-30-91 (Municipal Archives, Steisel files, box 16795, 37/47, file: '91 Sanitation.)

September 6, 1986: Some sources give the departure date as August, e.g., *South China Morning Post,* 6-9-93, p. 10.

A scheme for building a reef that Bahamian developers could put a resort on: A Bahamian resort developer, Tony Gallina, of Clearwater, FL, president of LSS International, Ltd.—presumably the same fellow who offered the *Khian Sea* a dump site—also offered a dumping spot for the *Mobro* (Little San Salvador, a small island near Andros and Eleuthera Islands), but was overruled by local health officials. (*Staten Island Advance,* 5-7-87, *Newsday,* 5-9-87, *Post,* 5-8-87.)

Two years and three months later: e.g., *Toronto Star,* 2-1-93, p. C4.

Gunboat encounters with the navies of several nations: Solid Waste Report, 6-3-93.

Changed its name: UPI, 11-1-89, "Grand jury investigating ship's missing cargo." The *Mobro,* too, was re-christened after its fateful voyage.

Its owners were convicted of dumping the load in the Indian Ocean: A portion of the eleven thousand tons was also dumped in the Atlantic Ocean; at least two thousand tons had previously been deposited on a beach in Haiti, where it was sold as "fertilizer" by individuals tied to the military government. *United States v. William P. Reilly,* CR No. 93-8, 9253, DC Delaware, 1-28-93, *United States v. William P. Reilly and John Patrick Dowd,* No. CR 92-53, DC Delaware.

Greenpeace played the Arthur Kell/chorus role: With an assist from Barry Commoner's CBNS—which appears to have inserted the story for the first time in the US media, opening the floodgates for the rush that followed. James Quigley, CBNS, letter to *New York Times,* 11-30-87, the first item located by Nexis in a search for *Khian Sea.* And just as there were multiple trash trains, there were also multiple ash ships (not just ships with multiple names) simultaneously at sea.

Lloyd promised to close the city's last-but-one incinerator: The waste management plan's analysis had established that these incinerators could have been rebuilt to incorporate steam-generating equipment and to meet current air-emissions standards more cheaply than a new plant could be constructed. City of New York, Department of Sanitation, *A Comprehensive Solid Waste Management Plan for New York City and Final Environmental Impact Statement,* appendix Volume 7.1: appendix 7-A.3, document #8; appendix 7-A.6, "Incineration."

"Every car is an incinerator": Queens Weekly, 8-20-92, Peter F. Vallone, "My Say"; Arthur Kell, *Courier,* 9-21-92, p. 38, guest column.

African-American incinerator supporters were traitors to their race: Martha K. Hirst, chief legislative representative, City Legislative Affairs, to David N. Dinkins, 8-27-92, 7:45 AM, quotes Susan Alter: "I am a white person representing a minority district. Some say I disempower. I don't disempower. Disempowerment of minorities comes from the Administration and my colleagues who vote for the plan.... As a white person, I ask you to vote against this plan." Hirst added, "(As you might guess, the African American Council Members' reactions were strong. Una Clarke was so angry she had to pass on her vote; Watkins, White and Foster all reacted to her statements in their remarks.)"

She also dropped six million more dollars through the meter of near term city budget commitments, and annual millions more thereafter: In the weeks leading up to the 8-26-92 vote, Lloyd and her negotiators added 8.2 million dollars to the FY 1994 budget; the night of 8-25/26-92 this amount went up to 12.0 million dollars, along with 1.7 million dollars in FY 1993. Among the other commitments not reflected in these totals were a two-dollar commitment for each ton of garbage burned at the Navy Yard incinerator (2.2 million dollars/year) "to be used for educational programs promoting recycling and waste reduction," and unestimated millions more for monitoring pollutants from the incinerator. Stanley E. Michels, chair, Committee on Environmental Protection to All Council Members, 9-3-92, "Solid Waste Management Plan;" Emily Lloyd to Philip Michael (city budget director), 9-8-92, "Waste Plan/Recycling Acceleration" (Municipal Archives, Dinkins papers, box 16795).

"Shame, shame": Reginald Patrick, *Staten Island Advance,* 8-27-92, p. A1.

Twenty policemen: Don Mathison, WNYC News (radio) tape, 8-29-92.

Grinning like a cheshire cat: The description of Bill Lynch is James C. McKinley, Jr.'s (*New York Times,* 9-1-92).

"Clean, Courageous Politics": 8-28-92.

"One of the greatest victories this city has seen in a long time": Richard Steier, *New York Post,* 8-28-92.

Lloyd's initial contact with Jorling's department: O'Connor to Lloyd, 9-9-92; Foster Maer, Brooklyn Legal Services Corporation to Jorling and O'Connor, 10-15-92 (Brooklyn Navy Yard permit hearing records).

Jorling committed a protocol breach of his own: Robert H. Feller, assistant commissioner for hearings, memo to "All Parties," 10-2-92.

Jorling's staff believed that there were insufficient nitrogen dioxide sources in the downstate reason to permit the city to demonstrate sufficient offsets for the Navy Yard incinerator: personal communication with a DEC staffer, 1992.

Kell filed for a preliminary injunction: United States District Court, Eastern District of New York, Community Alliance for the Environment . . . New York Public Interest Research Group v. Thomas C. Jorling . . . Emily Lloyd . . .; notice from Jorling to "All Parties," 11-3-92.

Jorling announced that the deadline was irrelevant after all: e.g., NYS DEC, *Reply Brief of Department Staff, DEC Project No. 20-85-0306,* 11-24-92, pp. 22-25.

Jorling stuck to this interpretation despite compelling arguments to the contrary from each of the environmental groups' attorneys: Jorling, *Fifth Interim Decision in the Proposed Brooklyn Navy Yard Waste-to-Energy Project Proceeding, DEC Project No. 20-85-0306,* 9-9-93, p. 10; Charles L. Kerr, *Sixth Post-Hearing Brief Submitted by The Natural Resources Defense Council, Inc.,* pp. 9ff; *Post-Issues Conference Reply Brief Submitted by the New York Public Interest Group, et al.,* pp. 15ff; *Reply Submission of The Environmental Defense Fund,* by James T. B. Tripp, 11-23-92, pp. 8ff.

The legislature passed a bill that revoked the exemption on which Jorling's excuse was based: The bill passed by the assembly contained a technical error (it gave the wrong year for the city law closing down apartment-house incinerators), and thus the assembly's passage of the bill was presumably invalid. NYPIRG staffers sitting up late that night in their NYC offices, following the legislative session by radio and phone, were immediately aware of the mistake, as they sat with bated breath eating pizza and hoping that it would not be caught. It was caught by the time the bill was introduced in the senate, but when legislative staff tried to make amends later that morning by having a correct version approved by the assembly, they were rebuffed. Brennan interview, June 1995.

The judge decided to bring the hearing to a close on a slow news day: Although the decision was signed by Robert O'Connor, administrative law judge, and mailed on 12-23-92, it was not released to the press until 12-24-92, so that the news story would appear on Christmas Day when few people would notice (Steven Lee Myers, *New York Times*, 12-25-92).

The bones of Revolutionary War heroes might be below the incinerator's intended foundation: A year before, federal government officials building a new office building a block north of City Hall had been distressed to find that their construction site contained the remains of untold hundreds of African-Americans buried there in colonial times, when the desolate plot was too far north to appeal to whites. This discovery cost the US Department of General Services a lengthy delay, the loss of a four-story pavilion, and considerable embarrassment at what many perceived as their callous lack of good grace about it all. e.g., Steven Lee Myers, *New York Times*, 5-23-93, p. A1; Karen Cook, *Village Voice*, 5-4-93, pp. 23ff.

During the course of the City Council's hearings on the waste management plan, Barry Commoner, sitting in the audience one day next to Arthur Kell, was startled to hear a Brooklyn historian say that there were probably graves of Revolutionary War heroes underneath the proposed incinerator site. Commoner immediately offered his assistance in tracking down new evidence, went to pull out documents himself at the Brooklyn Historical Society, and sent an intern to sift through the maps the historian had dug up, including, most importantly, a drawing produced by General Jeremiah Johnson in 1786 that seemed to show that graves might indeed be beneath the site's rubbly fill. Kell interview, 8-8-95; Commoner interview, 7-12-95.

The possibility of there being human remains in the soil had already been iden-
tified in the environmental analysis for the project: City of New York, *Final*
Environmental Impact Statement for the Proposed Brooklyn Navy Yard
Waste-to-Energy Facility, June 1985, p. 2-17 and appendix O, pp. 11, 18,
36, 42.

It contained the standard assurances that more in depth archeological
examinations would precede full site development and any findings handled respectfully with appropriate measures—the shoreline after all had
been completely altered from its colonial configuration by thousands of
tons of rock, sand, and gravel fill, and a thousand or so bodies had already
been recovered from the site and long ago been removed to the Prison
Ship Martyrs Monument in Fort Greene Park (William Bunch, *Newsday,*
12-28-92). Paterson disputes that that area was originally wetland and
offers evidence that suggests that he may be right (deposition, Brooklyn
Navy Yard project permit hearing, 1-28-93). But given the moisture and
acidity of the soil, according to anthropologist Peggy Caldwell of the
chief medical examiner's office, "There is probably very little left at Wallabout, although some teeth with their enamel might still be there"
(quoted in Howard Pitsch, *The Hill,* fall, 1993, p. 5). Even Commoner
confessed skepticism about anything being there, but as he pointed out,
from a legal perspective it was absolutely the right thing to do. Commoner interview, 7-12-95.

Lloyd promised to conduct additional field testing before the start of construction:
Lloyd to Julia S. Stokes, deputy commissioner for Historic Preservation,
NYS Office of Parks, Recreation and Historic Preservation, 3-22-93.

The scandal led to a full investigation. . . : NYC Department of Investigation, *Report of Investigation Regarding An Environmental Assessment of the Site*
for the Brooklyn Navy Yard Refuse-to-Energy Facility, 5-4-94.

. . . and got the site added to the state's list of Superfund sites: e.g., *New York*
Times, 1-1-95, p. C47; Joe Sexton, *New York Times,* 2-5-95, p. 56:1.

Giuliani delayed the appropriation for constructing the Navy Yard incinerator until
1998 . . .: John Sullivan, *New York Times,* 6-16-95, p. B4:1.

. . . and then, on further thought, to 1999: NYC Department of Sanitation,

Comprehensive Solid Waste Management Plan Draft Update and Plan Modification, 6-1-95, p. 4-24.

Robert Molinari, a one-term Democrat-turned-Republican: Susan Molinari, *Representative Mom. Balancing Budgets, Bill, and Baby in the US Congress* (New York: Doubleday, 1998), p. 17.

Susan Molinari's most recent coup had been securing 1.25 million dollars to produce a study of Fresh Kills's health impacts: Nicholas Dmytryszyn, environmental adviser to the Staten Island borough president, personal communication, 10-7-99.

Guy Molinari, a former Marine with a reputation as a loose-lipped cannon: His publicly expressed opinion of doctors who perform partial-birth abortions: they should have their brains suctioned from their heads; of a female candidate for New York State attorney general: "admitted lesbians" are unfit for office; of Rudy Giuliani after his betrayal of his own party to support Mario Cuomo: he should become a Democrat. e.g., Joyce Purnick, *New York Times,* 10-3-94, p. B8; *"Democrat" quote: New York Times,* 11-10-99, p. A1:1.

Until recently, even Guy Molinari had not dared hope for an end to the Fresh Kills landfill: "There will never be a cessation of the dumping of raw garbage at the landfill." Quoted in *Staten Island Advance,* 8-20-92, "BP: City Must Incinerate."

Only those in the room that day know what they said, and they are not telling: Guy Molinari and Rudy Giuliani both turned down, without explanation, requests for interviews. Of the other Giuliani administration officials with whom I spoke (none of whom were willing to have their comments attributed to them), none had any specific knowledge of such a meeting, but all shared my understanding that such a discussion had indeed taken place.

Fresh Kills absorbed nearly 40 percent of all the refuse generated every day in New York State: NYS Senate, www.senate.state.ny.us, Narrative N91602, 1997, "Solid Waste Management."

The bills' sponsors had expected opposition from the city's and state's executives: e.g., Assemblyman Robert Straniere, quoted by Carl Campanile in the *Staten Island Advance,* 5-2-96.

Fresh Kills was ordered closed. Just as the bill was used as window dressing to effectuate the deal struck in Giuliani's office, another fig leaf also was used as an excuse for the mayor's action: a lawsuit filed by Molinari charging that the Fresh Kills landfill violated sections of the Clean Air Act. Since it is scarcely conceivable that this suit would have caused the landfill to close, using it as an excuse for the closure is at best disingenuous.

The value of these one hundred million cubic yards of capacity: Edward W. Repa and Allen Blakey, "Municipal Solid Waste Disposal Trends, 1996 Update," *Waste Age,* January 1996, p. 51.

A puzzling prodigality: budget figures from Michael Rogovin, New York City Independent Budget Office (Rogovin to Miller, 10-25-99). The city's spending on the Board of Education was 3.296 billion dollars in 1994, 3.216 dollars in 1996. 816,589 persons received AFDC in December 1993, versus 652,954 in December 1997 (a decrease of 163,635); gross annualized savings—including federal and state funds—were 357 million dollars. Projected cost of export: e.g., Vivian S. Toy, *New York Times,* 5-30-96, p. B1.

"Among the most carefully scrutinized . . . infrastructure project[s] in the country": Fifth Interim Decision, 9-9-93.

The Navy Yard incinerator was buried in a one-sentence reference in the sixth paragraph on page seven of the second section of the late city edition: 5-31-96.

The environmental groups were almost as silent as the editorial writers were: The Natural Resources Defense Council, the Environmental Defense Fund, and NYPIRG all testified in the hearing on the council bill to close Fresh Kills, but only NYPIRG demonstrated unqualified support. The Environmental Defense Fund and the Natural Resources Defense Council, while generally supportive of the closure bill, cautioned that the precipitous shutdown, in the absence of planning, could lead to problems, particularly with export.

Guy Molinari won his next election by a lopsided margin: 68 percent to 32 percent, *New York Times,* 11-5-97, p. B3:6.

"The same legal rights as the rest of the country to refuse [New York's trash]": David J. Oestreicher, *Daily News,* 7-19-92.

A House bill to restrict interstate waste transport received an instant jolt of fresh momentum: HR 2323 (Lorie J. Nevares, "Washington Watch," *MSW Management*, May/June 1996, p. 14.; and September/October 1996, pp. 14-15.)

Many analysts expect that the initial reaction to the actuality of Fresh Kills's closure will be the most important factor in determining whether limitations ultimately are enacted: e.g., Kim A. O'Connell and Randy Woods, *Waste Age*, February 1997 (on www).

"To soften the angularity of the slopes": City of New York, Department of Sanitation, Fresh Kills Landfill Draft Environmental Impact Statement, 3-15-96, p. 32.

It will probably be thirty years or so before all sections of the site will be accessible: conversations with sanitation department and city planning officials, 1999.

EPILOGUE

Only seven containers: Other accounts said only three were unloaded. (e.g., William Bunch, *New York Newsday*, 7-23-92, p. 5.)

"Dried and mummified": Chris Wagner, Conrail spokesperson, to the Associated Press, *Los Angeles Times*, 7-18-92, p. A20. Like the *Mobro*, the trash trains generated miles of copy. The other details in this paragraph are from the following stories: *New York Post*, 7-11-92, p. 8; *Staten Island Advance*, 7-14-92; David J. Oestreicher, *Daily News*, 7-19-92; *Solid Waste Report*, 7-23-92; *Pittsburgh Post-Gazette*, 9-6-94, p. A5.

"Disease carrying flies.": Rita Giordano, "Living With Big Apple's Rot," *Newsday*, 7-23-92. The quote is from Dan Shomon, spokesman for the Illinois Environmental Protection Agency. Associated Press, *Los Angeles Times*, 7-18-92, p. A20.

The local trucking contractor handling the unloading operation missed the court-mandated deadline for getting the train unloaded because local residents staged a sit-in: William Bunch, *Newsday*, 7-23-92, p. 5.

"The people here have dictated they don't want any part of it": Washington Post, 7-16-92, p. A4.

"How offensive that when it comes to garbage, the train inevitably stops on Staten Island": David J. Oestreicher, *Daily News*, 7-19-92.

Federal legislators began to trade graphic conjurations of the dangers the trains held for their constituents: The senators are quoted by Helen Dewar, *Washington Post*, 7-23-92, p. A8.

After the dramatic all-night session was over, many in the city breathed a sigh of relief: e.g., *Daily News*, 8-31-92; WCBS radio editorial, 9-2-92.

"The cost of disposing of garbage could bury the city's economy": *Crain's New York Business*, 8-24-92, p. 10

"Disappointed" feelings: Tom Ridge of Pennsylvania in a 5-31-96 letter to George Pataki.

These neighbors began to make it clear that waste-transfer stations were another type of facility that could not be counted on as a solution to the city's waste-management problems: e.g., *New York Times*, 6-29-97, Section 13; p. 9:3; Dan Janison, *Newsday*, 11-18-97; James Bradley, *Village Voice*, 3-3-98, vol. 43, no. 9, pp. 25ff; Paul H. Shin, *Daily News*, 12-3-98.

Attorney general's predecessor was president of Waste Management, Inc., New York State division: e.g., *Waste News*, 8-2-99, p. 1.

Jersey-bound trucks: Tri-State Transportation Campaign, *Mobilizing the Region*, #254, 1-31-00. These figures are for all four Hudson River crossings. 360,000 truck trips were predicted for 2000 (*Mobilizing the Region*, #268, 5-8-00).

Diesel exhaust constituents considered carcinogenic: Supreme Court of the State of New York, County of New York, In the Matter of the Application of Eliot Spitzer, Attorney General of the State of New York, Petitioner, For a Judgment Pursuant to Article 78 of the Civil Index No. Practice Law and Rules and for Declaratory Relief Pursuant to CPLR §3001, Against Kevin Farrell, Commissioner of the New York City Department of Sanitation, and New York City Department of Sanitation, Respondents, Petitioner's Memorandum of Law, 1-27-2000, Point #6.

The EPA's study of health effects of emissions from Fresh Kills: US Department of Health and Human Services, Agency for Toxic Substances and Disease Registry, *A Panel Study of Acute Respiratory Outcomes, Staten Island, New York*, Draft Final Report, 8-20-99.

Eight hundred extra trucks: Eric Lipton, *New York Times*, 2-21-2000, A1:1.

One thousand fifty additional workers: Message of the Mayor, 2000, p. 152, as quoted by Alicia Culver, senior research associate, INFORM, "Summary for NYC Department of Sanitation, FY01 Executive Budget Hearing, May 3, 2000."

Fifty-five dollars per ton: New York City Independent Budget Office, *Analysis of the Mayor's Preliminary Budget for 2001*, p. 50. These estimates were purposely conservative to avoid revealing during contract negotiations how much the city would actually be willing to pay.

An additional twenty-eight million dollars: Big Apple Garbage Sentinel (http://garbagesentinel.org), 1-24-2000; *Mobilizing the Region*, #254, 1-31-00.

Seventy-two dollars: Bid data provided by Chris Boyd, director of environmental policy, Brooklyn Borough President's Office, 5-25-00. Bradley Jacobsen, *Waste Age*, April 2000, p. 80, gives the average as 71.38 dollars per ton.

Ninety-six dollars: New York City Department of Sanitation, *Comprehensive Solid Waste Management Plan, Draft Modification*, May 2000, table 4.2-1. The figure is $95.50, which Julian E. Barnes (*New York Times*, 5-2-00, B10:3) and Ann M. Gynn, (*Waste News*, 5-8-2000, p. 37) round down to $95.

Forty-two dollars: Andy Newman, *New York Times*, 9-28-99, B3:1.

Three hundred twenty-three million dollars: New York City Department of Sanitation, loc. cit.; Eric Lipton, *New York Times*, 5-7-00, 47:1. Even if the contract costs were to remain stable—not a likely possibility—the amount is certain to be considerably higher than that, since this figure does not include all the debt service on capital facilities that the Sanitation Department will have to develop for the export system.

One hundred twenty-seven million dollars: Culver, ibid. Overall, the city's projections for the sanitation department budget for 2001 increased by 42 percent (286 million dollars) between 1997 (a year after the closure of Fresh Kills was announced) and 2000; 79 million dollars of this increase (10 percent) occurred just in the three months after the preliminary budget was presented in January. These increases, according to the respected organization City Project, occurred "almost exclusively because of unacknowledged costs of waste export." In testimony before the City Council on May 22, 2000, Glenn Pasanen, associate director of City Project, also said, "Moreover, looking way ahead, the State Financial Control Board's March report on the Mayor's January budget plan estimated that waste export costs for FY 2003 and 2004 were underestimated by as much as $117 million and $126 million, respectively. Lowballing the costs of waste export has had at least two bad consequences beyond the new costs themselves. One, it has helped promote the false notion that the City can afford over a billion dollars in new tax cuts this year, and two, it has meant a further shift in City priorities—from human service spending to uniformed agency spending."

Reversing its prior position: Big Apple Garbage Sentinel, 2-8-99.

"$4 or $5 million": Mayor John T. Gregorio, quoted by Barbara Stewart, *New York Times*, 5-25-00, B1:2. The guaranteed minimum amount was 1.3 million dollars; other sources suggested that this amount could increase to 3.7 million dollars. (e.g., Jessica Green, *Gotham Gazette*, 5-29-00 [www.gothamgazette.com].)

Fifty-million-dollar transfer station: Barbara Stewart, *New York Times*, 5-1-00, B3:3.

Gregorio's son-in-law: e.g., Stewart, 5-25-00. (Recognizing the potential conflict of interest this might cause, the mayor sensibly excused himself from any deliberations on the proposal.)

"Put us in the butter tub.": Stewart, 5-25-00.

The nearest of whom lived 1.7 miles from the site: Stewart, 5-25-00.

Taxes might go down: Lipton, 5-7-00.

Mile-long train: Stewart, 5-25-00.

Carteret would not get a cent: Kathleen Hopkins, *Home News Tribune*, 2-16-00.

Plans for 15 percent: Lisa Rein, *Daily News*, 4-6-99. She quotes Lhota as saying: "The more upstate is involved, it deflates some of the arguments of Pennsylvania and Virginia."

Fitzpatrick to Lhota: 5-12-99 (http://homestead.com/concernedcitizens/files/gjf2.GIF).

Farmersville voters: http://homestead.com/concernedcitizens/newspage-new.html.

"New York City has now officially joined with private dump developers": ibid.

Lhota to Fitzpatrick: 5-19-99 (http://homestead.com/concernedcitizens/files/jjl1.GIF).

Eisenbud testimony: 6-17-99.

Four firms share 85 percent of US waste-industry revenues: Susanna Duff, *Waste News*, 2-14-00, p. 1.

Sixty-five billion dollars: Bob Brown, *Waste News*, 5-3-99, p. 1.

Three other firms: The other three firms are Browning-Ferris Industries, Inc; Allied Waste Industries, Inc.; and Republic Services, Inc. In November, 1999, however, Republic bowed out of the competition for New York City's long-term waste-export contracts, having "discovered during the city's most recent bidding for an interim disposal contract that its landfills were too far away to be competitive with rivals, CEO James O'Connor said." Bob Brown, *Waste News*, 11-22-99, p. 1.

Doubling of the percentage of US landfills in private hands: From 17 percent in 1984 to 36 percent in 1998. Susanna Duff, *Waste News*, 5-1-2000, p. 1.

60 percent went to private landfills: Edward W. Repa, *Waste Age*, April 2000, p. 264.

Landfills in Utah and Georgia have already weighed in at twenty-four hundred acres apiece: Sarah Halsted, "News Roundup," *Waste Age*, February 1998, p. 8; Randy Woods, "Will Waste Ride Florida's Rails?" *Waste Age*, April 1996, p. 111.

Mega-fills' costs: Duff, 2-14-00.

page 14: *New York Post*, Dan Halasy; page 16: Illustrations of Cholera Asphyxia; in its different stages. Selected from cases treated at the cholera hospital, Rivington Street, by Horatio Bartley, Apothecary and Chymist, 1832. Negative number 73417. Collection of the New-York Historical Society; page 21: "New York City.—How the Metropolis Invites Disease and Epidemics," *Frank Leslie's Illustrated Newspaper*, April 23, 1881; page 32: A. J. B. Parent-Duchatelet, *Hygiène Publique: ou, mémoires sur les questions les plus importantes de l'hygiène appliquée aux professions et aux travaux d'utilité publique.* Vol. 1. Paris: J. B. Baillière, 1836. Plate 1. Archives & Special Collections, Columbia University Health Sciences Division; page 35: Archives & Special Collections, Columbia University Health Sciences Division; page 39: Manhattan Manufacturing and Fertilizing Company trademark for "Phosphatic Blood Guano," *Country Gentleman* vol. 36 (1871); page 46: "Soap Factory." Engraving by J. F. Bernard after drawing by von Radel, 1740-1818; page 49: Unsavory Hunter's Point—The Factories and Refineries on Newtown Creek. Drawing, *Harper's Weekly*, 8-6-1881. Museum of the City of New York, 55.53.13; page 49: Department of Street Cleaning, 1920. Municipal Archives, Department of Records and Information Services, City of New York; page 53: Grace, W.R., seated portrait. Photograph, negative number 522. Collection of the New-York Historical Society; page 56: Department of Street-Cleaning Annual Reports, 1902-1911. Municipal Reference Center, City of New York; page 56: Pressing Garbage after Boiling. Half-tone, nd, from "The Utilization of City Garbage," by George E. Waring. Museum of the City of New York, Print Archives; page 60: Courtesy of the National Park Service, Frederick Law Olmsted Historic Site; page 60: Library of Congress; page 63: Waring, George E., Major of Garibaldi Hussars. Negative number 63206. Collection of the New-York Historical Society; page 70: Municipal Archives, Department of Records and Information Services, City of New York; pages 72–73: George Waring, *Street-Cleaning and the Disposal of a City's Wastes.* NY: Doubleday & McClure, 1897; page 74: Municipal Archives, Department of Records and Information Services, City of New York; page 77: "Dumping Ground at the Foot of Beach Street, NYC." Drawing by Stanley Fox, *Harper's Weekly*, 9-29-1866; page 83: Waring, *Street-Cleaning and the Disposal of a City's Wastes;* page 84: *Men of Affairs in New York.* NY: L. R. Hamersly & Co., 1906; page 86: *Department of Street-Cleaning Annual Reports, 1902-1911.* Municipal Reference Center, City of New York; page 86: Municipal Archives, Department of Records and Information Services, City of New York; page 87: Barrelling the Oil. Half-tone, nd. Museum of the City of New York, Print Archives; pages 94–95: *National Cyclopaedia of American Biography,* NY:

J. T. White, 1898; page 97: "Creation," the entrance to Dreamland, Coney Island. Negative number 59200. Collection of the New-York Historical Society; page 97: "Twilight, Dreamland," Coney Island, September 1904. Museum of the City of New York, Gottsho-Schleisner Collection, 54.77.1; page 98: Department of Street-Cleaning Annual Reports, 1902-1911. Municipal Reference Center, City of New York; page 100: Henry Mosler, 1903, Collection of the City of New York, City Hall. Courtesy of the Art Commission of the City of New York; page 107: Major General McClellan. Drawing by F. O. C. Darley, nd. Museum of the City of New York; page 107: Mayor George McClellan. Photograph: Brown Bros., nd. Museum of the City of New York, Print Archives; page 109: "The Electric Light in Houses—Laying the Tubes for Wires in the Streets of New York." Drawing by W. P. Synder, *Harper's Weekly*, 6-24-1882. Museum of the City of New York, 56.349.10; page 111: "The New York Elevated Railway—View in Franklin Square." Drawing by Theo. R. Davis, *Harper's* Weekly, 9-7-1878. Museum of the City of New York, 53.407.29; page 112: *Men of Affairs*; page 112: *National Cyclopaedia of American Biography*. New York Public Library; page 113: *Men of Affairs;* page 114: Courtesy Penguin Putnam, 1936; page 116: Henry H. Klein, *My Last Fifty Years*, NY: Isaac Goldmann Co., 1935; page 117: *National Cyclopaedia of American Biography*. NY: J. T. White, 1898; page 119: Municipal Archives, Department of Records and Information Services, City of New York; page 123: Caricature: George Brinton McClellan, Sr., on pedestal. Negative number 44645. Collection of the New-York Historical Society; page 124: Caricature: George Brinton McClellan, Jr., on pedestal. Negative number 38504. Collection of the New-York Historical Society; page 125: Senator McCarren. Photograph, nd. Museum of the City of New York, bequest of Dr. Clarence C. Rice; page 126: Napoléon at Fontainebleau on March 31, 1814, after receiving news of the entry of the Allies into Paris. Paul Delaroche, 1845. © Museum der bildenden Kunste, Leipzig. Reprinted with permission; pages 128–129: *The World's Work*, February 1914, vol. 27, no. 4; page 133: Mayor John F. Hylan. Photograph, nd. Museum of the City of New York; page 135: Chrysler Building, spire detail, c. 1930. Irving Browning, negative number 58090. Collection of the New-York Historical Society; pages 142–145: Courtesy Robert A. Bernstein, New York City Metropolitan Transportation Authority, Bridges and Tunnels; page 148: William J. Wilgus Papers, 1895-1947. Map showing Belt Railway and Jamaica Bay Terminal. Manuscripts Division; The New York Public Library; Astor, Lenox and Tilden Foundations; page 161: William J. Wilgus Papers, 1895-1947. Picture of Mr. Potato, 10/25/23: "Carrying Fruits and Vegetables to 8,000,000 People." Manuscripts Division; The New York Public Library; Astor, Lenox and Tilden Foundations.; page 168: The Eastern Parkway system design, from *East Parkway and Boulevards in the City of Brooklyn*, 1873. Courtesy Brooklyn Historical Society; page 174: William J. Wilgus Papers, 1895-1947. Volume, Regional Plan of New York-Volume II: Pencil Drawing of Causeway." Manuscripts Division; The New York Public Library; Astor, Lenox and Tilden Foundations.; page 181: New York Public Library; page 182: Municipal Archives, Department of Records and Information Services, City of New York; pages 183–191: Municipal Archives, Department of Records and Information Services, City of New York; pages 197–198: New York City Department of Parks, *The Future of Jamaica Bay*, 7-18-38; pages 207–208: Municipal Archives, Department of Records and Information Services, City of New York; page 211: Audrey C. Tiernan, *Newsday*, Inc. © 1987. Reprinted with permission; pages 216–218: Staten Island Institute of Arts and Sciences; page 220: *New York Times*/Steven Berman, 10-18-89; page 224: © 1970 Time Inc. Reprinted by permission; page 228: US Patent Office; page 232: Municipal Archives, Department of Records and Information Services, City of New York; page 245: Courtesy of Harry Szarpanski; page 248: *New York Times*/William Sauro; page 255: Municipal Archives, Department of Records and Information Services, City of New York; page 258: Courtesy Arthur Kell; page 264: © 2000 Village Voice Media; pages 267, 274: Courtesy Arthur Kell.

INDEX

Page numbers in italics refer to illustrations.

Hearst, William Randolph (*continued*)
  power, 124
  Smith and, 164, 165
  war on Tammany Hall, 113–14
Heiskell, Marian, 266
hemp, 34
Hempstead (New York), 237–38,
  239–40
herbicides, 240
Hewitt, Abram, 104
Hildreth, J. H., 79, 80
Hoover, Herbert, 134
horses
  disposal of carcasses, 33–34, 35, 40,
  54
  manure, 38, 47, 49–50
  slaughterhouses, 36–40
hospital wastes, 78
host communities, 286, 294, 295, 297
housing, public, 195–96, 198, 210
Housing Authority (New York City),
  210
Hroncich, Thomas, 3, 7, 299, 300
Hudson River
  transport between New York and
  New Jersey, 157, 294
  waste dumped in, 44, 67
human waste. *See* sewage
hydrogen sulfide, 80–81
hydropulpers, 237–38, 239–40
Hylan, John, 133, *133*, 134–35, 156,
  157, 163, 164

Idlewild Airport, 192–93, 204
immigration, 19, 95, 105
incinerators
  air pollution, 11–12, 233, 239–41,
  247, 254, 367
  amount of power generated, 230
  in apartment buildings, 233, 280
  of Brooklyn Ash, 118, 180, 231

Commoner's opposition, 11–12,
  239–41, 251
dioxin created, 11–12, 239–41, 254
electricity generated, 118–19, 129,
  231
in England, 74, 229–30
history in United States, 230–31,
  233, 357, 358–59, 360
in long-range waste management
  plan, 270, 272, 377
Moses' view of, 206, 232–33
New York municipal, 12–13,
  118–19, 129, 180, 231–32, 256, 351
New York municipal closed, 275,
  276, 280, 282, 351
opponents, 233
planned for New York, 134, 208–9,
  231–32
problems, 230–31
risk assessment by Commoner, 241
steam generated by, 118, 229, 239
See also ash, incinerator; Brooklyn
  Navy Yard incinerator plan
infectious diseases
  among poor, 20, 22–23, 27
  on Barren Island, 88
  contagionist views, 19, 55, 222, 229
  diptheria, 79, 88
  disagreements over causes, 18–19,
  36, 55, 303
  epidemics in England, 27
  microorganisms as causes, 36,
  80–81, 89
  prevention attempts, 79–80
  spread by mosquitoes, 223
  spread by untreated garbage, 79
  typhoid, 88
  typhus, 223
  vaccines, 19
  venereal disease, 158–59, 303
  yellow fever, 20–22, 89–90